Tilmann Riemenschneider

Tilmann Riemenschneider

HIS LIFE AND WORK

Justus Bier

THE UNIVERSITY PRESS OF KENTUCKY

ISBN 978-0-8131-5126-7

Library of Congress Catalog Card No. 80-5171

Copyright © 1982 by The University Press of Kentucky

Scholarly publisher for the Commonwealth,
serving Berea College, Centre College of Kentucky,
Eastern Kentucky University, The Filson Club,
Georgetown College, Kentucky Historical Society,
Kentucky State University, Morehead State University,
Murray State University, Northern Kentucky University,
Transylvania University, University of Kentucky,
University of Louisville, and Western Kentucky University.

Editorial and Sales Offices: Lexington, Kentucky 40506

To my friend and former colleague
Ernest Christopher Hassold
and my son Max Robert
helper in many ways

Contents

Preface

In a manner of speaking, the present volume was conceived in Germany half a century ago, to celebrate in 1931 the fourth centenary of Riemenschneider's death. At that time *Tilmann Riemenschneider: Ein Gedenkbuch* (A Memorial Volume) first appeared. Five German editions were published before World War II; a sixth, enlarged edition came out shortly after the end of hostilities in 1948.

When I came to this country as an immigrant, to join the faculty of the University of Louisville, I was invited to stay at the home of a colleague who soon became my dear friend, Ernest Christopher Hassold. Together Ernest Hassold and his wife harbored me until my own wife and son were able to join me the following year. That year was 1937, and the present English edition of the memorial volume is based on a translation of the *Gedenkbuch* made by Dr. Hassold then. In the ensuing years, however, more pressing needs claimed my attention: I had to acquire a more extensive knowledge of English in order to give my lectures at the university, which ranged over the whole history of art. Indeed, my first publication in an American journal did not appear until seven years after I had settled in Louisville. After teaching in Louisville for twenty-four years I became Director of the North Carolina Museum of Art in Raleigh, and there once again I came into contact with students of all ages just as I had during the years of my directorship of the Kestner-Gesellschaft in Hanover, which preceded my American venture. Teaching a class at Duke University—first there, and then as a seminar at the Raleigh museum—kept me in touch with the young. As the label of "Riemenschneider scholar" was firmly attached to me, there was always the question: "When will you write a Riemenschneider book for us that *we* can read?"

While the idea remained firmly in mind always, there were still priorities that had to be met: my German monograph on Tilmann Riemenschneider had to be completed. The first two volumes appeared in 1925 and 1930 in Würzburg and Augsburg respectively; volume three was published in Vienna nearly half a century later, in 1973; and just recently the fourth and final volume has appeared: *Tilmann Riemenschneider: Die Späten Werke in Holz* (Vienna, 1978).

With the present modest volume I hope to give English-speaking students an introduction to the life and work of Tilmann Riemenschneider,

the great German Late Gothic sculptor. An independent study grant from
the National Endowment for the Humanities has enabled me to bring my research up to date and to expand this survey in a number of ways pertinent to
its readership in this country. The most important of these has been the in-
clusion in this edition of those works by Riemenschneider that have entered
public collections in the United States and Canada since the 1930s. Most of
these works came from private German collections. Many have already been
discussed extensively in separate articles, but since these works now form a
sizable and distinguished body and are easily accessible to students of Riemenschneider in this country, I felt it worthwhile to treat them as a special
group here, and in cases where prior articles in English exist, to draw together and collate that material. The earlier publications are listed at the end
of each entry.

As though to compensate for wartime losses in Germany, most of which
occurred in the great fire that destroyed so much of the city of Würzburg on
March 16, 1945, several fine sculptures have shown up since then; four of
these postwar discoveries (one as recent as the early 1970s), which are now in
the museums in Heidelburg, Würzburg, Cologne, and Munich, have also
been included. Several other important pieces in German collections have
been added as well.

I have kept the original format of the German *Riemenschneider Gedenkbuch*, presenting only works created entirely by Riemenschneider himself or
works that clearly show his design and substantial participation in the carving. Once again I have used only photographs which reflect the true character of Riemenschneider's work, many of them taken by the late Leo Gundermann, with whom I often collaborated in their preparation. Details illustrating Riemenschneider's masterful surface carving and skillful use of light and
shadow are included rather than adding other works of lesser quality. For a
series of photographs showing the Rothenburg Altarpiece of the Holy Blood
in its restored state, I would like to thank Mr. Eike Oellermann, who led the
restoration team in the winter of 1964–1965. And for the revealing photograph of the war-damaged Cathedral in Würzburg, I am indebted to Dr.
Rudolf Kuhn of Würzburg. Though the original "notes on the plates" have
been expanded in many cases and brought up to date in respect to changes in
location and condition, often as a result of the last war or the recent interest
in restoring works by Riemenschneider, they are still only intended to com-
plement the very fine photographs. A chronological checklist of works, with
selected references, has been added for the first time; so too has a list of
monographs on Riemenschneider.

I wish to thank my friend Ernest Hassold for providing the basic translation for this edition, and for all his help and interest those many years ago. I

also wish to thank the North Carolina Museum of Art, its commissioners, its staff, and especially its former director, Moussa Domit, for their unfailing support of my Riemenschneider research, which has permitted me to complete a project of nearly half a century's duration. My special gratitude is due to my trusted editorial assistant, Sally Siewert, whose skill, patience, and good humor have guided me throughout this work. Inge Witt, my research assistant, has also helped in every way she could to ensure accuracy and up-to-date information. And I would like to thank Nancy Cashwell for her skillful typing of the final manuscript. Financial support for this work has been generously provided by the National Endowment for the Humanities and by a private foundation in Hanover, Germany, which wishes to remain anonymous.

This presentation of the life and work of Riemenschneider in English is also intended as an expression of thanks to this country, which offered me asylum and, in the University of Louisville, a new place to work in very critical years.

TILMANN RIEMENSCHNEIDER

An Introduction to His Life & Work

IN THE LAST decades of the fifteenth century and the early years of the sixteenth, which may be considered the period of transition from the Late Gothic to the Renaissance in northern European countries, Germany produced a remarkable number of gifted artists. This was not, perhaps, entirely a matter of chance, but resulted in part from the particular conditions prevailing at that time. Conflicting forces shaped the art of those years. A reaction against the refinements of the mannered style of the 1470s, with all its intricacy and elaborate configuration, led in two different directions. On the one hand there was an attempt to refashion that style along more masculine lines, which evolved ultimately into what has sometimes been called "Late Gothic Baroque"; and at the same time there was a more fundamental change that sought to express a mood of serenity in plastic forms that were both simpler and more natural. Apart from these attempts to transform or recast the Late Gothic style—essentially trying to infuse new life into it— there was also an avid interest in appropriating the new ideas and forms of the Renaissance which swept into northern Europe from south of the Alps. Clearly this combination of native developments and external influences offered rich possibilities for individual choice and did much to stimulate the growth of vigorous, distinctive personalities.

Like all his contemporaries, Tilmann Riemenschneider, even though his work seems so homogeneous and uniform in character, can be understood only against this diverse and complex background. About 1480 he seems to have moved away from the excesses of the Late Gothic current—its turbulence and tortuous forms, its often grotesque contortions of even the human figure—in the direction of a more structured composition and greater naturalism of form. The baroque extravagance of the 1480s was no doubt alien to his nature and his convictions as an artist. Both the exaggerated daintiness of Martin Schongauer (d. 1491) and the bathos that Michael Pacher (c. 1435–1498) had brought into northern art were rejected, and in their place Riemenschneider sought to convey a new mood of quiet, introspective contemplation and a direct expression of feeling, without sacrificing purity of form and without descending to the level of crude or sentimental and mannered representation. Such purification is in line with the aims of the generation of Albrecht Dürer as expressed a decade later. The difference, however, is that Dürer's generation had the benefit of contact with the Italian Renaissance to help them achieve their goals, while Riemenschneider was still trying to embody or develop new concepts within the framework of Late Gothic conventions.

The sculpture of Tilmann Riemenschneider and of his contemporary Adam Kraft (c. 1460–c. 1509) is evidence that Late Gothic art in Germany was certainly working towards ends similar to those of the art of the Renaissance, and that to some extent it prepared the way for the latter. At the same time, analysis of Riemenschneider's artistic development shows why the art of the Renaissance was bound to succeed, rather than these independent endeavors of the Late Gothic. Riemenschneider's attempt to give Late Gothic sculpture a new emotional content and to rid it of all playfulness and complacency is in fact a unique solution, one that works only in his case by virtue of his particular character, convictions, and abilities. Despite the powerful influence of his art and despite his many followers and imitators, neither Riemenschneider's own work nor that of his fellow adherents of the Late Gothic made a creative continuation of Late Gothic art possible. On the other hand, the contact of the younger generation with Italian art opened up entirely new possibilities, even for those artists who were not in direct contact with it as were Dürer (1471–1528) and the later members of the Vischer family.

Earlier, I mentioned divergencies in style when comparing Riemenschneider with Schongauer. Yet for all the difference of content and form, the artistic kinship of these two artists is striking. In many respects Riemenschneider is Schongauer's disciple. After the advance and progress made by the preceding generation of Konrad Witz (c. 1400–c. 1445), Schongauer's art is an attempt to set the clock back. While it does contain elements of a new artistic language, his work has many of the qualities associated with earlier Gothic art: the sentiment and tender mood, and the graphic expressiveness that is characteristic of a linear language dealing with two-dimensional representation. Following in the steps of Schongauer, Riemenschneider shows a similar romantic mixture of realism and idealism. Like Schongauer he negates the spatially-organized compositions of Renaissance art and its respect for basic anatomical structure. The three-dimensional element is even more conspicuously absent than in Schongauer; even Riemenschneider's great altar compositions are set on a relatively shallow stage. In addition, any realistic observation of or reference to the drab, unseemly, or harsh and ugly side of everyday existence that had crept into Schongauer's work is strictly avoided.

What compensates for these self-imposed limitations of Riemenschneider's art is not only the unique refinement of the actual carving but also the new depth and intensity of spiritual and humanistic content. Looking at the faces of Riemenschneider's figures we see far more than the anonymous collective soulfulness of the typical Gothic countenance; rather we see an individual character and sensibility, an awareness of a personal destiny, reflected in each face and gesture. Even so, there is something tentative about this quality. Whereas the virile figures of Dürer seem to assert their newly-won individuality and to have broken all ties with the collective consciousness of the past, Riemenschneider's figures retain an impression of tragic conflict. From the isolation of an individual fate they seem to find safety in a brotherhood of shared experience. It is this that gives them their distinct medieval quality and links them to the art of the past rather than the emerging art of the Renaissance. Side by side with the distinguishing gesture and the characteristics of a unique personality, there is imprinted on every one of these faces the same familiarity with sorrow, the same resignation and humble acceptance of—even a longing for—a destiny to be fulfilled only in the world beyond. Yet it is not this medieval humility and yearning that explains the lasting quality of Riemenschneider's work. His art appeals above all by virtue of its new content, its special brand of realism: there is an individual expression, an inner force and ardor written on the features of Riemenschneider's figures that make them people of our time, people who retain the power to move us.

Not much is known about Riemenschneider's life, in fact much less than about his work. The little we do know, however, touches upon fundamental qualities of his character and temperament. Like his work, the circumstances of his life were governed by the conventions and traditions of the Middle Ages. Riemenschneider enjoyed only a fraction of the fame during his life that surrounded an artist like Dürer, but even so he was clearly much more than an anonymous artisan in his own time. A Würzburg chronicle by Johann Reinhard[1] describes Riemenschneider as a master known far and wide, famous for his impressive tomb-monuments for two prince-bishops of Würzburg, Rudolf von Scherenberg and Lorenz von Bibra: the second of these, "a splendid stone" that the prince-bishop during his lifetime "had brought from Saltzburg and had hewn at Wirtzburg by a far-famed master there, Dillmann Riemenschneider by name, who had also made Bishop Rudolph's stone." The commissions Riemenschneider received prove that he was indeed "far-famed" and that his reputation extended well beyond Würzburg and the Franconian territories. In 1490, when he had been a master in the Würzburg Guild of St. Luke for only five years, he was engaged to carve the great altarpiece for the high altar of the parish church of Münnerstadt,[2] which lies considerably north of Würzburg, in the Thuringian region. And even before that he must have carved an altarpiece for Hessenthal,[3] situated in the Spessart Forest, northwest of Würzburg, near Aschaffenburg. Following the Münnerstadt retable, many towns in a wide area around Würzburg gave him their most sought-after commissions. From Rothenburg ob der Tauber and Windsheim, both of which are as near to Nuremberg as to Würzburg and could as easily have employed Nuremberg sculptors, from Creglingen in the Tauber valley, and from Aschaffenburg on the Lower Main River, Riemenschneider received commissions for a number of large altarpieces. For the Peterskirche (Church of St. Peter) in Erfurt, still further away, Riemenschneider carved at least two figures in alabaster. In 1499 one of his major commissions came about when the bishop of Bamberg engaged him to carve a tomb for the imperial saints, Emperor Henry II and his wife Cunegund, for Bamberg Cathedral.[4] This massive "tumba" took more than a decade to complete and was formally erected in Bamberg Cathedral in 1513. Hewn of stone, it consists of an elaborate lid portraying the imperial couple and five reliefs on the sides depicting scenes from their legends. The greatest proof of his reputation as an artist, however, is that Frederick III, elector of Saxony, also known as Frederick the Wise (1463–1525), made use of his services. The elector was a noted patron and connoisseur of the arts and ordered from Riemenschneider, the "image-carver at Wirtzburgk," a monumental, over-life-size crucifix for the Stiftskirche in Wittenberg. The elector decorated the Stiftskirche with works commissioned from some of the greatest artists of the time, both German and foreign, among the former Albrecht Dürer and Lucas Cranach the Elder (1472–1553). (The Riemenschneider *crucifixus*, for which thirty-four guilders, ten groschen, and six pfennig were paid, including transport costs, was unfortunately destroyed by fire on October 13, 1760, during the bombardment of Wittenberg in the Seven Years War.)

To the ordinary man in those days, no less than to connoisseurs, Riemenschneider's art must have had a strong appeal. How else can we explain the fact that his works were so often taken as models and his style so often imitated by other artists who had not necessarily worked under him? The guild lists of the time show thirteen apprentices trained by Riemenschneider, though there must also, of course, have been considerable numbers of journeymen who stayed with Riemenschneider for short periods before moving on to some other workshop. But this in no way accounts for the number of artists who produced works in his style—presumably in response to what the public and patrons found pleasing.

The area where Riemenschneider's style prevailed, where his carvings set the standard and model, extended far beyond the area governed by the prince-bishop of Würzburg. (As the title implies, the prince-bishop was not only the spiritual head of the diocese of Würzburg, but also the temporal ruler of the duchy of Eastern Franconia.) Riemenschneider's influence reached into Swabia and Thuringia, and in isolated cases it penetrated still further, as far as Lübeck and the Moselle valley, Sweden, Switzerland, and the South Tyrol. Only Nuremberg resisted his influence and even took a negative attitude: when a bust of St. Kilian by Riemenschneider was brought to a Nuremberg goldsmith as a model for a silver bust for the cathedral in Würzburg, the goldsmith considered the Riemenschneider countenance "too childish." In Nuremberg, with its respect for down-to-earth realism, the idealized quality of Riemenschneider's art undoubtedly seemed quaint and outmoded.

What seemed naive or "childish" to Nuremberg eyes seems to have been regarded as natural and pleasing in Würzburg and the surrounding region far into the sixteenth century. The inhabitants of this area were more caught up in medieval ways and thought. Gentle and ingenuous, these people differed temperamentally from those in Nuremberg, where a climate of mercantile aggression existed that made that society receptive and fruitful ground for the new spirit of self-confidence inherent in Renaissance ideology. That is not to say, however, that the people of Würzburg and the area that is now Lower Franconia were lacking in spirit or conviction. They could be roused almost to the point of fanaticism by the social ills of the age, as shown not only by their involvement in the Peasants' War of 1524–1525, but by earlier events also. One example is the Niklashausen revolt of 1476. In their thousands the peasants of this region thronged to hear a young musician, Hans Böhm, who claimed that the Virgin Mary had commanded him to "burn his kettle-drum" and "preach to the common man." Unfortunately, though, since this German Savonarola not only preached against "lecherous sinful dance" and "jewelry display, vainglory, silk ribbons, breast cloths and pointed shoes," but also involved himself in politics, declaring that "henceforth there should be no more Popes, Emperors, Kings, Princes or other ecclesiastical and temporal rulers, but all those done away with, and all men should be as brothers, no one having more than the other," the bishop at length stepped in, routed the peasants with his horsemen, and burned the preacher at the stake.

It is easy to see how Riemenschneider's work would have evoked a sympathetic response in people of this kind, with their mild, open, yet sometimes passionate, even zealous disposition. His art touched upon the basic emotions of people of all stations; at the same time it had a dignity and spiritual character and a depth of religious feeling that still endure today. The Last Supper in the Rothenburg Altarpiece of the Holy Blood, the Assumption of Mary in the Creglingen Herrgottskirche, the Lamentation in Maidbronn—these are the great expressions of a simple, devout faith.

It is clear to us that Riemenschneider's life was governed by the same ideals and convictions that are expressed in his work. Just as his sculpture bears witness to the deepest spiritual forces of the age, so his attitude and conduct during the Peasants' Revolt show him willing, without regard for his own safety or status, to support those who seemed to him to stand for the Christian ideal, which we see so eloquently embodied in his carvings of the Apostles.

What, then, was the course of this man's life, a life that shows such unity of emphasis in respect to his work and actions? With the exception of one momentous event during the Peasants' Revolt in 1525, it was the typical life of a medieval burgher and master of a craft who rises to a position of esteem and significance in his community. What we know about Riemenschneider is largely derived from public records, not from artistic or personal sources. There was no chronicler of the arts among Würzburg's historians and archivists of the time, nobody to equal Neudörfer in Nuremberg or Vasari in Florence; and Riemenschneider and his generation, unlike Dürer a decade later, left no diaries or other autobiographical material. Riemenschneider still considered himself no more than a master craftsman. Our knowledge of Riemenschneider's life is gained therefore from a painstaking assembly of details pieced together from entries in official and business records, contracts, and all types of protocols.[5] And all these sources, moreover, relate only to the years after Riemenschneider had settled in Würzburg. His youth is still obscure, and even though some light has been shed on the history of his family,[6] Riemenschneider's own movements up to the time of his taking up residence in Würzburg in 1483 remain largely a matter of hypothesis.

An entry in a book of the Würzburg Council,[7] relating to Riemenschneider's declaration to the burgomasters of Würzburg when he took his journeyman's oath on December 7, 1483, tells us that Riemenschneider came "from Osterode in Saxony," a small town on the southern slopes of the Harz Mountains in what is now Lower Saxony. There is also an Osterode document concerning a sale of property, dated December 1483 (the same month in which Riemenschneider settled in Würzburg) which refers to a "Tile Riemenschneider" who was evidently recently deceased; and from the striking correspondence of the names, we may assume that this Tile Riemenschneider was the sculptor's father. Largely in view of this evidence, it used to be thought that Riemenschneider was probably a native of Osterode. Further research has shown, however, that his father and his paternal uncle, Nikolaus Riemenschneider, originally came from Heiligenstadt im Eichsfeld, another small town, south of Osterode, and that Riemenschneider, although he must have spent part of his youth in Osterode, was most probably born in Heiligenstadt. The elder Tilmann Riemenschneider had owned a mill in Heiligenstadt, which he had probably inherited from his father. Twice, however, in 1471 and in 1474, all his land and property in the town and vicinity were confiscated because of his failure to pay his debts. Quite possibly it was troubles of this kind that made him leave Heiligenstadt and settle with his family in Osterode. There he became master of the mint. Problems continued to beset him, however, and on one occasion a curate of Brunswick had both him and his wife Margaretha excommunicated, an action which carried with it the threat of banishment from Osterode.

In all these difficulties the elder Riemenschneider received assistance from his brother Nikolaus, who was both an ecclesiastic and a public official. Having been ordained in the diocese of Mainz (which included Heiligenstadt in its jurisdiction), Nikolaus became a curate of the cathedral in Würzburg. He was also made an imperial notary, and from 1458 until his death in 1478 he was *Fiskal*, or chief fiscal administrator, for the bishopric of Würzburg. Nikolaus, it seems, also took an active interest in his nephew's welfare; very probably he wished him to follow in the clerical profession. Tilmann Riemenschneider appears, in fact, to have taken lower orders in the diocese of Mainz at some point, the same diocese in which his uncle had his schooling as a cleric. In 1479, one year after the death of Nikolaus, "Tilmannus Rimensneider, clericus Magutinensis diocesis" (cleric of the diocese of Mainz) is mentioned as the last previous recipient of the benefice of the Altar of St. Anne in the Hauger Stiftskirche in Würzburg. Presumably Nikolaus Riemenschneider, who had accumulated a number of such church livings for himself, helped to obtain this benefice for his nephew as a means of support during his student years. (To be eligible for a small benefice of this kind the young Riemenschneider did not have to be a practicing cleric, which required higher orders and a minimum age of twenty-five. Lower orders alone would be sufficient for this; and only at that level could he give up the priesthood and return to secular life.) By 1479 Riemenschneider evidently had to do without this benefice; perhaps it was withdrawn or came to an end with the death of his influential uncle, or perhaps he himself gave it up voluntarily as part of a decision to leave the Church and work instead with "wood and stone." A few years after this, in December 1483, as mentioned earlier, it is presumed that the elder Tilmann Riemenschneider died in Osterode. In that same month the younger Riemenschneider settled in Würzburg as a journeyman carver.

Riemenschneider's beginnings as a sculptor remain the most enigmatic part of his career. The knowledge outlined above about his family and their movements in the decades between 1470 and 1490, though it allows some inferences to be made, still leaves unanswered the questions we have about his formative years in the field of sculpture. We do not know for sure where the young Riemenschneider pursued his clerical studies; when or why he changed his interests; where and with whom he served his apprenticeship; and where and with which masters he spent the major part of his journeyman years, before he decided to settle in Würzburg. Nor do we know very much about the works that he did during these early years, including his first seven years in Würzburg, prior to 1490 when, starting with the Münnerstadt Altarpiece, documents begin to give us guidance for the chronology of his sculptures.[8]

Though we have no sure answers to these questions, certain reasonable assumptions, based both on the stylistic qualities of Riemenschneider's work and on what we do know of his family, can be and indeed have been made. The question of Riemenschneider's apprenticeship has been under discussion for well over a hundred years. The first biographer of Riemenschneider, Carl Becker,[9] assumed in 1849 that Riemenschneider and Adam Kraft shared the same artistic roots because of a certain similarity of concept in their works. The fact should be acknowledged, however, that the dramatic realism of Kraft and the lyric idealism of Riemenschneider point in opposite directions and indicate quite different beginnings. As another possibility, Eduard Tönnies[10] in 1900 proposed the workshop of Wolgemut (1434–1519) in Nuremberg as the place where Riemenschneider may have served his apprenticeship. He did not realize, however, that as a master painter Wolgemut was not allowed to train sculptor apprentices but could employ only fully-trained sculptor assistants when these were needed for altarpieces that contained figures that were both polychromed and carved. What has been considered the influence of Nuremberg style on Riemenschneider can be explained by the presence of assistants in his workshop who had been trained in that city.

It is evident from Riemenschneider's work after 1490 (as will be discussed later) that he spent some part of his formative years in Swabia, in Ulm in particular, but because of the distance between Swabia and both Heiligenstadt and Osterode, where Riemenschneider spent his earliest years, it is unlikely that he started his training in Swabia. The most logical place for Riemenschneider to have served his apprenticeship would seem to be the city of Erfurt.[11] Like Heiligenstadt, where the family originated, Erfurt belonged to the diocese of Mainz and most likely it was there that the young Riemenschneider underwent the early clerical studies which resulted in his becoming a "cleric of the diocese of Mainz." Not only was Erfurt the closest academic center to both Osterode and Heiligenstadt, but Nikolaus Riemenschneider, who undoubtedly supported his nephew's clerical career, had received his academic degrees from the University of Erfurt. The Würzburg benefice in the Hauger Stiftskirche could have been used to finance Tilmann Riemenschneider's studies in Erfurt or to help support him there as long as he could supply a substitute to take care of the altar service in the Stift Haug Church. Since Erfurt was also the artistic center of the region and noted in the field of stone carving, it could well have been there, in these early years, that Riemenschneider developed his interest in sculpture. There are stylistic and compositional elements in Riemenschneider's work which support the circumstantial arguments for Erfurt as the place of his apprenticeship, at least as a sculptor in stone. Stylistic correspondences indicate that Riemenschneider may have been apprenticed to a stone sculptor who was a lay member of the Erfurt monastery of St. Peter (for which Riemenschneider worked in later years). It is also likely that Riemenschneider worked with the stone carver who created the epitaph of 1480 in the Erfurt Lorenzkirche (Church of St. Lawrence) devoted to the memory of an Erfurt citizen, Berlt Stark. This relief represents The Agony in the Garden. Many of the motifs that occur in it are to be found in Riemenschneider's own later depictions of this theme which he carved for the parish church in Heidingsfeld and the Burkarduskirche (Church of St. Burchard) in Würzburg; the Heidingsfeld figures of Christ and St. James, and the St. Burchard figure of St. John the Evangelist are notable examples. In view of this correspondence, it is feasible that Riemenschneider worked on the Erfurt epitaph, helping with the design or assisting in its execution.

Erfurt would also help to explain Riemenschneider's interest in and use of alabaster as a material for carving. Riemenschneider was the only major German sculptor of the period around 1500 who used alabaster, and it seems reasonable to assume therefore that he was introduced to this material during his apprentice years. Certainly in Erfurt he would have had ample opportunity to see religious sculptures in alabaster. Alabaster was quarried not far from the city, and in the middle of the fifteenth century Erfurt was a center in the production of alabaster sculpture in Germany.[12]

The character of Riemenschneider's later work in stone and wood would indicate that he was trained independently in each of these two fields. By the time he finished his apprenticeship, probably in 1480, he had very likely accomplished the first part of this training and qualified as an assistant stone carver.

After a period in Erfurt, Riemenschneider seems to have spent some time working in the region of the Upper Rhine, perhaps in Strasbourg. The fame of Nikolaus Gerhaert von Leyden (active c. 1462–1473) may well have drawn him to that city. The great Netherlandish sculptor had left Strasbourg in the late 1460s in order to accept the commission for the tomb of Emperor Frederick III in St. Stephen's Cathedral in Vienna, but Riemenschneider must have worked with one of his successors there. The influence of Strasbourg sculpture can be seen all through Riemenschneider's work, from the early Hessenthal Lamentation group (about 1485–1490) to the late Maidbronn altarpiece. Clearly, the Strasbourg sculptures of Gerhaert and his school made a lasting impression on the young Riemenschneider and, like the graphic work of Schongauer, which also transmitted the ideas of Netherlandish artists, influenced his work for many years, long after he had left that region.[13] The Hessenthal Lamentation, which appears to be the first altarpiece carved by Riemenschneider after he settled in Würzburg, is related to a Gerhaert School work, the Hedelfingen Pietà of 1471. In Riemenschneider's mature period, to take just one other example, the Dettwang Crucifixion Altarpiece of 1512–1513 also reflects Netherlandish influence in Strasbourg. The related works here are a pair of alabaster groups—the remains of a Crucifixion—representing the Virgin Mary, John, and the other Marys in one group, and the centurion with pharisees in the other. Both are preserved in the Frauenhaus Museum in Strasbourg.

From Strasbourg, Riemenschneider appears to have moved on to the city of Ulm in Swabia. He must of course have known what South Germany had to offer a sculptor eager for contact with the great masters of his time. The opportunity to work with, or at least close to, such a famous master as Michel Erhart (1469–1518 in Ulm), whose workshop practiced both stone and wood carving, probably attracted Riemenschneider to that city. Other good reasons would have been his desire to learn the art of wood carving and the fact that Ulm was very liberal in accepting apprentices in a second field without prescribing a fixed period for the apprenticeship. Riemenschneider was free to study "kurz oder lang" (for a short or a long time), and whenever he had finished the work required for acceptance as a fully-trained wood carver he could present himself to the guild masters and be declared a "Geselle," thereby moving up to the level of an assistant in this second field, too.

I consider it probable that Riemenschneider in fact worked and trained with Michel Erhart in Ulm. As in the case of Erfurt and Strasbourg, the first observations about Riemenschneider's connection with Ulm were based solely on stylistic evidence. Wilhelm Vöge observed close stylistic affinities between Riemenschneider and the carver of the figures in the shrine of the Blaubeuren High Altarpiece (of 1493–1494) and concluded from this that Riemenschneider and this sculptor must have worked together in the same workshop for a time.[14] Since I tend to believe that it was Gregor Erhart, the son of Michel Erhart, who carved the shrine figures of the Blaubeuren Altarpiece just before leaving Ulm for Augsburg in 1494, it seems reasonable to assume that the Ulm workshop of Michel Erhart was their common meeting-ground and that it was here that Riemenschneider trained and worked as a wood carver.[15]

Like the Upper Rhenish qualities in Riemenschneider's work, the Swabian elements are clearly discernible. Early works by Riemenschneider's own hand, such as the Grumbach tomb-monument in Rimpar, the figure of St.

John the Baptist in Hassfurt, the wing reliefs from the Münnerstadt Altarpiece showing The Meeting in the Garden and Supper in the House of Simon, the group of Mary Magdalene and the angels from the shrine of that altarpiece, as well as the Evangelist figures from its predella, and even the figure of Eve from the Marienkapelle in Würzburg, all suggest Swabia as well as the region of the Upper Rhine. In particular, the tomb-monument of Eberhard von Grumbach (which is Riemenschneider's earliest work connected with a definite date) points back to Ulm: the erect figure of Riemenschneider's knight is unmistakably related to the trim, elegant St. George in the Liebieghaus in Frankfurt am Main, which has been included in the body of works now ascribed to Michel Erhart.[16] Certainly, like the Netherlandish sculpture of Strasbourg, works created in Ulm—such as Michel Erhart's Mary with the Protective Cloak and the groups representing The Mass of St. Gregory and The Beheading of St. Catherine, now in the Staatliche Museen in West Berlin, as well as the busts of prophets and sibyls on the sides of the Syrlin choir stalls in Ulm Cathedral, which have also been attributed to Michel Erhart—became a decisive and lasting influence on the young Riemenschneider. The delicacy of Riemenschneider's art may well have derived from the refined carving in unpolychromed wood of the Ulm choir stall busts; equally, these busts may have taught Riemenschneider to portray people as individuals and to search for the power of personal expression.

Besides this, there exists other, more conclusive evidence of Riemenschneider's connection with Michel Erhart of Ulm. We know of a Crucifixion altarpiece by Riemenschneider, fragmented now, that has to be dated in the early 1480s and which can be determined as having stood in the abbey church of Wiblingen, near Ulm. In light of this I assume that this altarpiece was carved by Riemenschneider while he was an assistant in Ulm. It certainly appears that Riemenschneider carved almost the entire work, and if we consider the fact that Michel Erhart apparently entrusted his son Gregor to carve the greater part of the later Blaubeuren Altarpiece, he may well have given the task of the Wiblingen Altarpiece to Riemenschneider. Several fragments from the Wiblingen Altarpiece, which originally contained a Crucifixion in the shrine and a Deposition in the predella, have been identified: the two wing reliefs depicting The Agony in the Garden and the Resurrection are now in the collection at Schloss Berchtesgaden. (Though of a somewhat different character in the total composition, these reliefs nonetheless clearly show Riemenschneider's participation.) The two lateral groups from the Crucifixion scene in the shrine are now in Schloss Harburg in the collection of Prince Öttingen-Wallerstein. The centerpiece from the shrine, the Crucified Christ, was discovered in the church of St. Anton im Fünfhaus, near Vienna, in 1956; and the two lateral groups from the Deposition in the predella, one of which is known to have come from the abbey church in Wiblingen, are in the Staatliche Museen of West Berlin (see note 8). The group from the left side of the predella Deposition shows a woman weeping and drying her tears and another woman bent over what must have been the dead body of Christ, which is now missing and was originally the central figure connecting the two groups. The right-hand group shows Nicodemus holding the shroud on which Christ had been laid out, another woman wringing her hands, and John the Evangelist. This right group is the one ascertained to have come from the abbey church in Wiblingen; the character of both groups evinces a strong relationship between the work of Michel Erhart and the young Riemenschneider (compare, for example, Michel Erhart's Beheading of St. Catherine and Mass of St. Gregory, in Berlin), which also supports the thesis that the Wiblingen altarpiece was carved by Riemenschneider during his assistantship in Ulm.

In this discussion of Riemenschneider's early years as a carver I have noted the pervasive effect of both Swabian and Upper Rhenish sculpture in his work. The question remains whether there are any affinities of style or mood to the sculpture of northern and central Germany, the areas where he originated and eventually settled.

Examination of Würzburg sculpture of the period immediately before Riemenschneider shows no connection between the two. The monuments for the Prince-Bishops Gottfried von Limpurg (d. 1455) and Johann von Grumbach (d. 1466) in Würzburg Cathedral, which still belong to the monumental phase of German sculpture, about the middle of the century, are of a harsher and more severe and angular character than that which Riemenschneider brought to Würzburg. That is not due merely to the difference in generation: Adam Kraft, a contemporary of Riemenschneider's, would have preserved the tenor of these monuments even while working in the new style. Riemenschneider, in fact, introduced an entirely new note into Würzburg sculpture, a note which seems to me not so much northern as Swabian in character and origin. In Swabia, and specifically under such a master as Michel Erhart, Riemenschneider's style could develop in contact with a spirit akin to his own gentle, sensitive temperament; and as I have indicated above, the Swabian culture he experienced in his journeyman years clearly had a much more decisive effect on him than that of either the Harz region, where he spent his youth, or Erfurt, where he served his apprenticeship. It is significant that in the fundamental formal aspects of his art, as, for example, the figural organization of his shrines, Riemenschneider differs entirely from the North German art of his age. In northern and central Germany the shrines of altarpieces, even at that time, were crowded with many small figures; Riemenschneider, in contrast, employs relatively fewer, larger figures. Whether and to what extent Riemenschneider's origins are felt in the spirit or tenor of his work, in spite of the adopted sculptural forms of South German art, remains an open question.

Returning now to the historical aspects of his life, Riemenschneider's decision to settle in Würzburg seems a natural choice in the circumstances. Such a decision would be in keeping with the sober and clear way of thinking that is reflected in some of Riemenschneider's personal business documents, and which may seem to us today, though not to his contemporaries, surprisingly pragmatic when compared to the spiritual character of his art. No doubt he was influenced by the practical consideration that the thriving city of Würzburg, the seat of the ruling prince-bishop and at that time without a prominent artist, might offer valuable commissions, wealth, and esteem. In addition, he probably thought he would not be looked on as a total stranger there, since he already had connections with the city as the recipient of a Würzburg benefice and the nephew of the recently deceased "Fiscal" of the diocese. It is possible, moreover, that there were also other, more distant relatives of the family in Würzburg; the name Riemenschneider is recorded there several times in the fifteenth century. Like Tilmann, the other Riemenschneiders must originally have been immigrants to Würzburg and not natives of that city. The word "riemenschneider" means "cutter of strips of leather" and originally referred to a particular kind of artisan before it was used as a family name. The occupation "riemenschneider" described was that of a harness-maker, but while "riemenschneider" was commonly used to denote this craft in Lower Saxony, in Würzburg the practitioners of the same trade were traditionally known as "sporer" or "spur-maker." (This information was of particular importance before Riemenschneider's origins were determined by documentary evidence, when it was assumed that he came from Würzburg.)

On the question of age, we may assume that Riemenschneider was in his early twenties when he came to Würzburg. As we have seen, his years as an apprentice and journeyman sculptor and the course of his travels in that period can only be reconstructed on the basis of stylistic evidence. Similarly, even to determine the year of the sculptor's birth we have to rely in part on stylistic considerations, since we have only one statement relating to his age, and that is somewhat ambiguous: in connection with an arbitration he attended as a witness in 1528, he declared that he "had sat forty years at Würzburg" and "was sixty years old." This statement, however, has to be an approximation. We know that Riemenschneider came to Würzburg in 1483, so that by 1528 he had been there, not "forty years" but forty-five. Accordingly, "sixty years old" should be taken to mean that he was in his sixties, particularly since it can be proved that a number of other witnesses also gave only their approximate ages. Had Riemenschneider been sixty in 1528, he would have been born in 1468 and therefore would have been only fifteen when he arrived in Würzburg. But at the age of fifteen he could not have finished his apprenticeship and journeyman years. He must have been at least twenty when he arrived in Würzburg. He cannot, therefore, have been born in 1468, but at the latest in 1463, and at the earliest in 1459. The character of his art would also indicate a birthdate about 1460. Riemenschneider is not a contemporary of Dürer, Cranach, Baldung, Backofen, and Grünewald (all born in or just after the decade of the 1470s) but belongs to an older generation. He stands beside Adam Kraft, who was also born about 1460, and beside painters such as Bernhard Strigel and the so-called Master of the Peringsdörfer Altarpiece. They too were men of the transitional era, more bound to their Gothic heritage than was Dürer's generation, yet already imbued with the new concept of humanism which was totally unknown to the preceding generation of Schongauer and his contemporaries.

What was Riemenschneider's life like after he settled in Würzburg? When he arrived there at the end of 1483 he first joined the workshop of a Würzburg master as an assistant. We do not know which workshop this was, but on December 7 he is recorded as taking the journeyman's oath to perform "the duty of artisans with faithfulness" before the burgomasters of Würzburg. The nature of his oath makes it clear that Riemenschneider was already beyond the apprentice stage, which is confirmed by the fact that he is not listed as such in any of the guild books; but as a newcomer to the town he was prohibited, by the guild rules, from setting up his own workshop. It was not long, however, until he became independent. Early in 1485 he married Anna Schmidt (née Uchenhofer), the well-to-do widow of the Würzburg goldsmith Ewalt Schmidt. This marriage to the widow of a Würzburg master enabled him to become a citizen (*ex gratia*) of Würzburg on February 28, 1485, and also, in accordance with the local guild regulations, a master in his own right. The only way to become a master in Würzburg, for someone who was not the son of one, was to marry the widow or daughter of a Würzburg master, though not necessarily one in the same guild. Schmidt, for example, belonged to the guild of gold- and silversmiths, while Riemenschneider became a member of the Guild of St. Luke's, which comprised painters, sculptors, and glaziers.

From her previous marriage, Riemenschneider's wife Anna brought him three sons and a fine house called "zum Wolfmannsziechlein," or "Wolfman's Ewe." This was a spacious building in the present Franziskanergasse, with enough room for workshops and accommodation for his apprentices and assistants, as well as family quarters. Riemenschneider lived in this house for the rest of his life. The house was severely damaged during World War

II but has now been rebuilt around the one wall that remained standing. Ten years after their marriage, his wife died, leaving him a young daughter in addition to his stepsons. This daughter, Gertrud, later married a legal officer, a "Hofschultheiss," who is buried in the same grave-plot as his father-in-law. Of his stepsons, one seems to have died young, one became a priest, and one a goldsmith like his father before him. For this last stepson Riemenschneider occasionally furnished carved models.[17]

Riemenschneider stayed a widower for just over two years. However, his determination to find a new wife for himself and a mother for his sizable family is documented at the outset. A contract of February 24, 1495, concerning the division of his first wife's estate, clearly states that Tilmann Riemenschneider had "courage and will to enter again into the state of matrimony," since for him and his children it was "difficult and damaging to their health to keep house with servant-girls." In spite of this, he did not marry again until around Easter of 1497. From this union with a young wife, Anna (née Rappolt), came three sons and another daughter. All the sons became artists. Georg, the eldest, following his father, was accepted into the Guild of St. Luke's in Würzburg in 1522. In 1534 he became head of this guild and as such initiated a register of all the master workshops and their apprentices in Würzburg: according to this list he himself had only one apprentice, while his father trained thirteen. He is known to have carved tomb-monuments, including that of his father in 1531. The second son, Hans, who was probably born about 1500, also became a sculptor. He moved to the city of Nuremberg, however, and nothing is known about his activities in Würzburg. The youngest son, Bartholomäus, evidently had the most independent spirit and artistic talent. He became a painter and decorator who probably studied in Augsburg and was later active in Bolzano in the South Tyrol. He seems to have been well known in this region for his altarpieces and intricately painted ceramic stoves, which show the influence of Renaissance style.

Riemenschneider's second marriage must have lasted less than a decade, for in 1507 he married for the third time, on this occasion the widow of a blacksmith, Margarete Würzbach, who added a smithy to the family property. After the death of this third wife, Riemenschneider at the age of almost sixty, in 1520 or 1521, took a fourth wife, Margred (maiden or family name unknown), who survived him. Shortly before this marriage he apportioned two-thirds of his holdings among his five children: between them they received two houses and ten and a half "morgen" of vineyards, while for himself he kept his first house and seven and a half "morgen" of vineyards. (The "morgen," according to Bavarian standards, is equal to 0.84 acres.)

In the years after his arrival in Würzburg, as he had perhaps hoped, Riemenschneider had the help and patronage of some of his late uncle's friends. Johann von Allendorf, for example, who was chancellor to the prince-bishop of Würzburg and an executor for Nikolaus Riemenschneider, in 1494 commissioned a carving of the Fourteen Helper Saints for the chapel of a Würzburg hospital he had endowed. A fragment of this group with the figures of saints Christopher, Eustace, and Erasmus is now in the Cloisters Collection of the Metropolitan Museum of Art in New York.[18] Riemenschneider's services were also well used by the prince-bishop of Würzburg, Lorenz von Bibra. The tomb-monuments Riemenschneider carved for him and, at his request, for his predecessor, Rudolf von Scherenberg, are still in Würzburg Cathedral. For Lorenz von Bibra, who had lived in Italy and had many of the traits of a Renaissance prince, Riemenschneider also created a cast portrait medal which appears to be the first of its kind in Germany.[19] The sculptor also received important commissions from the City Council of Würzburg for the council's church, the Marienkapelle: namely, the stone figures of the twelve Apostles, Christ, and John the Baptist, which originally decorated the buttresses of the church, and the figures of Adam and Eve, which flanked the south portal, facing the Marktplatz.[20] (The latter figures replaced statues from the previous century, apparently found unsatisfactory in light of the new realism of the age.) There are indications, too, of other commissions for the Marienkapelle, and also documents referring to Riemenschneider's work for the high altar of the cathedral, which unfortunately has been destroyed.

On the civic rather than the artistic side, Riemenschneider's life is closely interwoven with the history of Würzburg itself, particularly with the events of the tragic and momentous years of 1524 and 1525. But while we know quite a bit about the commissions he was engaged on during the decade of the 1490s, his activities as a citizen become a matter of public record only after 1504. In that year (the same year that the young Dürer was being honored in Venice), Riemenschneider was elected a member of the City Council of Würzburg, having by that time achieved sufficient standing in the city to be selected by the Cathedral Chapter from six candidates proposed by the council. When the Emperor Maximilian, who was known for his patronage of the arts, visited Würzburg in 1505, Riemenschneider was one of the councilors who welcomed the emperor at the city gates. Over the next two decades, in addition to taking care of his thriving workshop, Riemenschneider held various offices that were the responsibility of the city councilors: in turn he was building supervisor (in charge of the building operations of the city), comptroller of fishing waters, custodian of the Marienkapelle (the council's church), tax-assessor, civilian head of the city's military force, and hospital overseer. Several times—in 1509, 1514, and 1518—he served on the Upper Council, the members of which were the city magistrates; and for the year 1520–1521 he was elected to the city's highest office as burgomaster or mayor, chosen presumably not only because of his experience in public life but because he enjoyed the trust and confidence of the prince-bishop, the Cathedral Chapter, and the other burghers of Würzburg.

These years of civic responsibilities and honors were also the years of Riemenschneider's artistic maturity, when he created such works as the Creglingen, Dettwang, and Maidbronn altarpieces, and clearly they were a successful and prosperous time for him.[21] In 1525, however, his fortunes changed abruptly. In that year, when the Peasants' Revolt swept over Germany and Würzburg was forced to take a stand, Riemenschneider took the part of the peasants and aligned himself with the group of council members who opposed the demands of the prince-bishop, Konrad von Thüngen, who wished to assemble troops from all over the duchy in Würzburg. Riemenschneider was opposed to admitting these forces and would not agree to send Würzburg men against the rebellious peasants. Following the victory of the princes, with whom Konrad von Thüngen was allied, Riemenschneider and the ten other councilors who had sided with him were all expelled from the council. Riemenschneider's troubles, however, did not end there. He was accused of starting a subversive and seditious rumor, and when Würzburg had to surrender to the princes, Riemenschneider almost paid for this alleged offense with his life. The rumor he was charged with spreading was that "there were mighty cannons in Katzenwickers" (the bishop's city estate); and when word of this got around, "the cry went up that when the horsemen came and were admitted into the city they would train these cannons on the city and force the citizens to accede to their demands. Thereupon there arose an uproar and riot as if the horsemen were already present and before the gate." Riemenschneider was not only imprisoned on account of this charge, but detained long after other captives had been released. He was dragged from one jail to another, terrorized by almost daily preparations for his execution, which the young knights would arrange as a means of entertaining themselves, and finally subjected to harsh interrogation. He saved his life by refusing to confess even under threat of torture, and by insisting that he had not originated the rumor but had repeated it after first hearing it from one Hans Bermeter. Riemenschneider was finally released from prison on August 8, 1525. Bermeter, who was known to be the leading rebel and dissident in Würzburg, was later arrested in Nuremberg at the request of the prince-bishop of Würzburg. Bermeter then tried to put the blame on Riemenschneider, but without success: "On Thursday after St. Kilian's day, 1527, he was condemned, and executed with the sword as an insurgent."[22]

It is not easy to determine what actually caused Riemenschneider to take the part of the peasants. Political reasons may have had something to do with the attitude of those burghers who, like Riemenschneider, sympathized with the rebels: for instance, a dislike of their dependence upon the prince-bishop and the Cathedral Chapter, though personally, of course, Riemenschneider had been well treated by the ecclesiastical authorities; the troubling memory of past attempts to gain independence and the continued hope of becoming a free imperial city, no longer under ecclesiastical rule, which was a status achieved by many a smaller city in that region.[23] Mixed with all of this must have been the anger felt by the burghers at the ever-increasing privileges enjoyed by the clergy, and by the nobility, from whose ranks at this time the clergy were exclusively drawn. In his role as tax-assessor, Riemenschneider had effectively opposed the bishop's plan of exempting from city taxes the properties of noblemen or clergymen that were in fact liable to such tax.

But however much this kind of social consciousness and political concern may have influenced Riemenschneider's attitude, it surely was not the decisive factor. In the final analysis—if we can judge from Riemenschneider's own works as the true mirror of his character—his sympathy with the rebels must have stemmed from his religious convictions. Works such as the Rothenburg Last Supper, the Creglingen Assumption of the Virgin, and the Maidbronn Lamentation for Christ reflect an unpretentious piety and a simple deep-seated faith that must have been at odds with much of the courtly ritual that the Church had developed. The contrast between the complacency of the religious dignitaries controlling the city, proud of their connections with the Franconian nobility, and the humility of the Apostles, as expressed in grave images by Riemenschneider, was surely too great not to have driven him to some kind of political action during the tumultuous years of the Peasants' Revolt.[24]

How did Riemenschneider survive imprisonment and torture? We have no documented work by him from the years after his release, and we have no knowledge of the effect these terrible experiences had on his work. But we do know that he was not broken by his ordeal, and that, contrary to the myth which has arisen, he was still able to work with his hands and continue carving. There is, in fact, one documented commission relating to the years after 1525: an order of 1527 from the convent at Kitzingen to repair and reassemble the altarpieces that had been torn down or damaged during the iconoclastic disturbances of the Peasants' Revolt.[25] There is also a record of payment made to Riemenschneider for a carving of two infants, probably to replace figures lost from an altarpiece of the Holy Clan (or Holy Kinship), which must have been part of this commission. It is sad, and not a little ironic, however, that the only commission we know Riemenschneider to

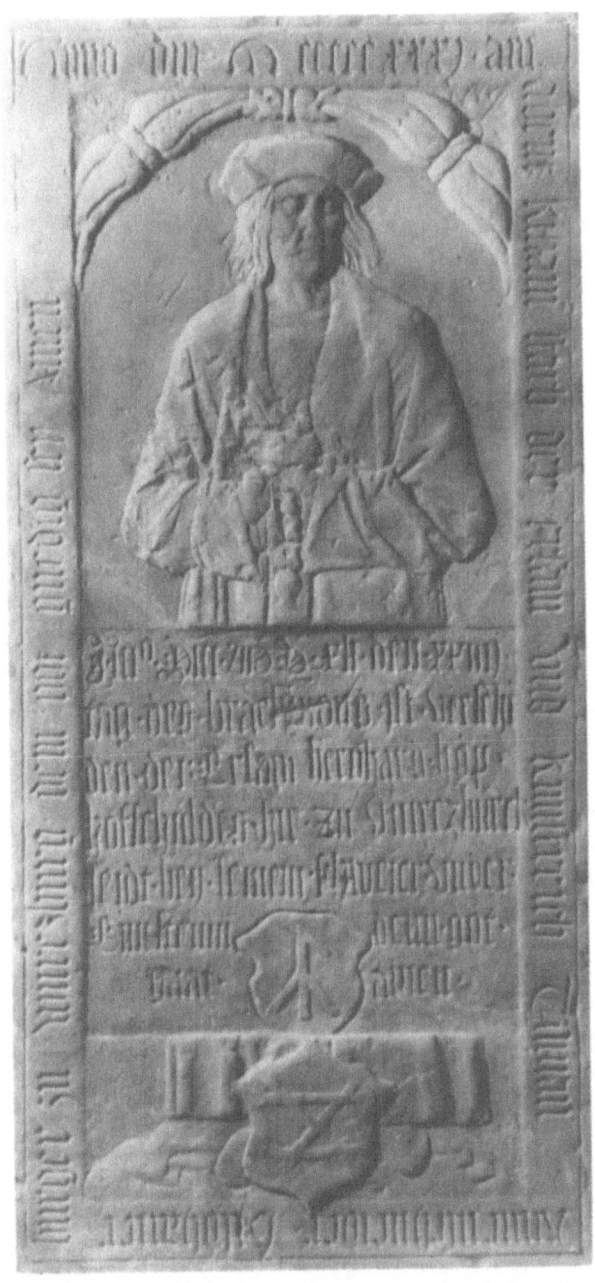

The tombstone of Tilmann Riemenschneider (d. 1531), carved by his son Georg. Now in the Mainfränkisches Museum, Würzburg.

have received in these years should be of this nature. It is still more ironic that Riemenschneider's last major work, the Maidbronn Lamentation Altarpiece, which must have been completed before the outbreak of the Peasants' Revolt, and which is such a moving document of the sculptor's spirit in those years, became in a way, by virtue of an inscription added to the predella in 1526 when the altarpiece was erected, a monument celebrating the triumph over the Peasants' Revolt and the victory of the forces Riemenschneider had opposed.

Riemenschneider lived for another six years after the suppression of the rebellion and his release from prison. He died on July 7, "on the eve of St. Kilian's day," 1531, at the age of about seventy. For several centuries he was completely forgotten. It was not until the early nineteenth century with the advent of the Romantic era and the discovery of his tombstone (in 1822) that the special qualities of his work were once again appreciated. Today in his own country he is considered to be one of the truly great artists Germany has produced.

The history of Tilmann Riemenschneider's life does not in itself provide an understanding of his artistic development. Though unique in certain respects, this development has to be thought of as directly related to and within the context of the general developments in the art of his age. Riemenschneider's sculptures, for all their difference in mood, spirit, and form, can take their place beside the most significant works of the German and Italian Renaissance. They are not merely an echo of a past artistic language, but represent instead the culmination and perfection of Late Gothic art and its highest aims. It is indicative of the creative energy and impulse of this last phase of Late Gothic art that it evolved of its own accord—out of an inner strength and not because of some outside influence—along the lines of the new art of the Renaissance. And the ultimate triumph of Renaissance art would be hard to imagine if these artistically most mature and pure works of the Late Gothic had not paved the way. This innate evolution in the direction of the new art can be traced in both Riemenschneider and Adam Kraft, two men quite different in temperament yet showing a similar course of artistic development. From his early, crowded and multi-figured Schreyer Epitaph, with its painterly depth, to the reliefs depicting the Stations of the Cross created shortly before his death, which rely on fewer figures in clearly defined spatial zones, Kraft's art runs almost parallel to Riemenschneider's development from his Münnerstadt and Rothenburg altarpieces to those of Creglingen and Dettwang, from the tomb-monuments of Grumbach and Scherenberg to those of Schaumberg and Bibra. The Rothenburg Altarpiece of the Holy Blood, created between 1501 and 1504 (Plate 23A), still shows the same crowded organization as Kraft's early work. Significant features are the almost equal value given to each individual figure in the closely interwoven composition of The Last Supper (Plate 23B) and the even density of forms in every available space, whether it be predella, shrine, wings, or superstructure. Unfortunately, the shrine composition of the Münnerstadt Altarpiece, an even earlier work, cannot be used for comparison since only parts of it have been preserved, but, to judge from the description in the contract, it seems to have been as filled with figures as Kraft's Schreyer Epitaph.[26]

It is important to note at this point that even these early altarpieces by Riemenschneider show two basic and fundamental innovations. In the first place, the play of light and shadow over the natural surface of the carved wood replaces the ornate splendor of paint and gilt. As Veit Stoss (1447?–1533) was to do later in his career,[27] Riemenschneider, from the beginning, preserved the natural appearance of the pale lindenwood, adding only touches of black and gray color to the pupil and iris of the eyes, and red to the lips and nostrils.[28] These touches enliven the features and intensify the emotional expression of his figures but are of no consequence as "color." In cases when it was not possible to leave the finished sculpture unpainted, as Riemenschneider preferred, the polychroming had to be done in a painter's workshop, by decree of the City Council of Würzburg. At about this time there was a parallel development to Riemenschneider's practice in the evolution from the colored woodcut to the woodcut in black and white in the work of the young Dürer. And to a certain extent this new treatment of the surface complemented the other innovation of the period, which restricted altarpieces to one presentation only. Previously, at least on closing the shrine, a different view would appear on the back of the wings, or various transformations were made possible through the use of several pairs of wings, giving different appearances for weekdays, Sundays, Christmas, and Easter. Both these innovations—foregoing the use of polychromy and gilt and of multiple sets of wings—came into being because of the Late Gothic desire to achieve, in its final phase, a purer artistic effect without sacrificing the mystical element inherent in the richness and splendor of appearance. It was the yearning for this mystical quality (a specifically Late Gothic characteristic) that had earlier produced the hinged polyptych which allowed a sequence of transfigurations and through its changing scenes preserved the desired sense of mystery. In spite of the restriction to one appearance, the same mystical sense pervades Riemenschneider's altarpieces, and gains a particular intensity from the way the element of light is exploited by the carving, so that the impression is not of something fixed and immutable but rather of a mysteriously shifting and changing scene. Such an effect would be impossible if color and gilt were used, since these together permit only the crudest

contrasts of light and shadow. Only by leaving off the polychromy and gilding could the light and shadow come into full play. At the same time this allowed a delicate refinement of the surface carving, extending to the smallest
variation in contour or depth, which produced the expressive countenances
so typical of Riemenschneider's art. This kind of refinement and subtlety
would have been quite lost under layers of tightly-woven canvas, gesso, and
polychromy.[29]

These innovations, first made in the Münnerstadt Altarpiece, are to be
found in all later altarpieces by Riemenschneider: the Altarpiece of the Holy
Blood in Rothenburg, as well as those in Creglingen, Dettwang, and Maidbronn. Carved from a single stone slab, though still tripartite in appearance,
the late Maidbronn retable (Plate 46A) is the one altarpiece that is radically
different (in both form and material) from the type of wood triptych Riemenschneider had used up to that time. But already in the Creglingen and
Dettwang works a new design begins to appear: the composition of the
altarpiece as a whole, as well as its individual parts, is more tightly structured and more strictly defined than in the earlier Rothenburg Altarpiece of
the Holy Blood. The organization of the shrine composition (Plates 33B,
41A) is particularly significant in this respect: individual figures are drawn
together into groups and the empty space between single figures and between groups is a deliberate and important part of the design. Tension between mass and empty space becomes the basic compositional feature in these
mature works. Light and shadow assume a new and growing significance
also. Even in the early works it was essentially the play of light and shadow
on the close-knit, intricate forms, producing quick, dramatic contrasts, that
defined the composition. The pattern of light and shadow in these cases,
however, was always determined by the carved, tactile form; space was defined entirely by plastic means, whereas in the mature works light and
shadow are themselves used to create the illusion of space.

It should be emphasized here that even in these mature works the spatial
setting remains no more than a suggestion; the perspective and depth of Renaissance art was entirely foreign to Riemenschneider. More and more he
tended to exclude all effects of depth in his work. A comparison of the Münnerstadt relief of The Meeting in the Garden (Plate 20C) with Schongauer's
engraving of that scene, or of the other relief from that altarpiece, Supper in
the House of Simon (Plate 20D), with contemporary woodcuts, shows that
this tendency existed from the beginning. Some spatial depth, however, can
be seen in other early relief compositions, and Riemenschneider's early work
in general shows the same restless, intricate arrangement of forms, in the
breaking of the drapery folds and the twisting and turning of bodies,[30] that
characterizes the prevailing style of the 1480s. Later on, in his mature and

late works, Riemenschneider increasingly eliminates all accents suggesting recession in space and tends to an arrangement of the figural parts on one frontal plane.[31]

The change in Riemenschneider's style, from the early to the mature, is first observed in the sculptures of the Rothenburg Altarpiece of the Holy Blood (1501–1504). Both the relief depicting The Agony in the Garden (Plate 23P) and the figure of Mary from the Annunciation group above the shrine (Plate 23J), which were carved in the years 1502 to 1504, demonstrate his new style. Forms are here simplified and expanded: the cascades and flurries of small, broken folds still found in the shrine group of The Last Supper (Plate 23B), created a little earlier, in 1501–1502, give place to a more quiescent, clearer arrangement of the drapery. The concave forms and calm, uncluttered areas that appear in the mantle folds of Mary and Christ (Plates 23J, 23P) as well as the figure of St. Anne that is believed to come from the Rothenburg Altarpiece of St. Anne (Plate 29) are a particularly significant feature. In addition, the individual figures are more harmoniously set and integrated into the surrounding space; in The Agony in the Garden, as in later reliefs (for example, those on the tomb of Henry and Cunegund in Bamberg Cathedral, Plates 40D, E) the figures appear in a more natural arrangement than in the earlier reliefs.

The tomb-monument for Konrad von Schaumberg (Plate 25B), who died in 1499 on his way back from the Holy Land, was created about the same time as these initial altar works in Riemenschneider's mature style. This work may profitably be compared with the earlier tomb-monuments of Eberhard von Grumbach (Plate 17) and Prince-Bishop Rudolf von Scherenberg (Plate 22A). In the Grumbach and Scherenberg monuments an uneasy tension is created by the positioning of the figures in relation to the surrounding area: we see how the figure of Grumbach strains in places beyond the confines of the slab, while the image of Scherenberg is narrowly encased and constrained by the lions, armorial shields, and angels depicted in the rim of the frame. In the Schaumberg tomb-monument, on the other hand, as well as in the slightly later work for Elisabeth Stieber (Plate 30),[32] the tectonic integration of the figure is sought: in flowing outline the knight stands out from the surrounding area, in like manner to the groups of figures in the shrine compositions of the Creglingen and Dettwang altarpieces. Here too the figure is felt to be set in space, with some depth to it, and the empty area around it is an integral part of the overall design.

The evolution of Riemenschneider's work, in spirit as well as in form, is also clearly demonstrated by the Grumbach and Schaumberg tomb-monuments. Eberhard von Grumbach appears as a slightly dandified though well-built knight of the Late Gothic era, with his broad shoulders and narrow hips, encased in armor from head to toe; one might say he looks like a figure out of the engravings of the Master of the Hausbuch, with little as yet distinctively Riemenschneider's about him. The Grumbach figure is largely the product of impressions gathered during the sculptor's formative years as a journeyman. Konrad von Schaumberg, on the other hand, with his bare head, cascading curls, and relaxed stance, is in keeping with the emerging spirit of buoyancy at the turn of the century. Yet in some ways he is more "medieval" than the self-confident, upright figure of Grumbach. The curvilinear outlines of the Schaumberg image, intentionally reminiscent of High Gothic figures, give it an ethereal and weightless quality, just as the young knight's face, for all its vigor and manliness, reflects spiritual rather than temporal concerns. Beside this expressive countenance the face of Grumbach appears blank and lifeless. In the same way, the figures from the Münnerstadt Altarpiece, and even the figure of Adam from the Marienkapelle, seem equally inhibited and restrained in their expression when compared to the more eloquent countenances of Riemenschneider's later years.[33]

In the period of Riemenschneider's last works in his early style—those such as the Scherenberg tomb-monument of 1496–1499, and the Last Supper group for the Altarpiece of the Holy Blood of 1501–1502—his main concern seems to have been to delineate individual characters, to try to portray or give expression to the complexity of human experience, and to enlarge and deepen his own sensibility and awareness (see Plates 22B, 23B-I). In the period of the Creglingen Altarpiece and a little before, from about 1503 to 1510, Riemenschneider restricts himself to a smaller number of figural and facial types, which have evolved out of his own feelings and experience. By limiting his scope in this way, the psychological and spiritual content of his work at this time is deepened and intensified (see Plates 33C-J, 33P).

Compared to the emotional fervor and poignant expression of the Creglingen Altarpiece, the language of the next decade is more modulated and restrained. Heralded in the figures for the high altar of Würzburg Cathedral (1508–1510) and in the Heidingsfeld Agony in the Garden (1510), this new development is fully revealed in the Dettwang Crucifixion Altarpiece (1512–1513), the later parts of the imperial tomb in Bamberg (1499–1513), and the Steinach crucifix (1516) (Plates 34–42).

In this decade, Renaissance art, which until then had not in any way affected or interfered with Riemenschneider's natural development, began to exert some influence on him. Adam Kraft, by his death in 1508, was spared having to confront the new art then in ascendance; but Riemenschneider ultimately had to come to terms with it. Certain works of these years show the effects of this influence and indicate that for a time Riemenschneider was confused and unsure of his direction. The tomb-monument of Lorenz von

Bibra (Plates 43A-D) is the prime example of this, and illustrates the conse-
quent loss in warmth and vitality when Riemenschneider attempted to work
in an idiom alien to his temperament. The appointment of an assistant to
carve the frame of this monument in Renaissance motifs, whether voluntary
or at the request of the prince-bishop himself, would in itself indicate that
Riemenschneider was going through a period of doubt and uncertainty. And
even the severe, dignified figure of the prelate, though clearly a carefully de-
liberated piece of work, contains contradictions that were inevitable when
Riemenschneider tried, against his inclinations, to conform to the spirit and
canons of the new age. The Renaissance putti he carved on the Bibra monument tend to the melancholy angel figures of the Late Gothic (Plate 43D),
and in the same way the image of Lorenz von Bibra demonstrates a similar
desire to accept the new values without being able to break away from old,
deep-rooted convictions. Riemenschneider's willingness to portray the self-
assertive Renaissance man with both feet planted firmly on the ground ran
contrary to his inner nature; he was neither temperamentally suited nor particularly able to express such down-to-earth vitality. On the other hand,
when he is portraying devout, youthful beauty, as in his figures of Adam or
Konrad von Schaumberg, and types such as St. John the Evangelist and the
angel figures, Riemenschneider is always totally convincing. He is equally
successful with the emotionally mature figures, such as St. Philip (in the
Creglingen Altarpiece) and Bishop Kilian (from Würzburg Cathedral),
whose faces reflect the spiritual torments and chastening they have endured,
or with the aged and frail figure of Rudolf von Scherenberg, who seems almost no longer of this world.

After this period of uncertainty and self-doubt, Riemenschneider went
back to following the dictates of his own nature. The final evolution in his
style is seen in the Virgin with the Christ Child (Plates 16A-C), carved (we
may assume) in 1521 as the model figure for the Volkach Madonna in a Rosary (Plate 44). The stone figure of the Virgin with the Christ Child from a
canon's residence in Würzburg (1516–1522) and the Maidbronn Lamentation Altarpiece (1519–1523) (Plates 45–46) show the new style in full assurance. The strict organization apparent in both these works, the tectonic and
plastic clarity of the individual figures and groups of figures, and the simpli-
fication of form are distinguishing characteristics of Riemenschneider's style
in its final period—a style in which ideas of the Renaissance have been assim-
ilated, rather than imposed and forced as they were in the Bibra tomb-monument.

The design and composition of the Maidbronn Altarpiece, with its effect
of an unfolding triptych, actually goes back to and resembles the tripartite
compositions of earlier Late Gothic altarpieces. The density of the figures is

reminiscent of the closely-interwoven arrangement of The Last Supper in the Altarpiece of the Holy Blood, but the grouping is now more articulate and there is both greater clarity and plasticity of form. In returning to his own ways and convictions, there is a resurgence of Riemenschneider's former vitality and intensity of feeling. The Maidbronn Lamentation Altarpiece is the work of a great and comprehensive vision, deeply and eloquently human in its appeal. Though more quiet and controlled, it can hold its own against the fervor and restless rhythms of the Creglingen Assumption Altarpiece. In it Riemenschneider draws together all the resources he had developed throughout his long life.

NOTES

1. See "Johann Reinhards wirtzburgische chronicke" in J.P. Ludewig, *Geschicht-Schreiber von dem Bischoffthum Wirtzburg* (Frankfurt, 1713), p. 867.

2. See Justus Bier, *Tilmann Riemenschneider, vol. 1, Die Frühen Werke* (Würzburg, 1925), pp. 9–59, plates 4 ff. The Münnerstadt altarpiece is also treated in the present book on pp. 82–84. This is the only altarpiece by Riemenschneider that is fully documented. Contracts and receipts are now in the Münnerstadt parish archives. A list of other documented works by Riemenschneider appears on pp. 114–26 of this volume. All documents relating to the works are reproduced in the four volumes of the author's monograph on Tilmann Riemenschneider (see p. 113, below).

3. See Justus Bier, *Tilmann Riemenschneider, vol. 3, Die Späten Werke in Stein* (Vienna, 1973), pp. 147–51, illustrated on p. 134: also idem, "A Pietà by Tilmann Riemenschneider," *Bulletin of Rhode Island School of Design* 46, no. 3 (March 1960): 3, fig. 4.

4. See Justus Bier, "Riemenschneider's Tomb of Emperor Henry and Empress Cunegund," *The Art Bulletin* 29, no. 2 (June 1947): 95–117, 287.

5. For documents relating to Riemenschneider's life, see Carl Streit, *Tylmann Riemenschneider: Leben und Kunstwerke des fränkischen Bildschnitzers*, 2nd ed. (Berlin, 1888).

6. See P. Schöffel, "Zur Herkunft Tilmann Riemenschneiders," *Altfränkische Bilder* 45 (Würzburg, 1939).

7. Book of the Würzburg Council, number 4, in the municipal archives in Würzburg.

8. See Justus Bier, "Zur Frage der Jugendwerke spätgotischer Bildhauer: 1. Zum Frühwerk Riemenschneiders; 2. Zum Frühwerk des Veit Stoss," *XIVe Congrès International d'Histoire de l'Art 1936: Actes du Congrès*, 1 (Laupen-Bern, 1936): 57–59.

The works that are attributed to Riemenschneider's early years, 1480–1490, are the ones most in need of further investigation. With this as a particular objective, the Staatliche Museen (State Museums) of West Berlin are conducting a long-term investigation of the Riemenschneider works in their collection. Scientific methods first employed in the 1960s to determine the original condition of the Rothenburg Altarpiece of the Holy Blood are being used again by a team of art historians and restorers selected for this project. Their findings will be of particular interest in the case of the two Deposition fragments from the predella of the Wiblingen Crucifixion Altarpiece which I consider a very early work of about 1480–1483.

9. Carl Becker, *Leben und Werke des Bildhauers Tilmann Riemenschneider* (Leipzig, 1849). About Riemenschneider and Adam Kraft, see p. 5.

10. Eduard Tönnies, *Leben und Werke des Würzburger Bildschnitzers Tilmann Riemenschnei-der*, Studien zur Deutschen Kunstgeschichte, 22nd issue (Strassbourg, 1900), pp. 45 f.

11. Both Edwin Redslob and Max H. von Freeden make similar suppositions. See Edwin Redslob, "Riemenschneiders Jugendstil und die Erfurter Kunst," *Kunstchronik* (1951), pp. 253 f; and Max H. von Freeden, *Tilmann Riemenschneider: Leben und Werk*, 4th ed. (Munich and Berlin, 1972), p. 11.

12. The small alabaster figures of St. Barbara (Böttcherstrasse, Bremen) and the Virgin and Angel of the Annunciation (Rijksmuseum, Amsterdam), attributed to Riemenschnei-der's own hand, can be dated in the 1480s. Riemenschneider apparently returned to Erfurt at a later date, or dates, to contract the carving for the Church of St. Peter of the two alabaster sculptures now in the Musée du Louvre and the Cleveland Museum of Art. For a discussion of Riemenschneider's works in alabaster, see Justus Bier, "Riemenschneider's St. Jerome and His Other Works in Alabaster," *Art Bulletin* 33, no. 4 (December 1951): 226–34.

13. See Justus Bier, "Riemenschneider's Use of Graphic Sources," *Gazette des Beaux-Arts*, 6th ser., 50 (October 1957): 203–22. Much work remains to be done on the question of the influence of German graphic art on Riemenschneider's sculpture. Mention should be made, however, of a recent pertinent publication in Russia: Ch. A. Mezentseva, *Znachenie pechatnoi grafiki dlia razvitiia nemetskoi skul'ptury 1450–1550 godov* (The Significance of Graphic Art for the Development of German Sculpture from 1450 to 1550) (Leningrad, 1972). I am grateful to Lawrence E. Feinberg of the Department of Slavic Languages and Literatures of the University of North Carolina at Chapel Hill for his valuable translation.

14. See Wilhelm Vöge, "Der Meister des Blaubeurener Hochaltars und seine Madonnen," *Monatschefte für Kunstwissenschaft* 2 (1909): 11 ff.

15. Other scholars have attributed the Blaubeuren Altarpiece to either Michel Erhart or his son Gregor. Anja Broschek in a recent contribution, *Michel Erhart: Ein Beitrag zur schwä-bischen Plastik der Spätgotik, Beiträge zur Kunstgeschichte* 8 (Berlin and New York, 1973): 2, dis-cusses the difficulty of distinguishing the work of these two sculptors.

16. Gertrud Otto, "Der Bildhauer Michel Erhart," *Jahrbuch der Preussischen Kunstsamm-lungen* 54 (1943).

17. See Justus Bier, "Riemenschneider as a Goldsmith's Modelmaker," *Art Bulletin* 37, no. 2 (June 1955): 103–12, 237.

18. See Justus Bier, "Riemenschneider's Helpers in Need," *Metropolitan Museum of Art Bulletin* 21, no. 10 (June 1963): 317–26.

19. See Justus Bier, "Riemenschneider und die Schaumünzen des Lorenz von Bibra," *Müncher Jahrbuch der bildenden Kunst*, 3rd ser. 7 (1956): 95–110. The cast medal shows a portrait of Lorenz von Bibra and is dated 1511. Cast medals were in general use only from about 1518.

20. Of the figures in this series of the Apostles, only James the Elder is still at the Marien-kapelle in Würzburg; Christ, John the Evangelist, Peter, and Andrew are in Würzburg Ca-thedral, and the nine remaining figures are in the Mainfränkisches Museum in Würzburg. The figures of Adam and Eve are also now in the Mainfränkisches Museum.

21. Max H. von Freeden, in *Tilmann Riemenschneider*, pp. 13–14, points out that in Rie-menschneider's second decade of public service there appear to have been fewer autograph works and more workshop pieces.

22. Ludewig, *Geschicht-Schreiber*, p. 876.

23. For example, Rothenburg ob der Tauber and Nuremberg were both free imperial cities at that time. Würzburg was not in fact secularized until 1801.

24. As Thomas Mann describes it in the following passage from "Deutschland und die Deutschen," *Die Neue Rundschau* (Stockholm), October 1945, pp. 10–11 (translated):

> At that time there lived in Germany a man who has my special sympathy, Tilmann Riemenschneider, a master of religious art, a sculptor and woodcarver, widely famous for the faithful and expressive excellence of his works, his profound altar painting and chaste reliefs which ornamented the places of worship all over Germany. The master had won high regard, both as a man and as a citizen, in his immediate environs, the city of Wuerzburg, where he was a member of the Council. He never expected to take a hand in politics, in world affairs—the thought lay far from his natural modesty and from his love for his free and peaceful work. There was nothing of the demagogue about him. But his heart, that beat warmly for the poor and oppressed, forced him to take the part of the peasants, whose cause he recognized as just and pleasing in the sight of God, against the lords, the bishops and princes, whose favor he could easily have retained. Moved by the great and fundamental contrasts of the time, he felt compelled to emerge from his sphere of purely spiritual and esthetic artistic life and to become a fighter for liberty and justice. He sacrificed his own liberty for the cause that he held higher than art and the dignified calm of his existence. It was his influence, chiefly, that determined the city of Wuerzburg to refuse military service to the "Burg," the Prince-Prelate, and, in general, to assume a revolutionary attitude against him. Riemenschneider paid dearly for it. For after the crushing of the peasant revolt, the victorious powers whom he had opposed took cruel revenge upon him; they subjected him to prison and torture, and he emerged from the ordeal as a broken man, incapable of awakening the beauties in wood and stone.

25. See A. Pfrenzinger, "Riemenschneider und Kitzingen," *Bayerland* 36, no. 22 (1925): 703.

26. See Bier, *Tilmann Riemenschneider*, 1: 92 f. An example of similar overcrowding is found in the shrine of the Altarpiece of the Tailors' Assistants ("Schneidergesellen") in the Annenmuseum in Lübeck.

27. See E. Oellermann, "Die monochromen Holzbildwerke des Veit Stoss," *Maltechnik-Restauro.*, "Internationale Zeitschrift fuer Farb- und Maltechniken, Restaurierung und Museumsfragen" (Munich: G.D. Callweg), 82, no. 3 (1976): 173–82.

28. Recent discussions have focused on the question of whether Riemenschneider used a pigmented glaze in order to unify the appearance of the whitish lindenwood. Eike Oellermann, the restorer of the Rothenburg Altarpiece of the Holy Blood, found such a glaze—a "lasur" as he calls it—spread over the sculptures of that altarpiece and the right wing of the Dettwang Altarpiece of the Crucifixion. He also believes to have found a similar glaze on the Evangelist figures from the Münnerstadt Altarpiece. See Eike Oellermann, "Die Restaurierung des Heilig-Blut-Altares von Tilmann Riemenschneider," *24. Amtsbericht des Bayerischen Landesamtes für Denkmalpflege* (Munich, 1966), pp. 81–82; and Charles E. von Nostitz, Jr., "Two Unpolychromed Riemenschneiders at the Cloisters," *Metropolitan Museum Journal* 10 (1975): 51–53, 59–62. See also Walter Paatz, *Süddeutsche Schnitzaltäre der Spätgotik* (Heidelberg, 1963); Marlene Benkö, "Ungefasste Schnitzaltäre der Spätgotik in Süddeutschland," unpublished dissertation, University of Munich, 1969; and Johannes Taubert, "Zur Oberflächengestalt der sogenannten ungefassten Holzplastik," *Städel Jahrbuch* (1967), N.F. 1.

29. Charles von Nostitz makes the same points in his investigation of Riemenschneider's unpolychromed sculpture and its historical significance: "Two Unpolychromed Riemenschneiders," pp. 61, 62. A specific instance is discussed in the case of the Three Helpers in Need at the Cloisters: von Nostitz cites the "refined subtleties in its carving, the details

which would have been obscured by polychromy, and the faint traces of paint on the eyes," as grounds for assuming that this group—like much of Riemenschneider's sculpture—was meant to remain unpolychromed (p. 53).

30. See, for example, the figure of John the Baptist (Plate 18); and compare the Münner-stadt Angels (Plate 20A) with the Creglingen Angels (Plates 33B, D), which are of a much simpler design yet convey a greater feeling of movement.

31. The same tendencies are seen in figures of the Madonna: compare, for instance, the Werbach Madonna of about 1490 (Plate 19) with the Madonna and Child from a Würzburg Stiftskurie, 1516–1522 (Plate 45) or the Gramschatz Virgin and Child of about 1510–1515 (Plate 38A). The theme of the Virgin with the Christ Child occupied Riemenschneider throughout his working life, and the sizable body of his representations, ranging from the early 1490s to the late 1520s, affords an instructive example of the evolution in his style. An illustrated survey of the most important figures is found in Justus Bier, "Riemenschneiders Marienstatuen und die Clemens-Madonna im Kölner Kunstgewerbemuseum," *Wallraf-Richartz-Jahrbuch* 37 (1975): 41–64.

32. See Justus Bier, "Tilman Riemenschneider's Monuments of Heinrich and Elisabeth Stieber," *Art in America* 31, no. 4 (October 1943): 172–83.

33. To trace this development, compare Adam of 1493 (Plate 21C), St. John the Evangelist in the Creglingen Assumption Altarpiece (Plate 33H), the Franconian Apostle (Plate 35E), and finally St. John the Evangelist in the Maidbronn Lamentation Altarpiece (Plate 46C).

PLATES

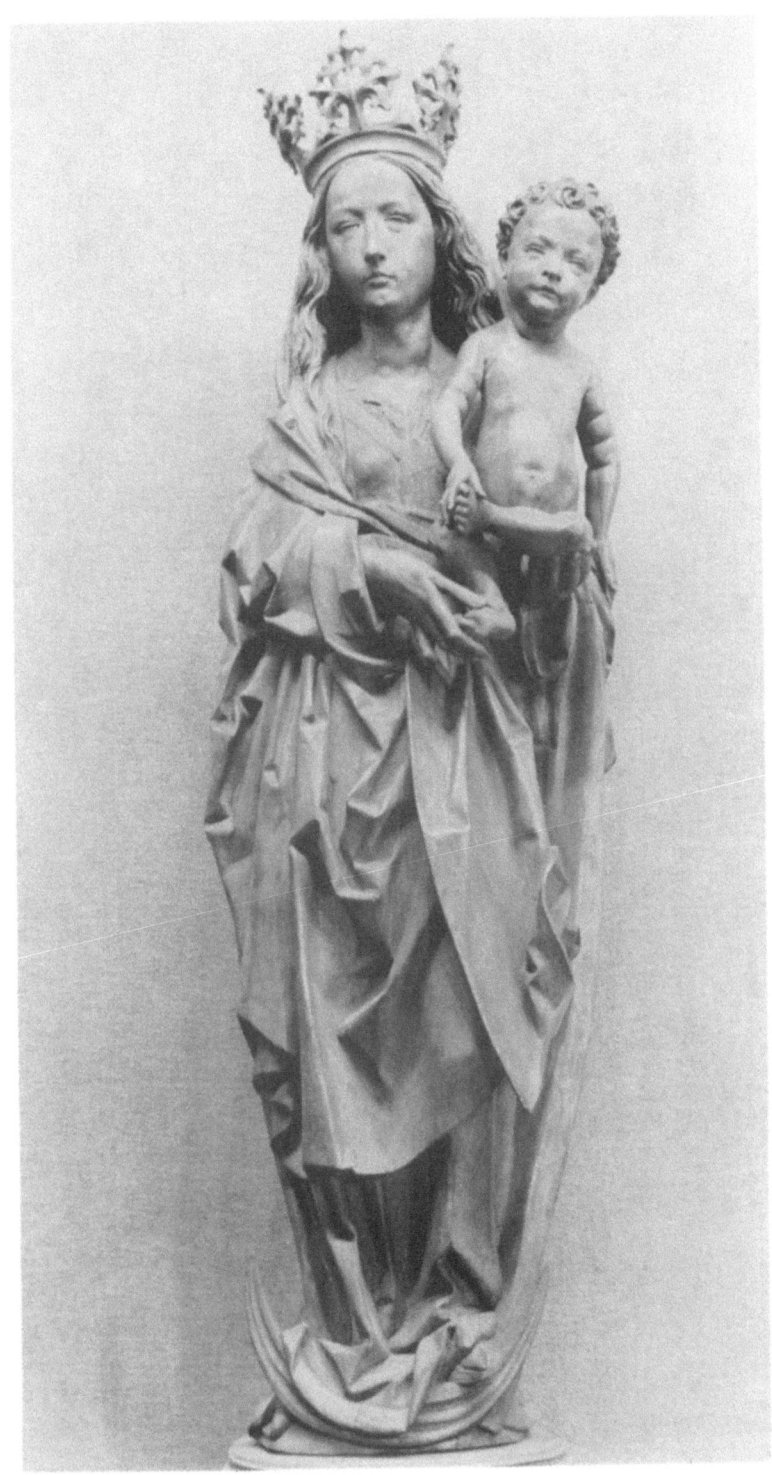

1. The Virgin with the Christ Child. About 1490–1492. Lindenwood. Museum of
Fine Arts, Boston.

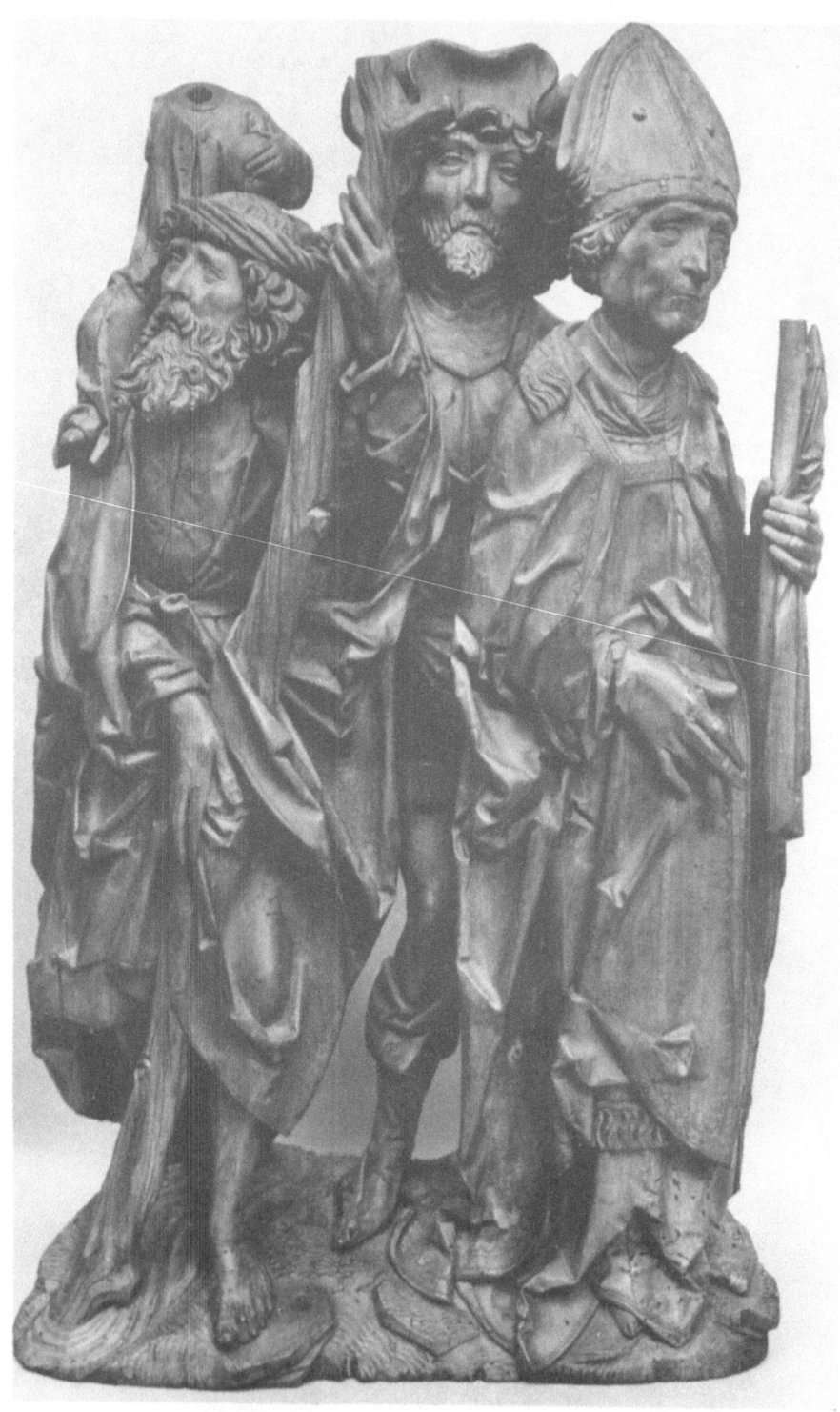

2A. The Three Helpers in Need (St. Christopher, St. Eustace, St. Erasmus). 1494. Linden-wood. Metropolitan Museum of Art; Cloisters Collection, Purchase, 1961. *Opposite:* Two details. *Top:* 2B. St. Christopher carrying the Christ Child. *Bottom:* 2C. St. Eustace.

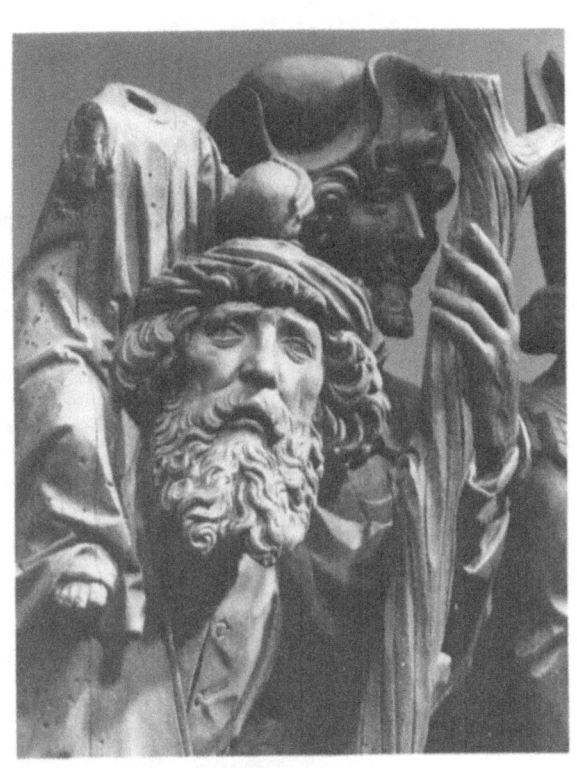

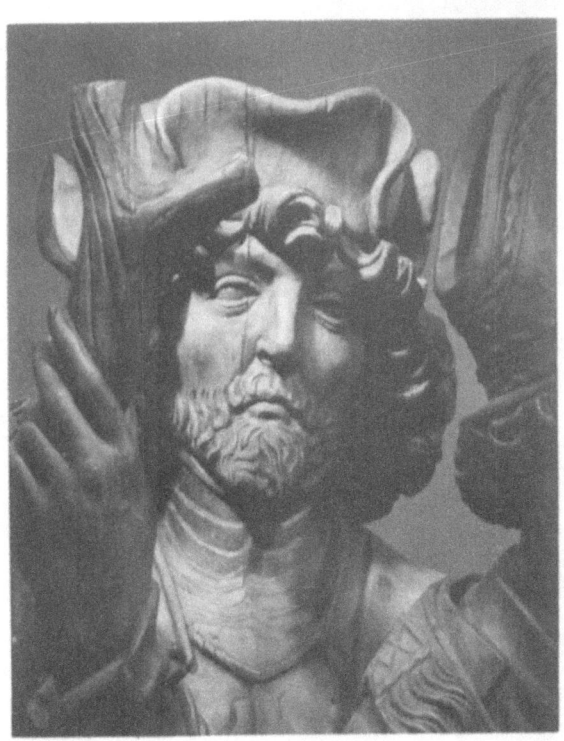

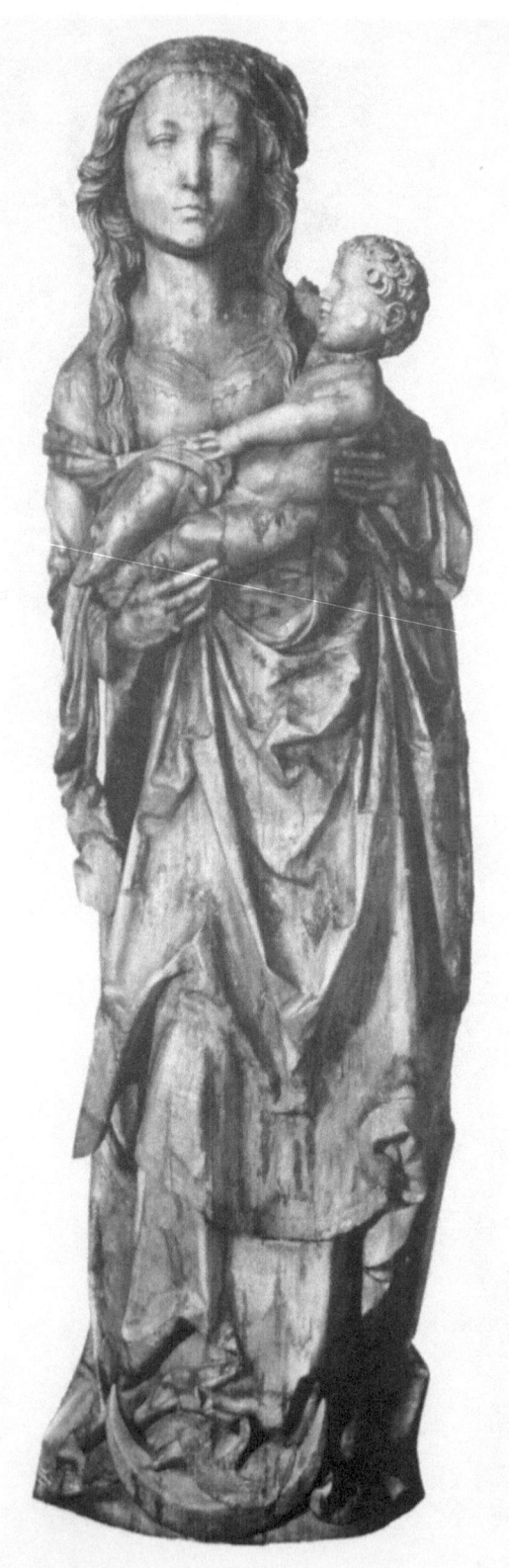

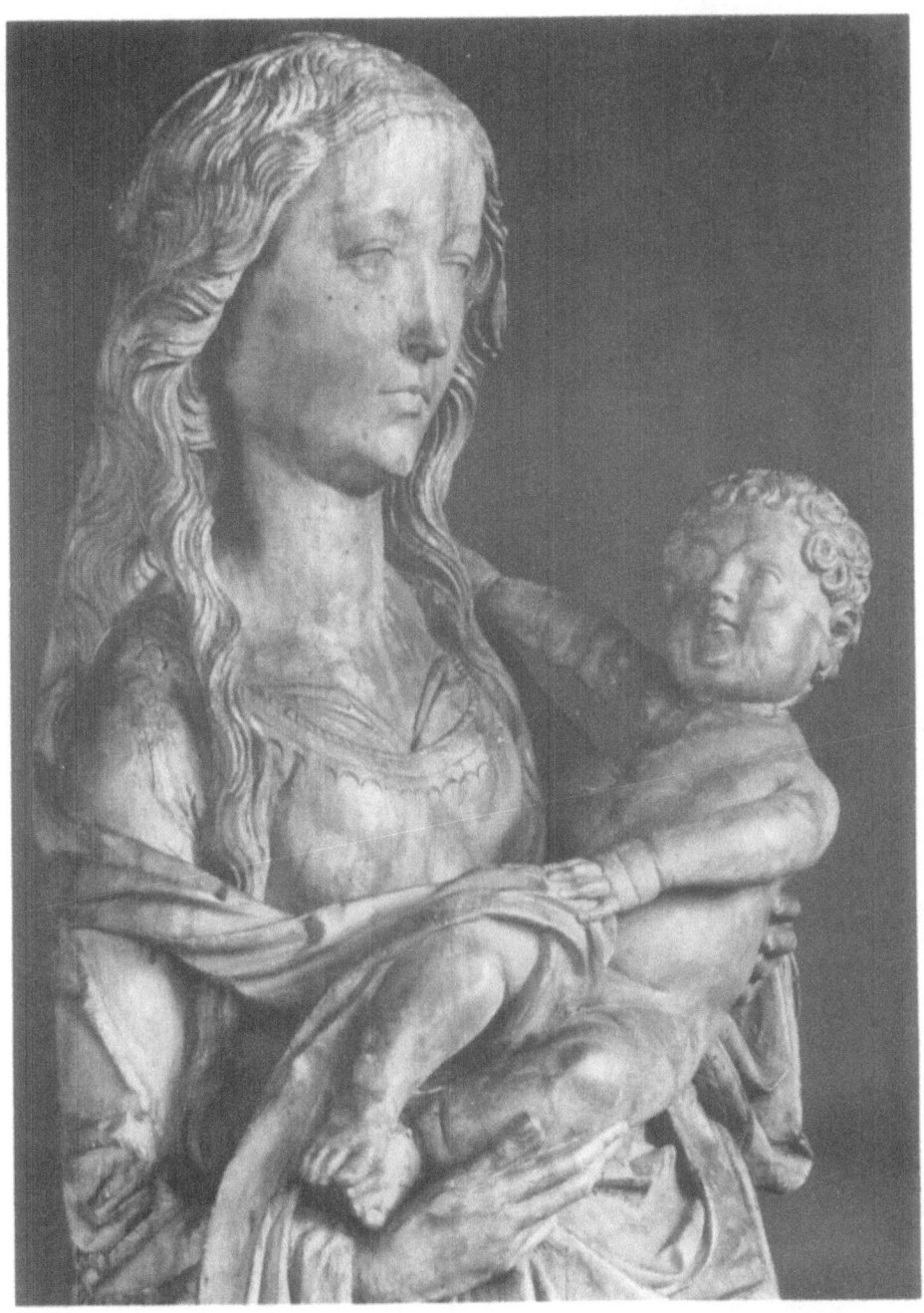

3A and B. The Virgin with the Christ Child. Late 1490s. Lindenwood. Helen Foresman Spencer Museum of Art, University of Kansas, Lawrence; gift in memory of Professor Harry C. Thurnau through the estate of Myrtle Elliott Thurnau.

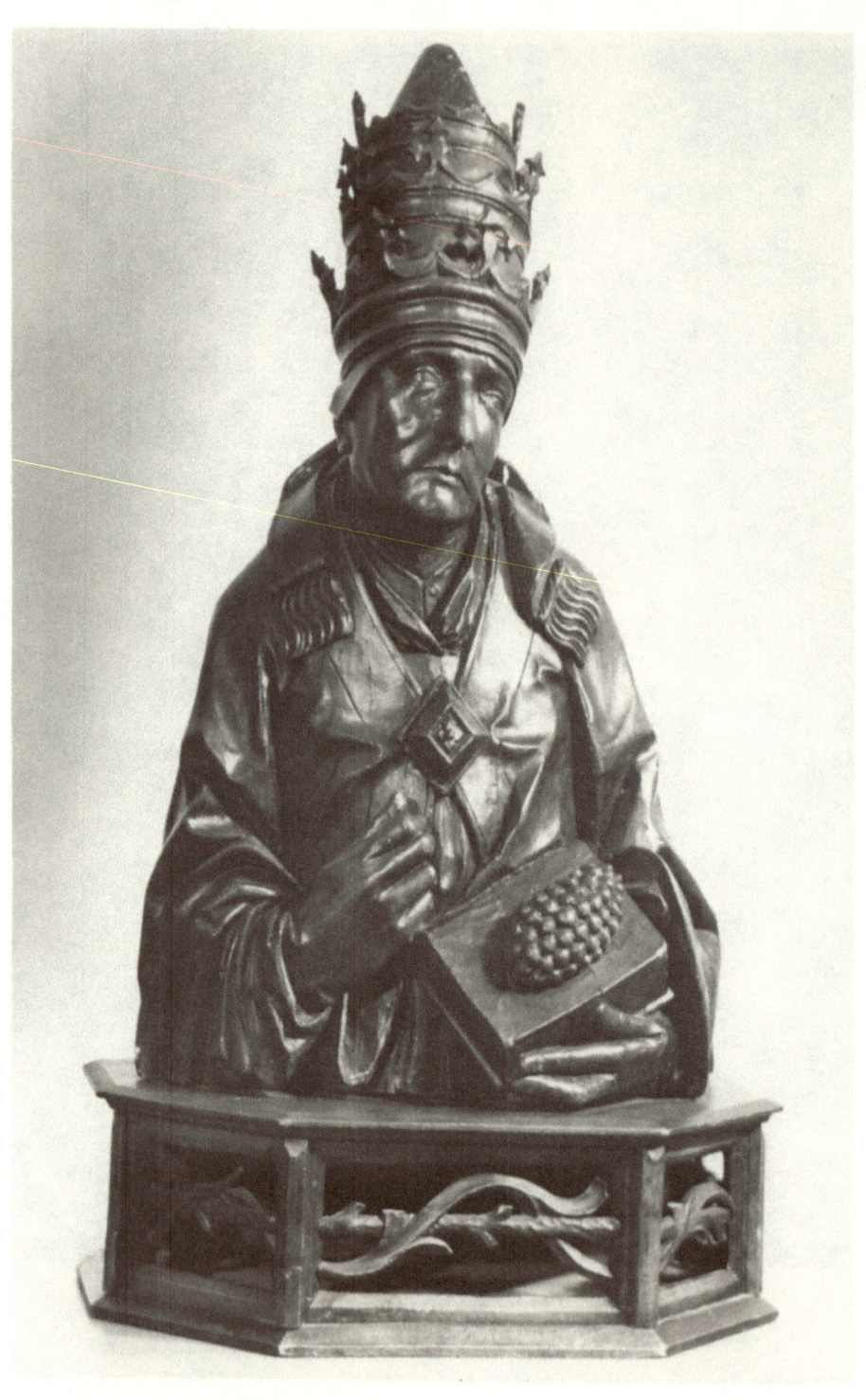

4. St. Urban. About 1500. Lindenwood. Allen Memorial Art Museum, Oberlin College;
R.T. Miller, Jr., Fund.

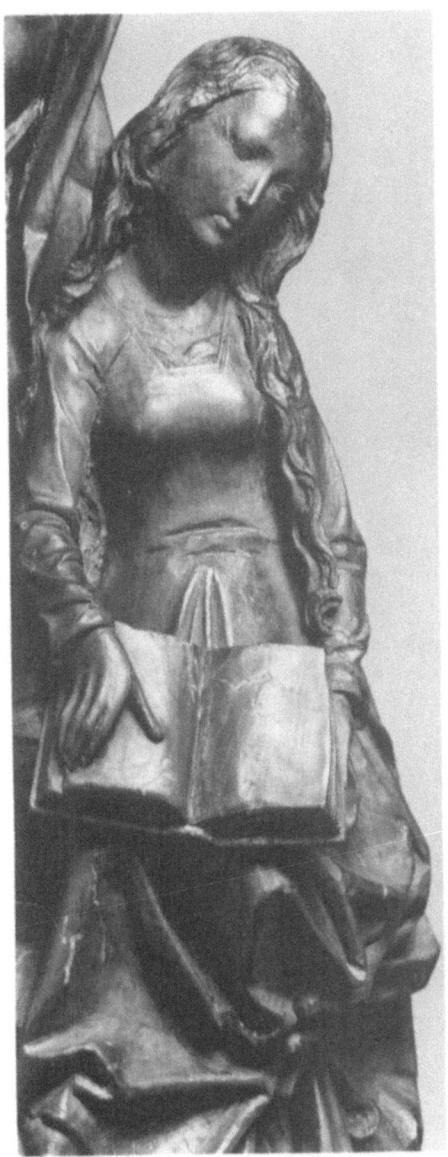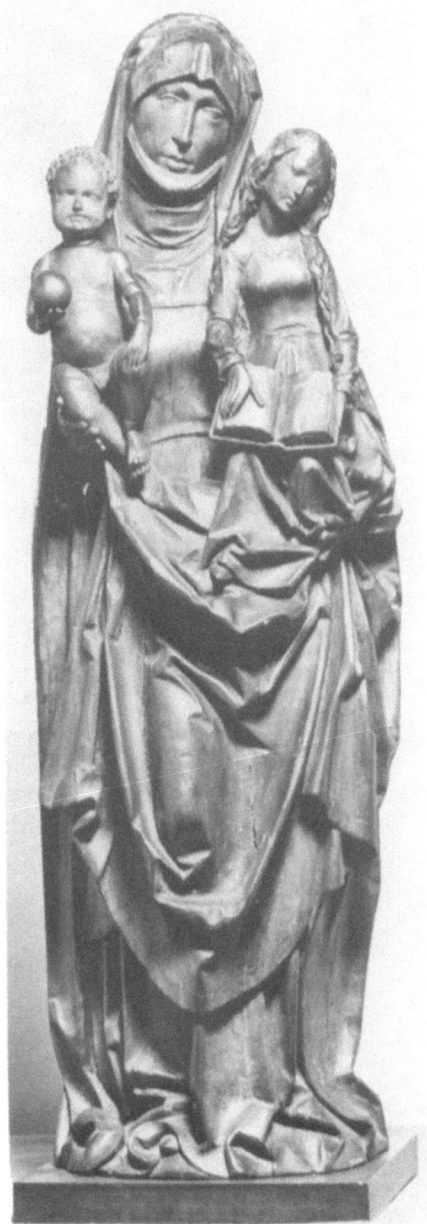

5A and B. Anna Selbdritt. About 1502–1504. Lindenwood. Walters Art Gallery, Baltimore.

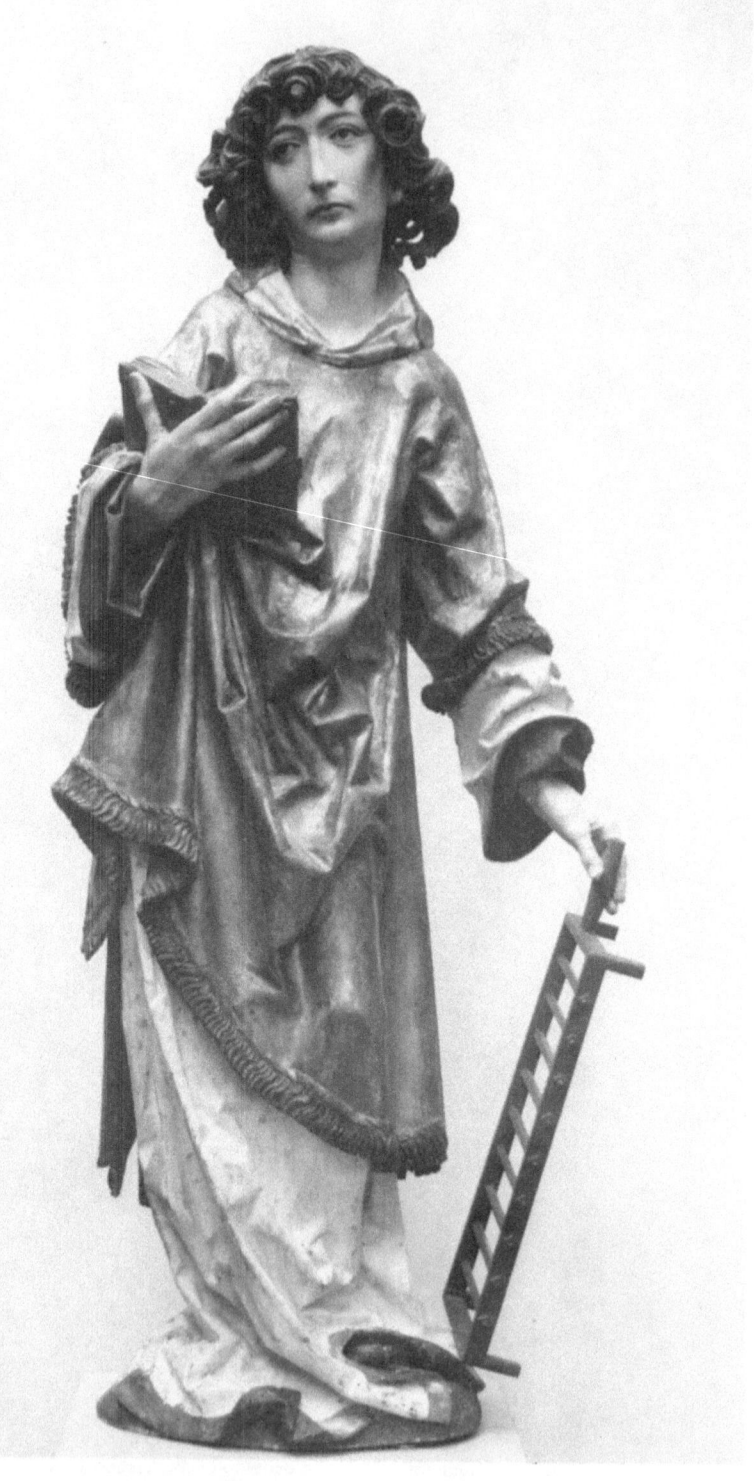

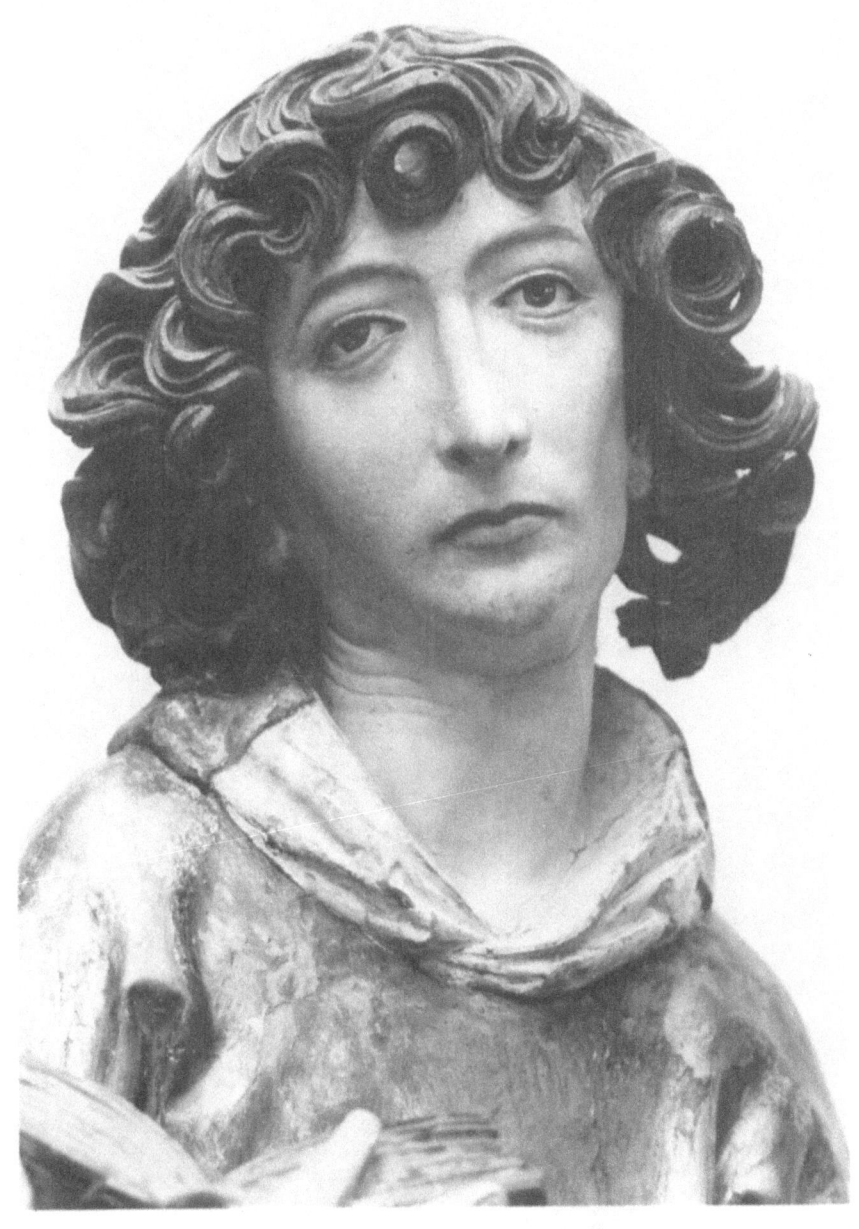

6A and B. St. Lawrence. About 1502. Lindenwood. Cleveland Museum of Art;
from the Leonard C. Hanna, Jr., Bequest.

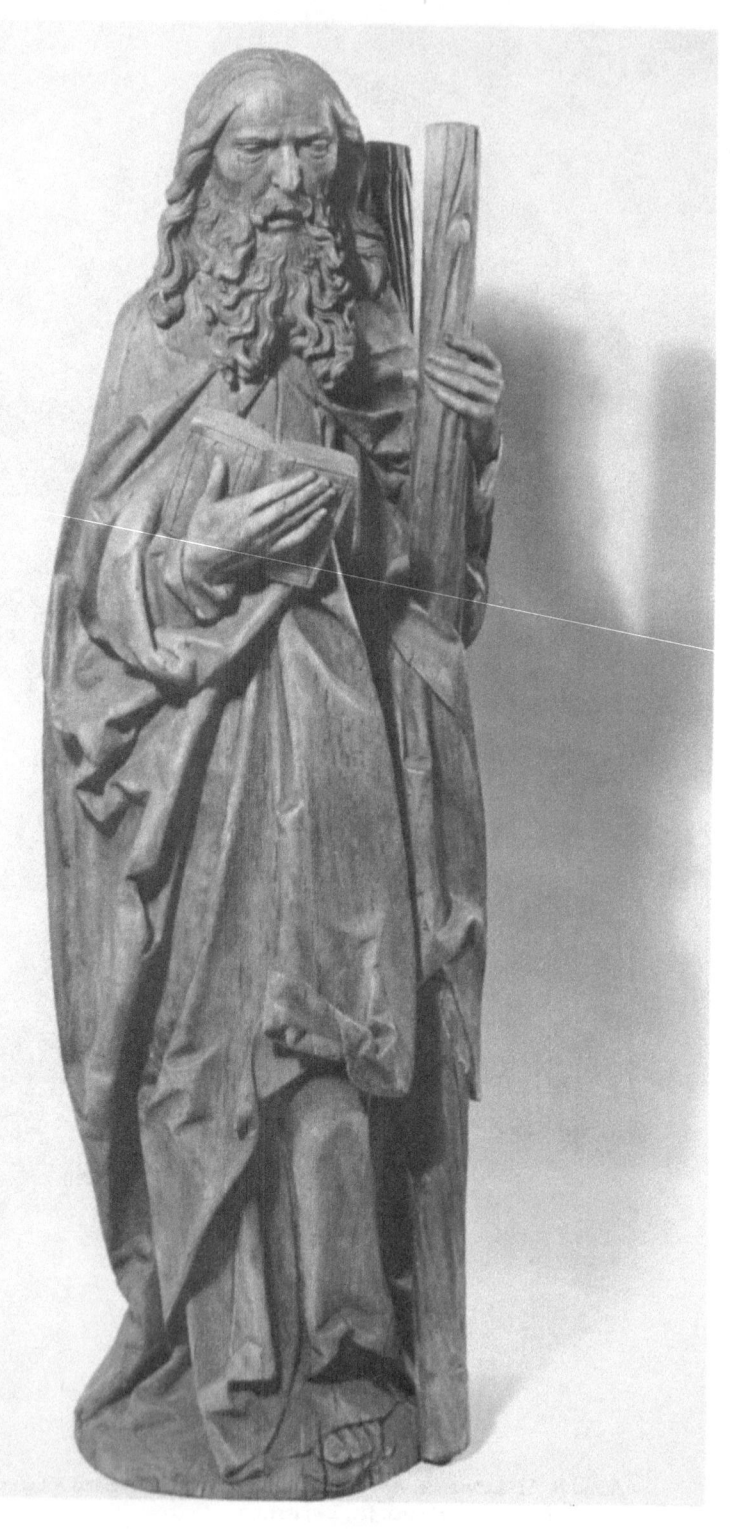

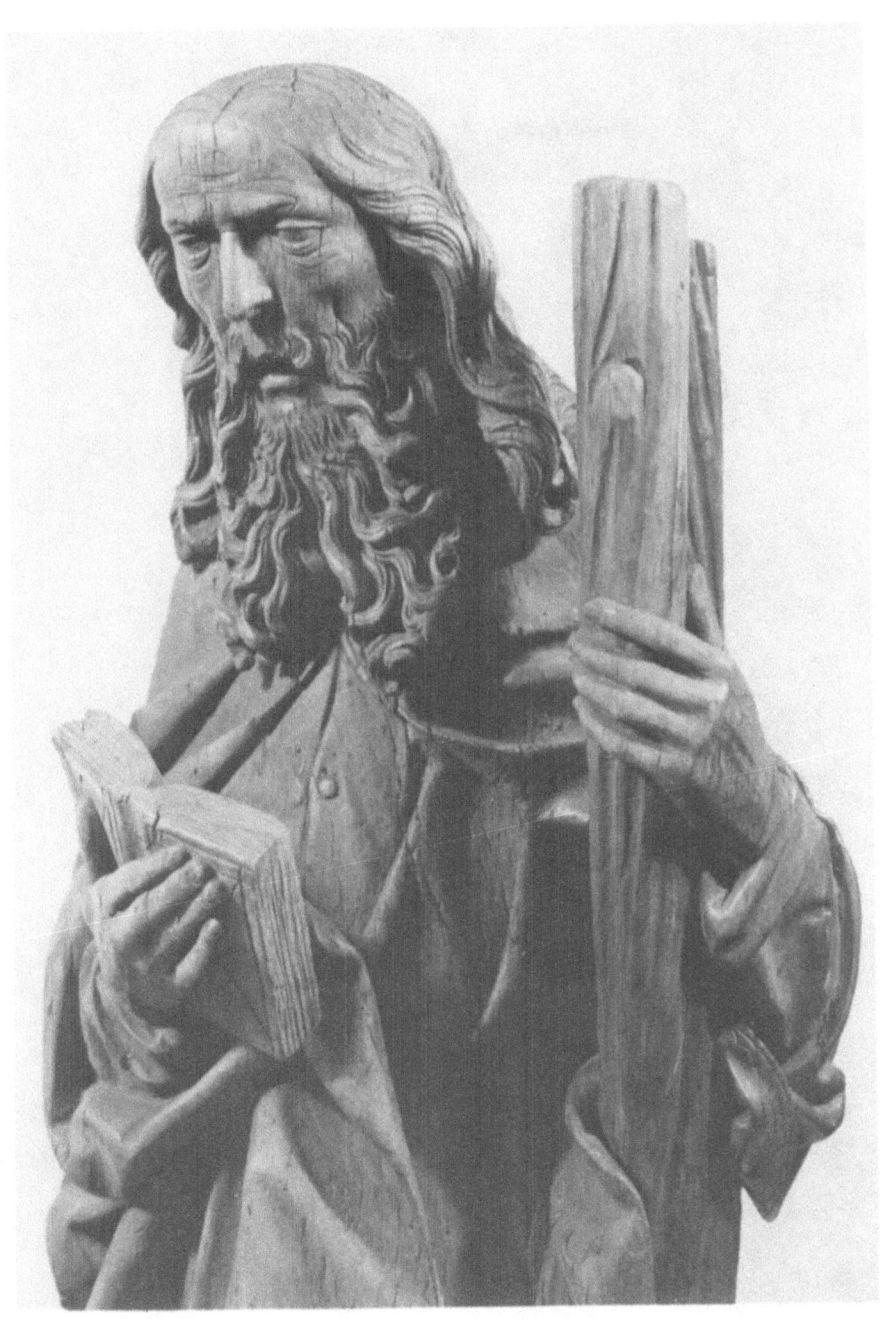

7A and B. St. Andrew. About 1505. Lindenwood. High Museum of Art, Atlanta; Samuel H. Kress Collection.

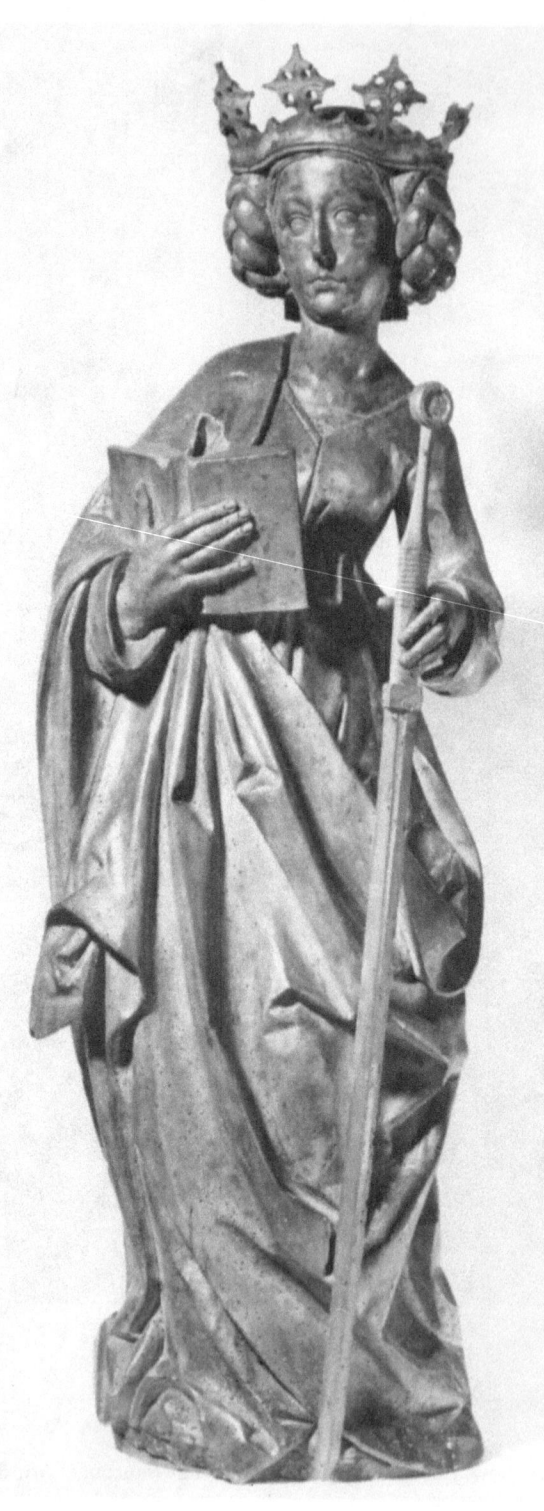

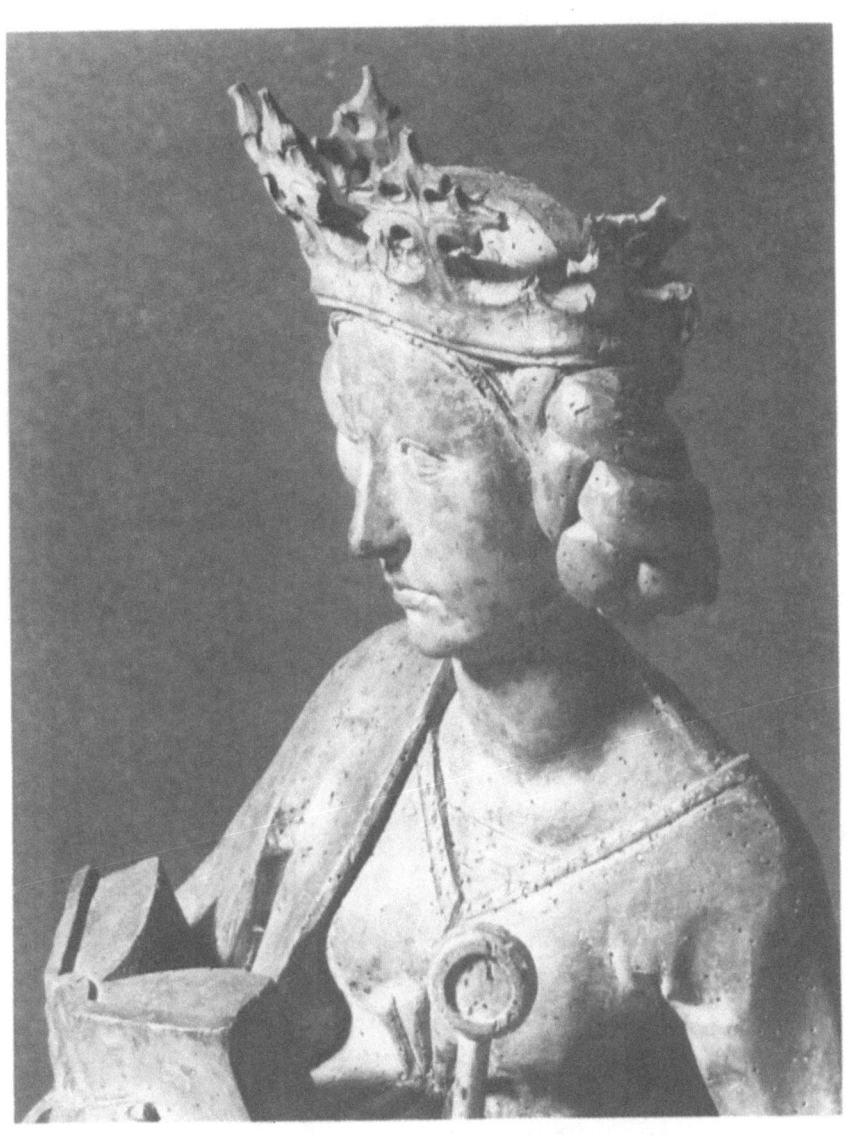

8A and B. St. Catherine. About 1505–1510. Lindenwood.
North Carolina Museum of Art, Raleigh.

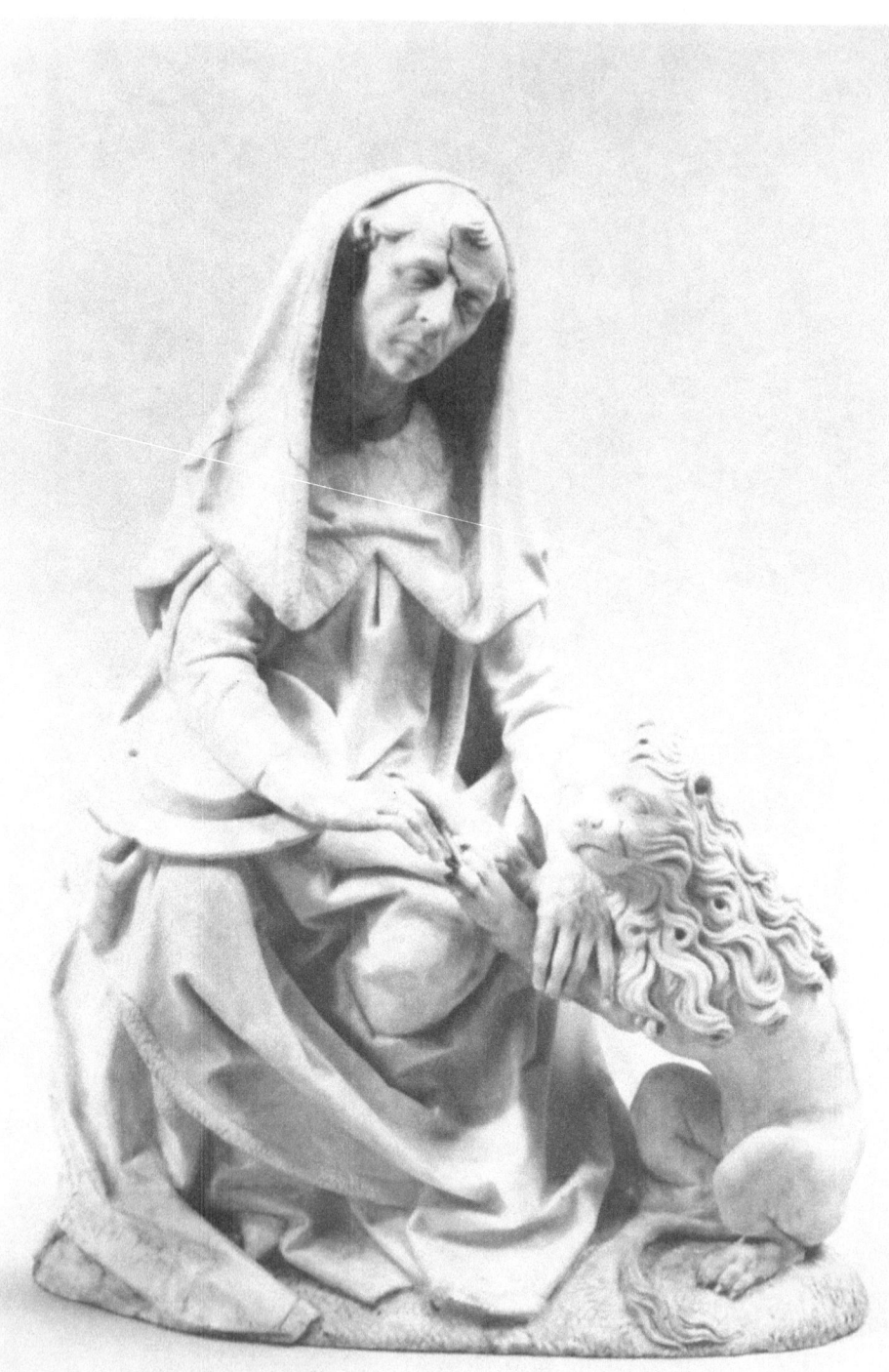

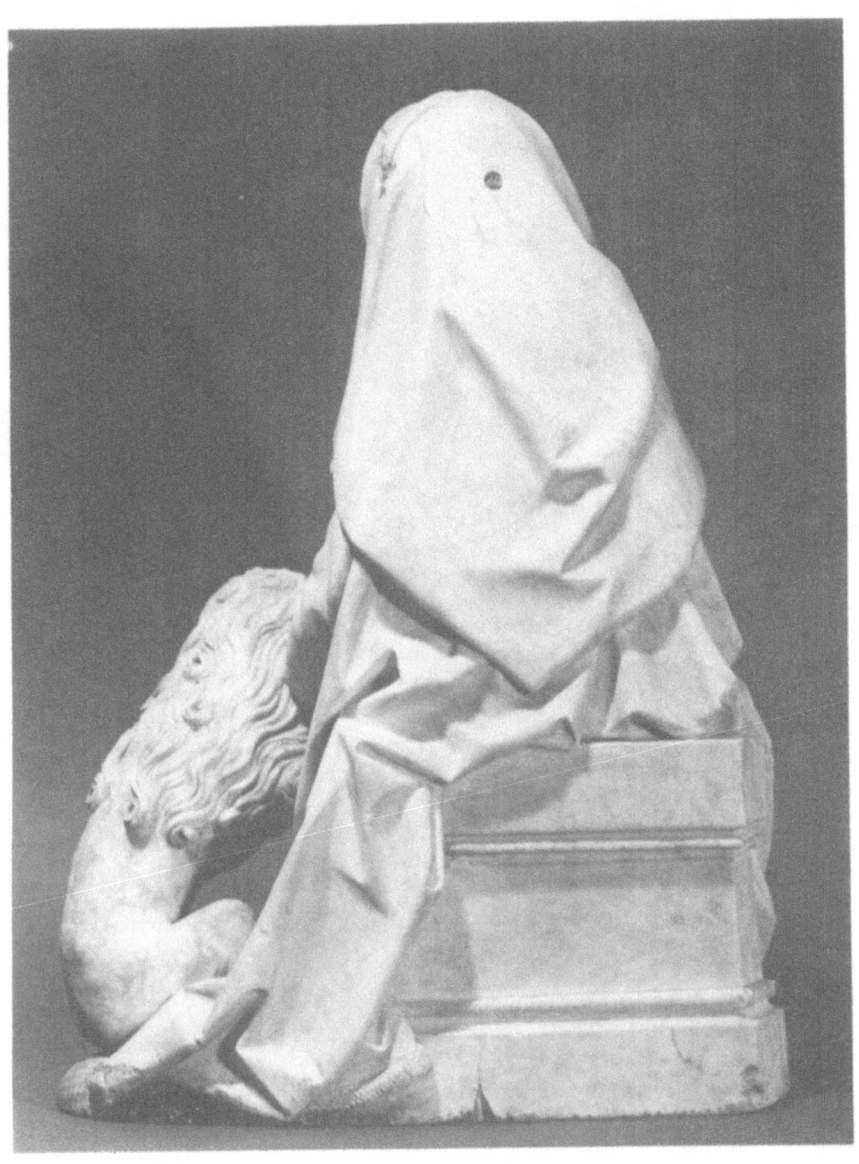

Opposite: 9A. St. Jerome and the Lion. About 1505–1510. Alabaster. Cleveland Museum of Art; purchase from the J.H. Wade Fund. *Above:* 9B. Back view.

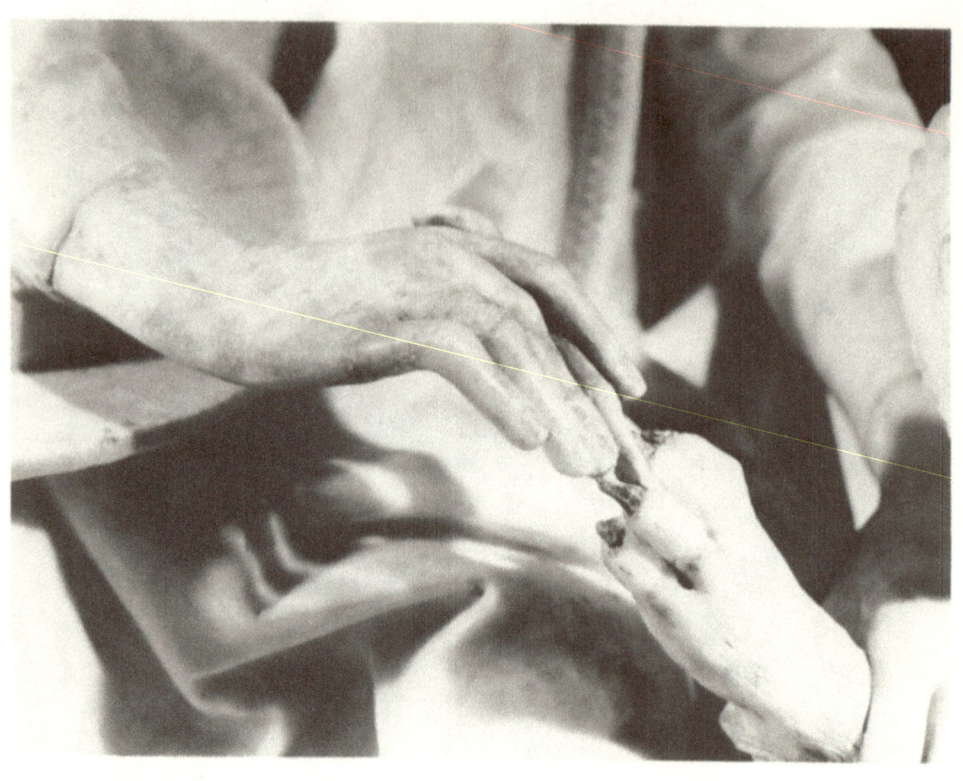

9C and D. Two details of St. Jerome and the Lion.

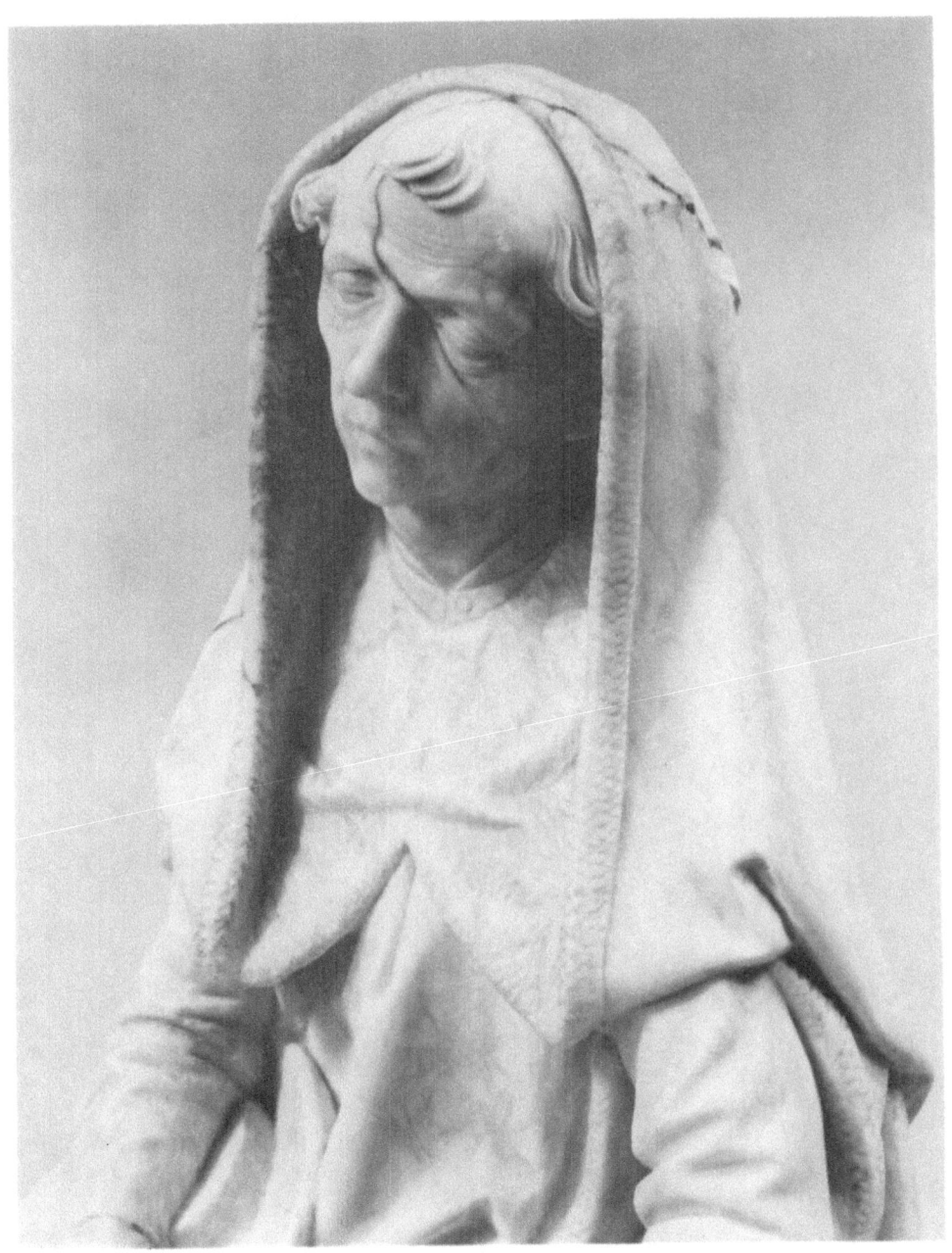

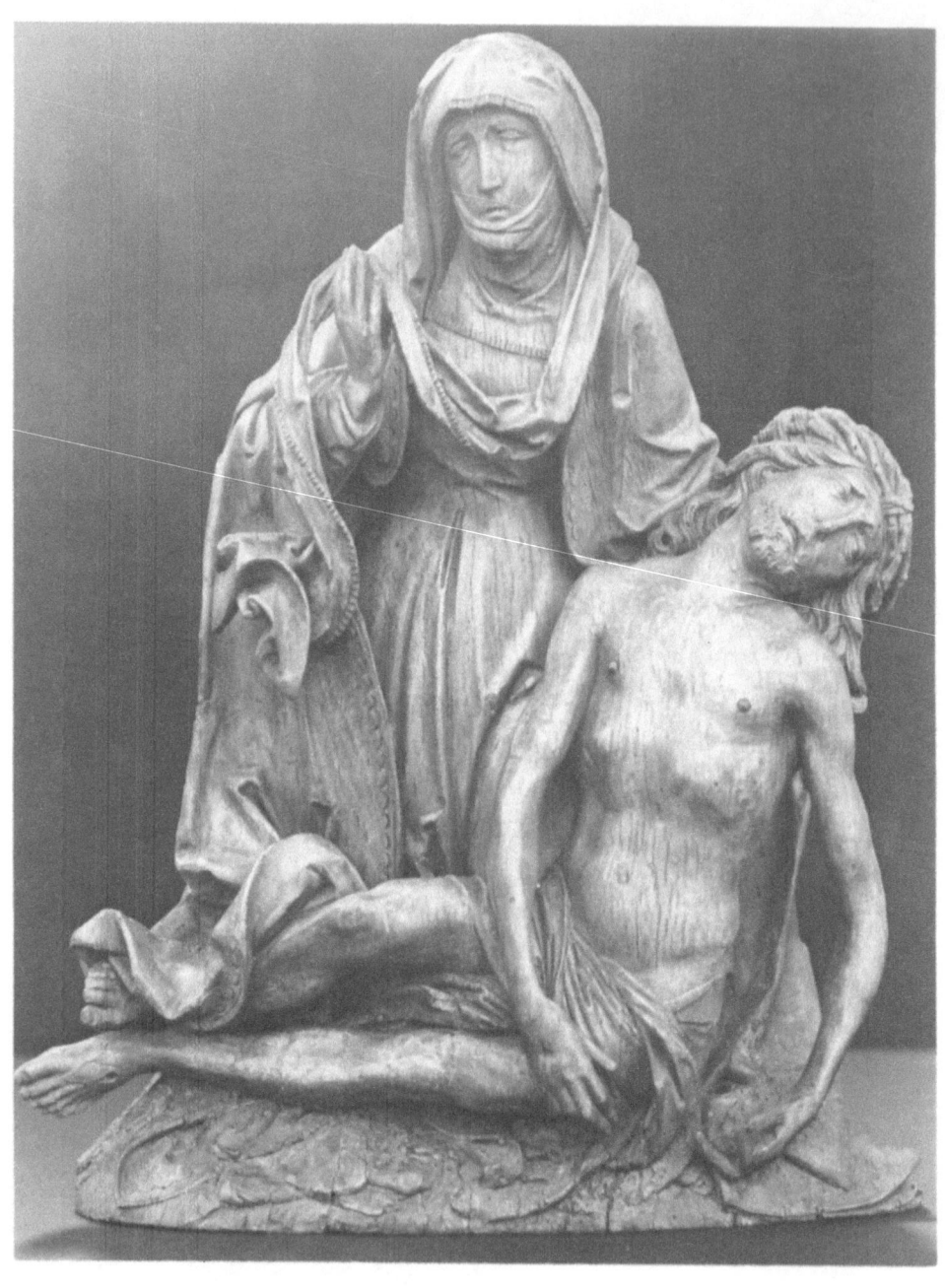

10A. Pietà. About 1505–1510. Lindenwood. Museum of Art, Rhode Island School of Design; Museum Works of Art Fund. *Opposite:* 10B. Side view.

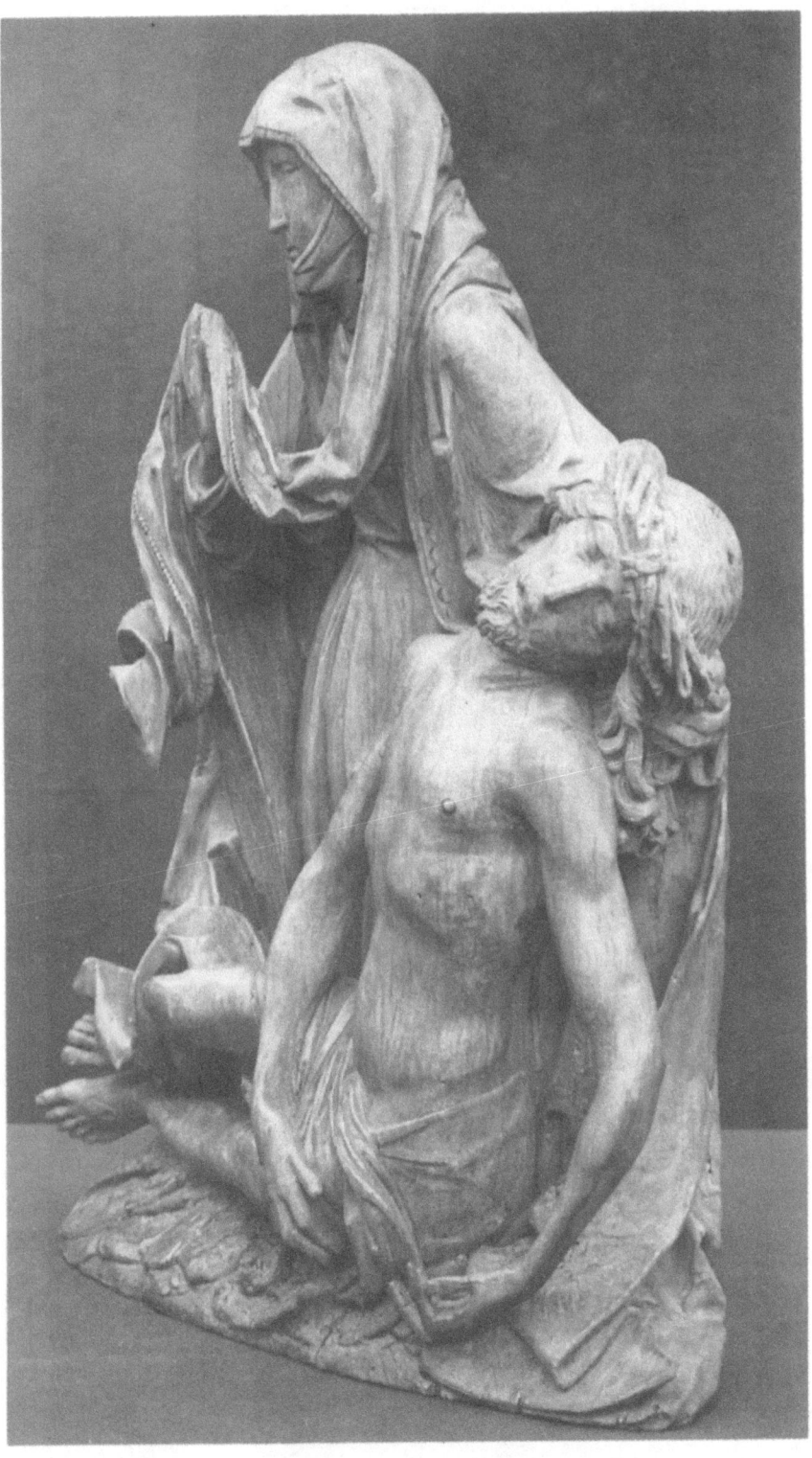

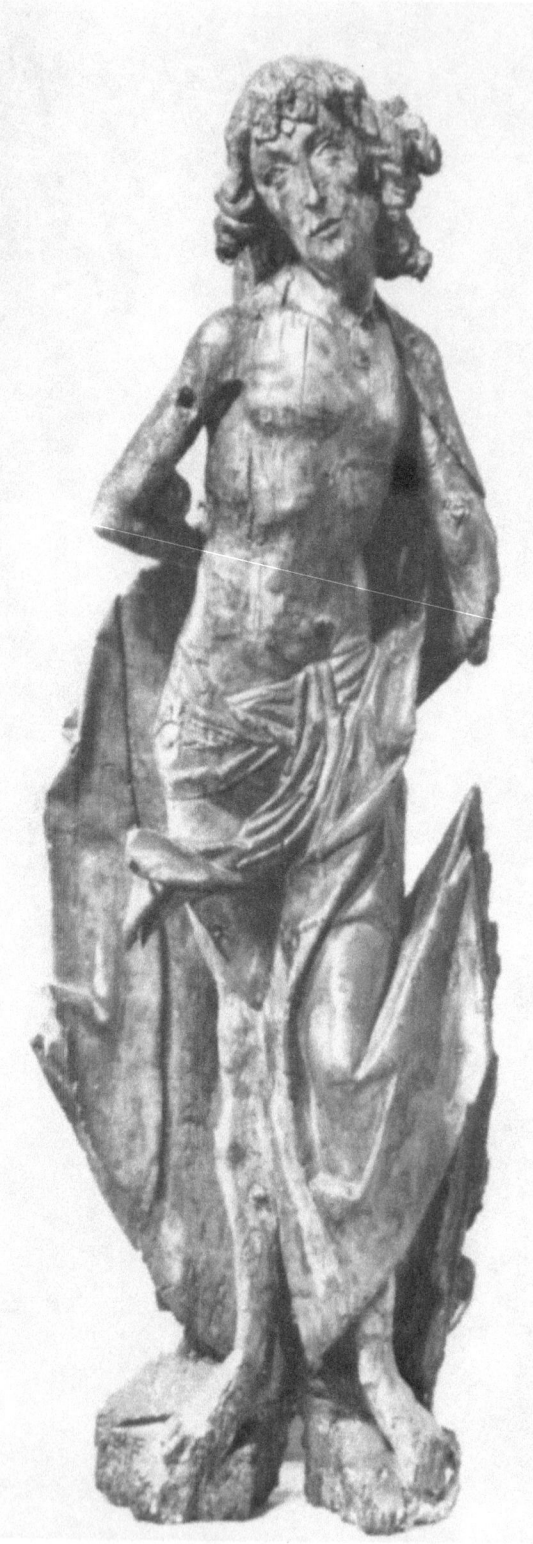

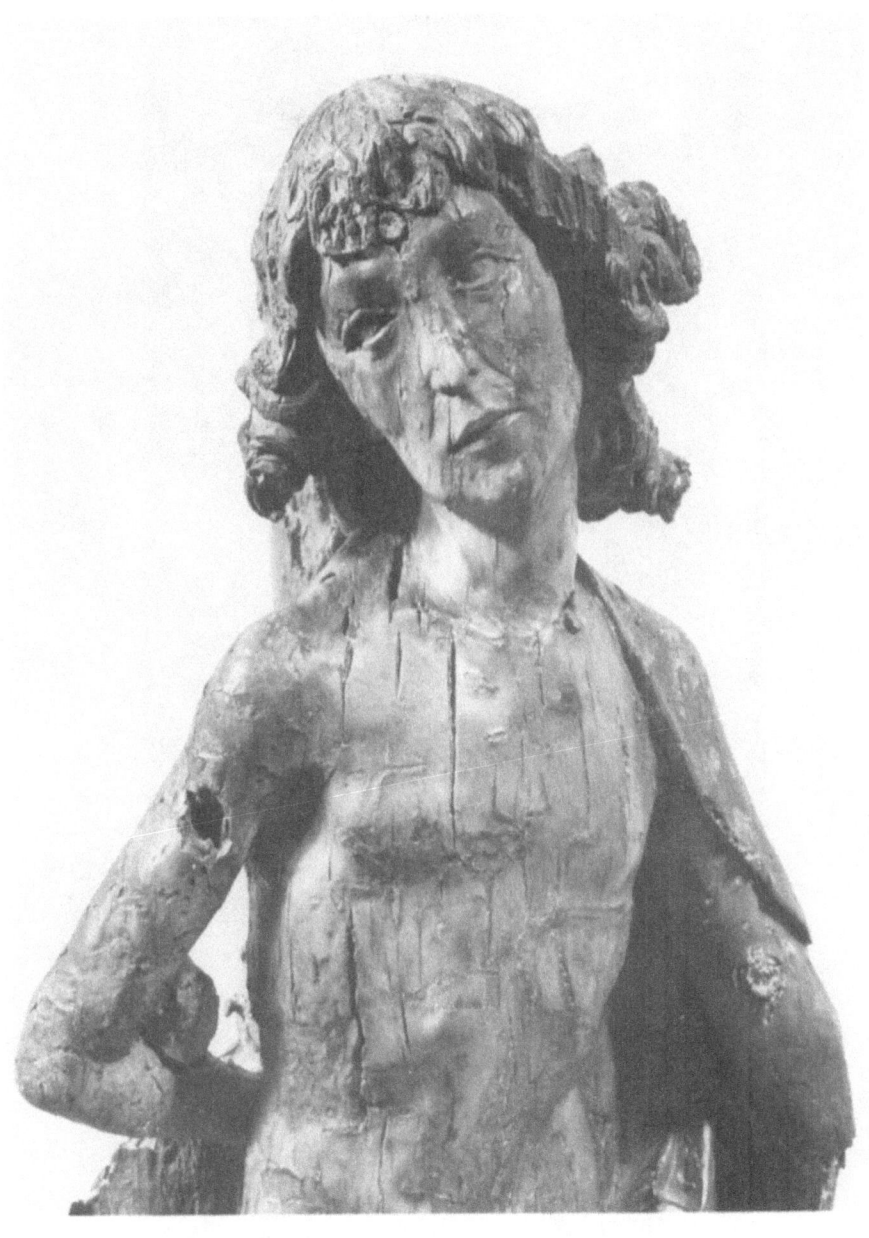

11A and B. St. Sebastian. About 1505–1510. Lindenwood. Montreal Museum of Fine Arts.

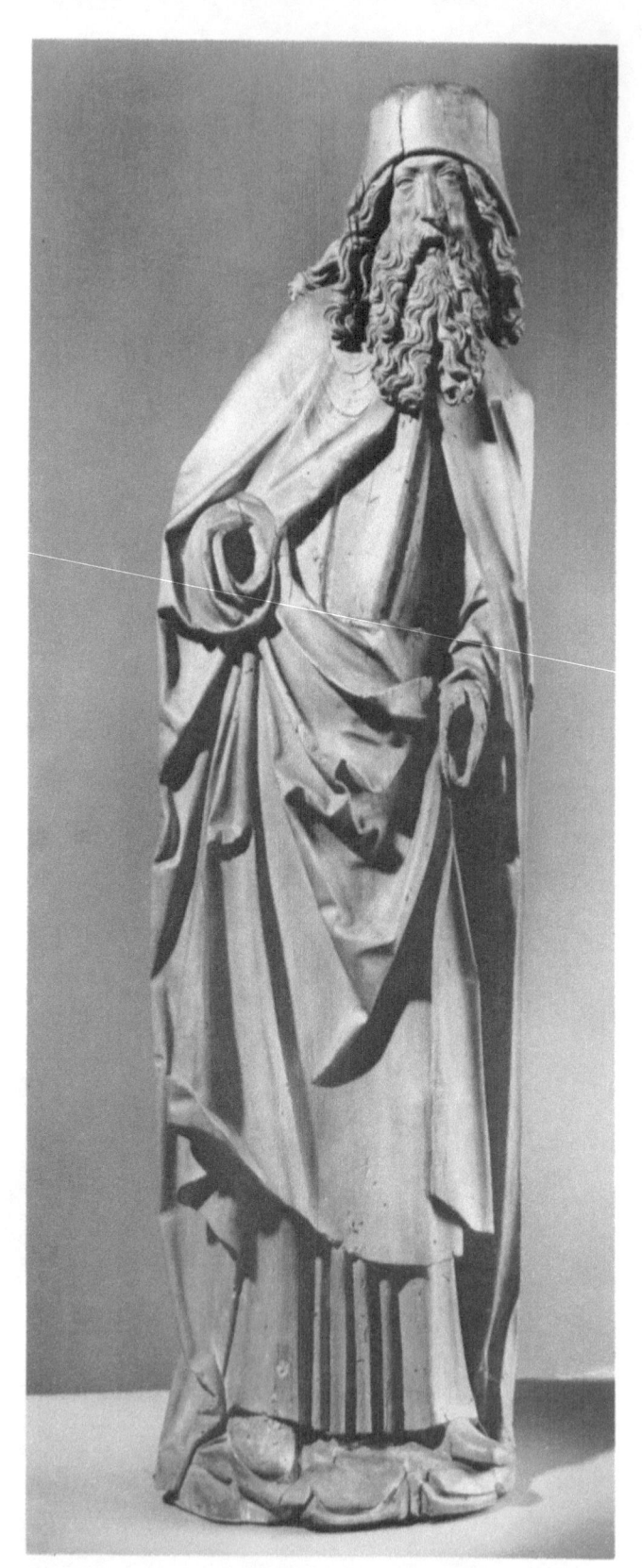

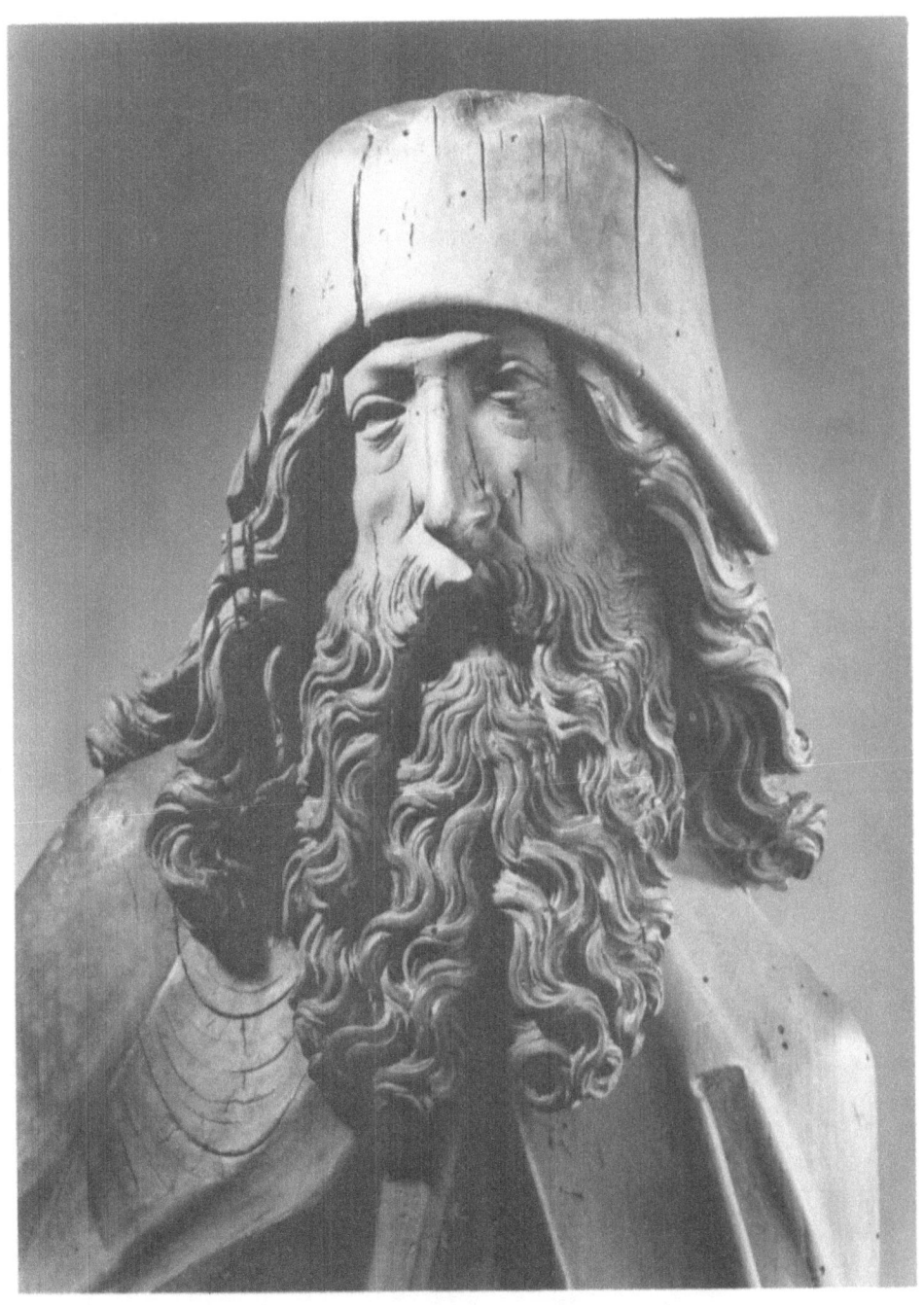

12A and B. St. Anthony Abbot. About 1510. Lindenwood. Courtesy of the Busch-Reisinger Museum, Harvard University.

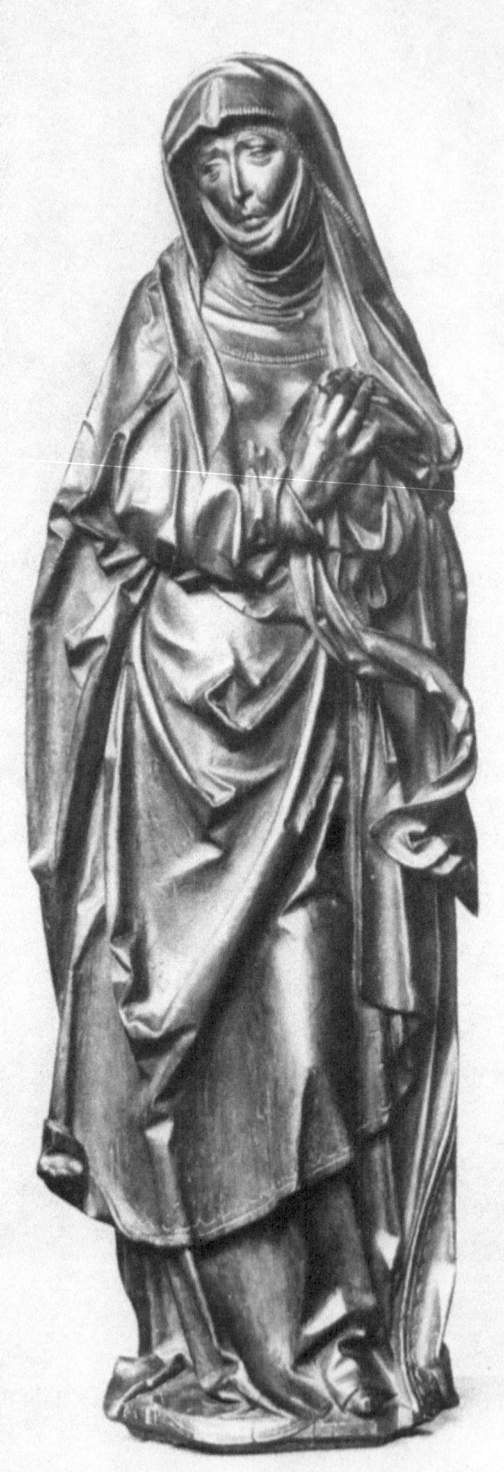

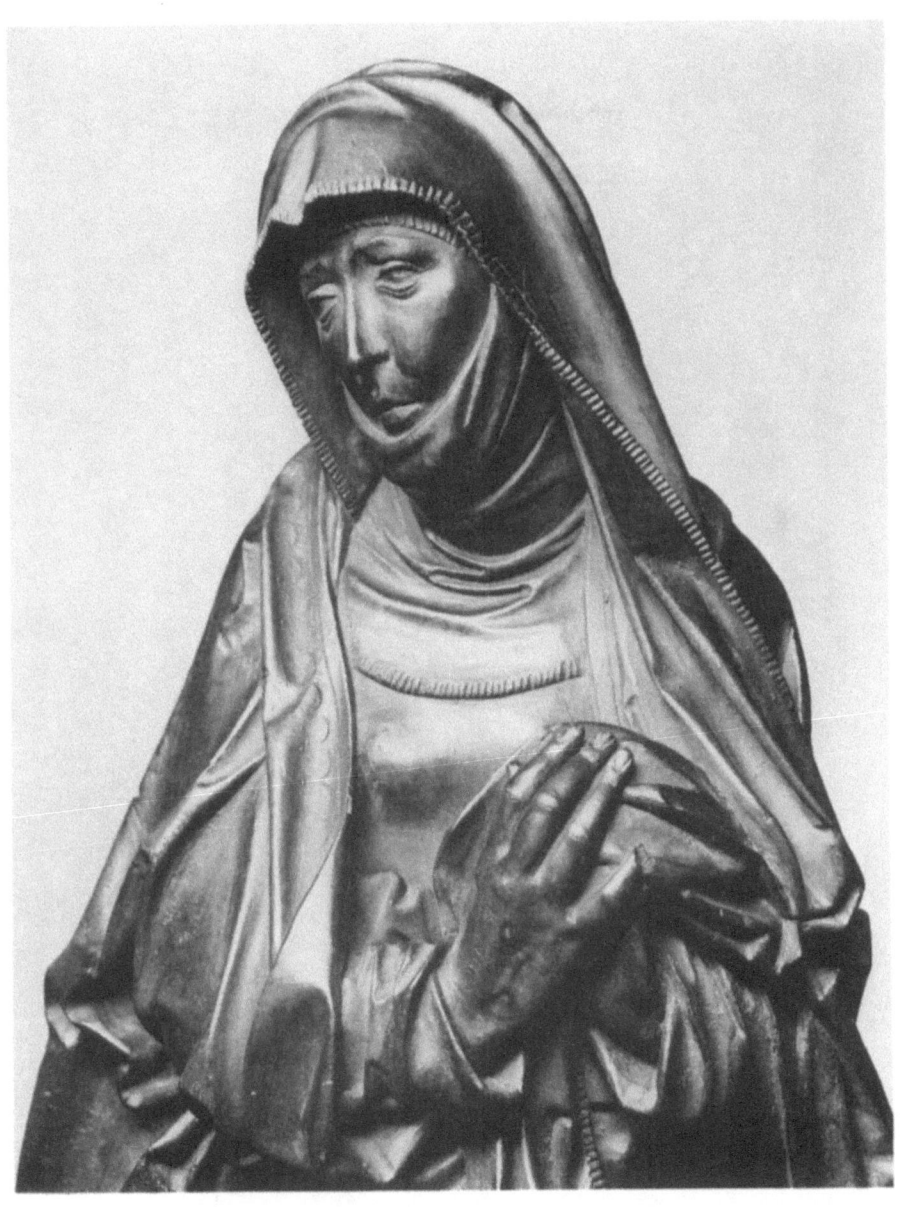

13A and B. The Mourning Virgin. About 1510. Lindenwood. Nelson Gallery-Atkins Museum, Kansas City, Missouri; Nelson Fund.

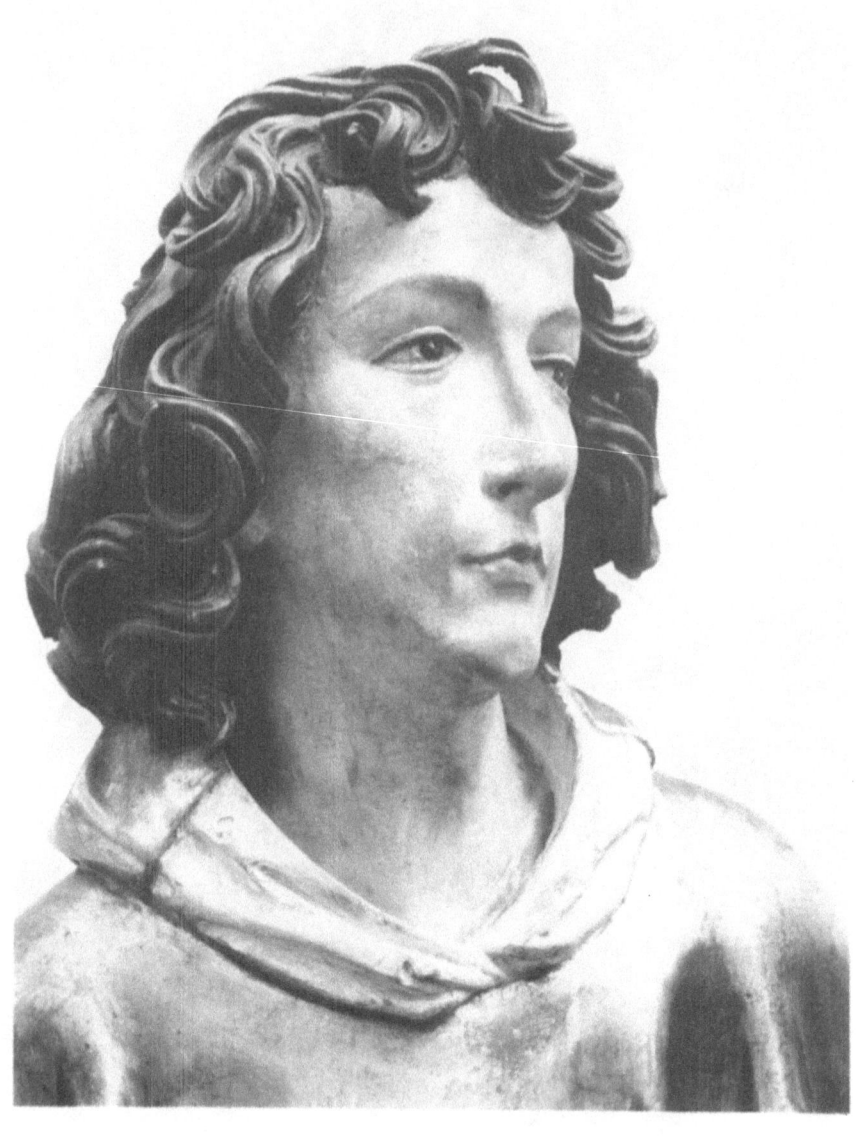

14A and B. St. Stephen. About 1510. Lindenwood. Cleveland Museum of Art; from the Leonard C. Hanna, Jr., Bequest.

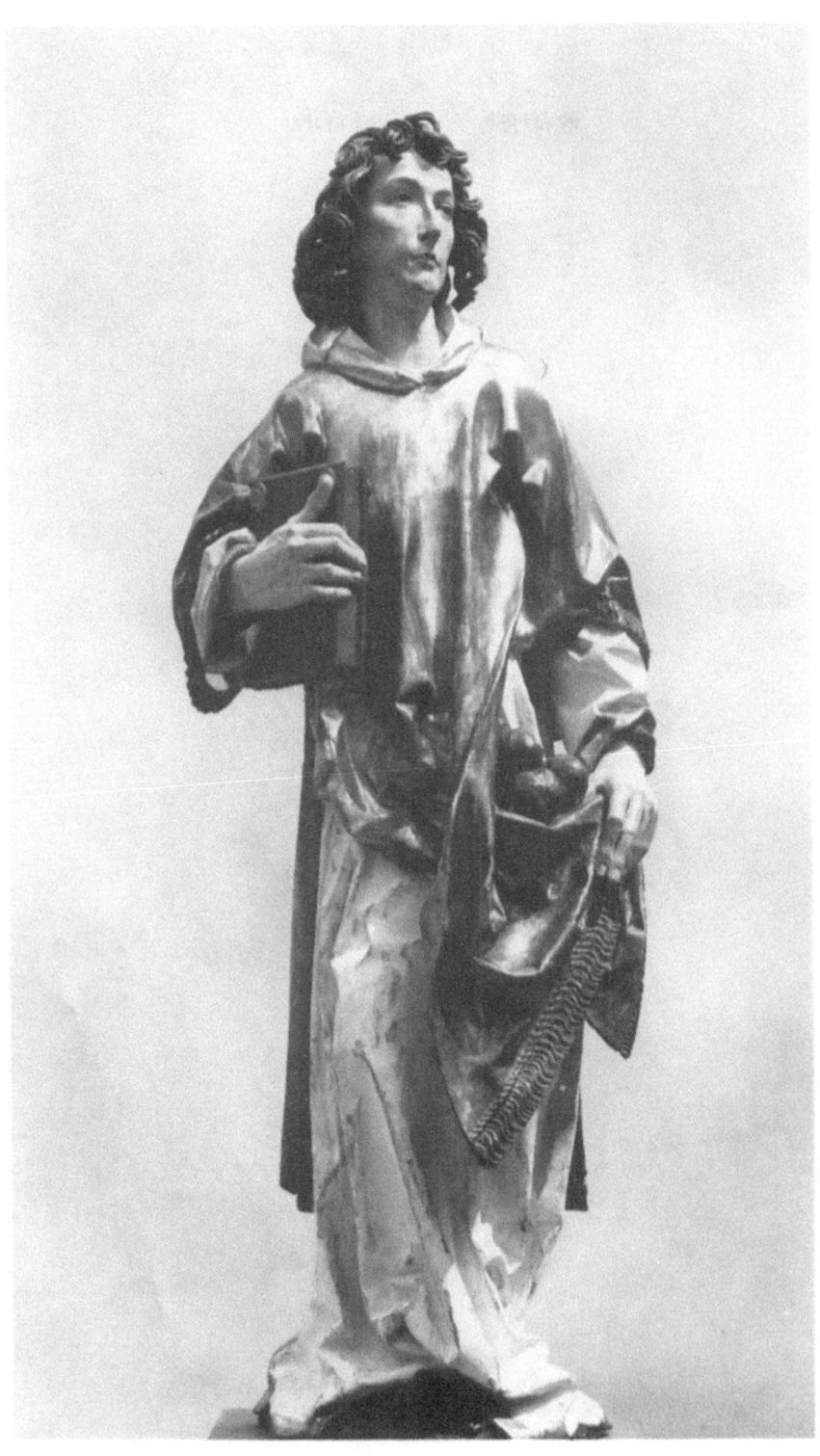

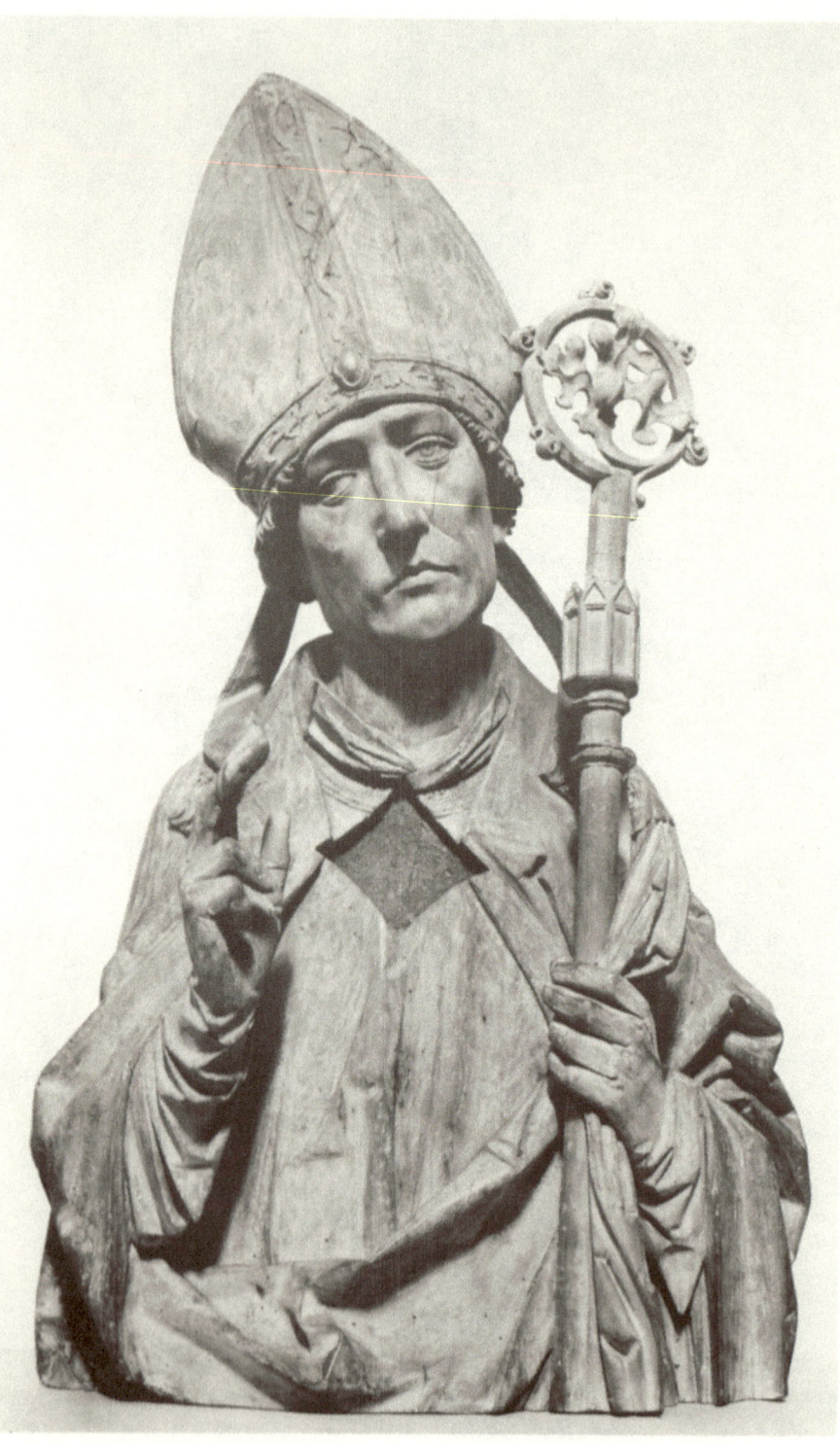

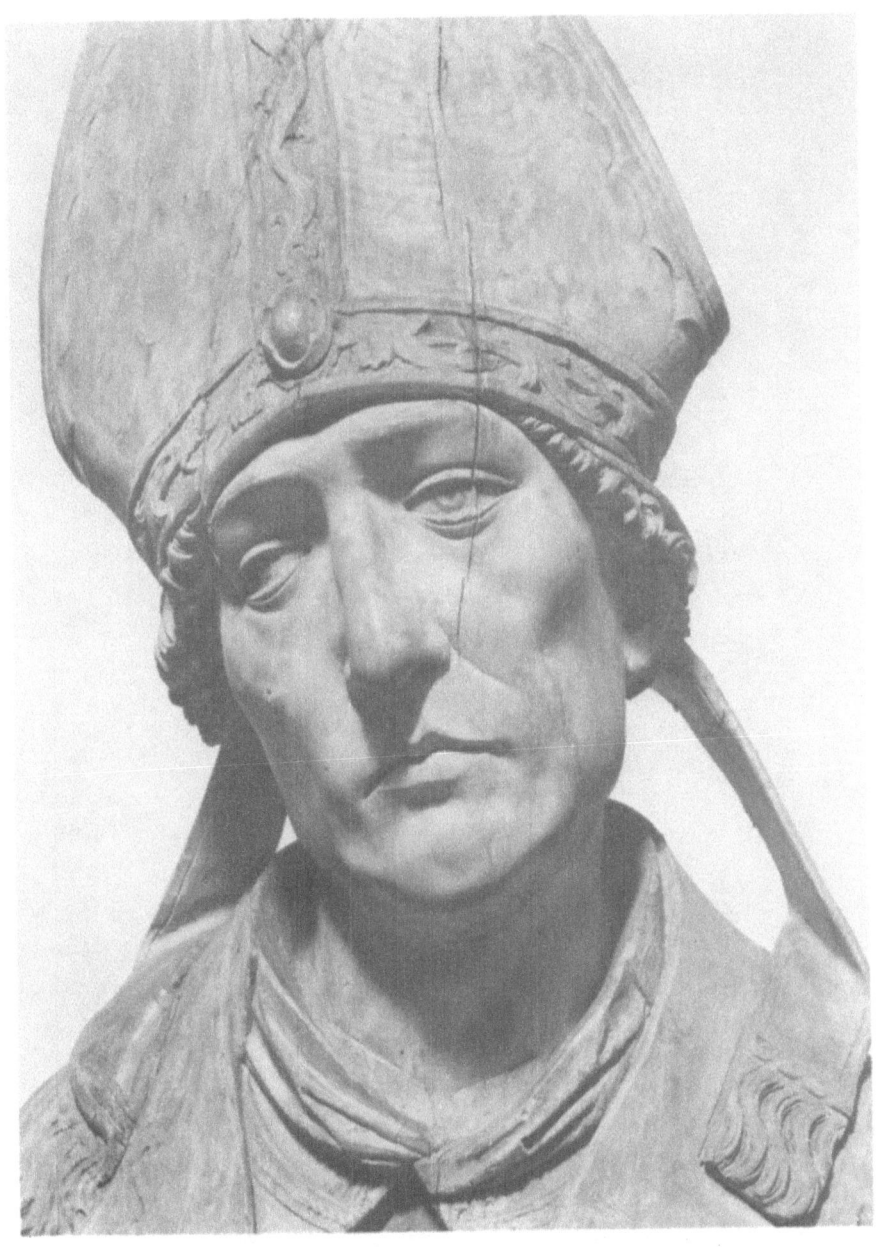

15A and B. St. Burchard. About 1519–1523. Lindenwood. National Gallery of Art, Washington, D.C.; Samuel H. Kress Collection.

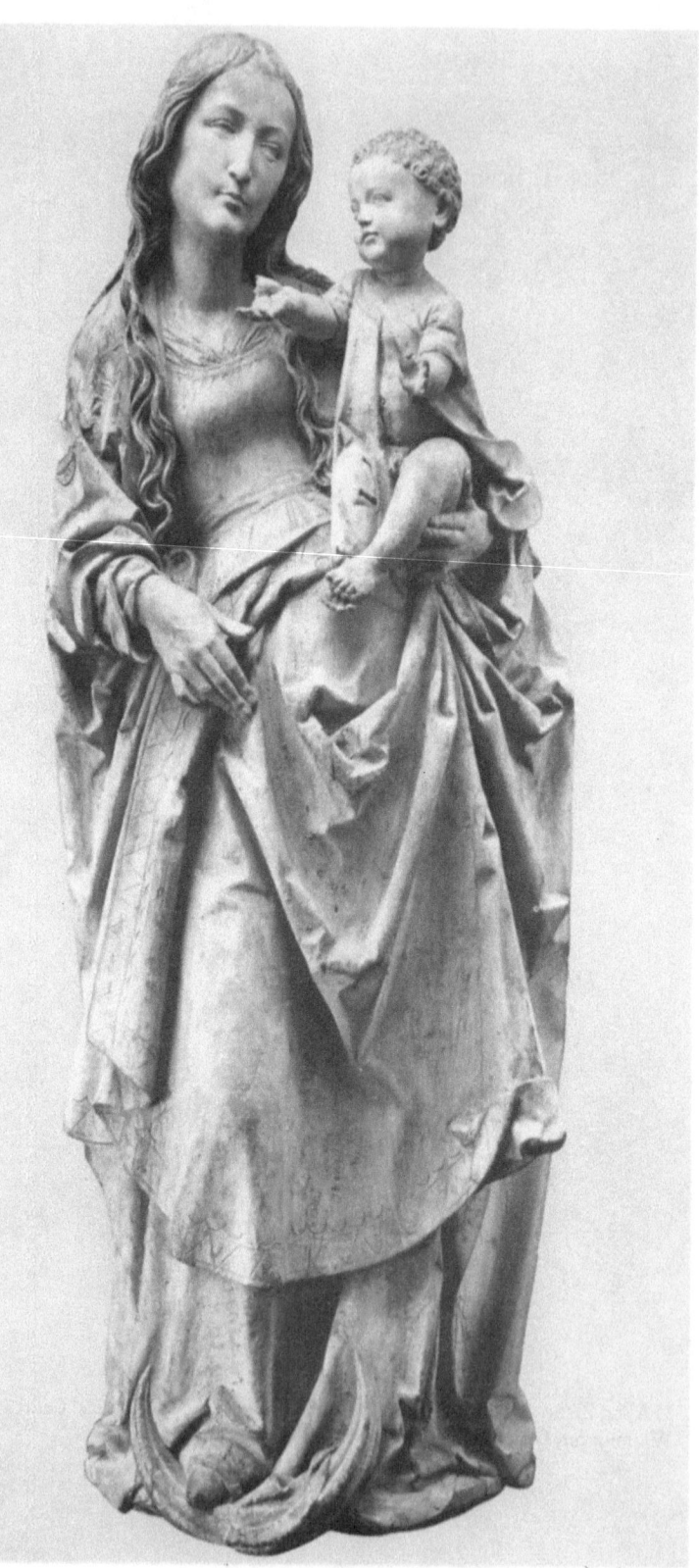

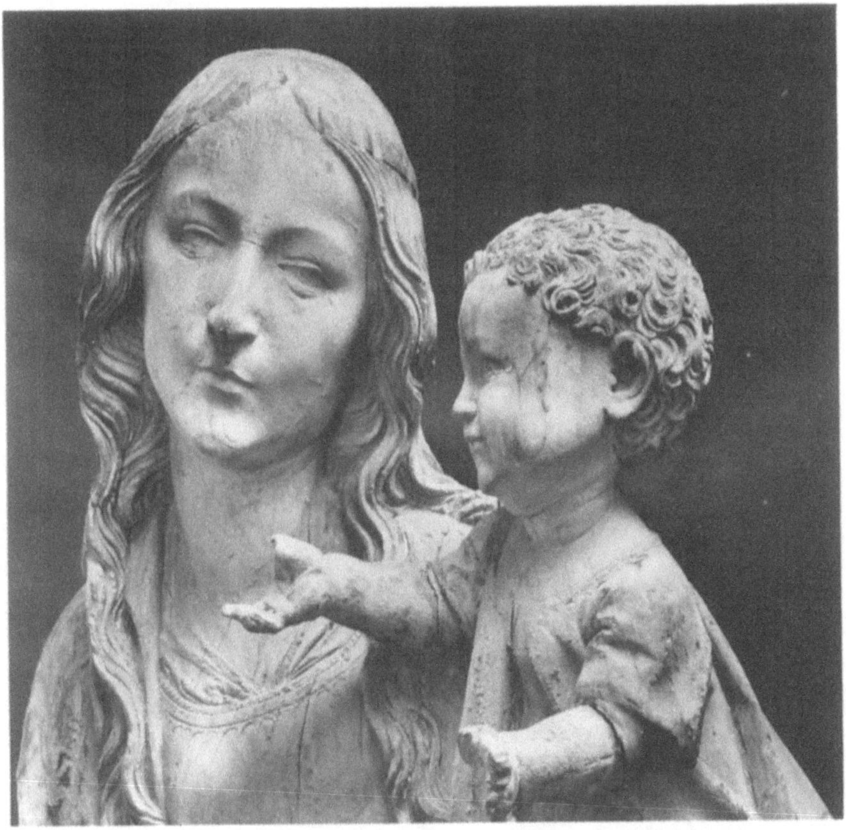

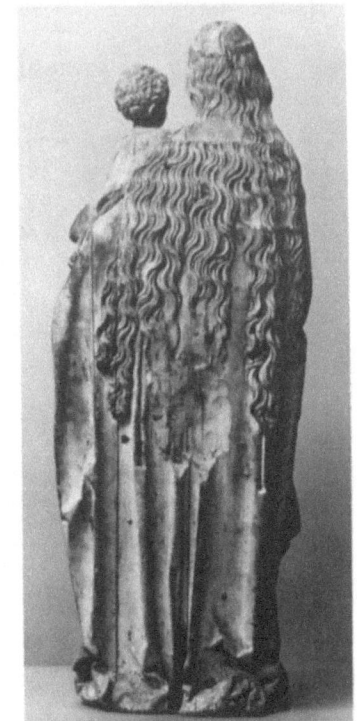

16A and B. The Virgin with the Christ Child.
1521. Lindenwood. Courtesy of the Dumbarton
Oaks Collection, Washington, D.C.
Right: 16C. Back view.

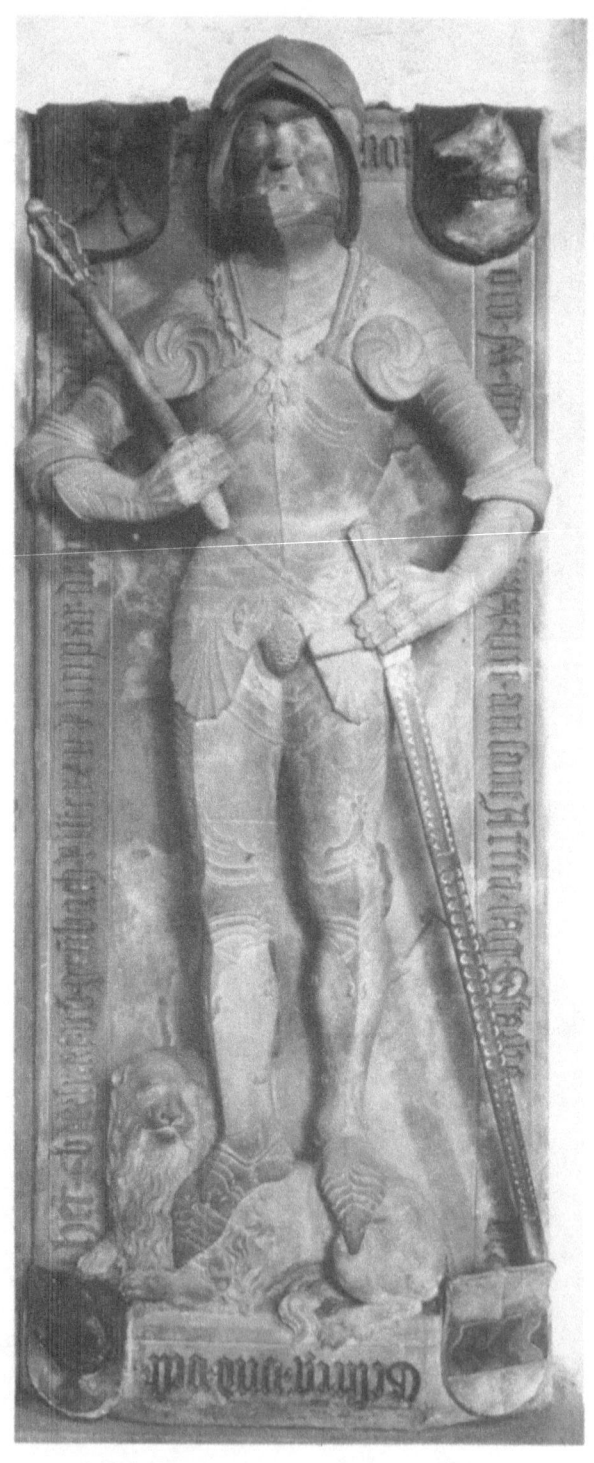

17. Tomb-monument of Eberhard von Grumbach
(d. 1487). About 1488. Sandstone. Parish Church, Rimpar.

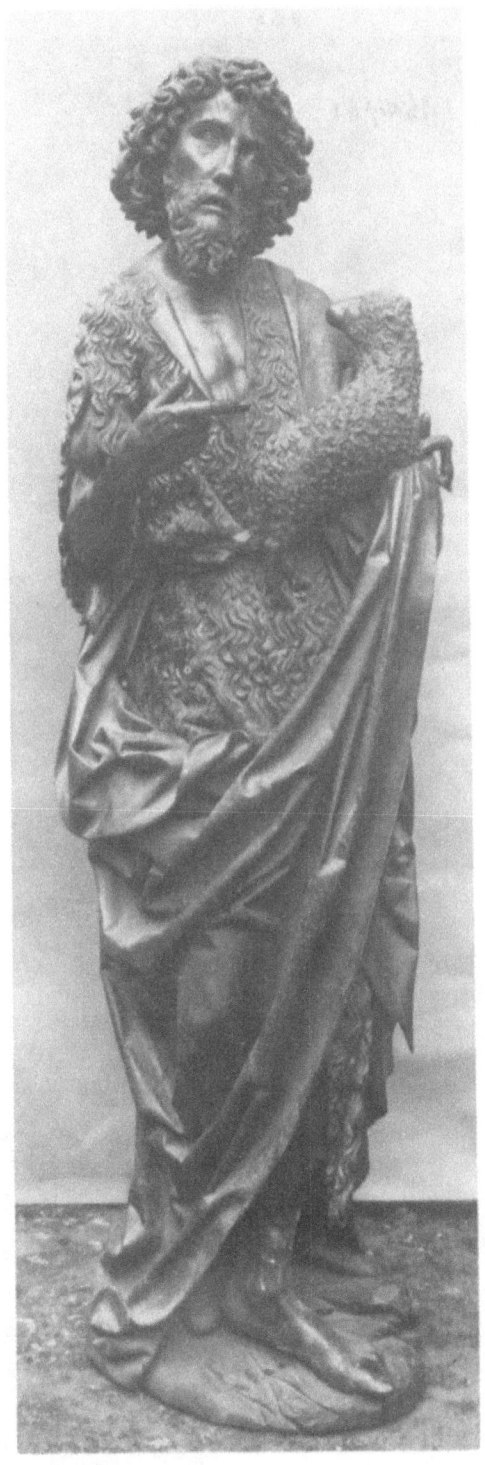

18. John the Baptist. Before 1490. Lindenwood.
Parish Church, Hassfurt.

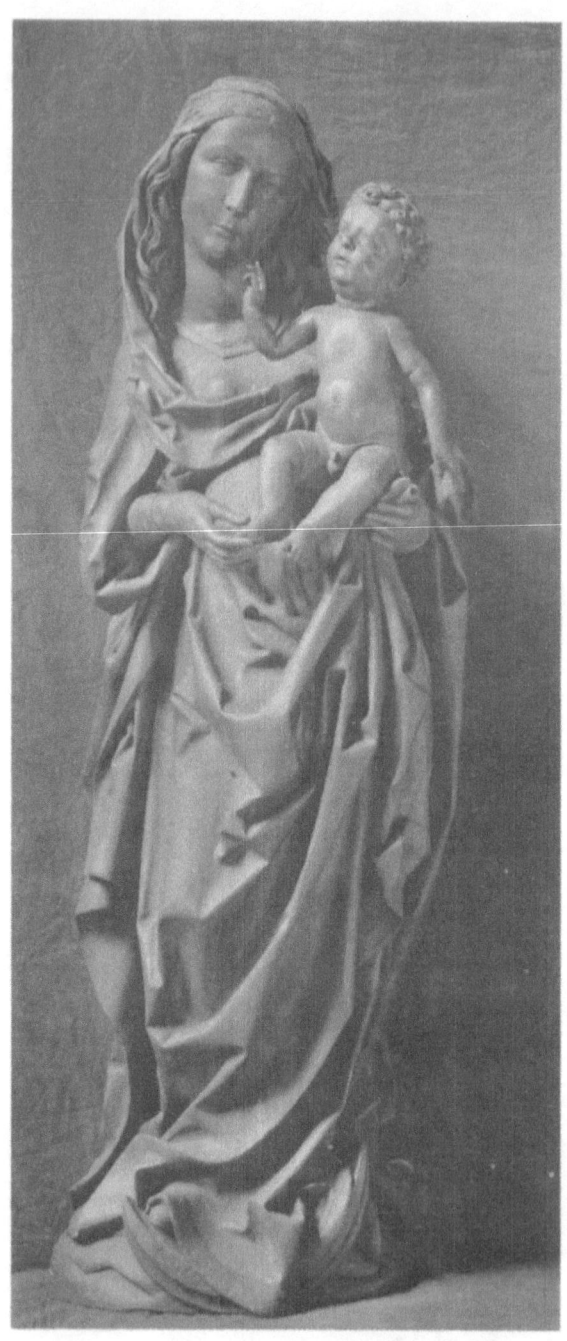

19. The Virgin with the Christ Child. From Werbach im
Taubertal. About 1490. Lindenwood. Formerly Deutsches
Museum, Berlin. Destroyed in 1945.

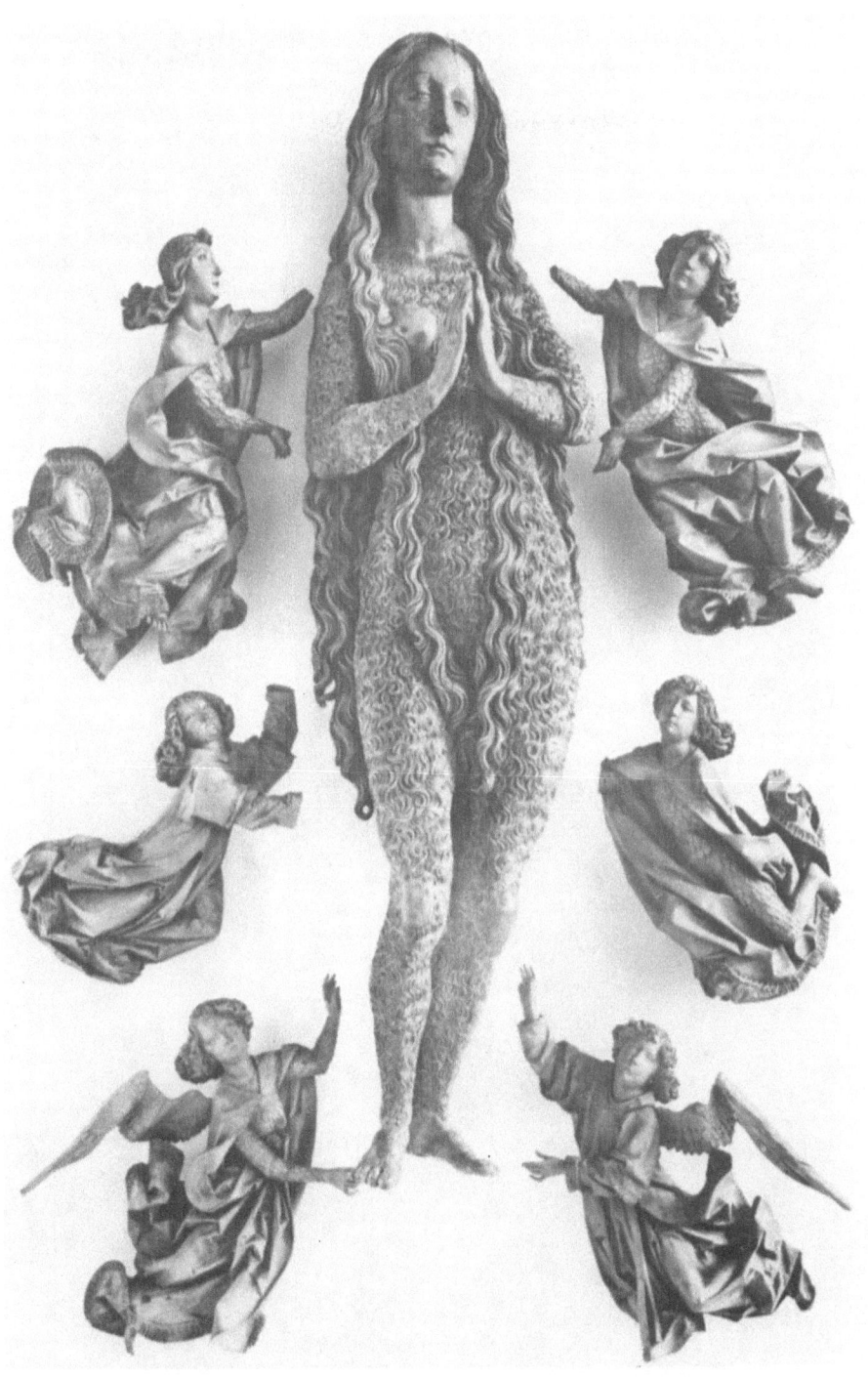

20A. Mary Magdalene borne aloft by angels. From the shrine of the Münnerstadt Altarpiece. 1490–1492. Lindenwood. Bayerisches Nationalmuseum, Munich. After restoration.

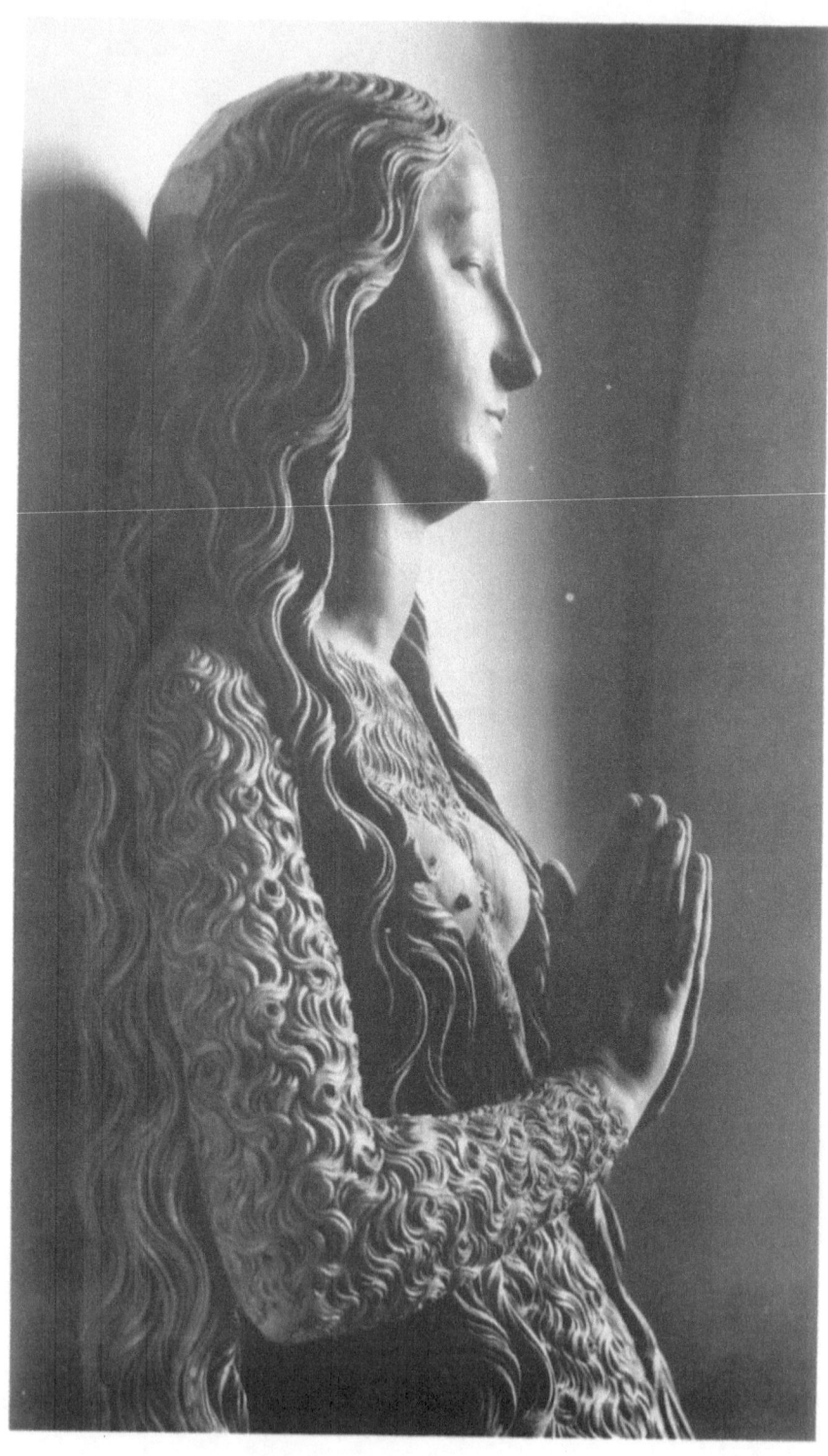

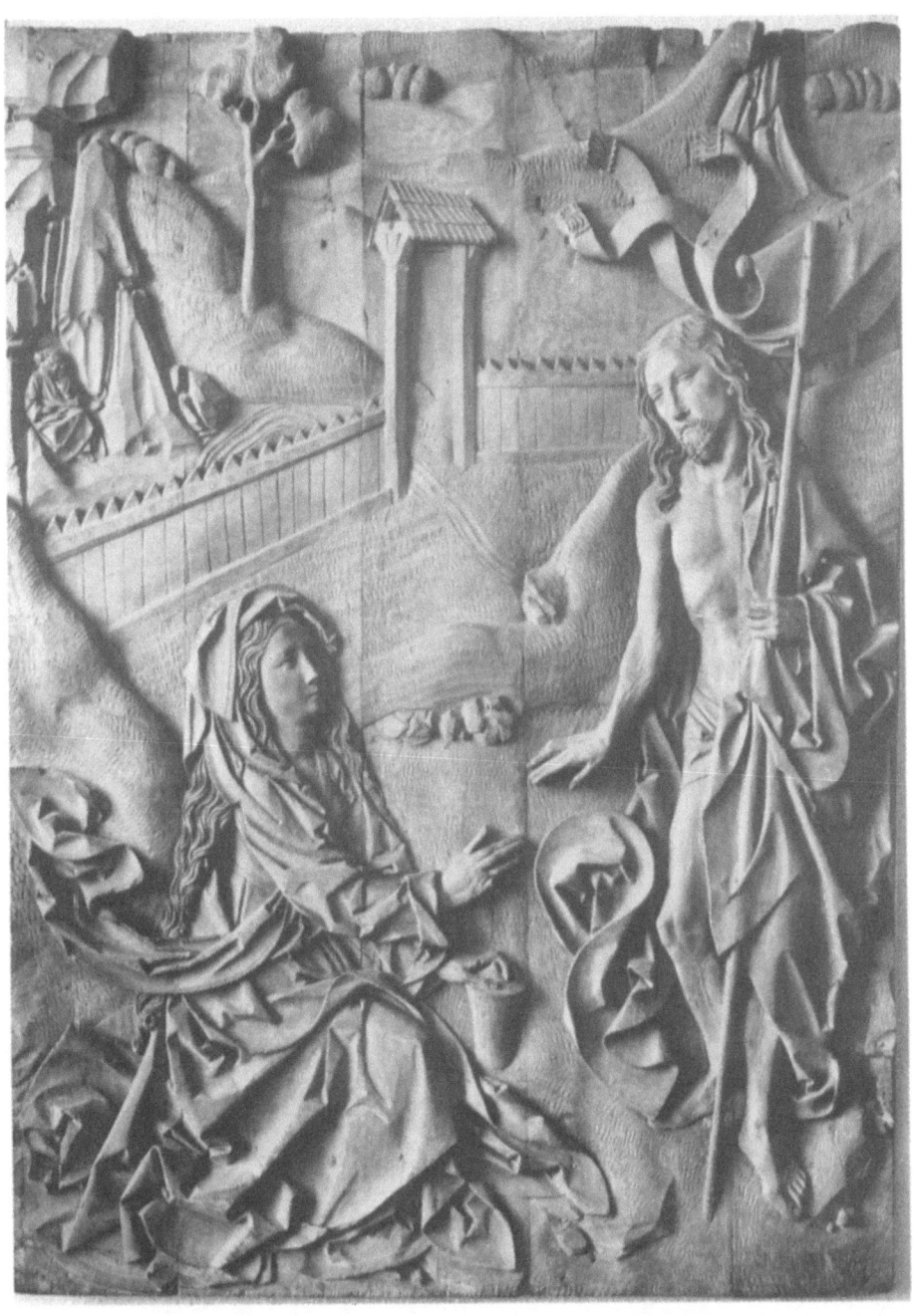

20C. The Meeting in the Garden. Wing relief from the Münnerstadt Altarpiece. 1490–1492. Lindenwood. Skulpterenabteilung, Staatliche Museen, West Berlin.

Opposite: 20B. Mary Magdalene from the Münnerstadt Altarpiece, detail.

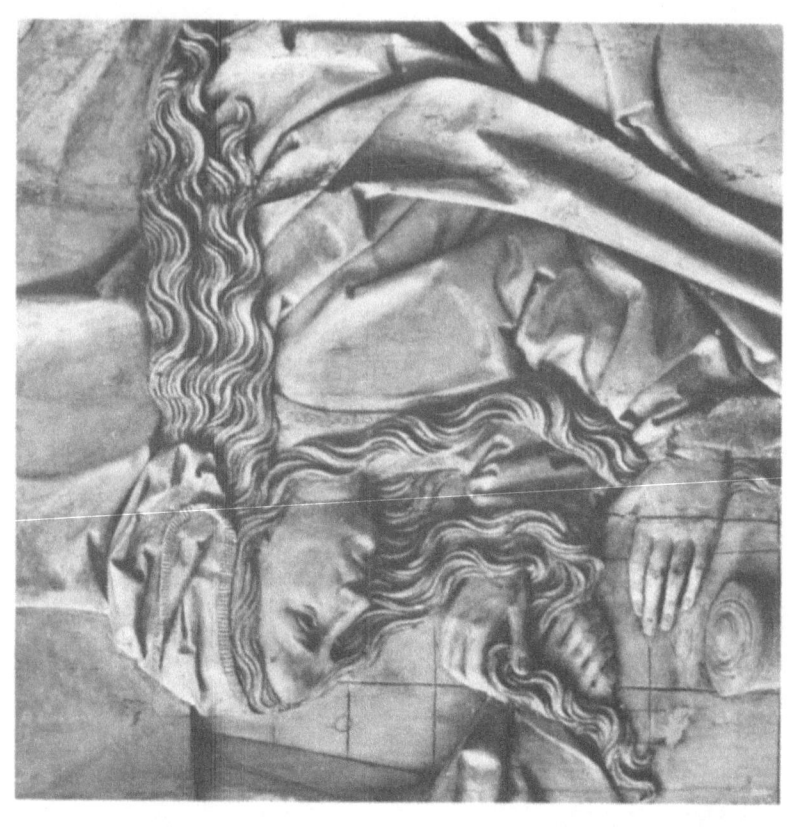

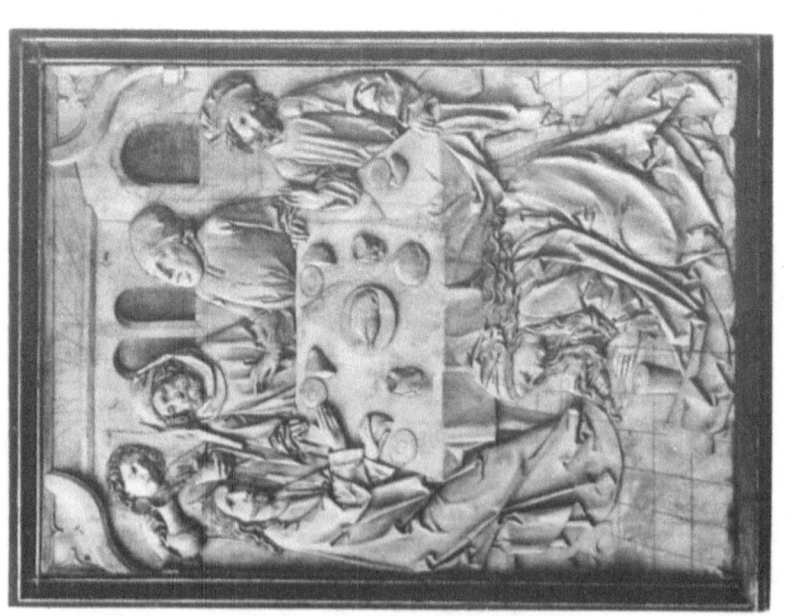

Left: 20D. Supper in the House of Simon. Wing relief, Münnerstadt Altarpiece. 1490-1492. Lindenwood. On loan to the Bayerisches Nationalmuseum, Munich, from the Bollert Collection. *Right:* 20E. Mary Magdalene anointing Christ's feet, detail of Supper in the House of Simon.

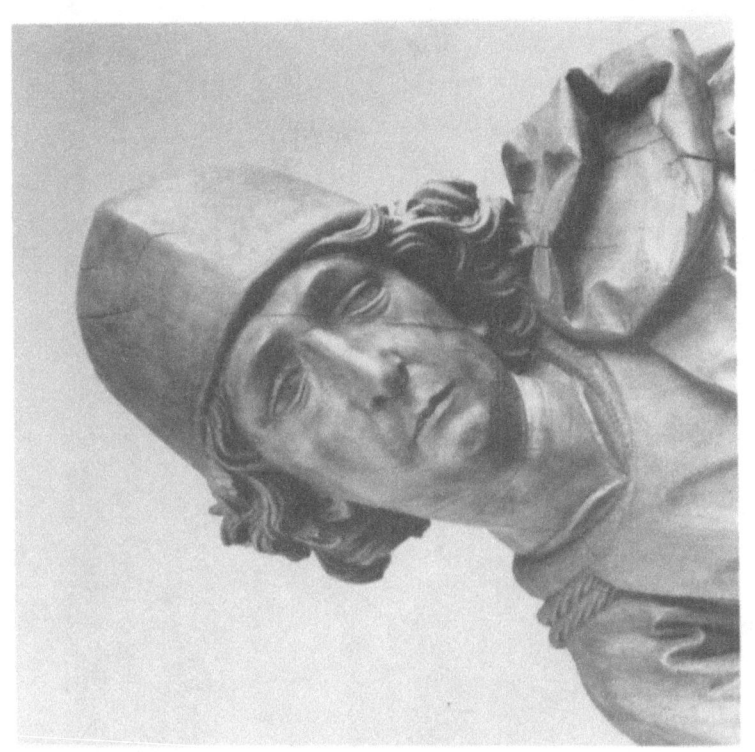

20G. The Evangelist Luke from the Münnerstadt Altarpiece (detail of Plate 20I).

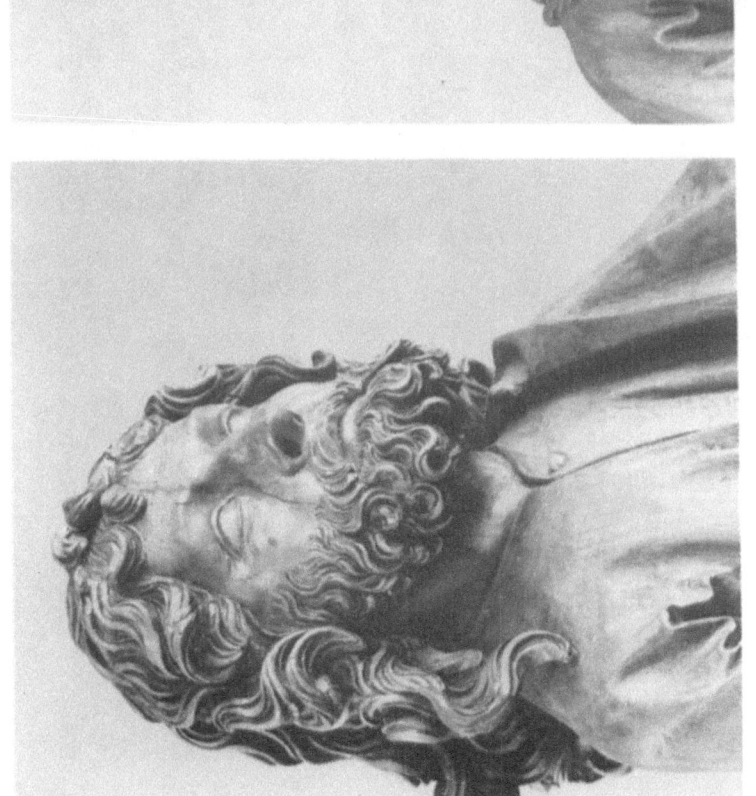

20F. The Evangelist Matthew from the Münnerstadt Altarpiece (detail of Plate 20H).

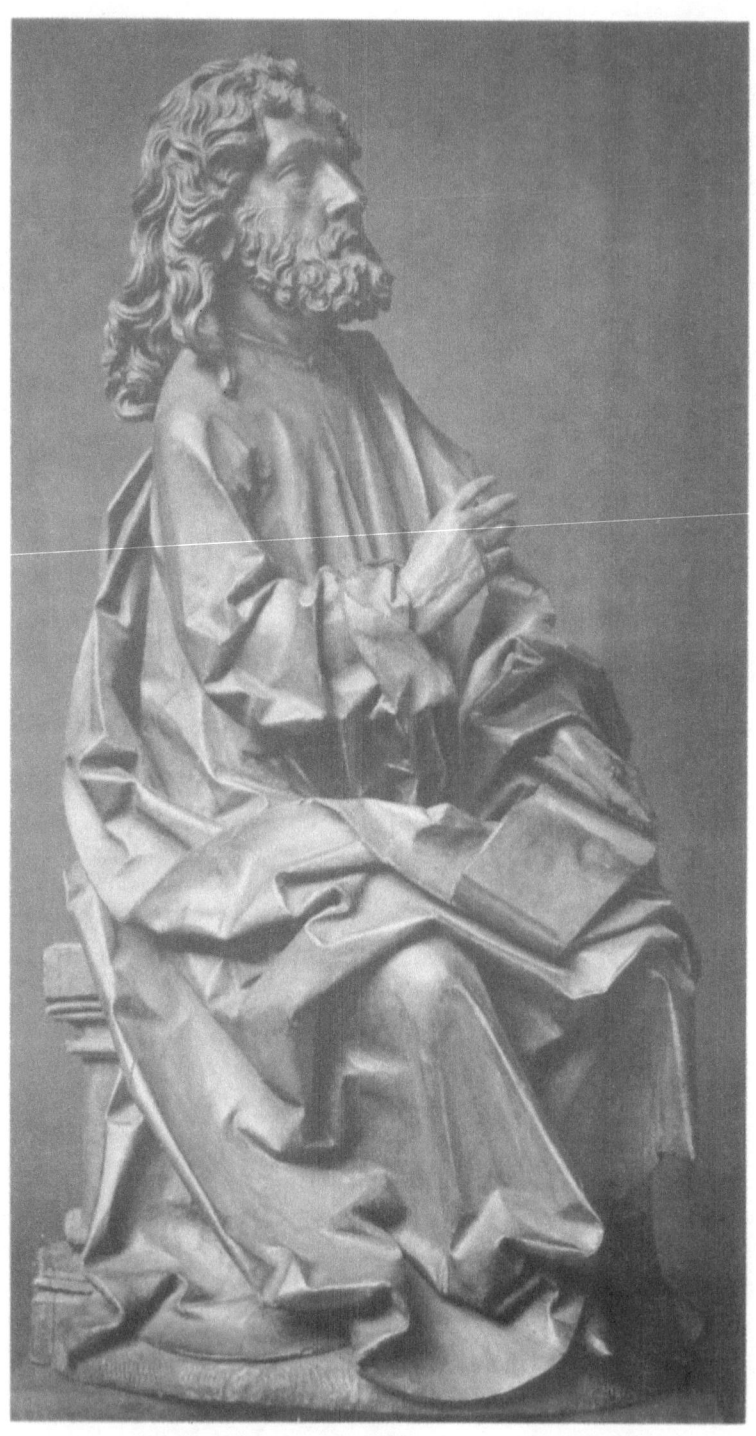

20H. The Evangelist Matthew. From the predella of the Münnerstadt Altarpiece. 1490–1492. Lindenwood. Skulpturenabteilung, Staatliche Museen, West Berlin.

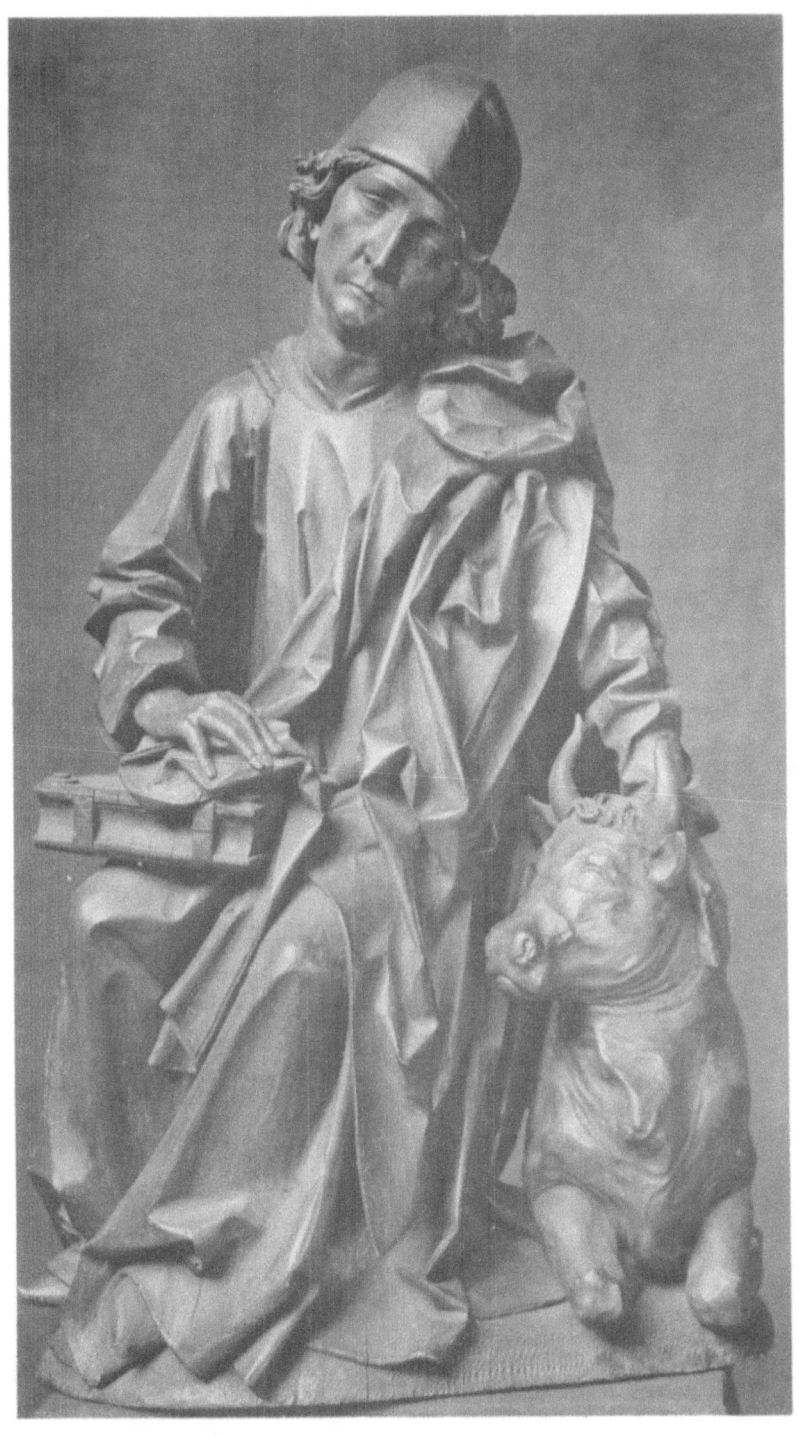

20I. The Evangelist Luke. From the predella of the Münnerstadt Altarpiece. 1490–1492. Lindenwood. Skulpturenabteilung, Staatliche Museen, West Berlin.

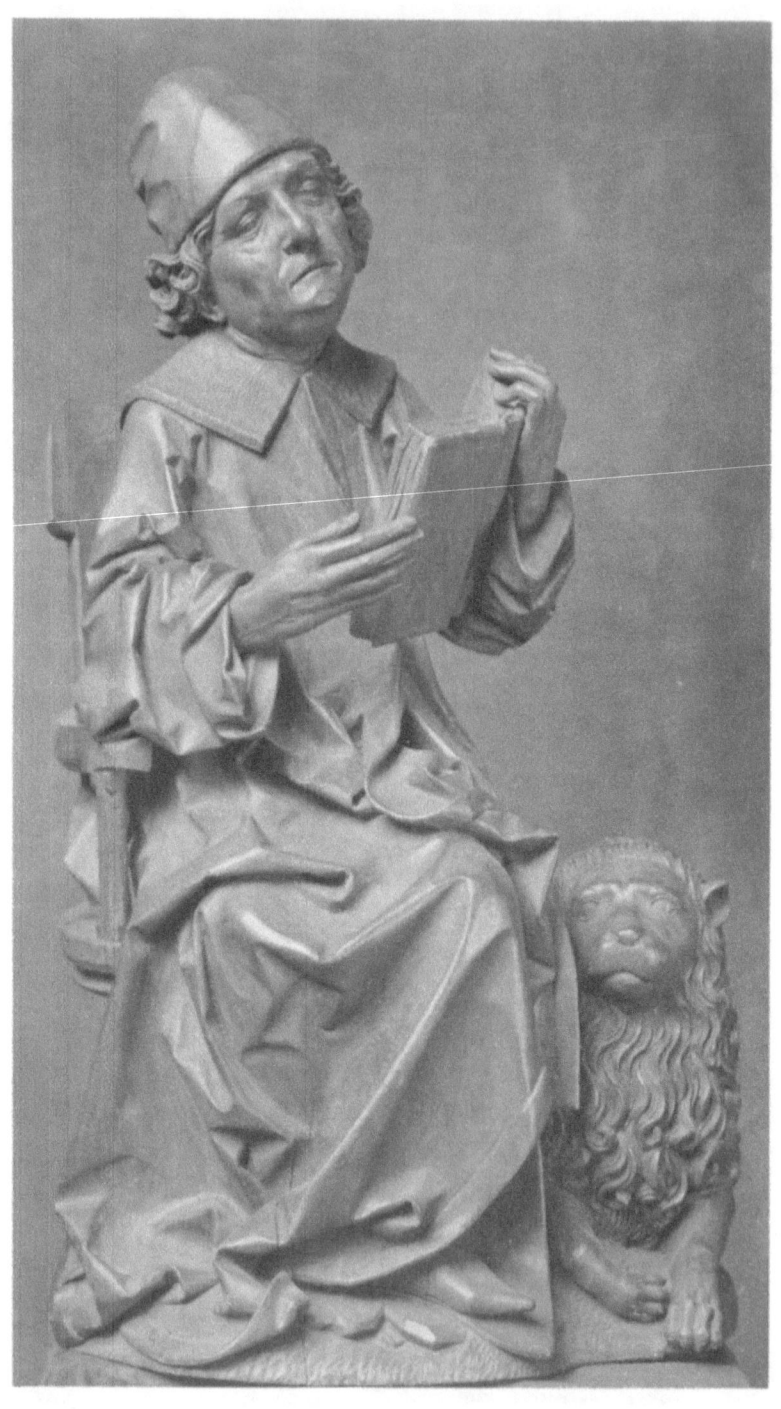

20J. The Evangelist Mark. From the predella of the Münnerstadt Altarpiece. 1490–1492. Lindenwood. Skulpturenabteilung, Staatliche Museen, West Berlin.

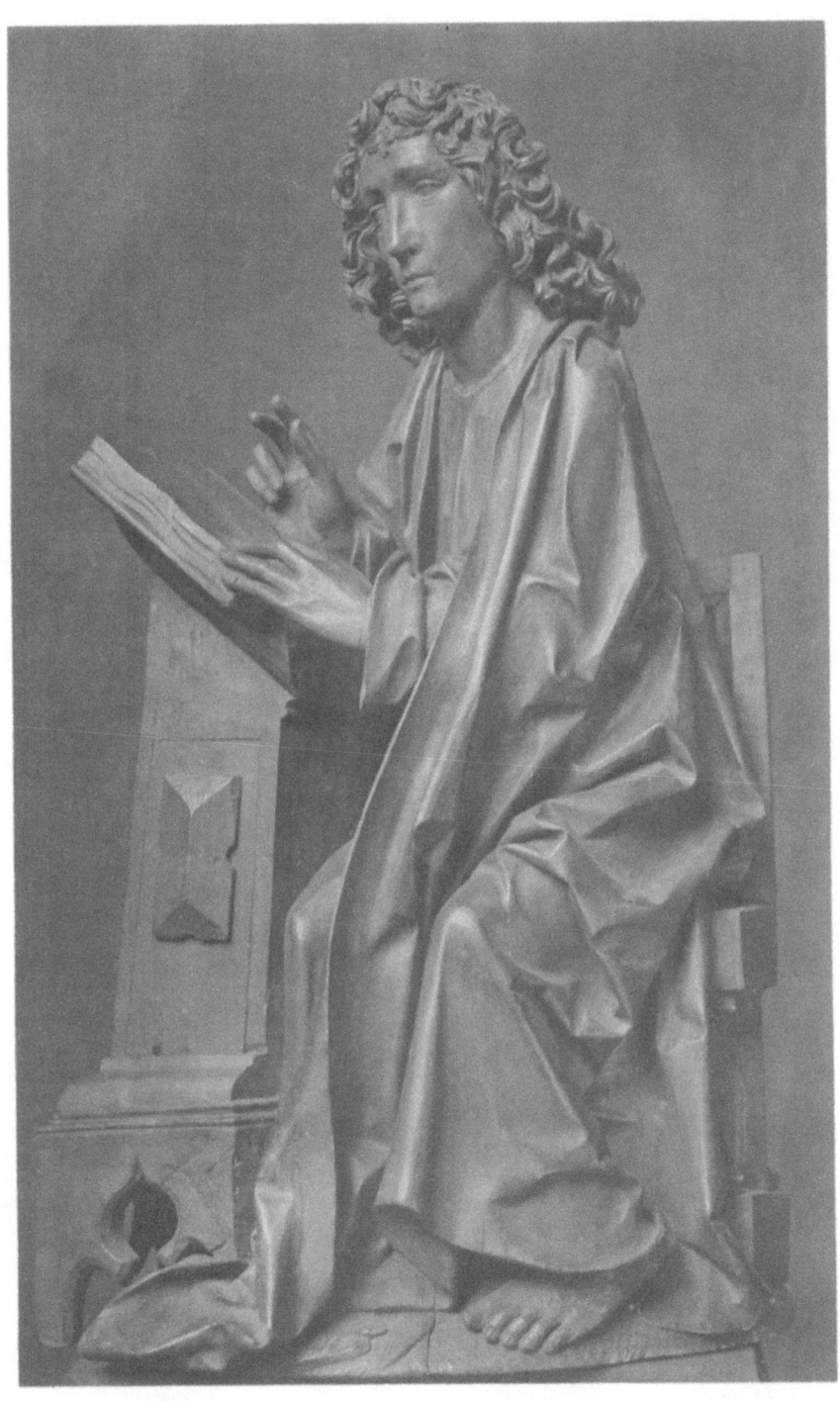

20K. The Evangelist John. From the predella of the Münnerstadt Altarpiece. 1490–1492. Lindenwood. Skulpturenabteilung, Staatliche Museen, West Berlin.

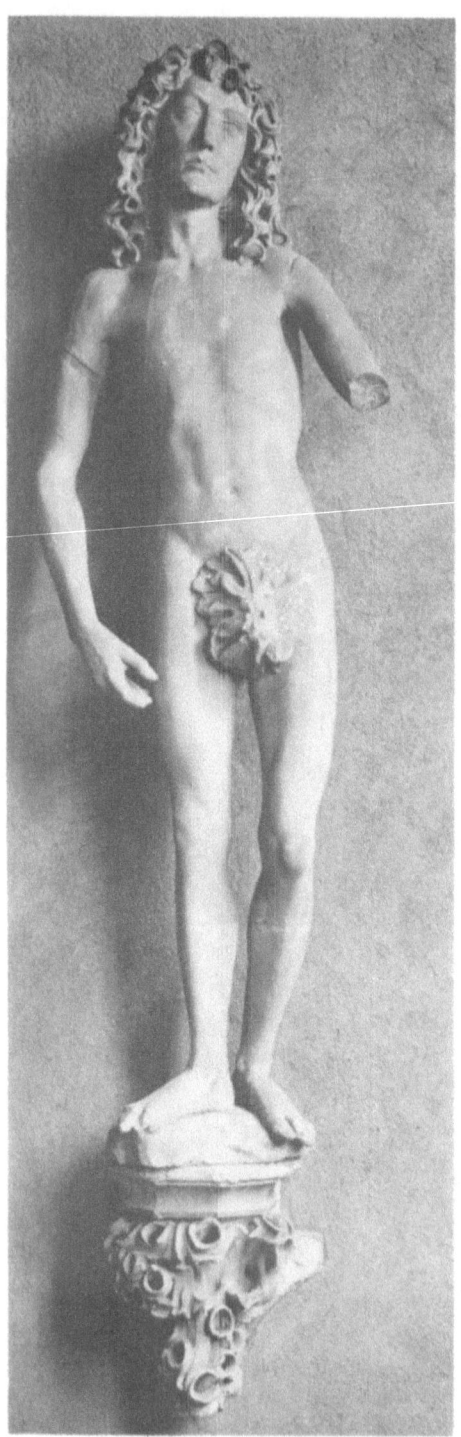

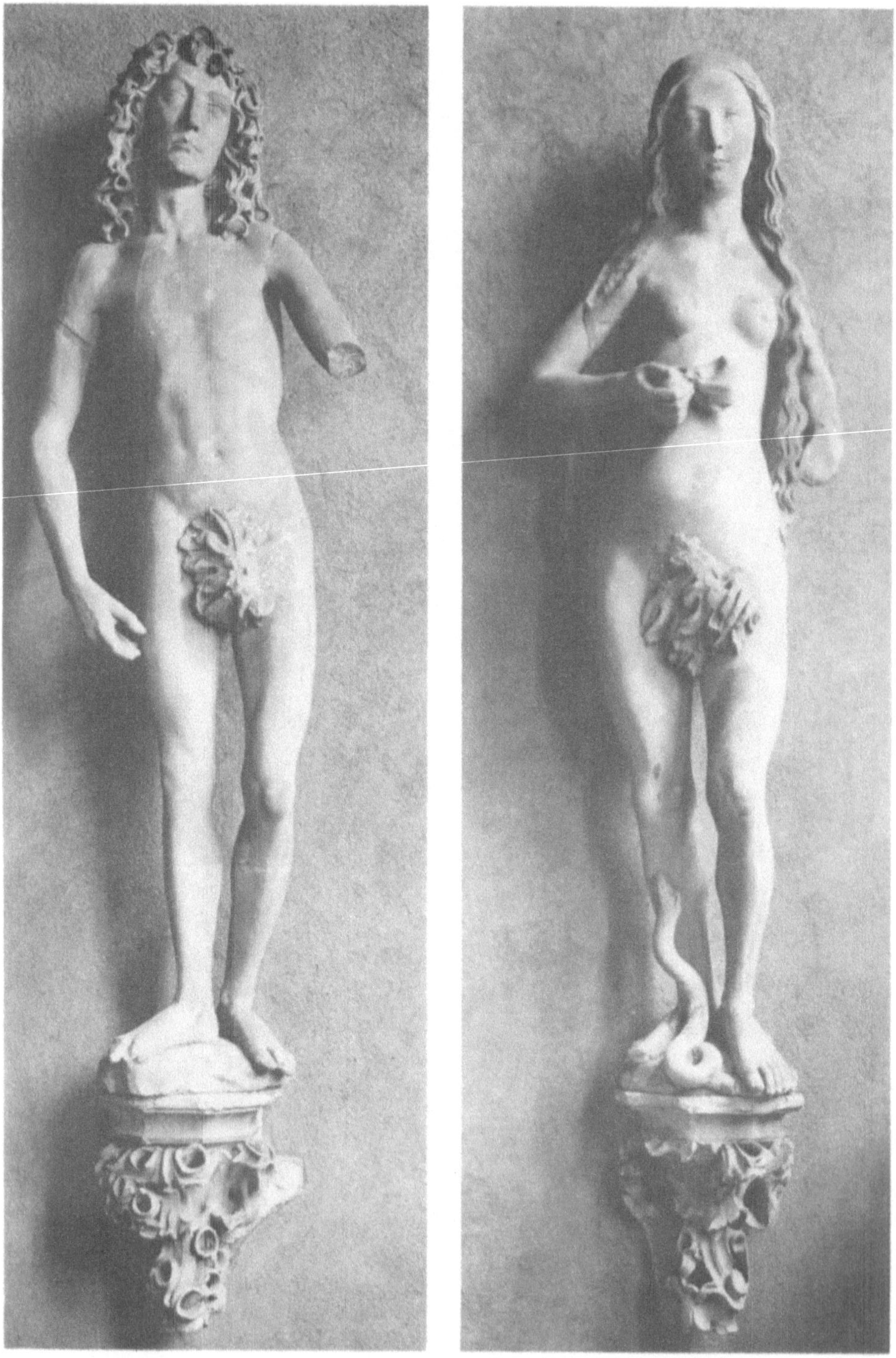

21A and B. Adam and Eve. From the Marienkapelle in Würzburg. 1491–1493. Sandstone.
Mainfränkisches Museum, Würzburg. *Opposite:* 21 C and D. Adam and Eve, details.

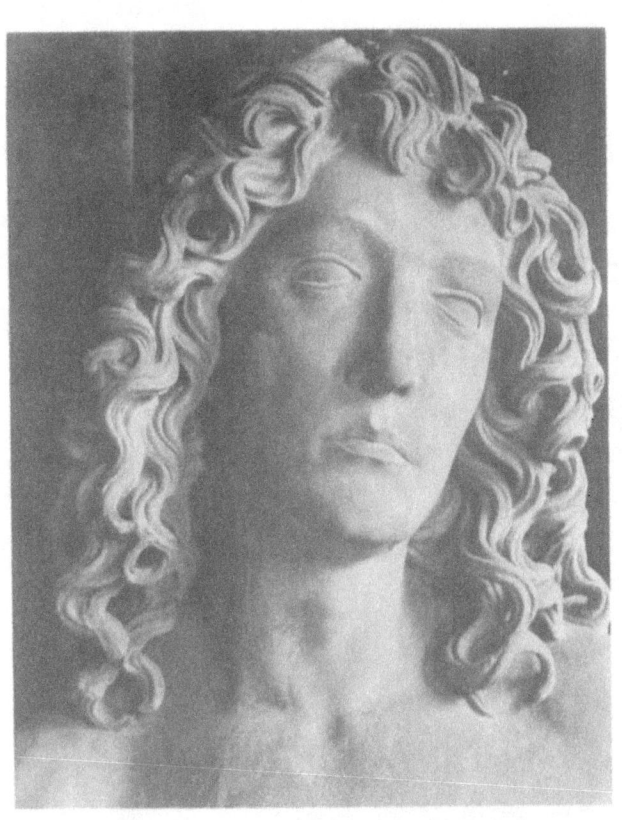

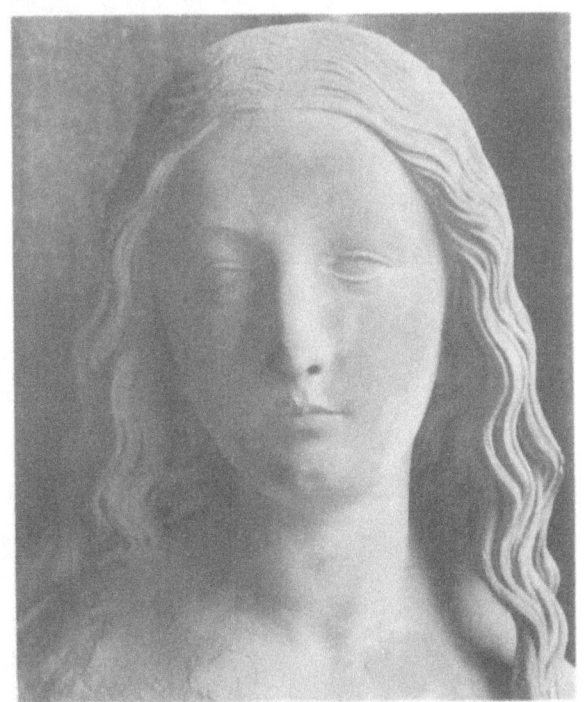

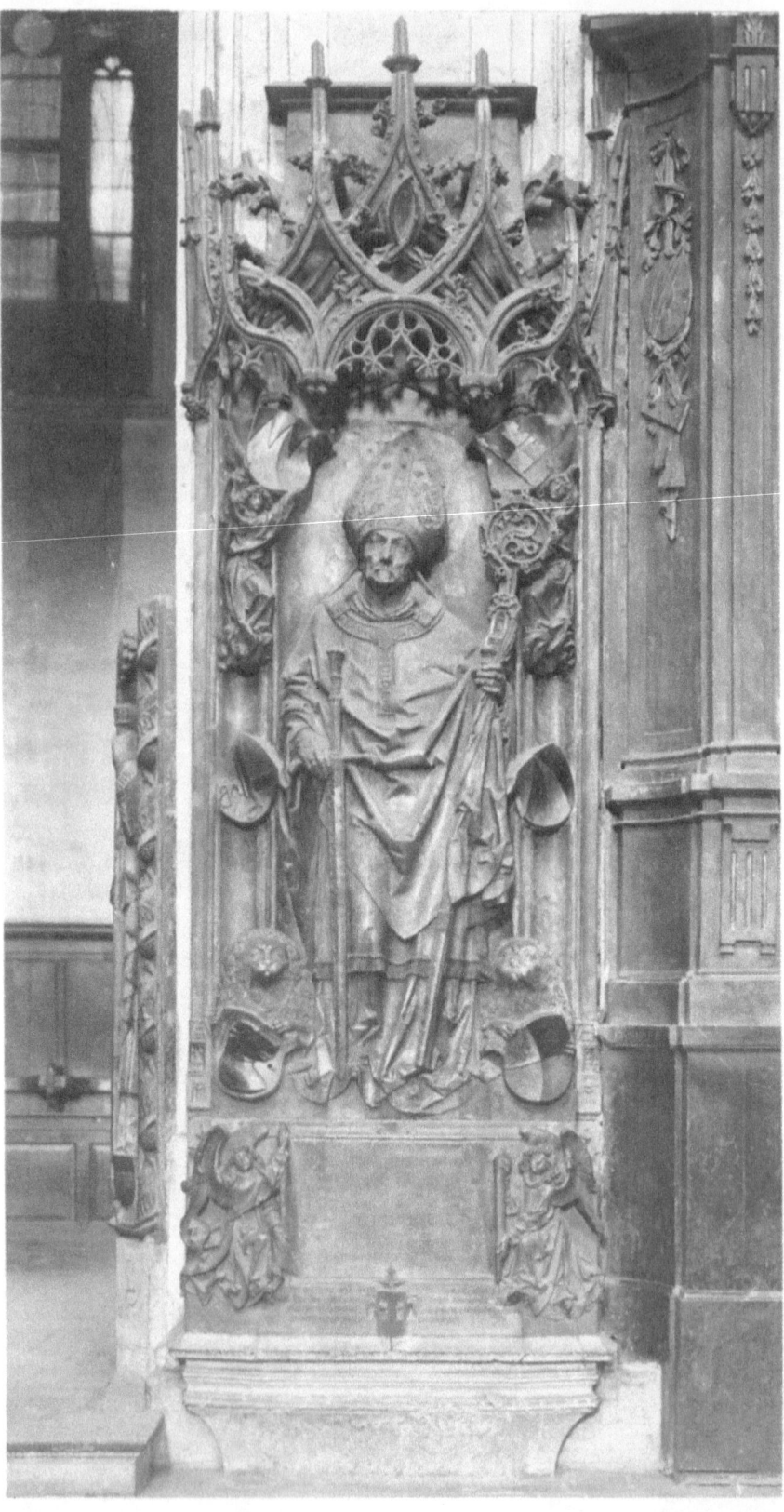

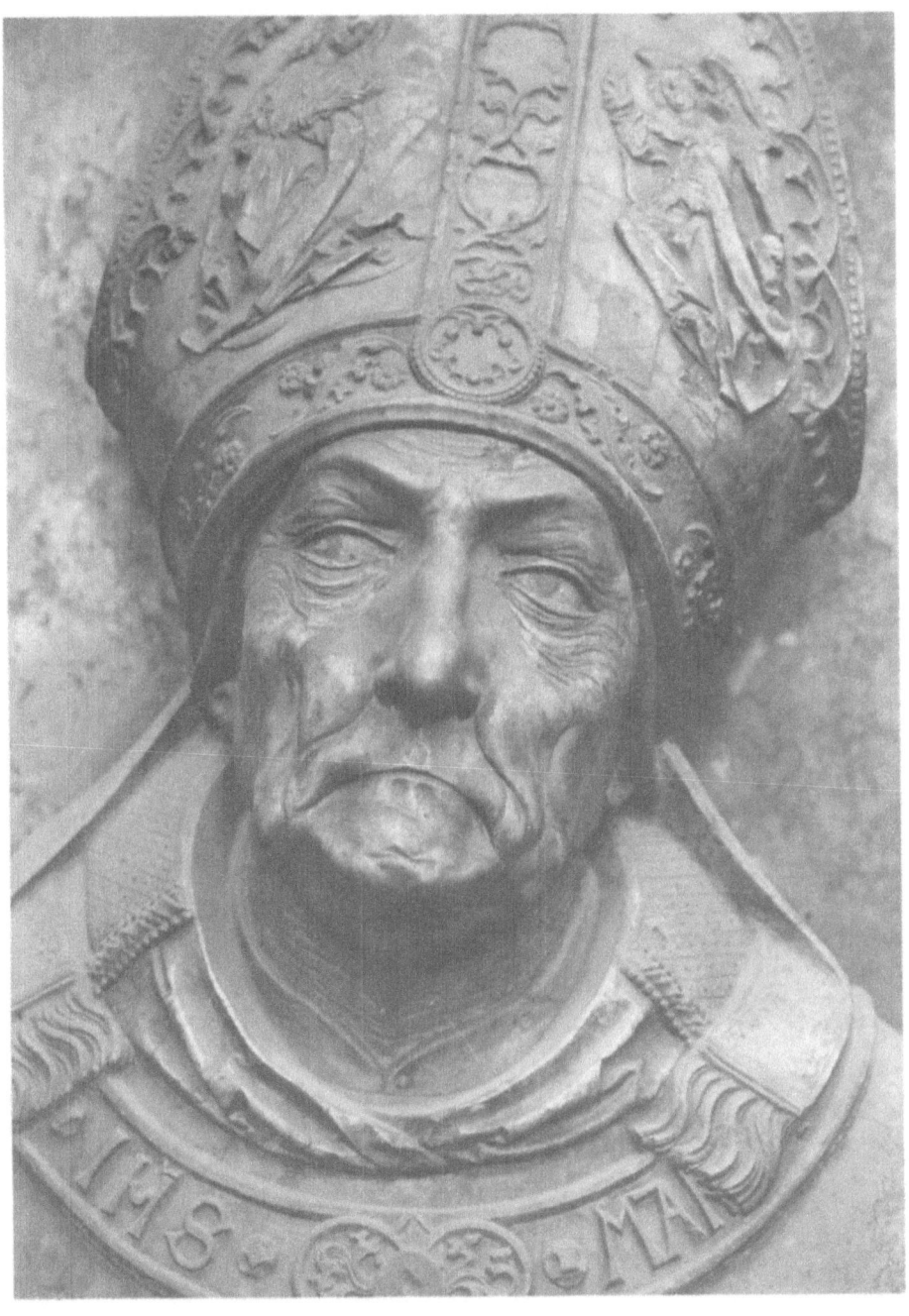

Opposite: 22A. Tomb-monument of Rudolf von Scherenberg (d. 1495). 1496–1499. Sandstone and marble. Würzburg Cathedral. *Above:* 22B. Prince-Bishop Rudolf von Scherenberg, detail of his tomb-monument.

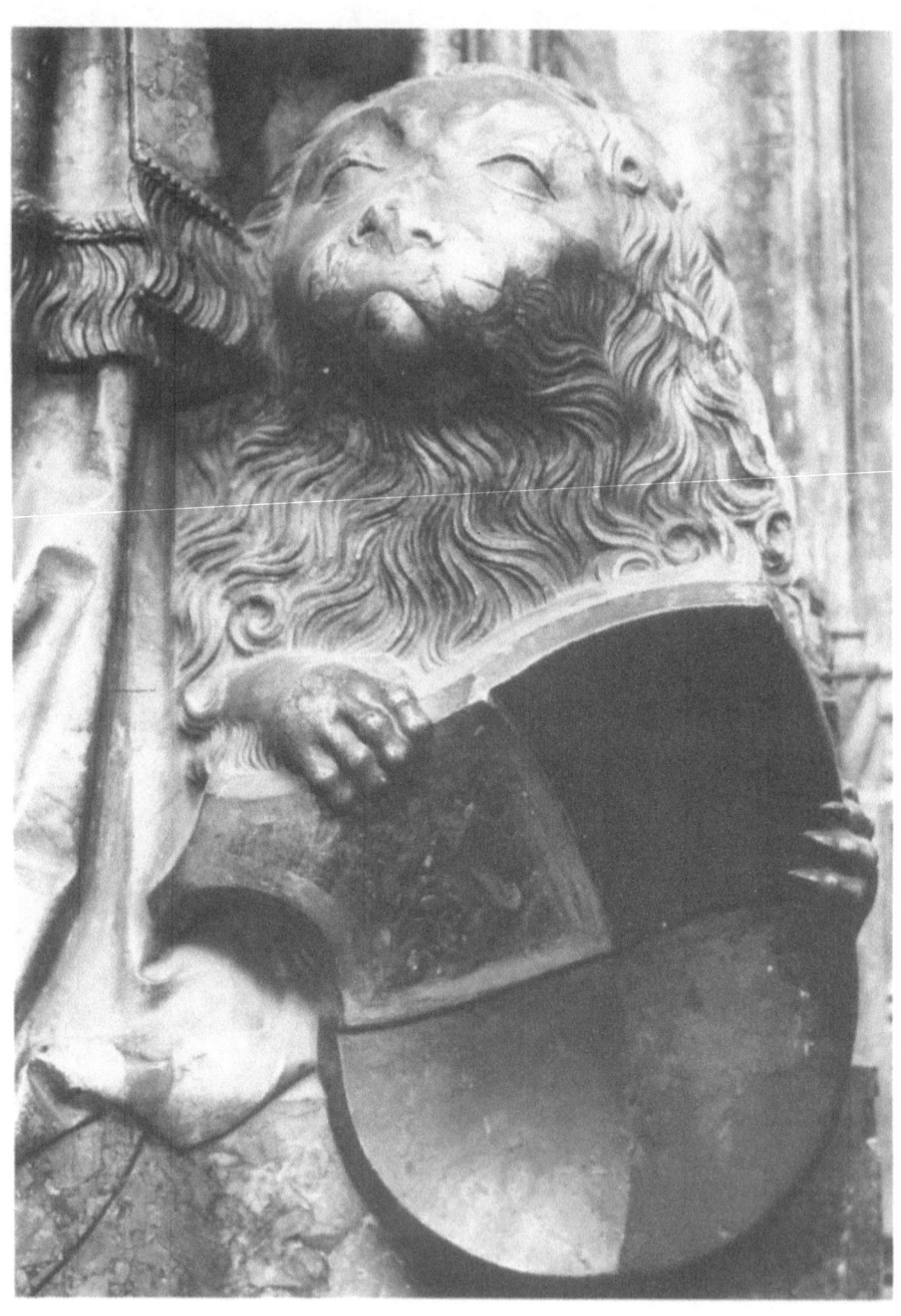

Details from the Tomb-monument of Rudolf von Scherenberg. *Above:* 22C. Lion holding coat of arms. *Opposite:* 22D and E. Angels holding the epitaph.

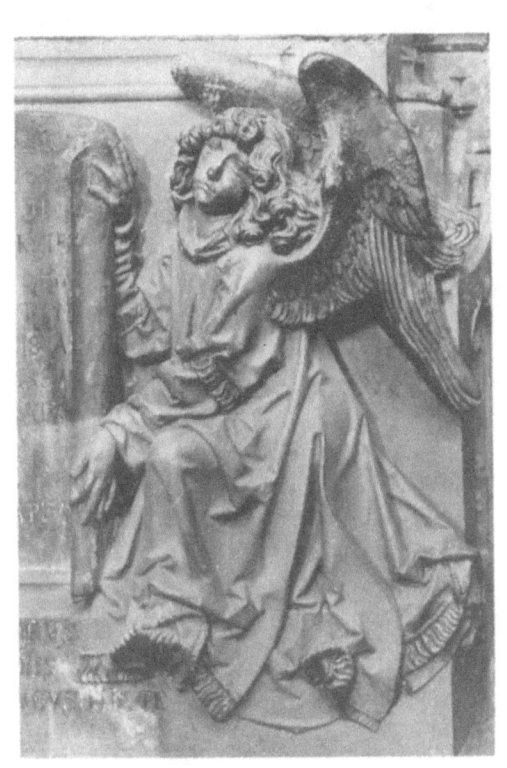

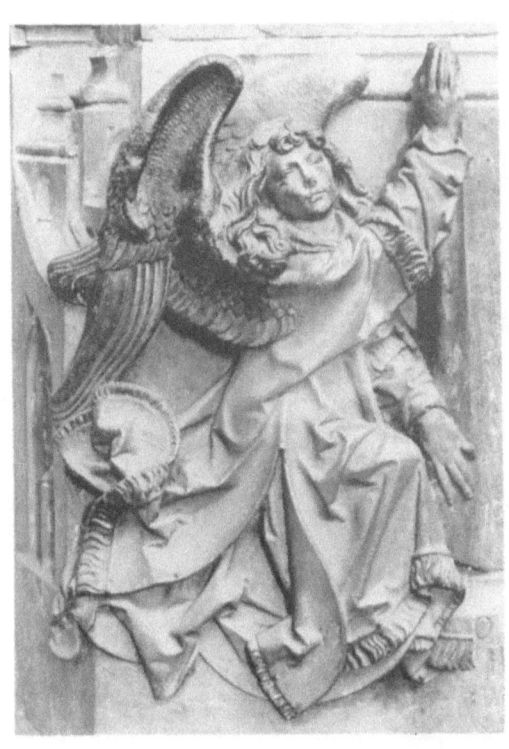

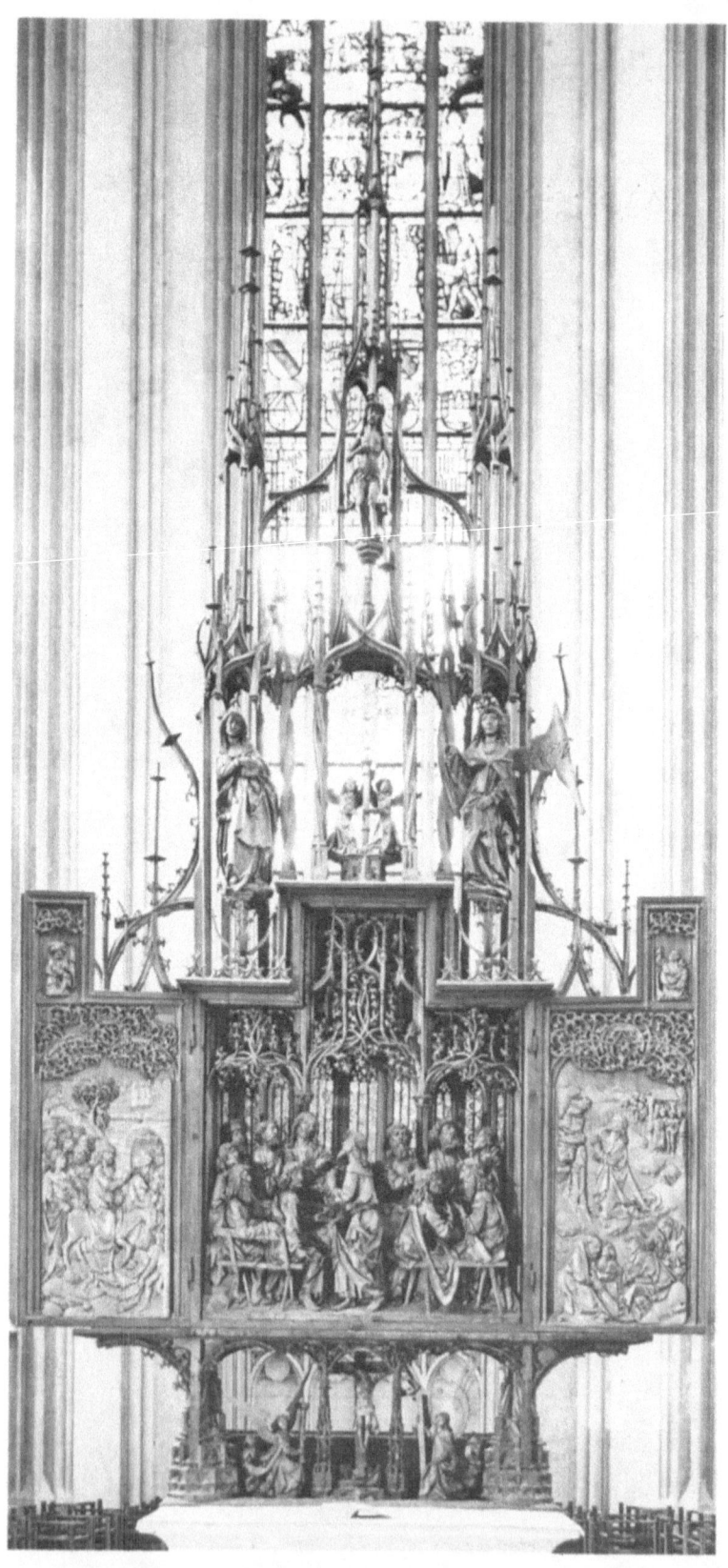

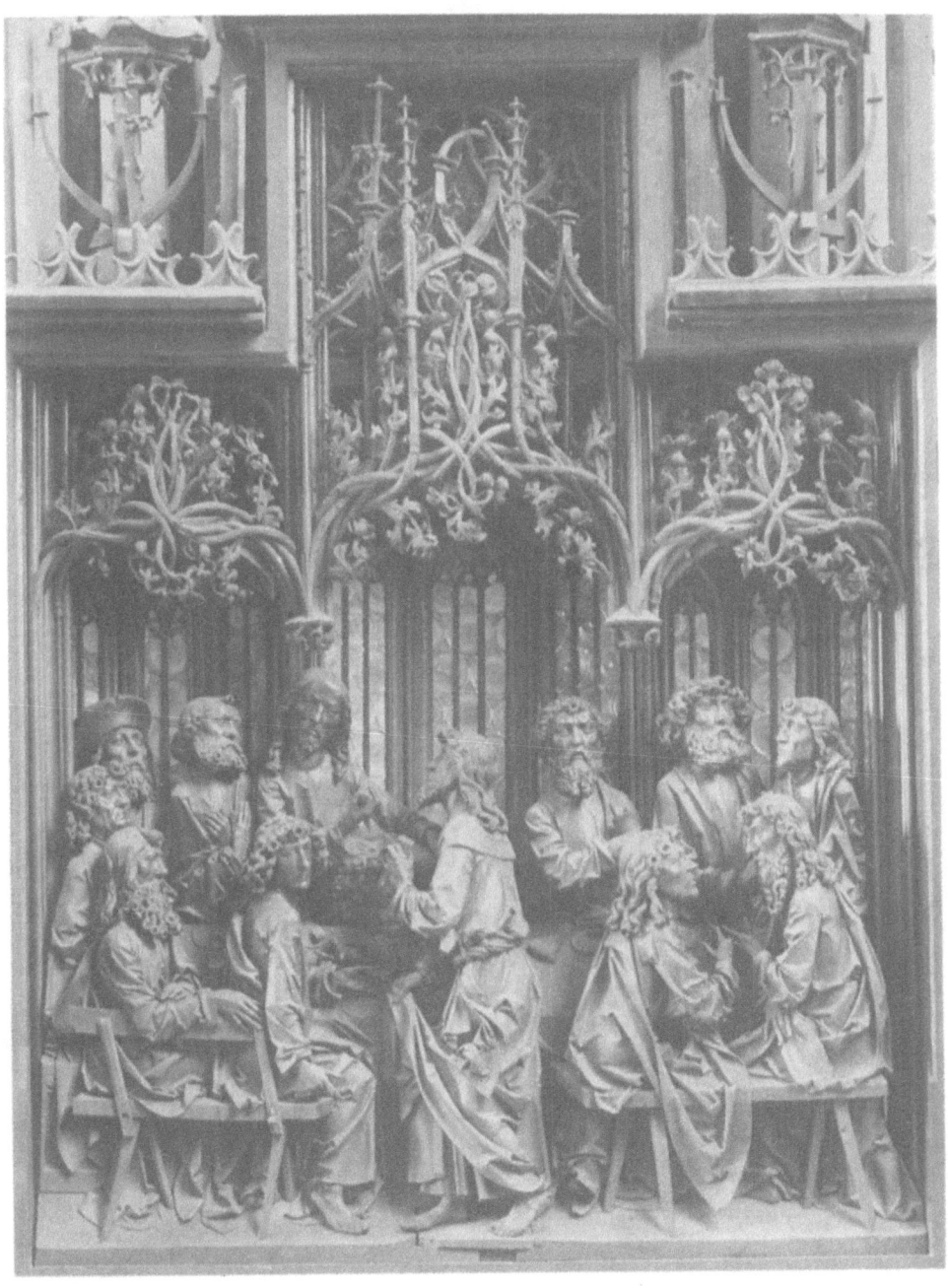

Opposite: 23A. Altarpiece of the Holy Blood. 1499–1504. Lindenwood. St. Jakobskirche, Rothenburg ob der Tauber. After restoration in the early 1960s. *Above:* 23B. The Last Supper. In the shrine of the Rothenburg Altarpiece of the Holy Blood. 1501–1502.

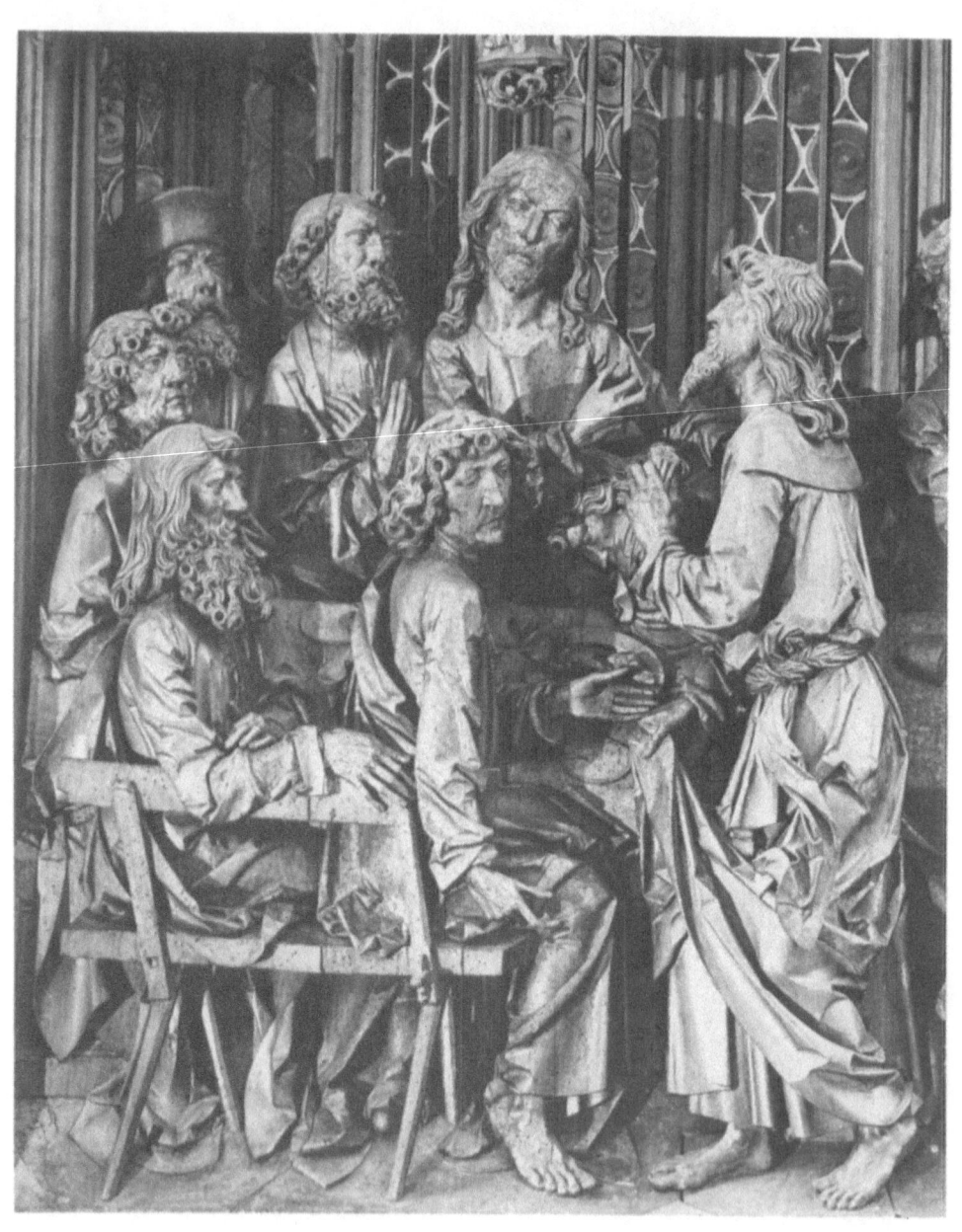

23C. Group of Apostles around Christ, detail of The Last Supper, Rothenburg Altarpiece.

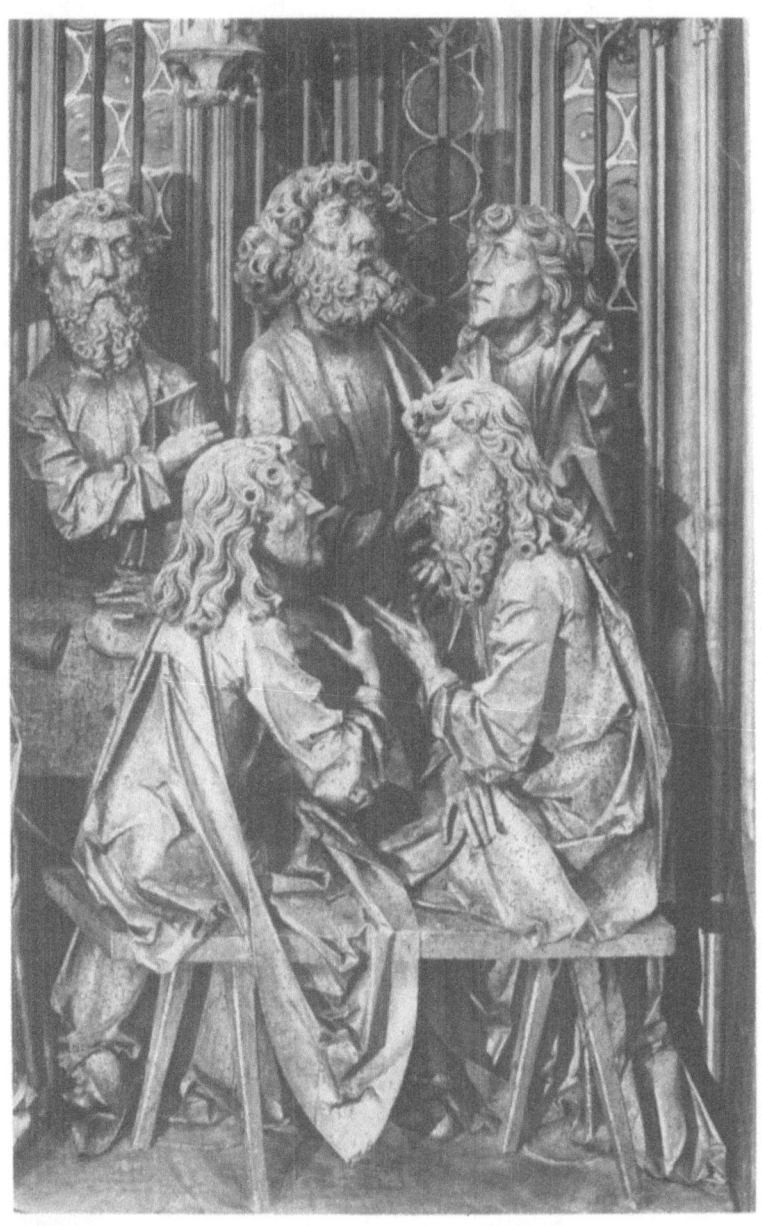

23D. Group of Apostles, detail of The Last Supper, Rothenburg Altarpiece.

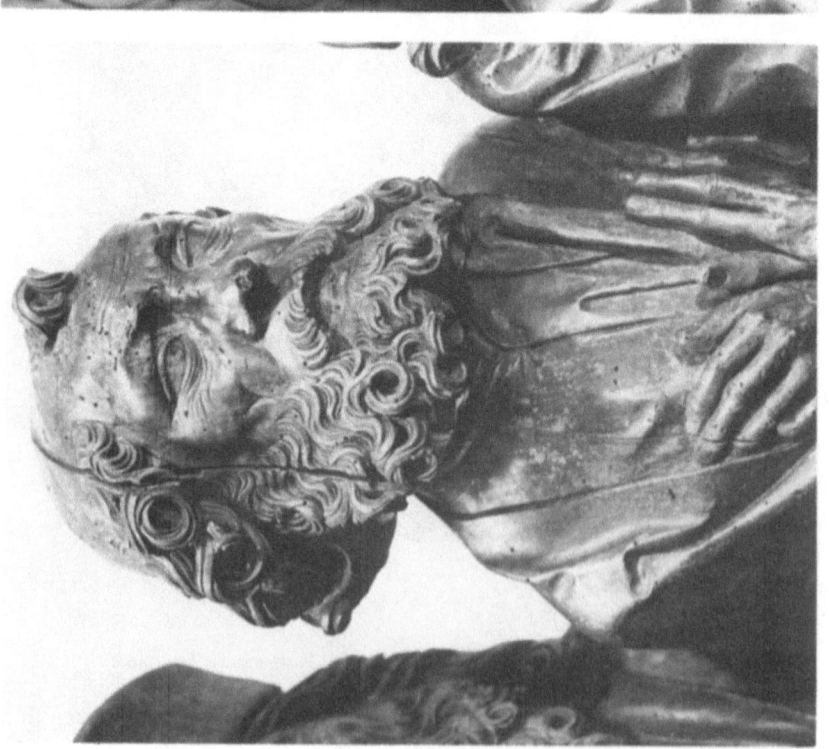

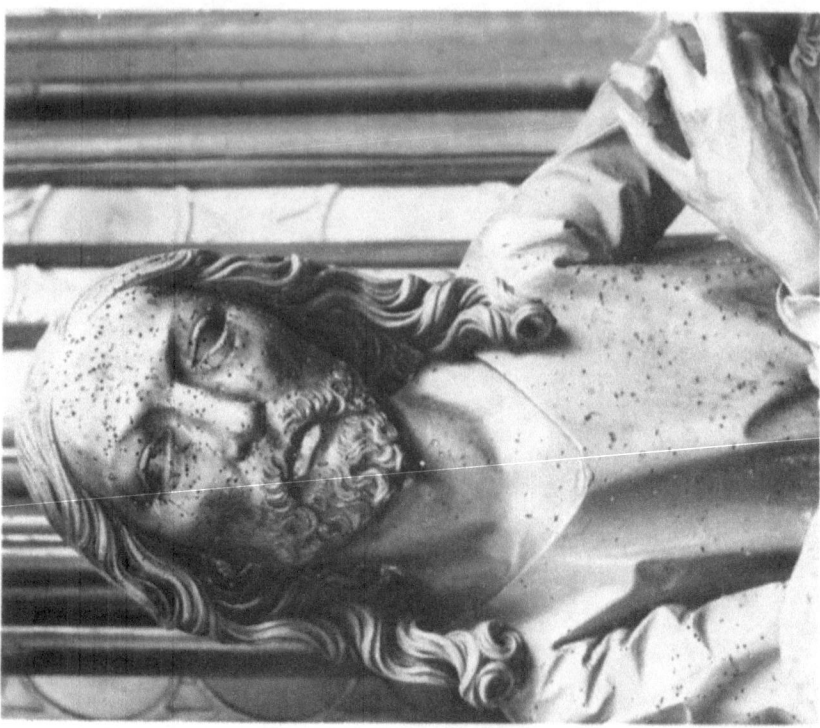

Four details of The Last Supper, Rothenburg Altarpiece.
Above: 23E. Peter declaring his innocence.

23F. Christ offering the bread to Judas.

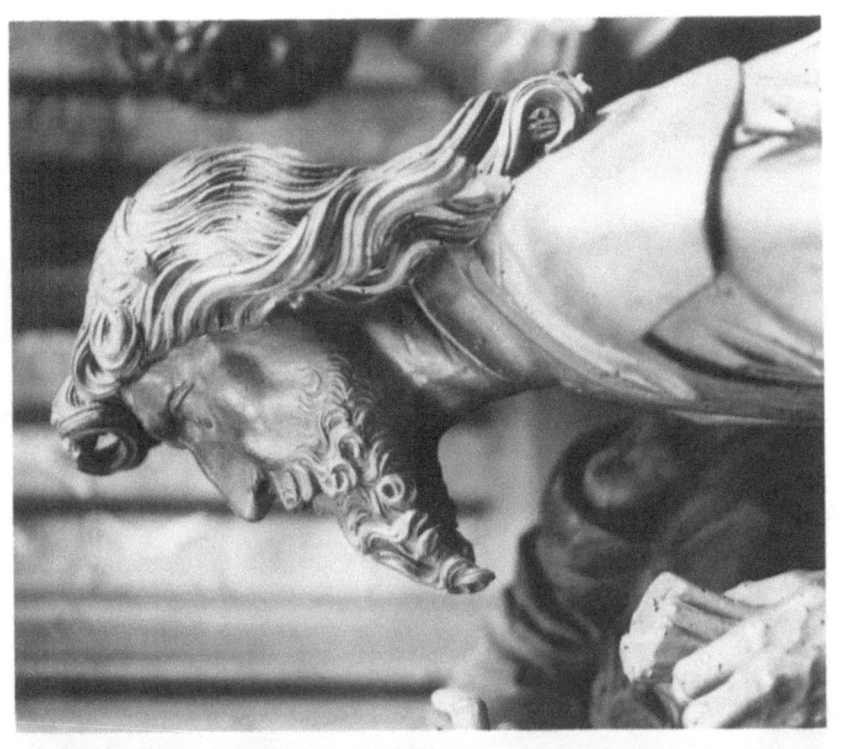

23H. Judas receiving the bread.

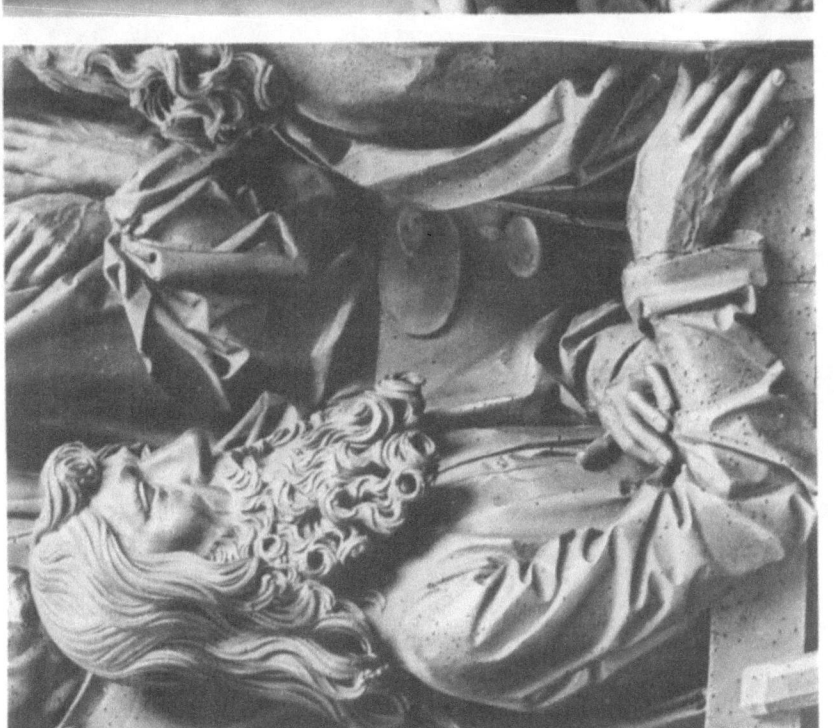

23G. One of the Apostles (Andrew?).

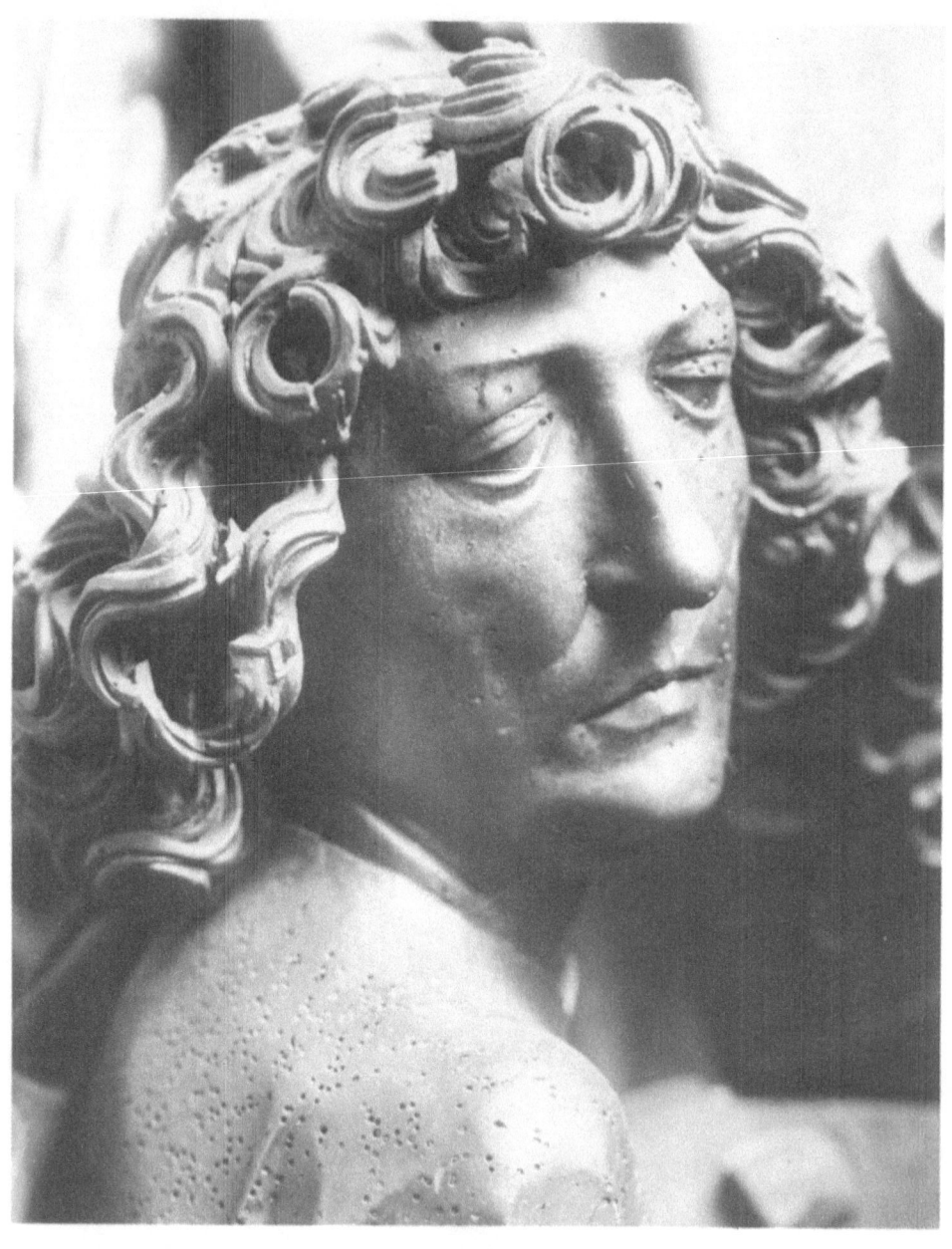

23I. One of the Apostles, detail of The Last Supper, Rothenburg Altarpiece.

Opposite: 23J. Mary, detail of The Annunciation (Plate 23K). In the superstructure of the Rothenburg Altarpiece. After restoration.

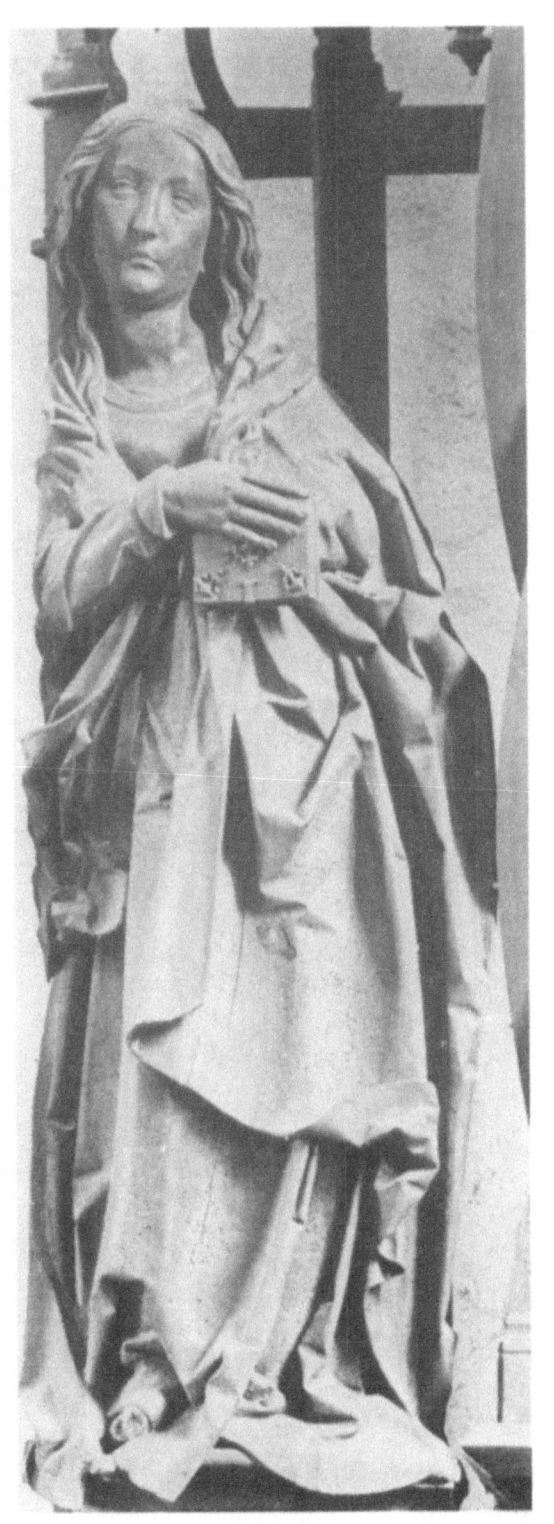

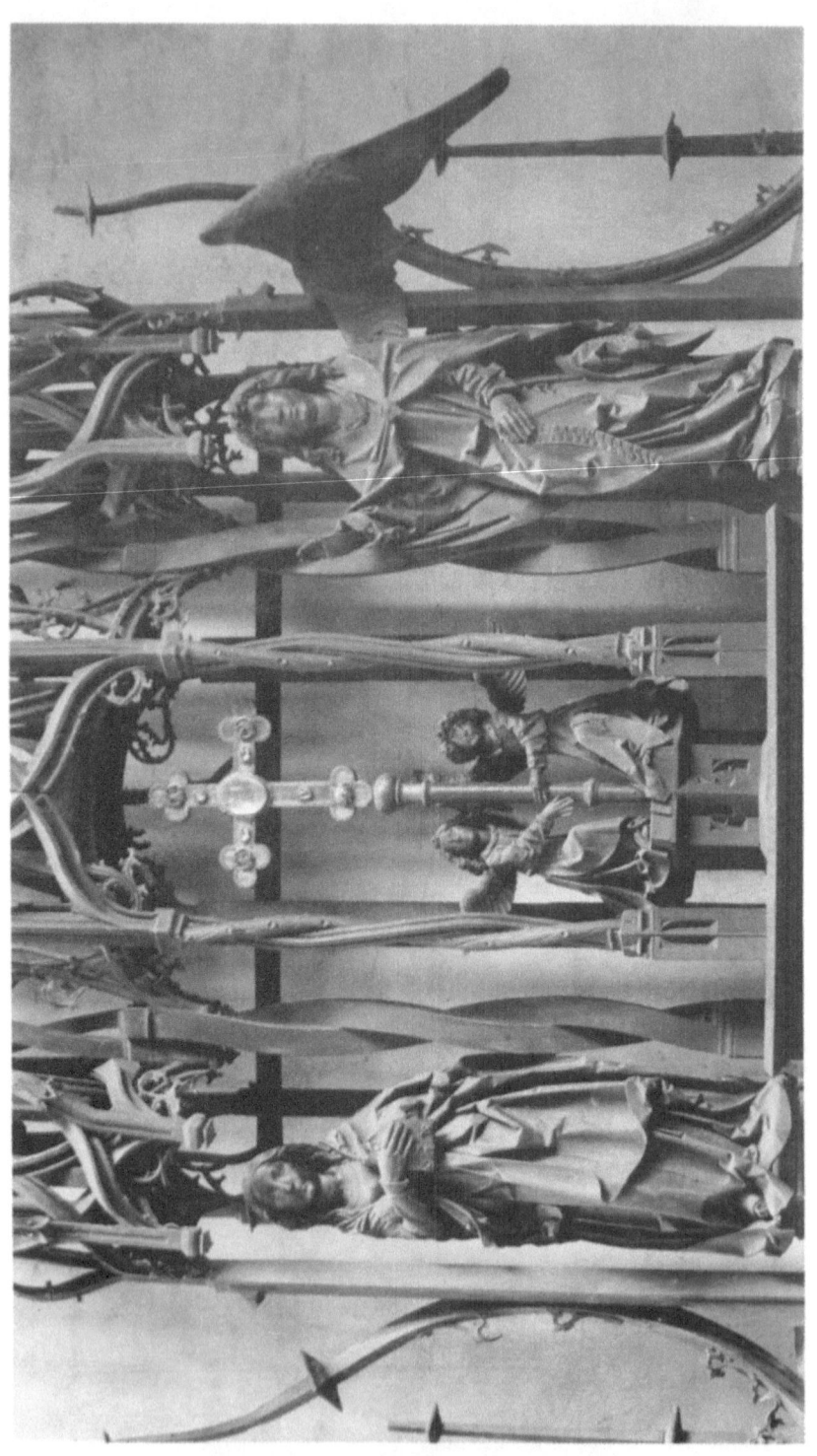

23K. The Annunciation and Angels with reliquary cross. In the superstructure of the Rothenburg Altarpiece. 1502–1504. After restoration. *Below:* 23L and M. Angels with the pillar and cross of Christ's martyrdom. In the predella of the Rothenburg Altarpiece. 1501–1502.

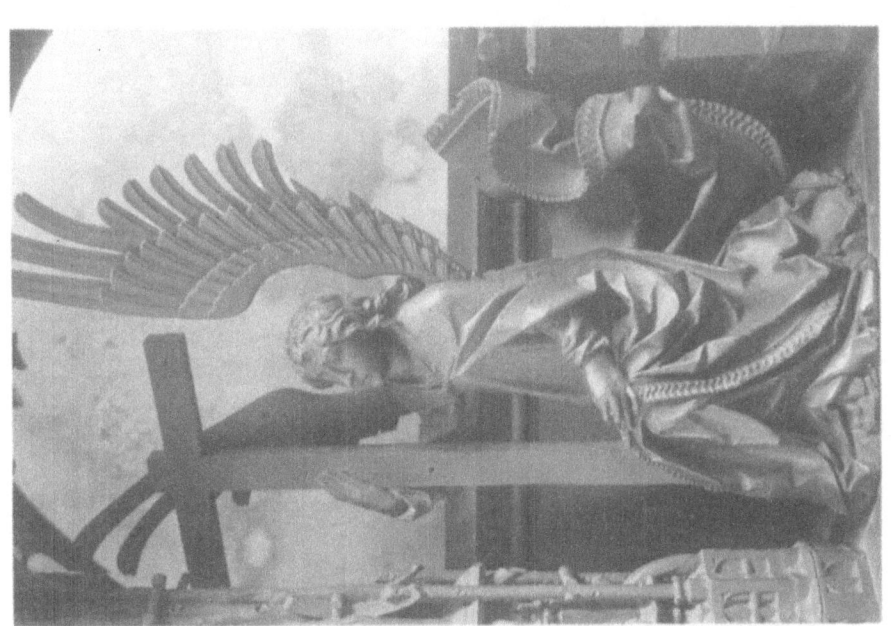

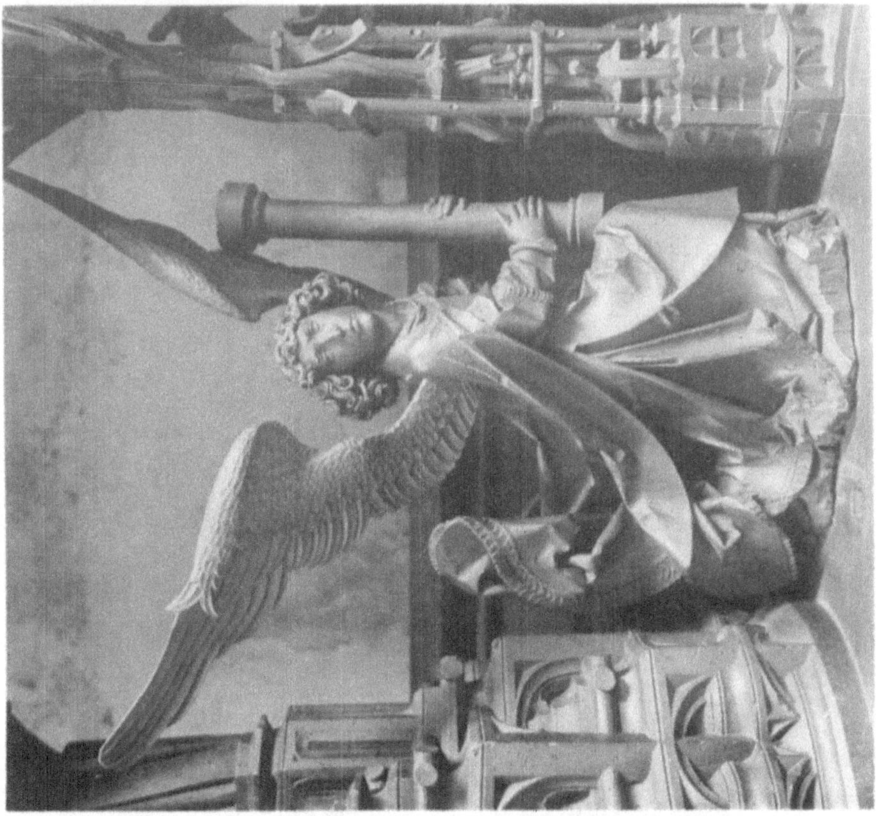

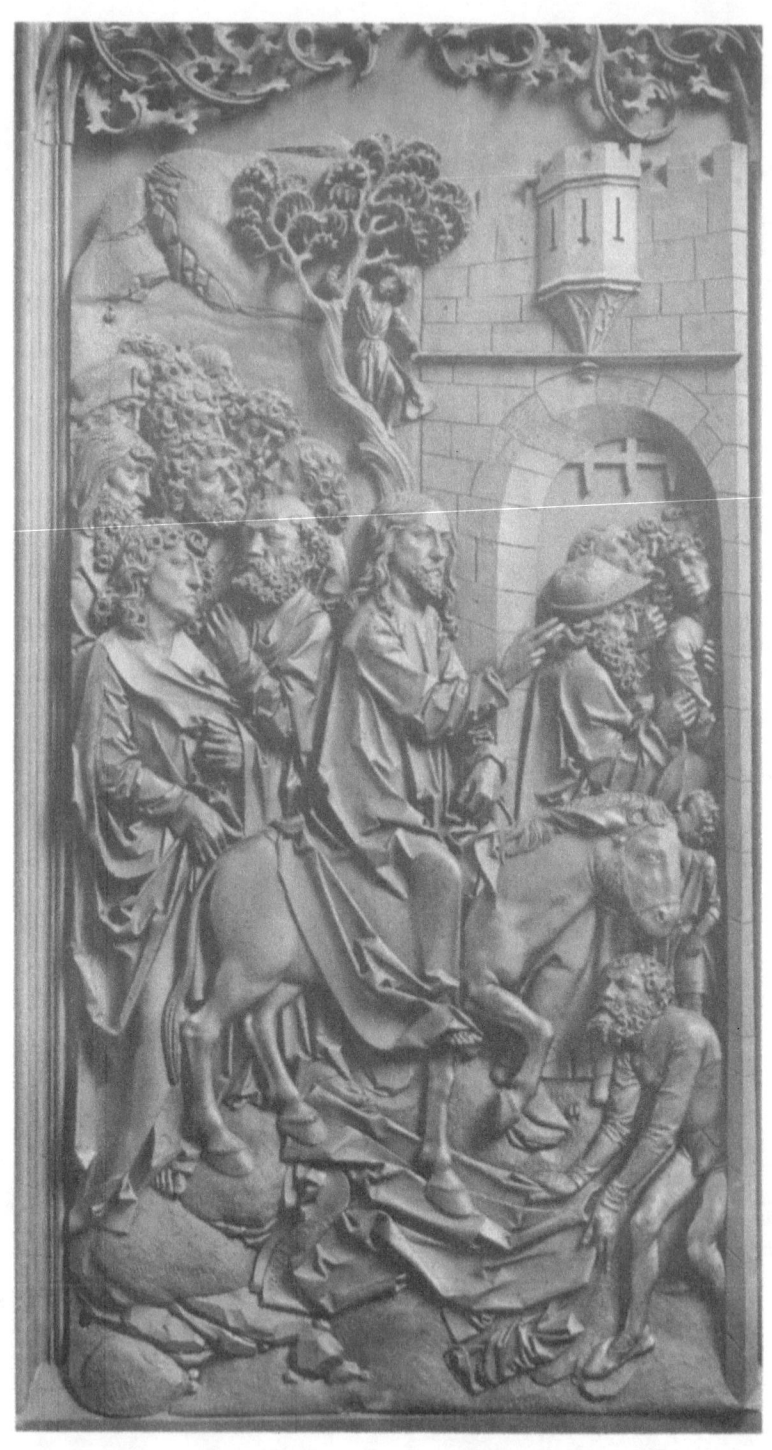

23N. Christ's Entry into Jerusalem. Left wing relief of the Rothenburg
Altarpiece. 1502–1504.

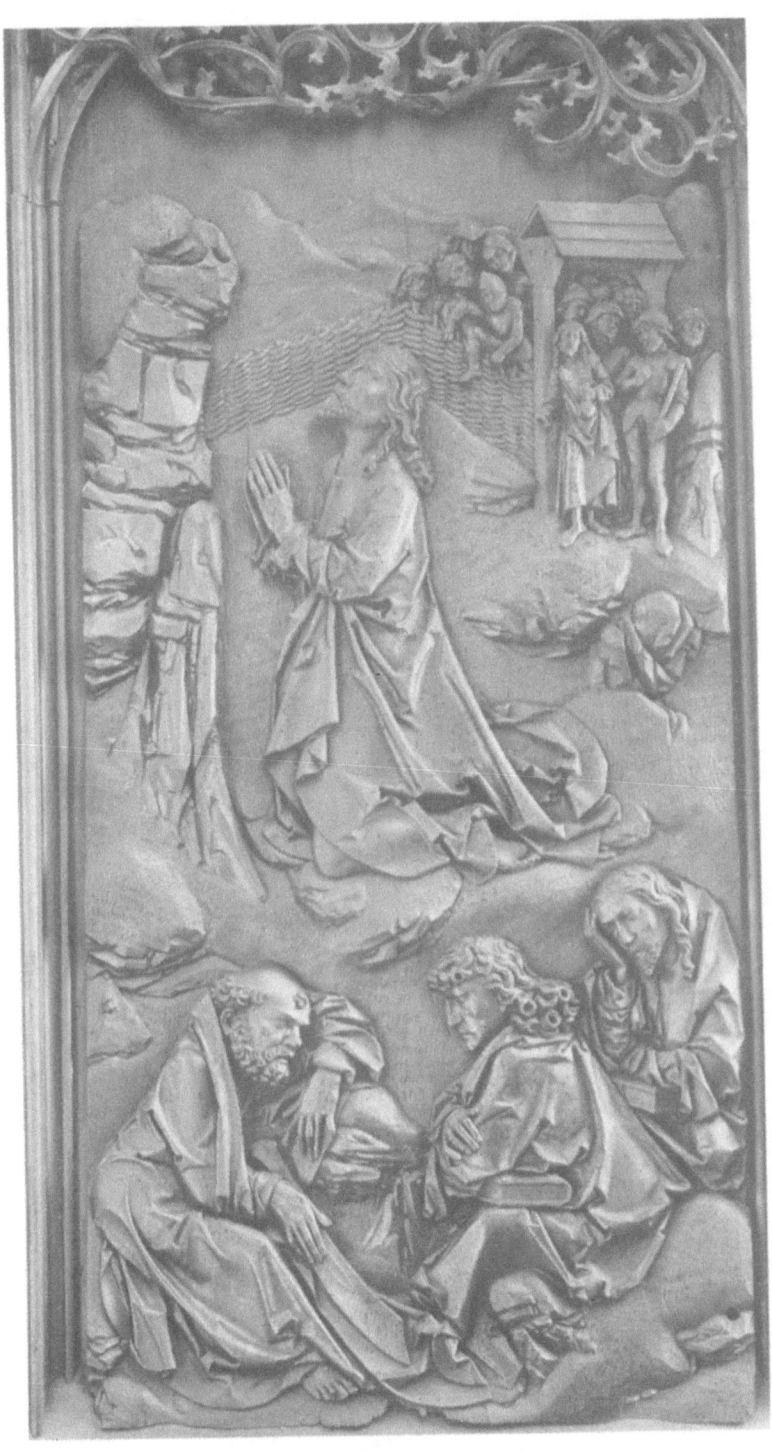

23P. The Agony in the Garden. Right wing relief of the Rothenburg
Altarpiece. 1502–1504.

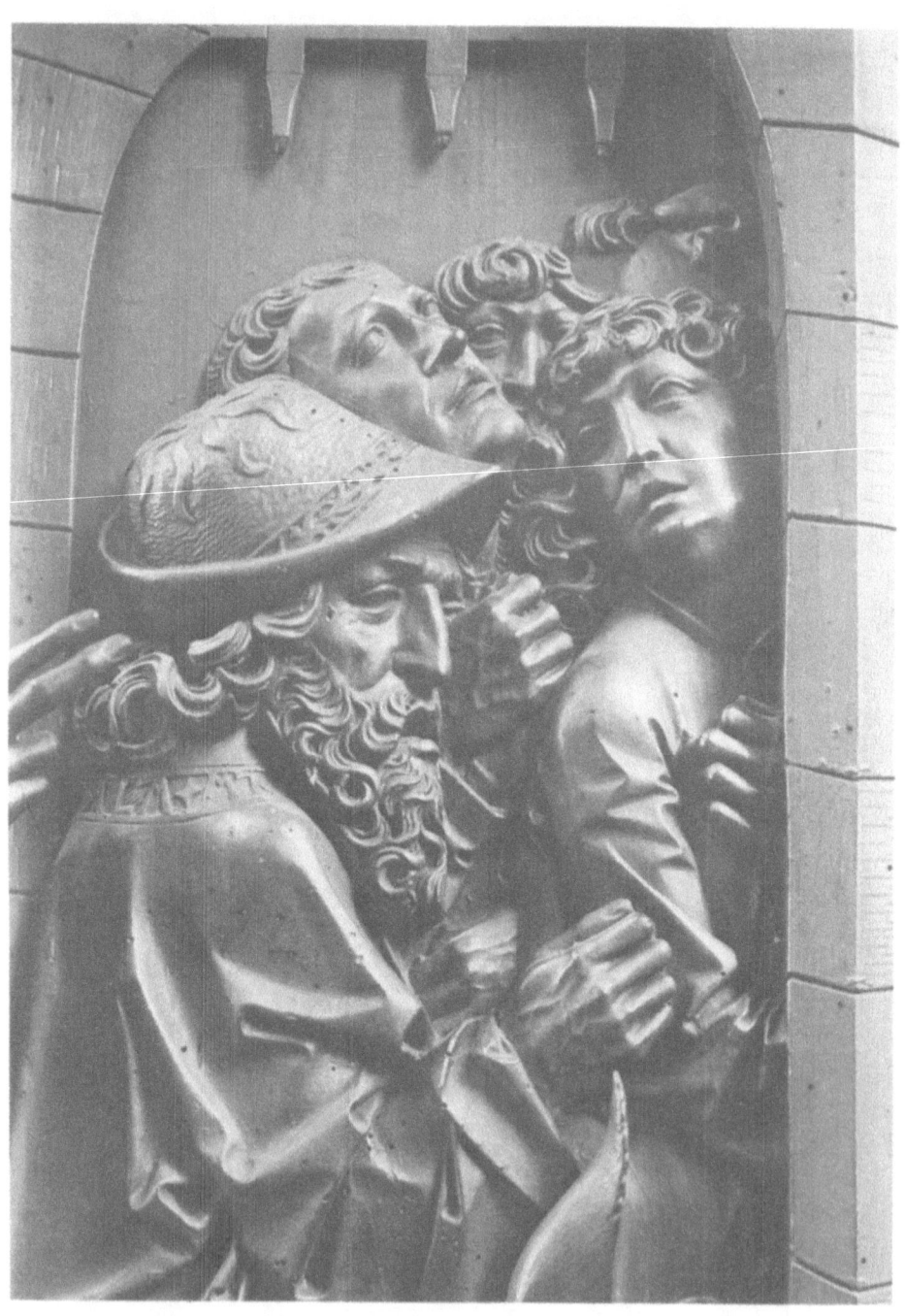

23Q. Jews at the gate into Jerusalem, detail of Christ's Entry into Jerusalem, from the Rothenburg Altarpiece.

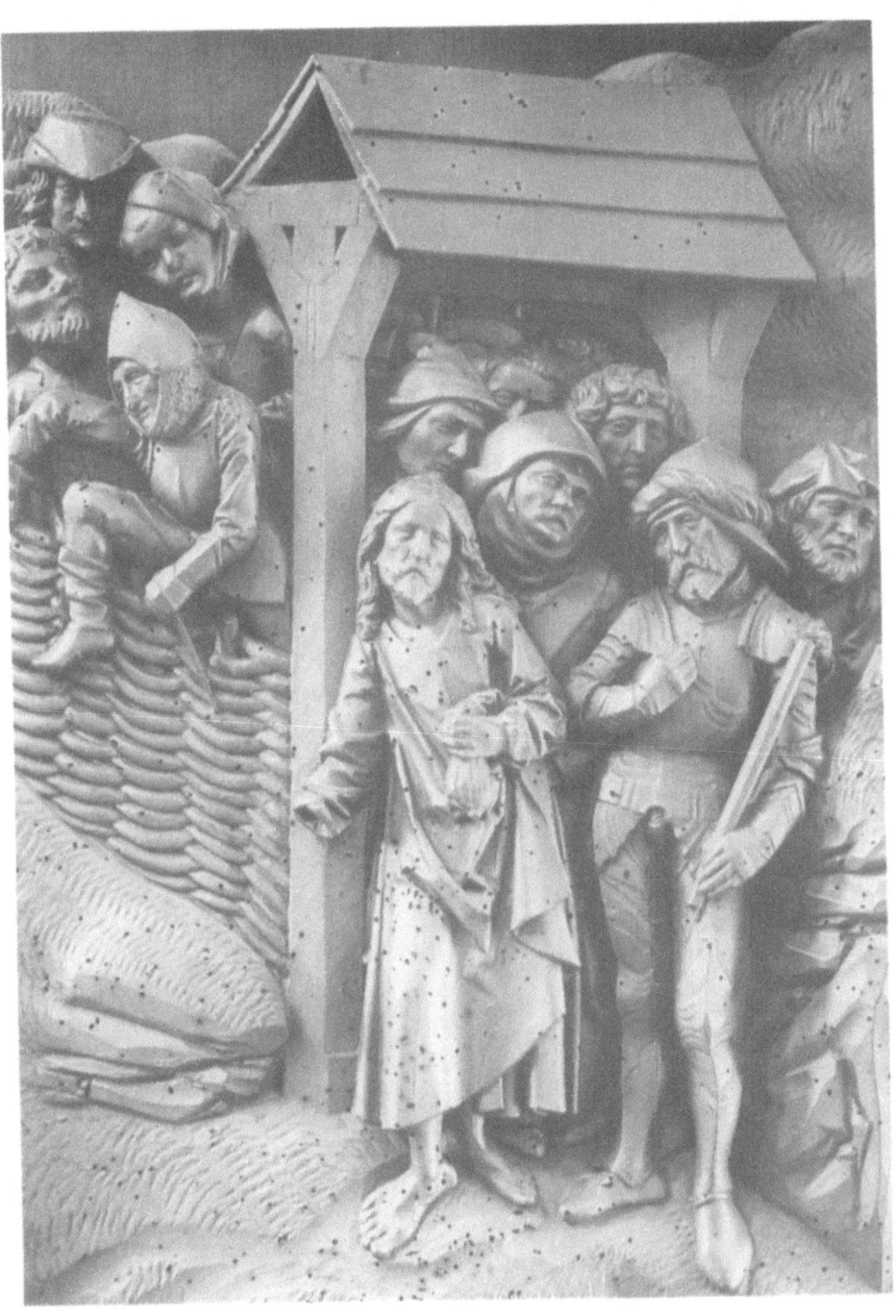

23R. Judas and the group of soldiers coming to take Christ, detail of The Agony in the Garden, from the Rothenburg Altarpiece.

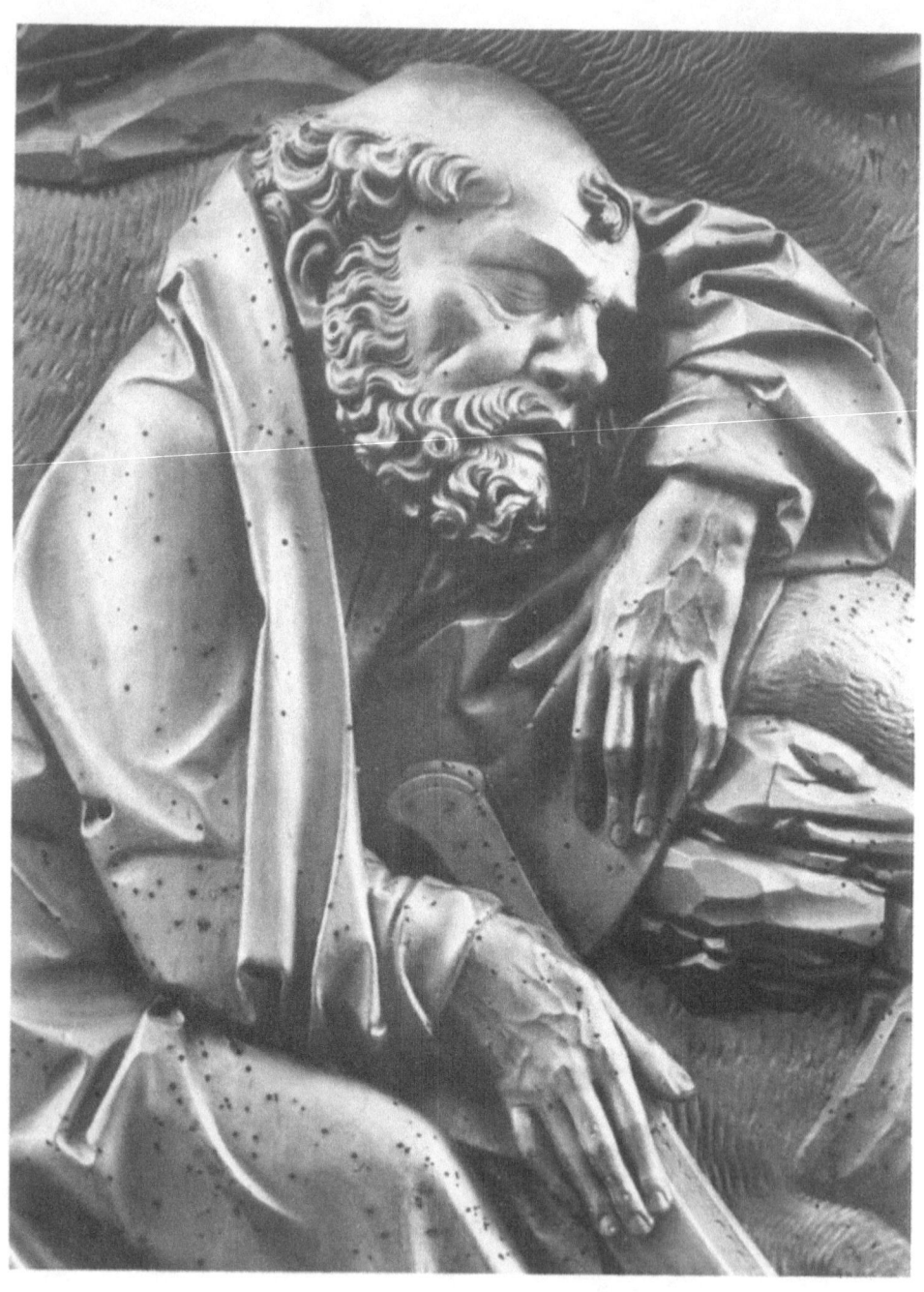

23S. Peter asleep, detail of The Agony in the Garden, from the Rothenburg Altarpiece.

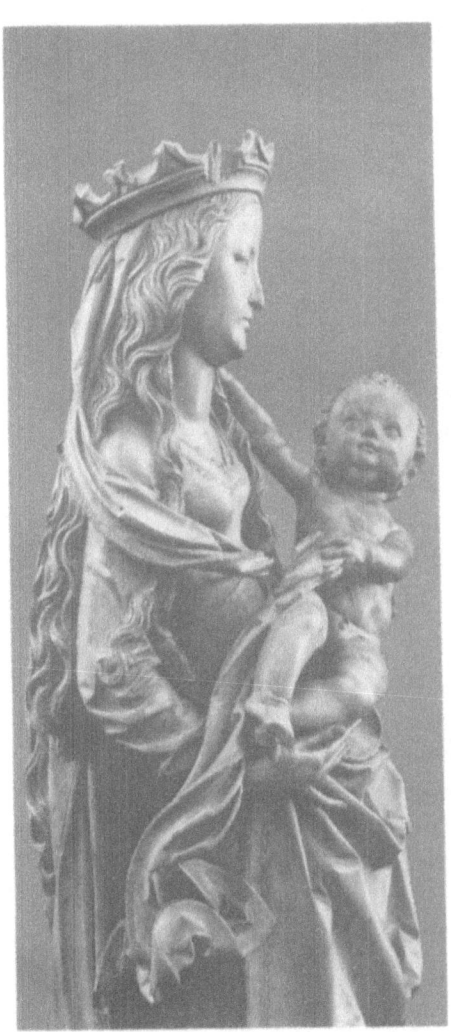
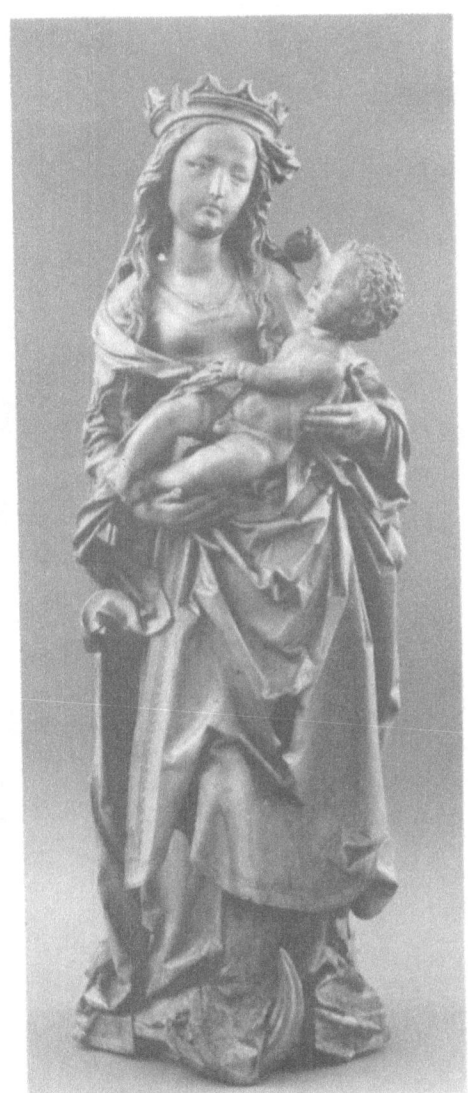

24A and B. The Virgin with the Christ Child. About 1501–1502. Lindenwood. Kunstgewerbemuseum, Cologne.

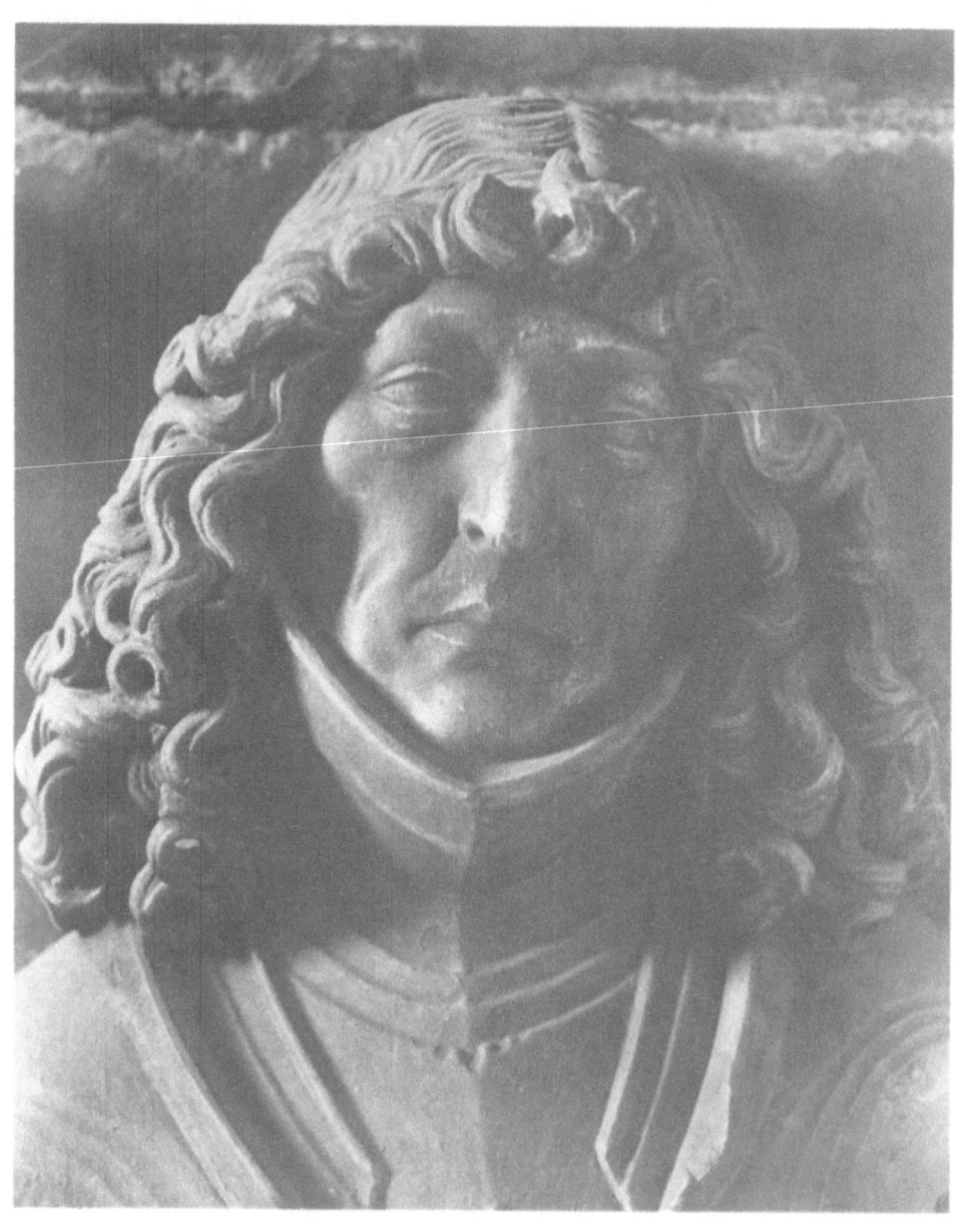

25A and B. Tomb-monument of Konrad von Schaumberg (d. 1499). After 1502. Sandstone.
Marienkapelle, Würzburg.

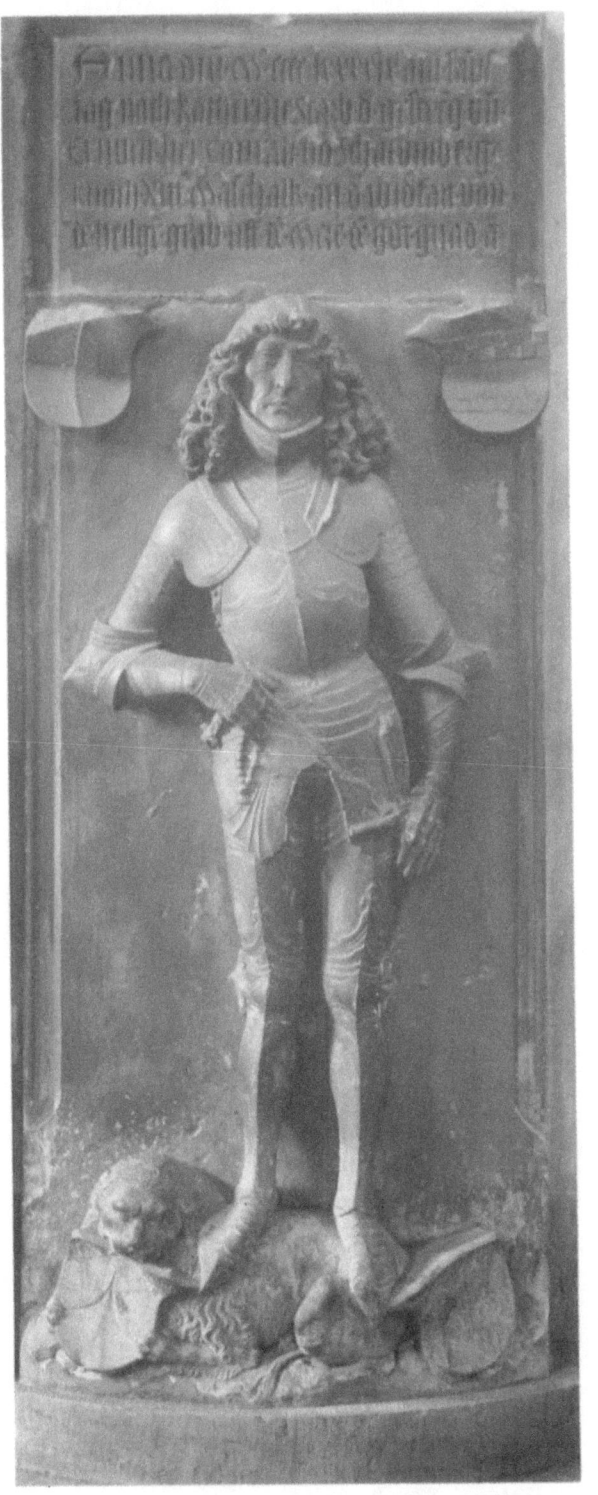

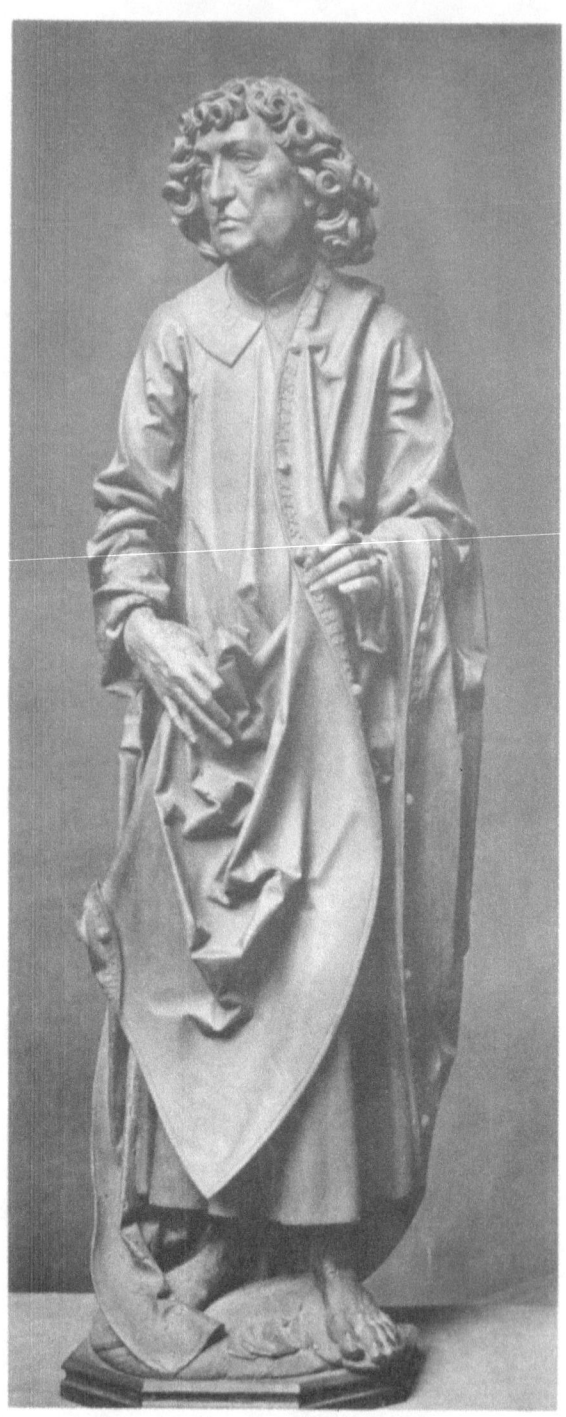

26A. "Sant Mathias." Model for the stone figure of
Matthias from the Marienkapelle, Würzburg. After
1502. Lindenwood. Skulpturenabteilung, Staatliche
Museen, West Berlin.

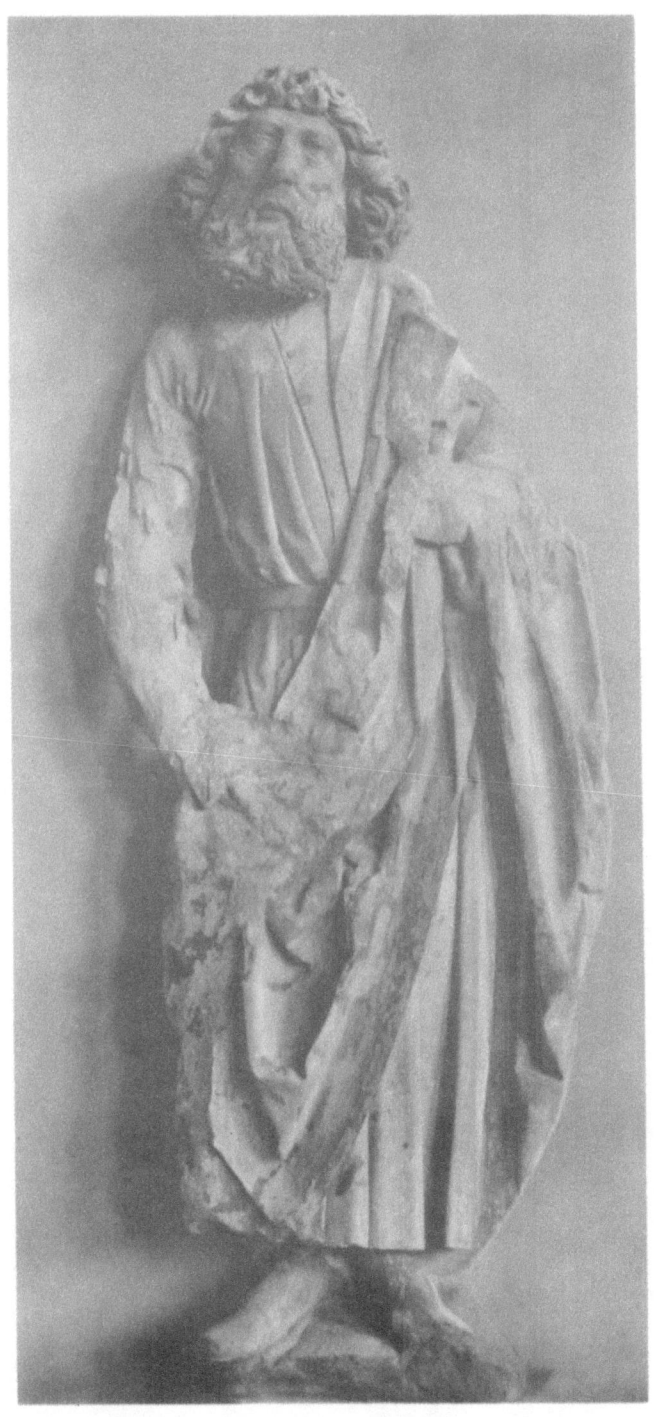

26B. The Apostle Bartholomew from the Marienkapelle,
Würzburg. 1500–1506. Sandstone. Mainfränkisches Museum,
Würzburg.

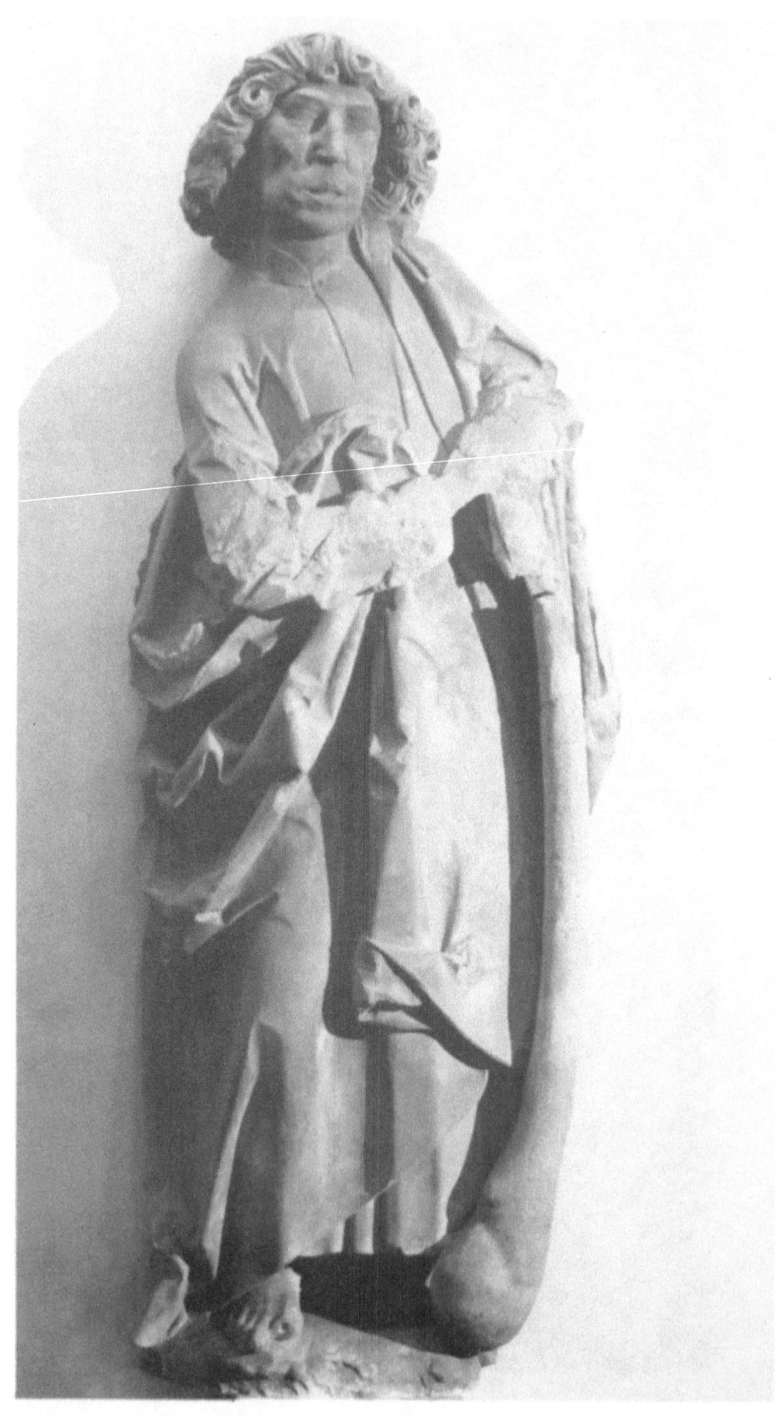

26C. The Apostle Jude Thaddaeus from the Marienkapelle, Würzburg. 1500–1506.
Sandstone. Mainfränkisches Museum, Würzburg.

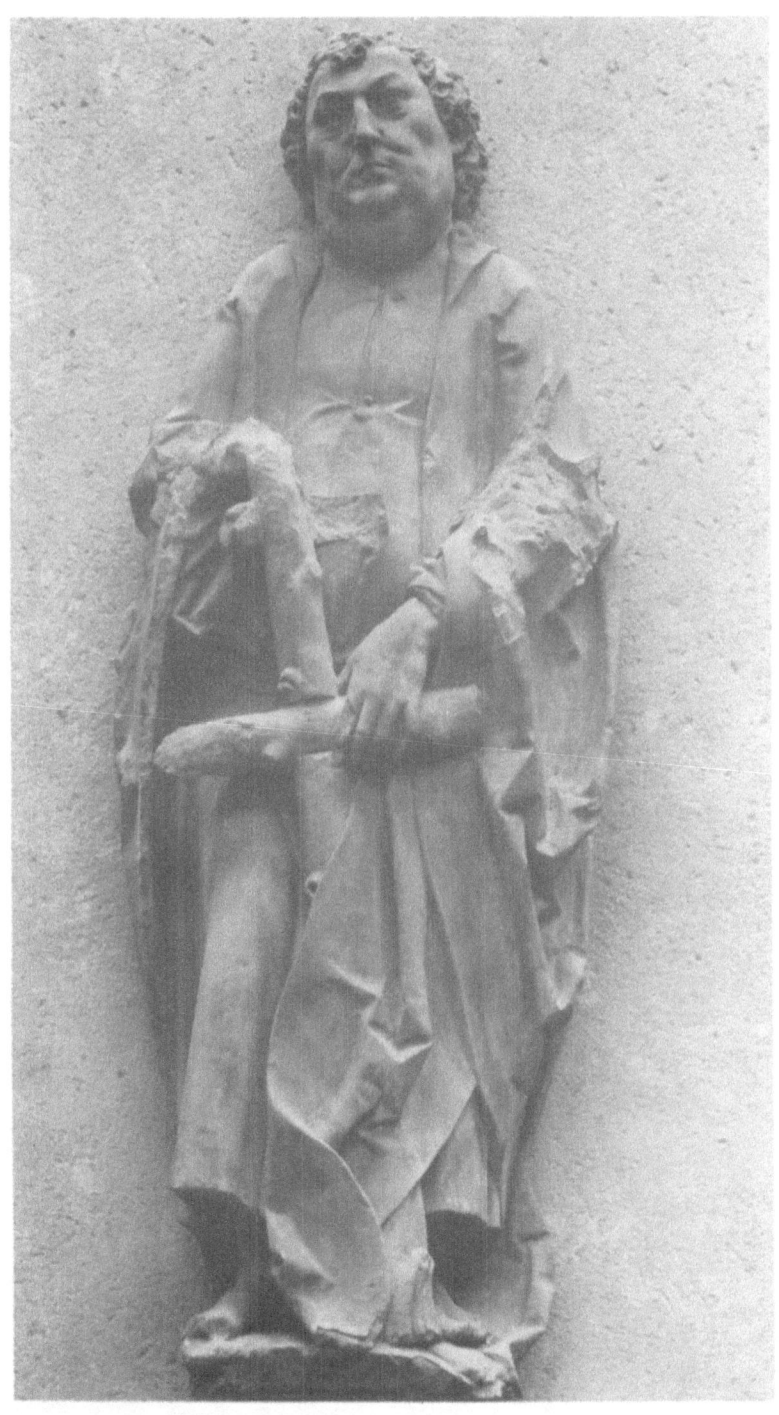

26D. The Apostle Philip from the Marienkapelle, Würzburg. 1500–1506. Sandstone. Mainfränkisches Museum, Würzburg.

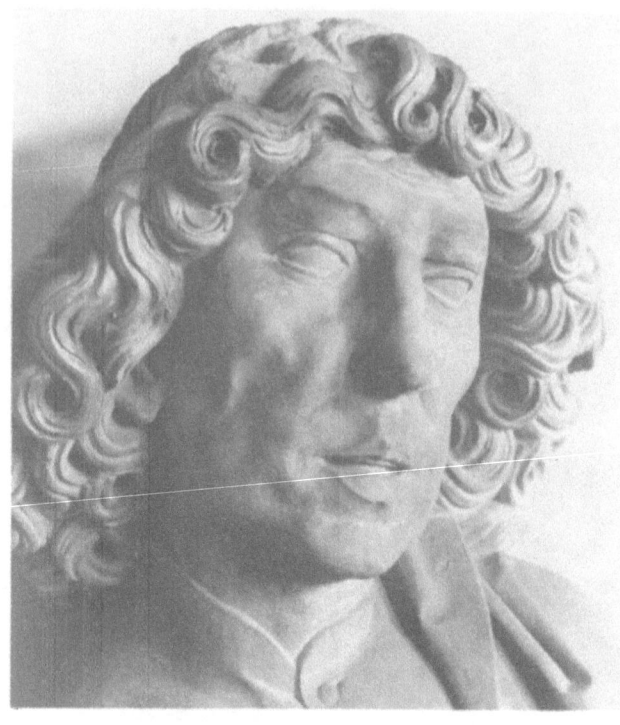

Above: 26E. The Apostle Jude Thaddaeus, detail.
Below: 26F. The Apostle Philip, detail. Both from the Marienkapelle, Würzburg.

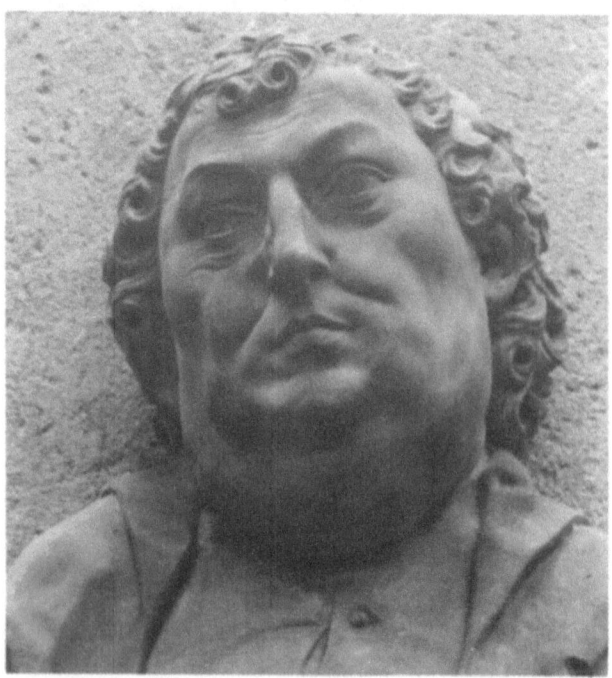

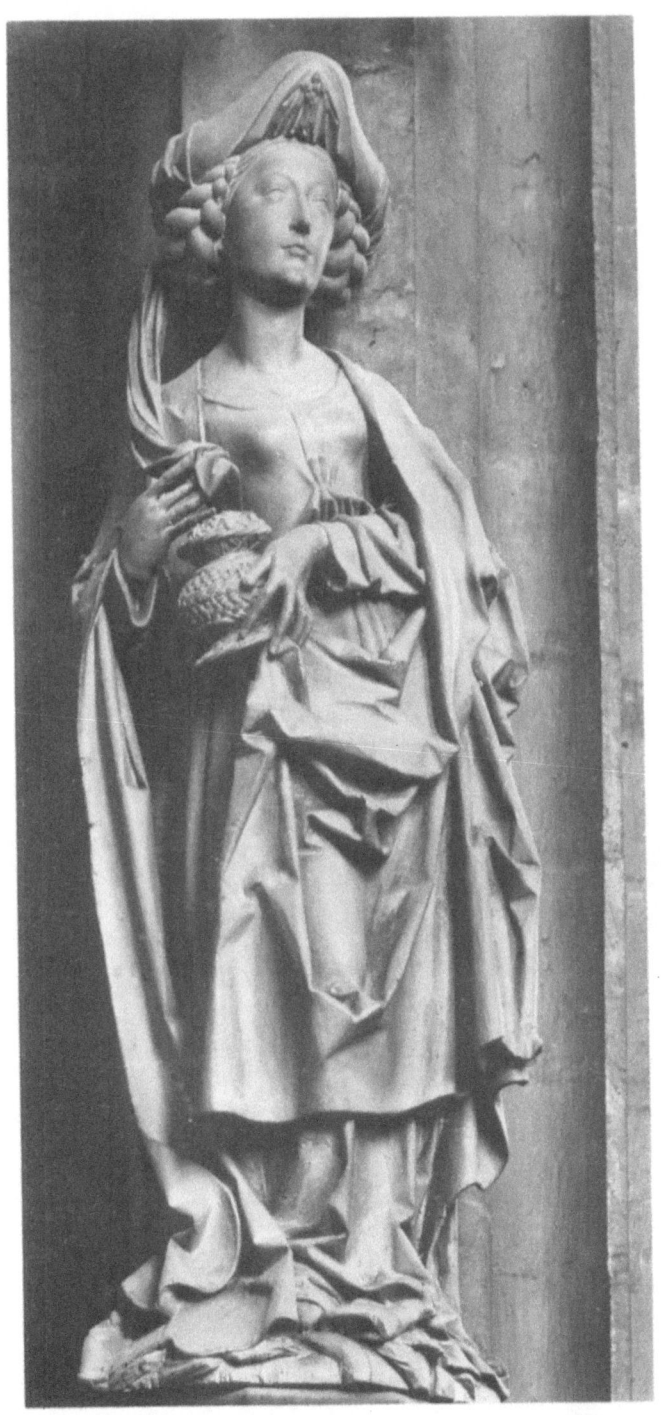

27. St. Dorothea. From the Marienkapelle, Würzburg.
About 1500–1505. Lindenwood. Destroyed in 1945.

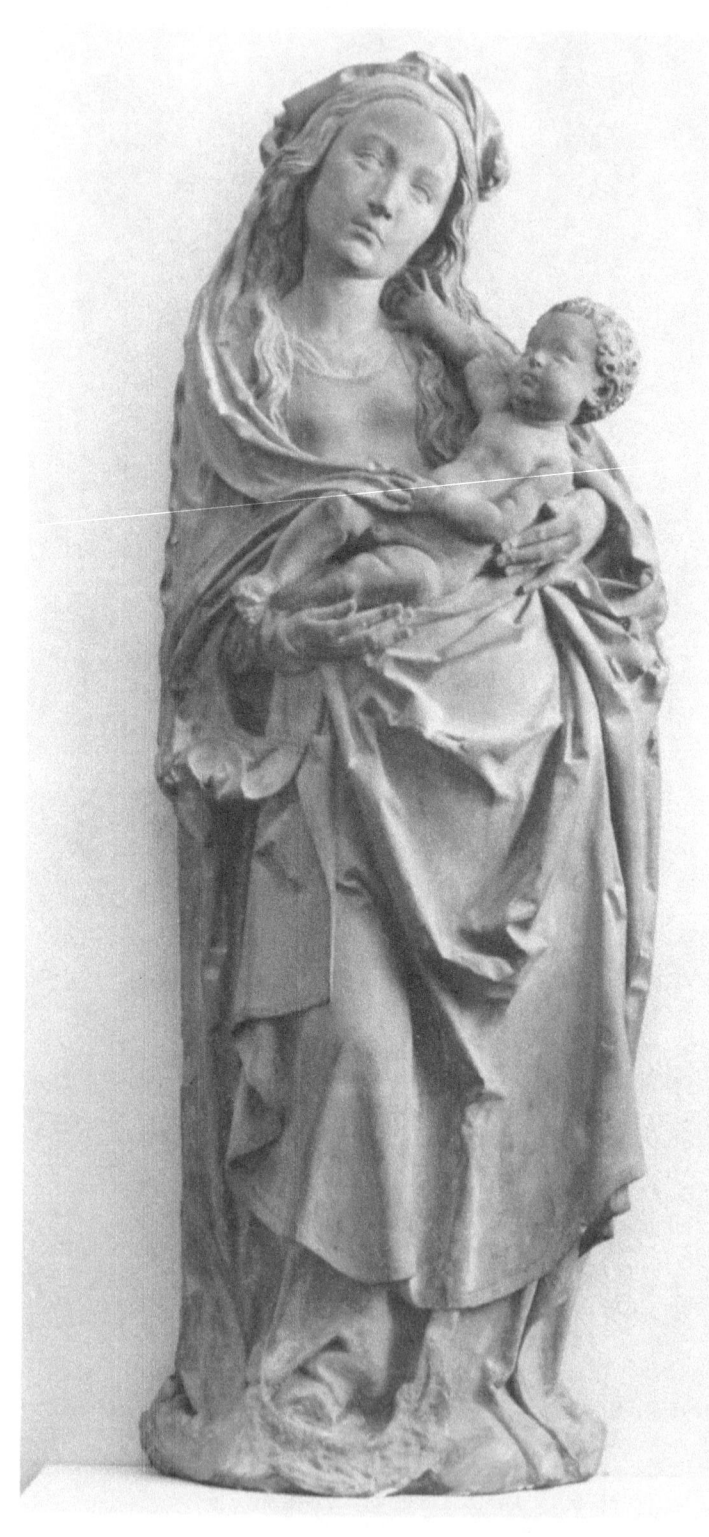

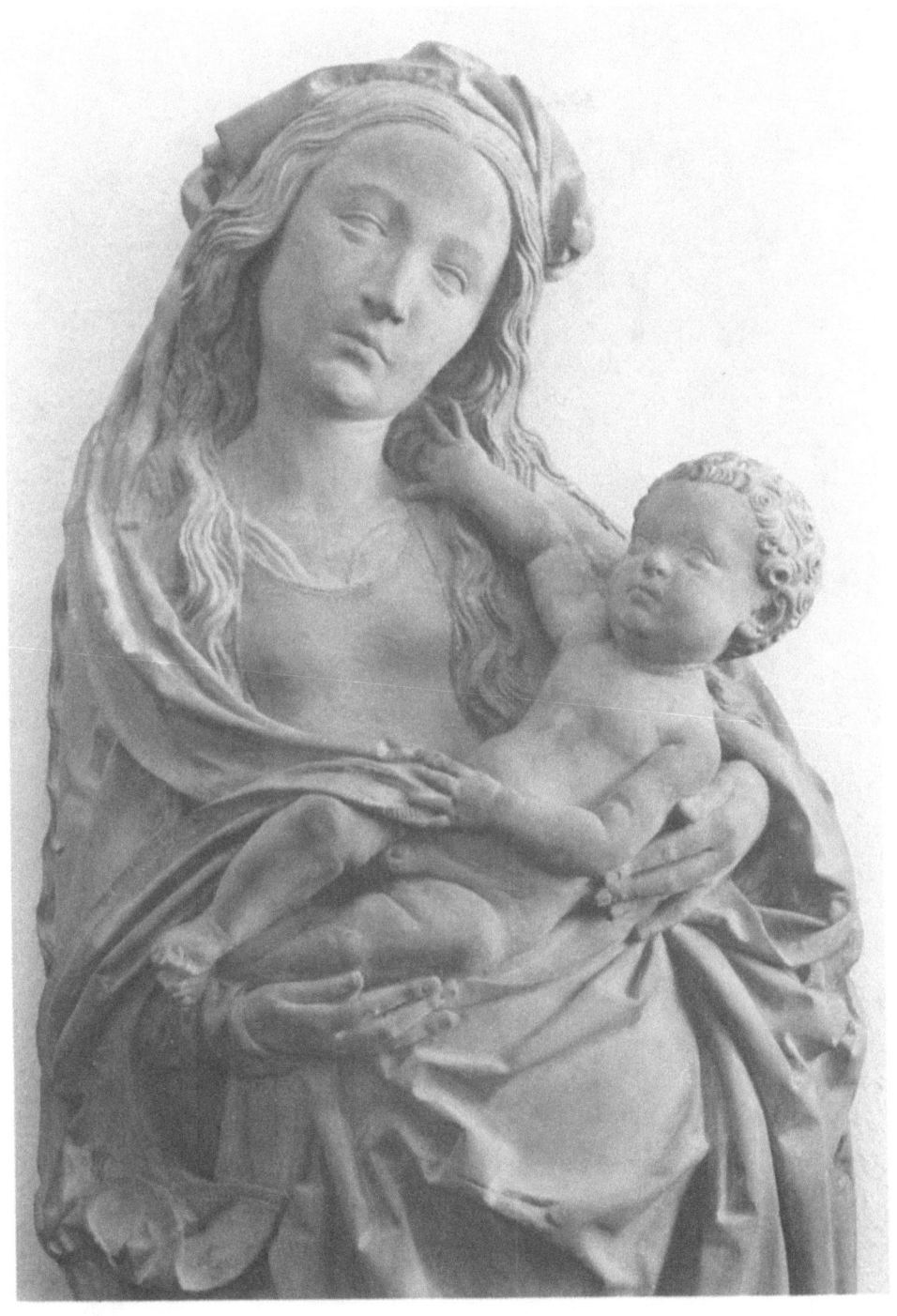

28A and B. The Virgin with the Christ Child. About 1505. Sandstone.
Mainfränkisches Museum, Würzburg.

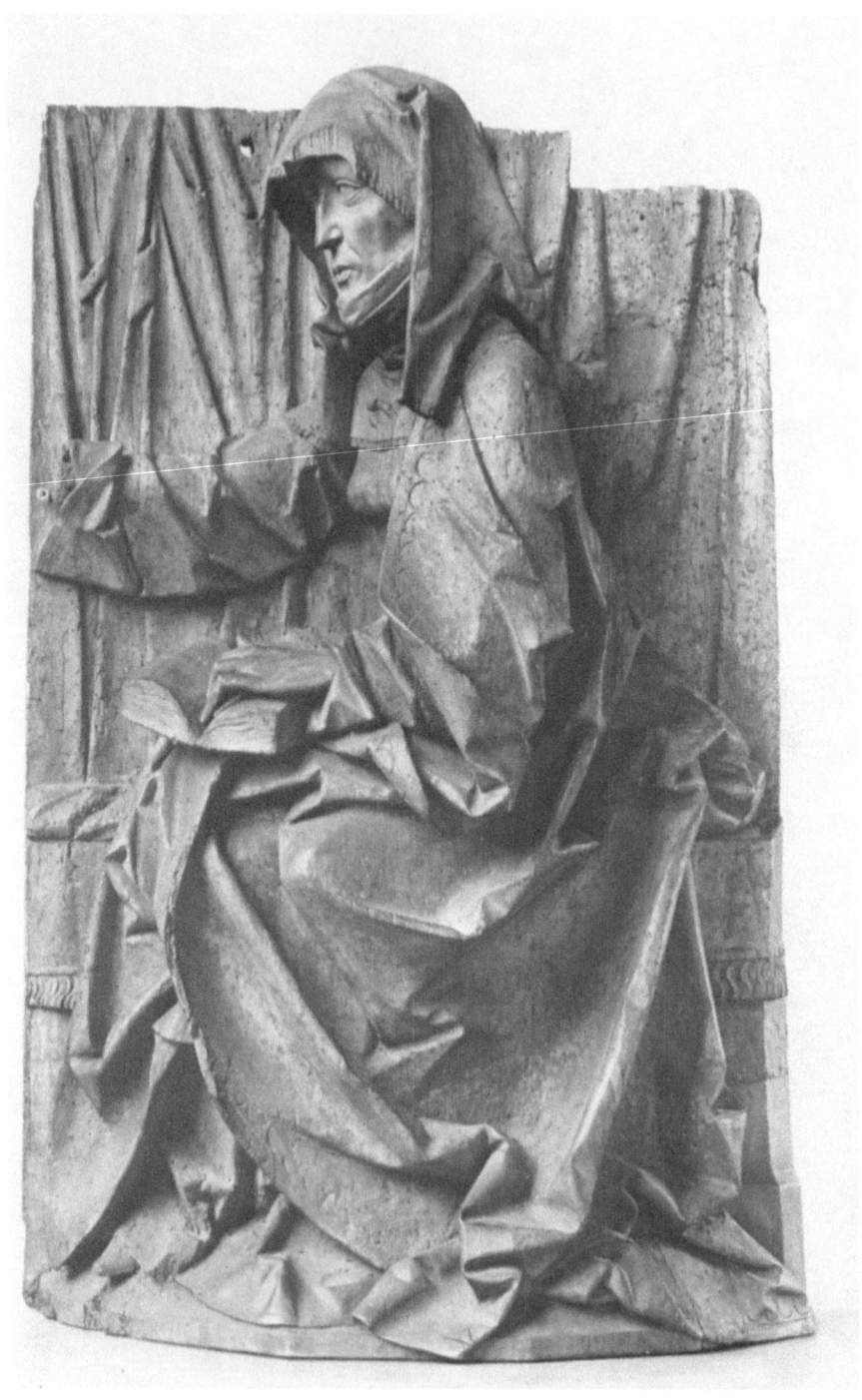

29. St. Anne. About 1505–1506 (?). Bayerisches Nationalmuseum, Munich.

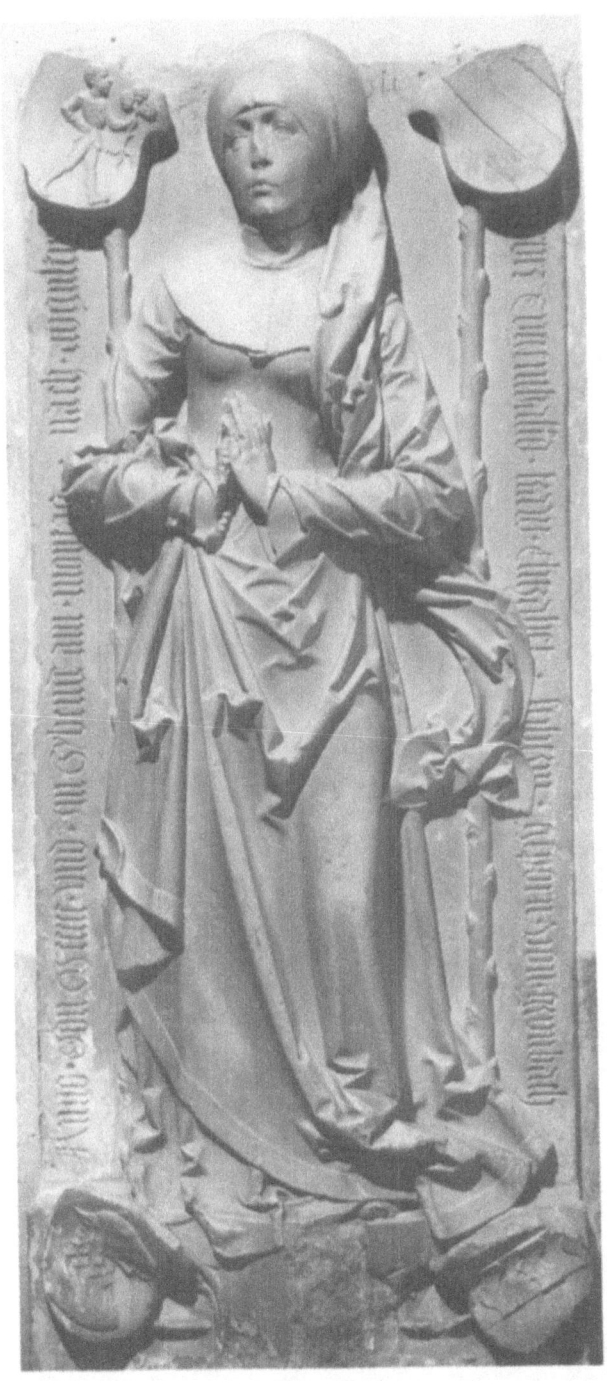

30. Tomb-monument of Elisabeth Stieber (d. 1507). Sandstone.
Parish Church, Buttenheim.

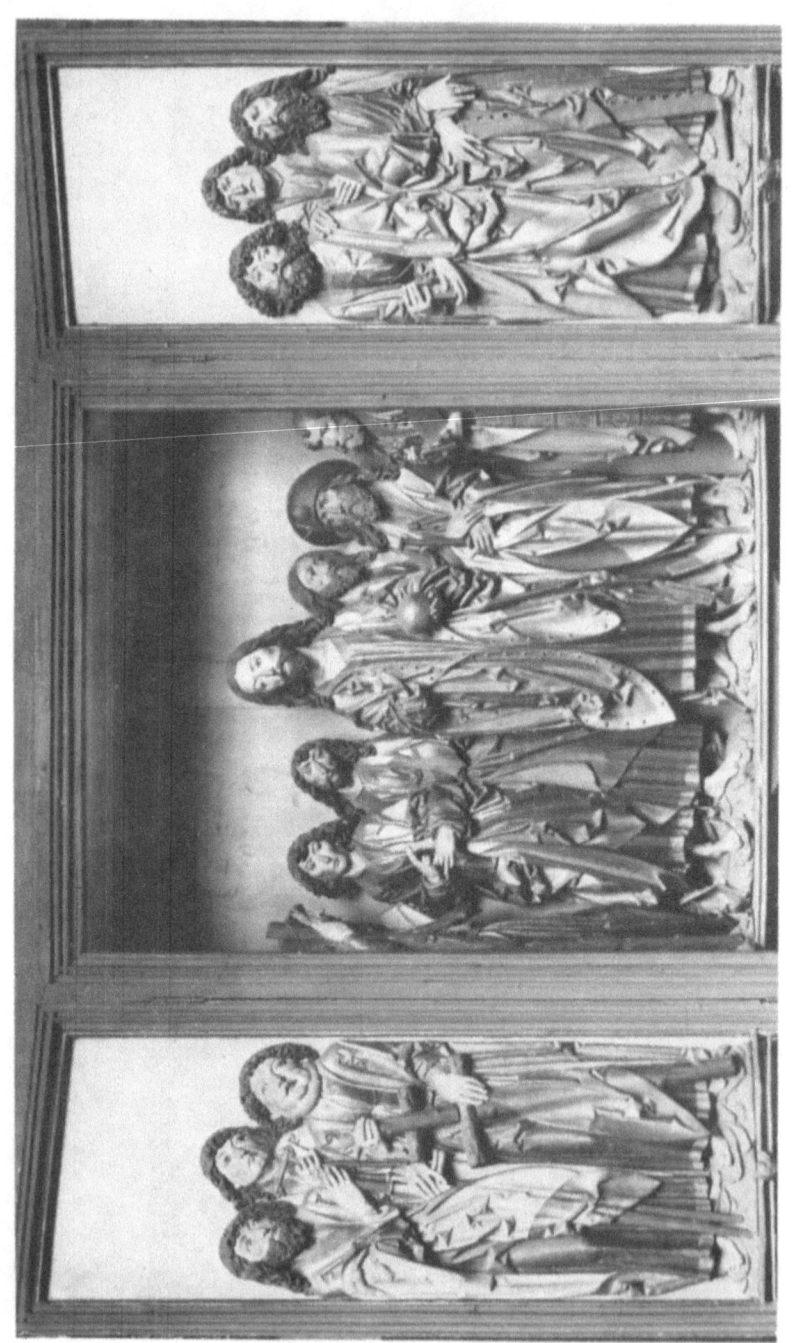

31A. Altarpiece of the Twelve Apostles. From the former Church of St. Kilian, Windsheim. Before 1509. Lindenwood. Kurpfälzisches Museum, Heidelberg. Before restoration. *Below:* 31B. Altarpiece of the Twelve Apostles from Windsheim, after restoration.

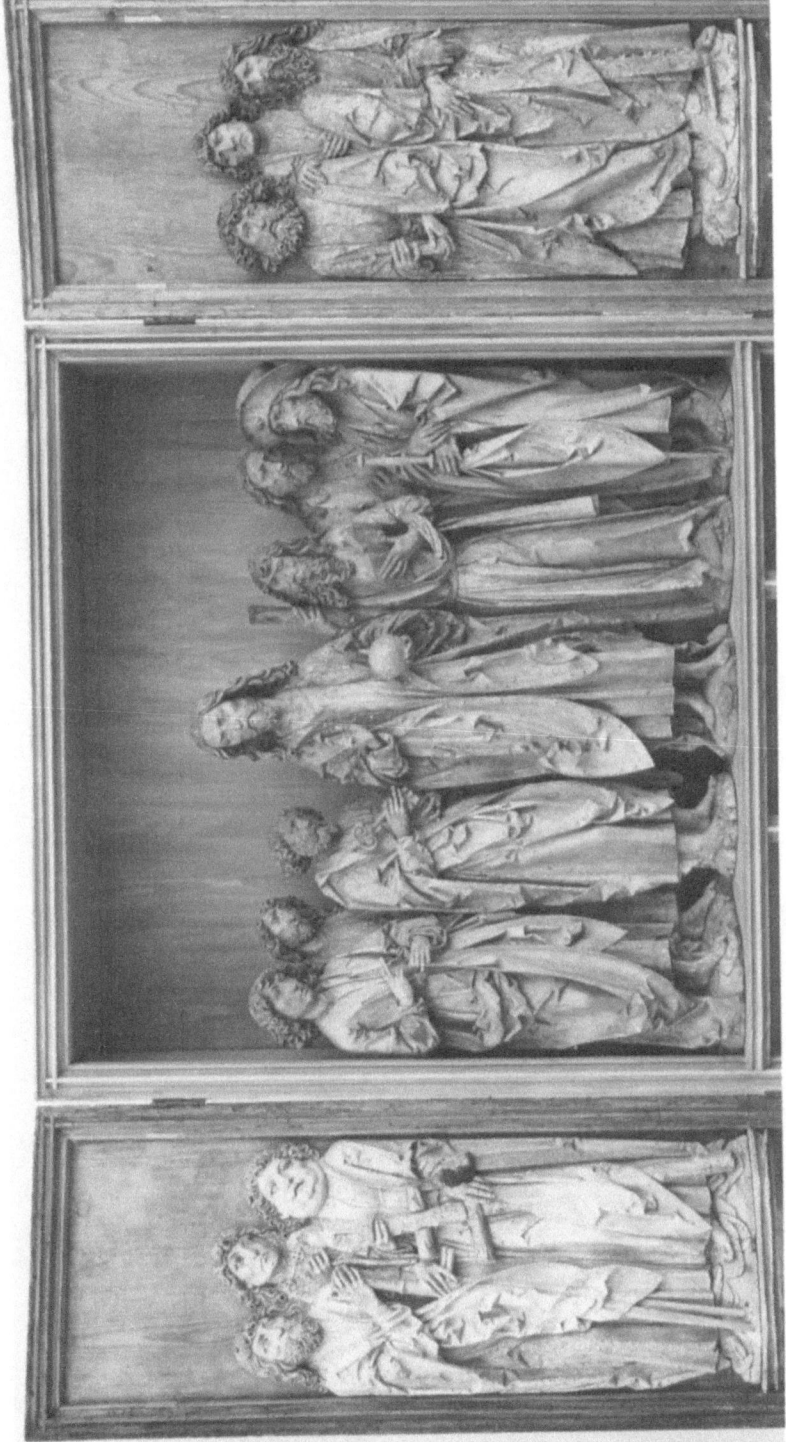

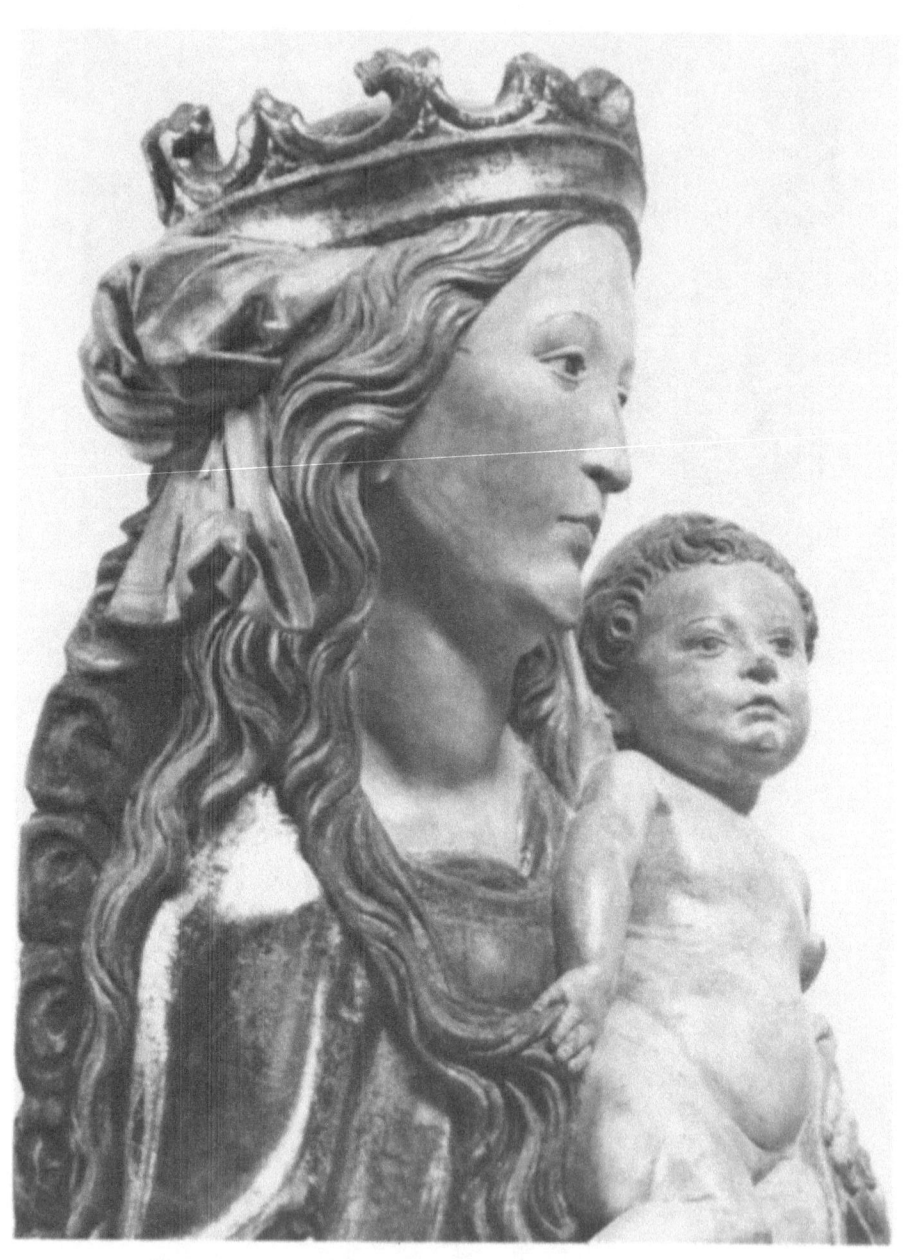

32A and B. The Virgin with the Christ Child. About 1505–1510. Lindenwood.
Bayerisches Nationalmuseum, Munich.

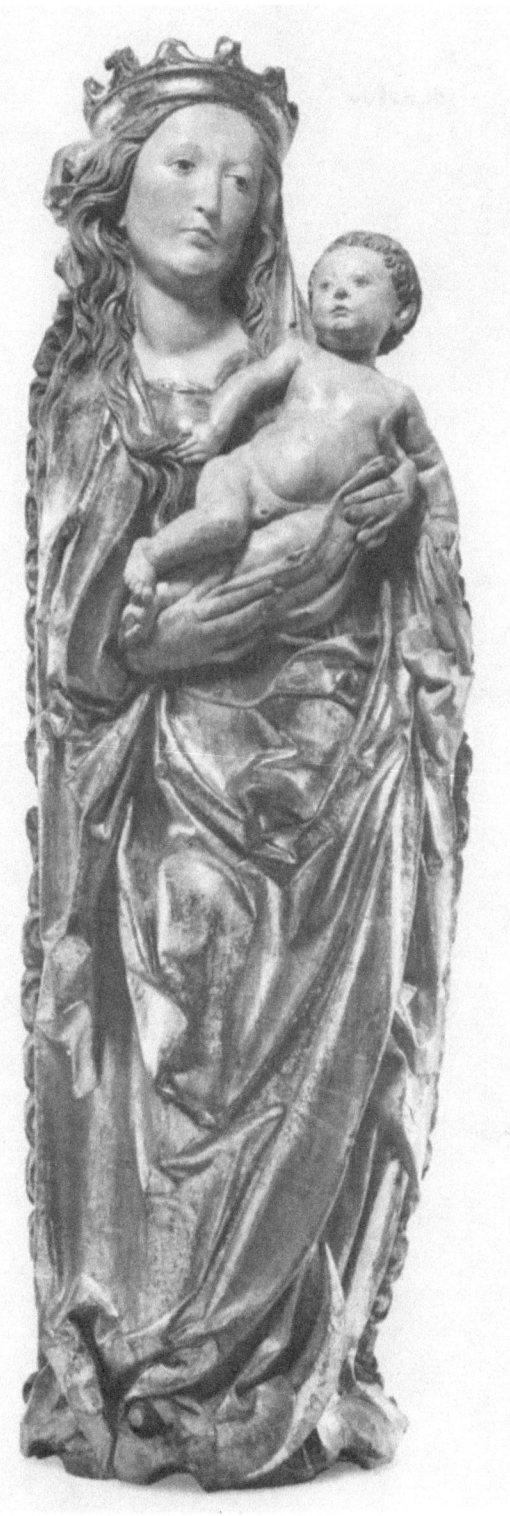

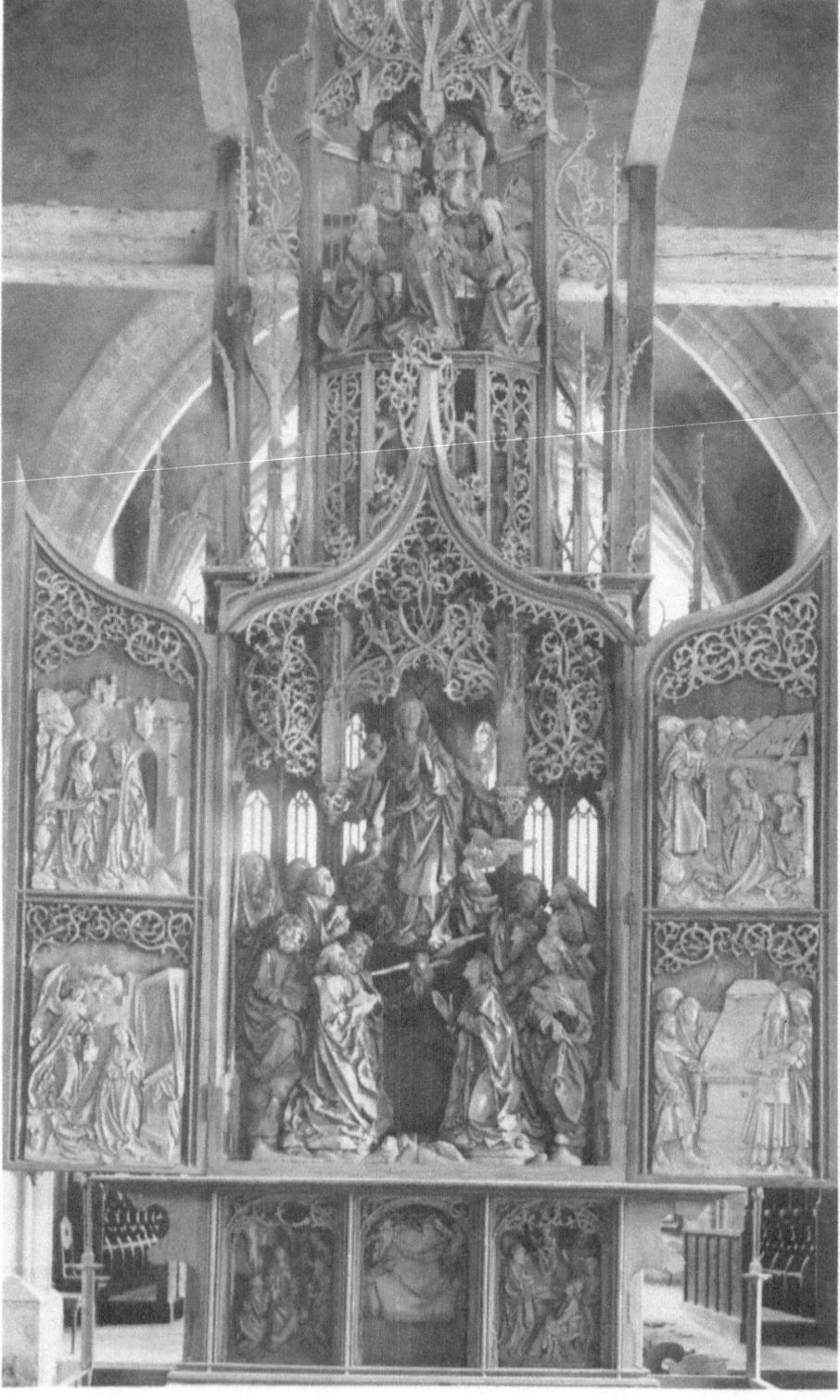

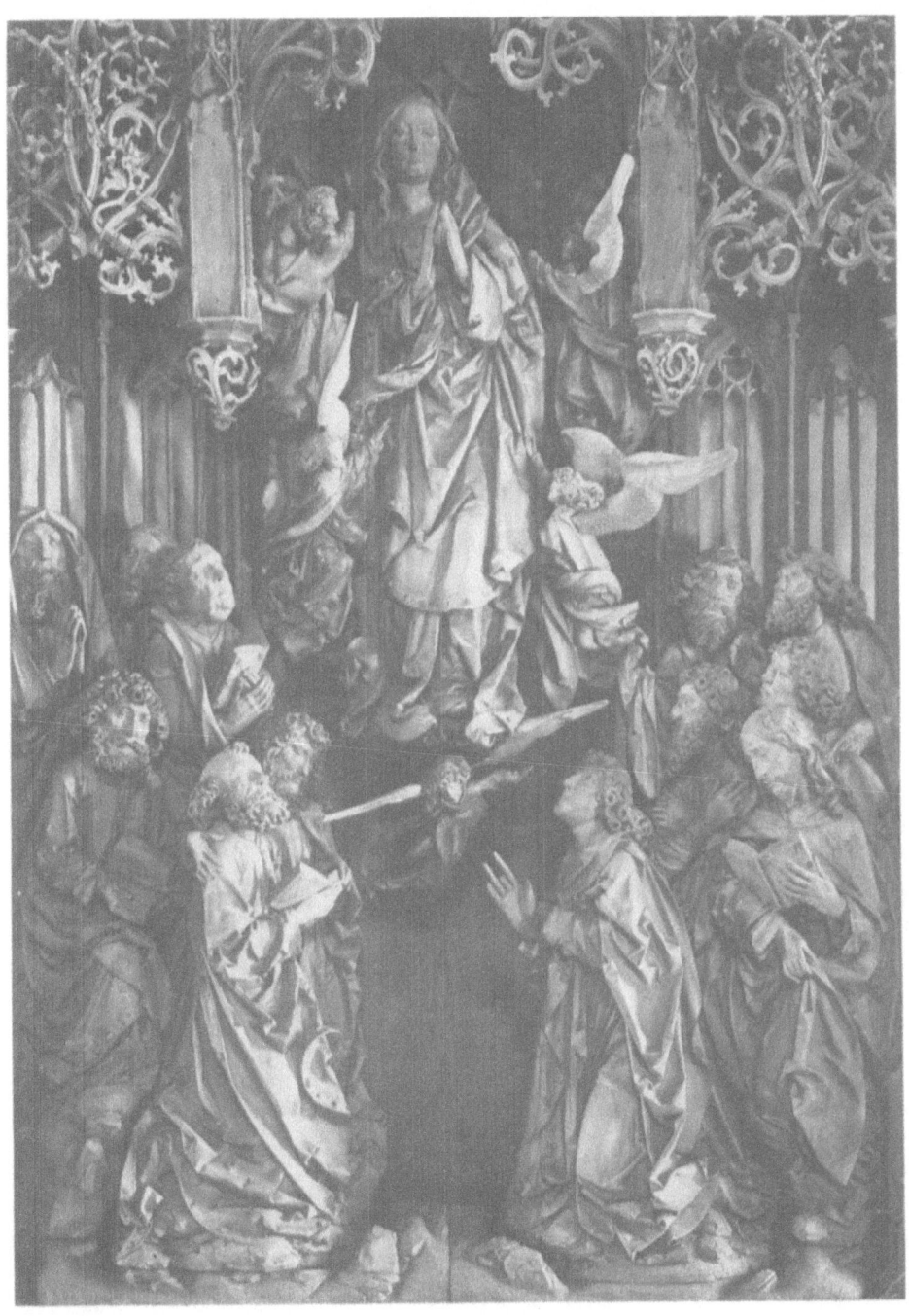

Opposite: 33A. Altarpiece of the Assumption of the Virgin. About 1505–1510. Lindenwood. Herrgottskirche, Creglingen. *Above:* 33B. The Assumption of the Virgin. In the shrine of the Creglingen Altarpiece.

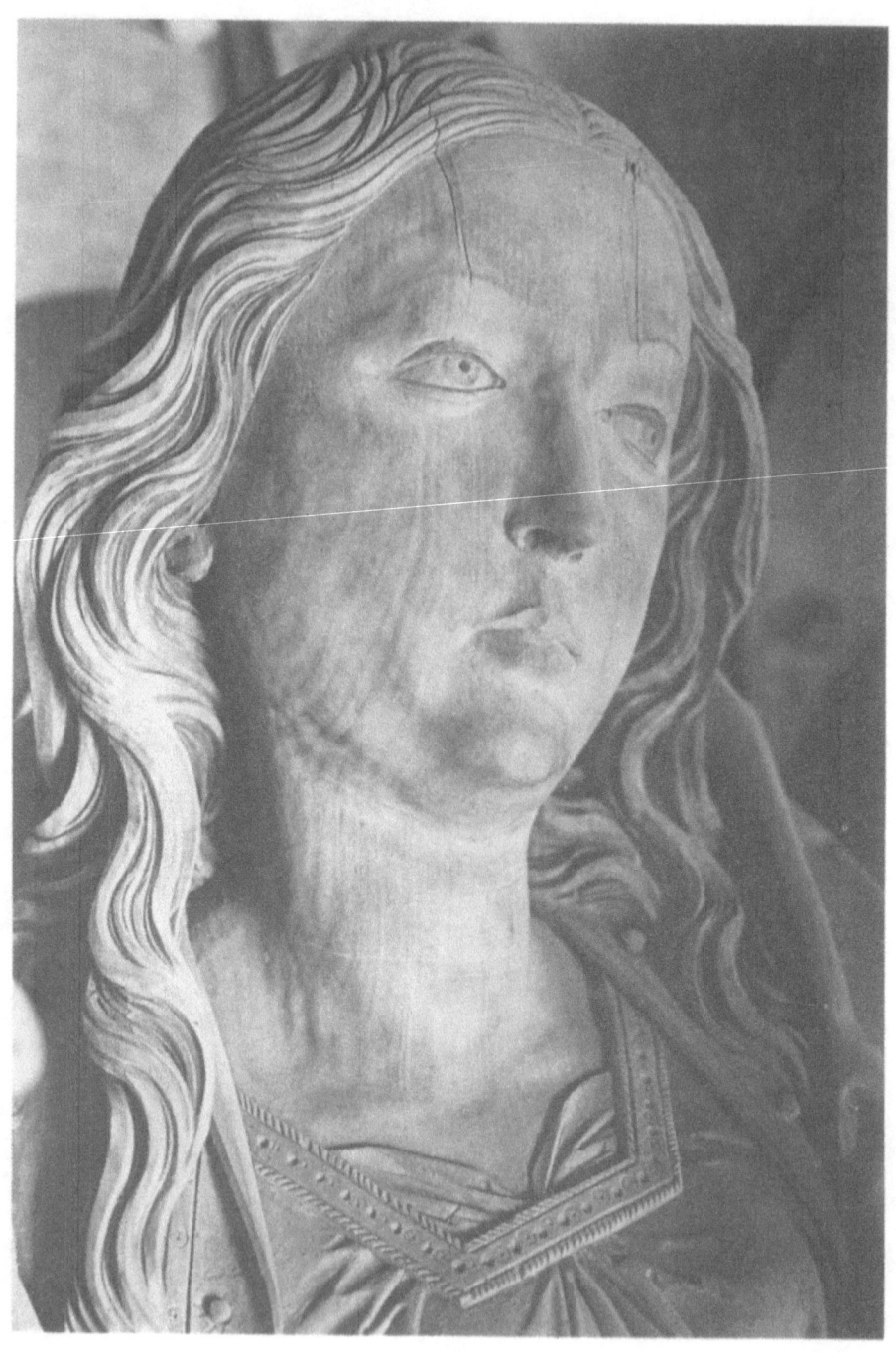

33C. Mary, detail of the shrine, Creglingen Altarpiece.

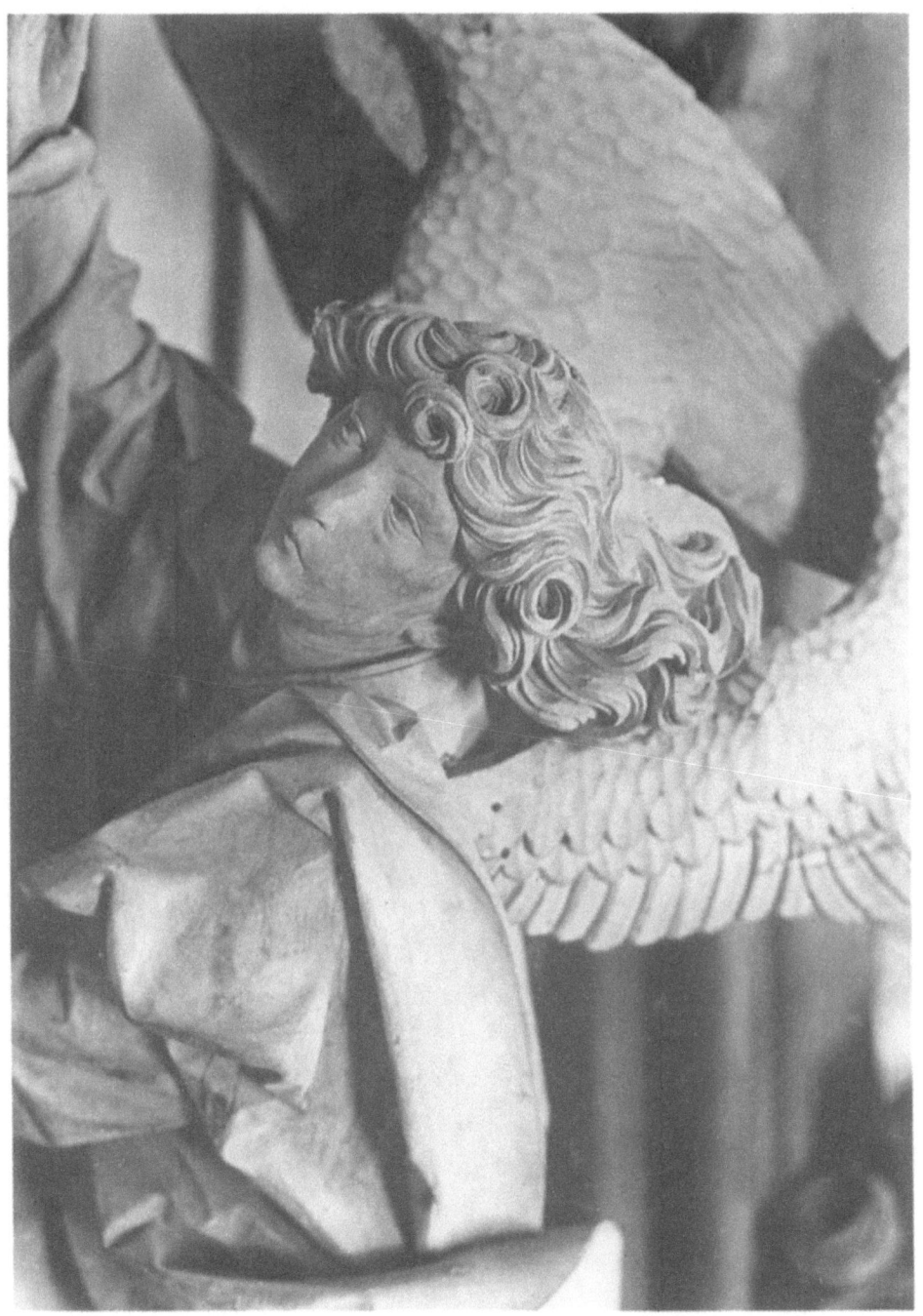

33D. Angel, detail of the shrine, Creglingen Altarpiece.

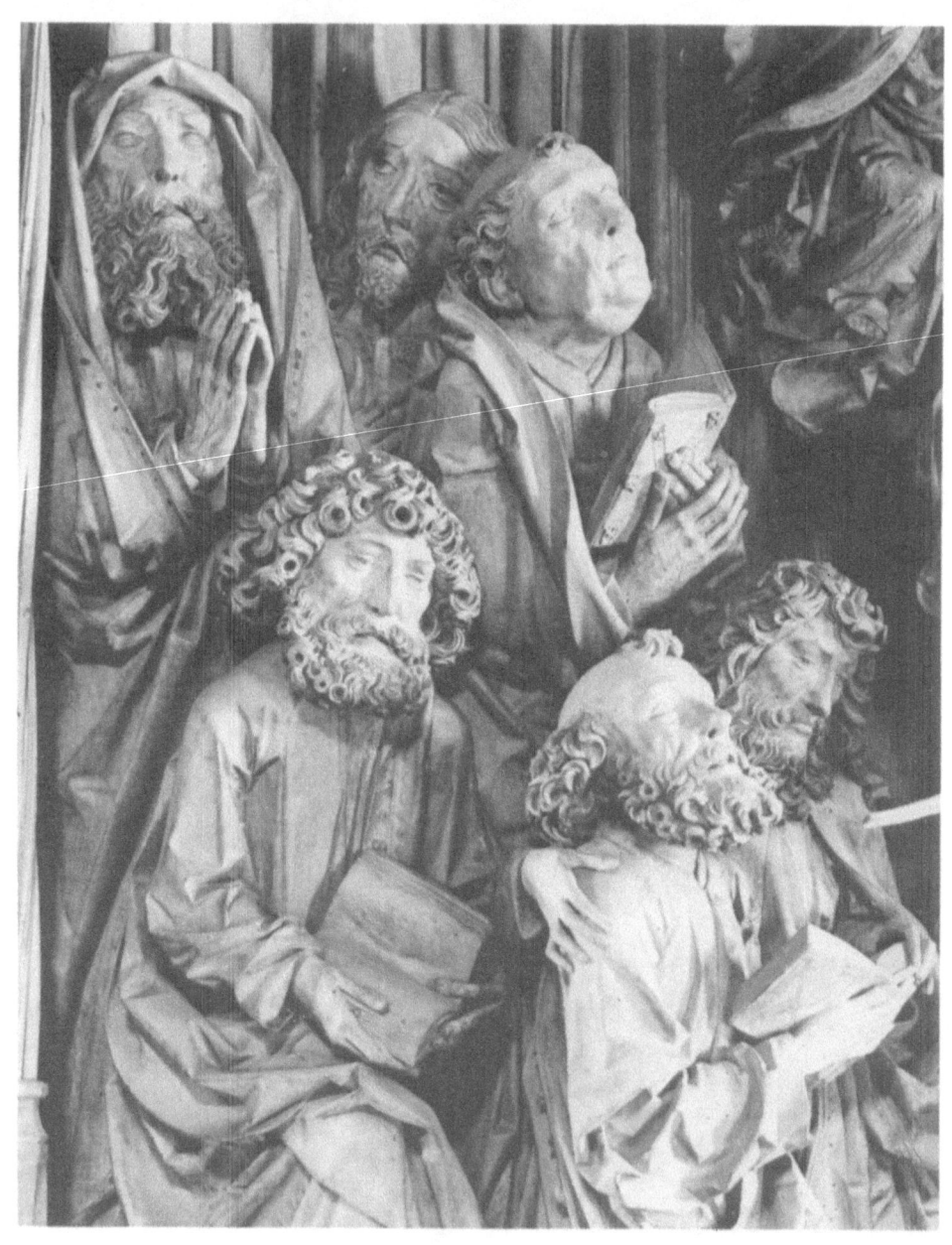

33E. Group of Apostles, detail of the shrine, Creglingen Altarpiece.

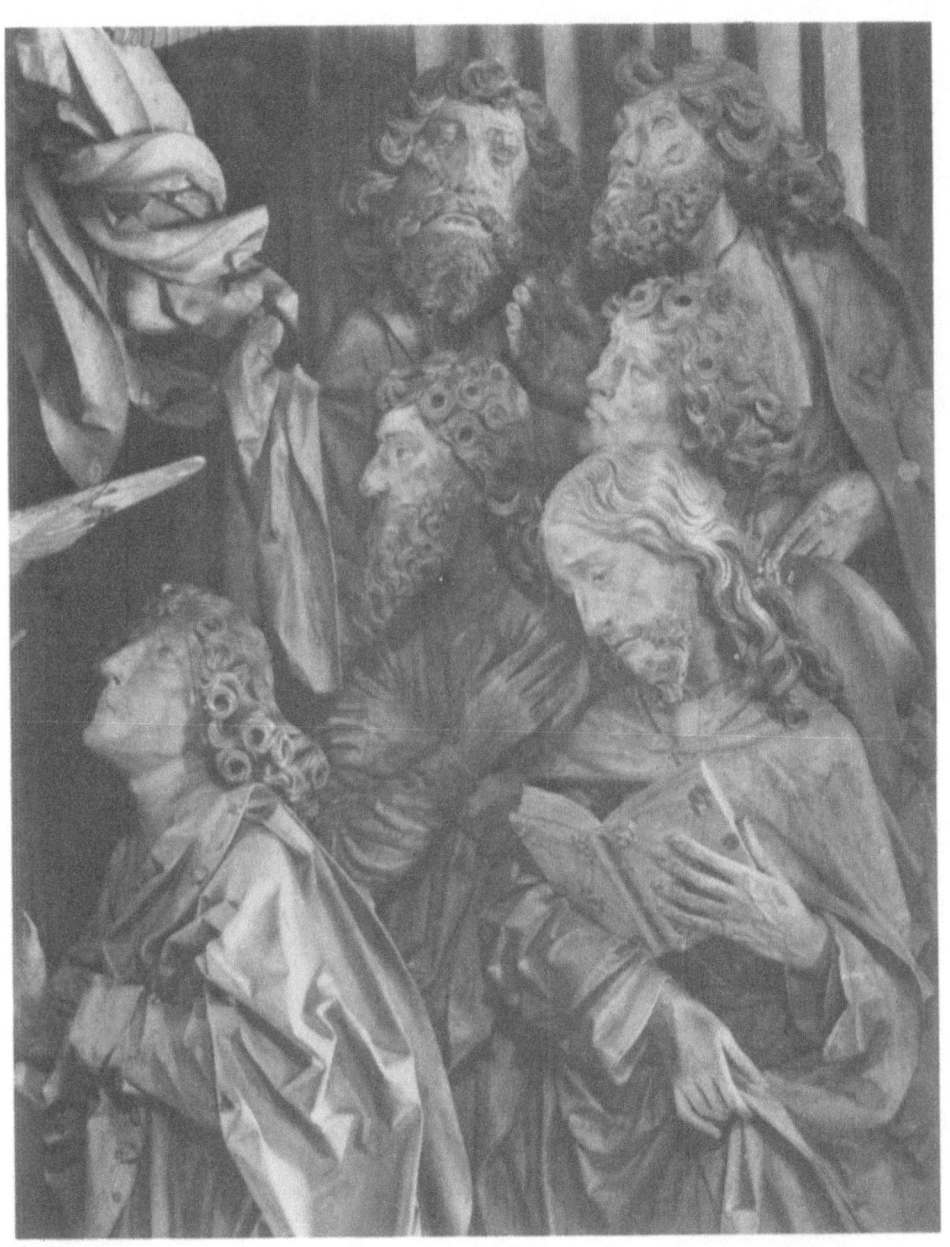

33F. Group of Apostles, detail of the shrine, Creglingen Altarpiece.

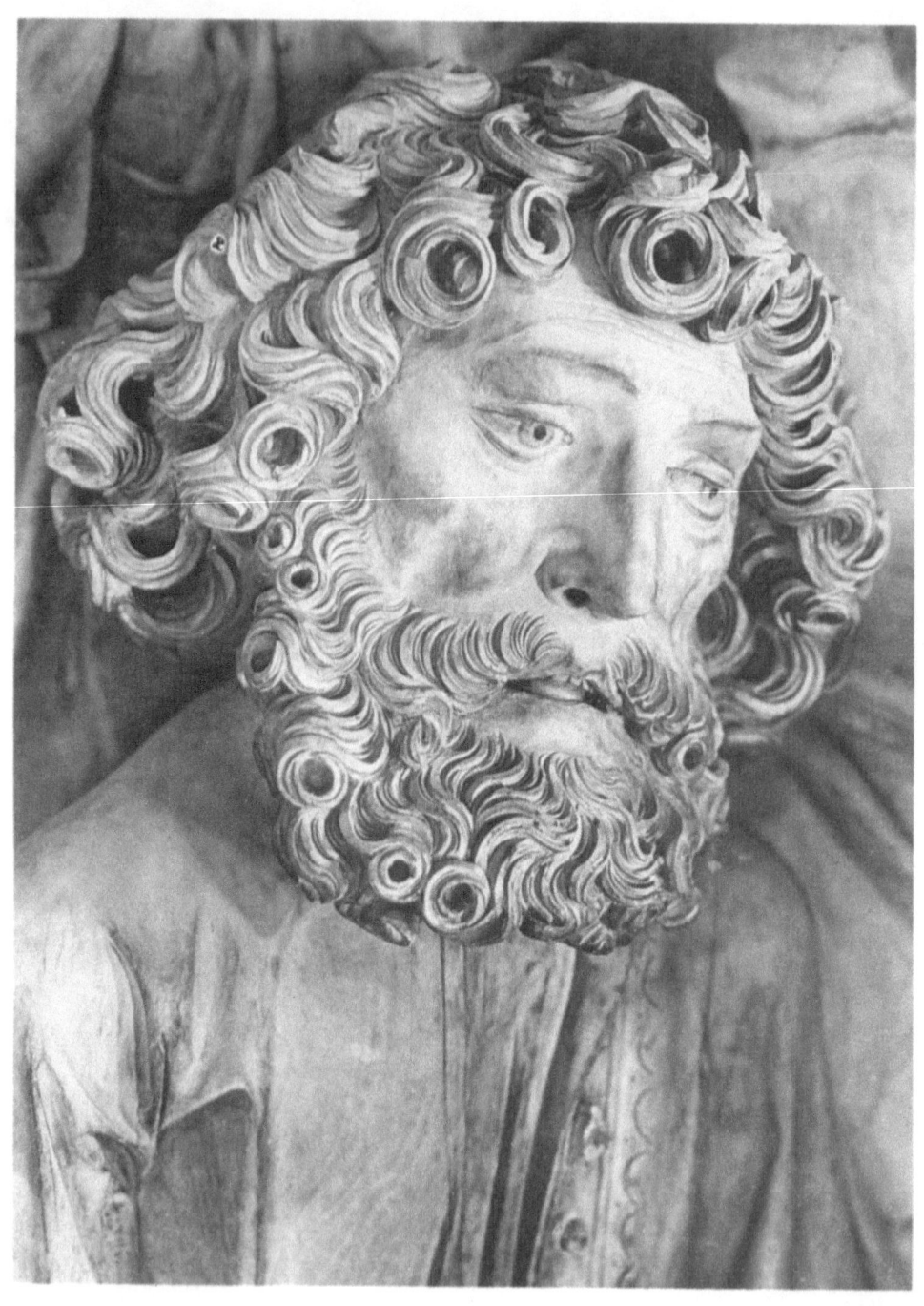

33G. One of the Apostles (Bartholomew?), detail of the shrine, Creglingen Altarpiece.

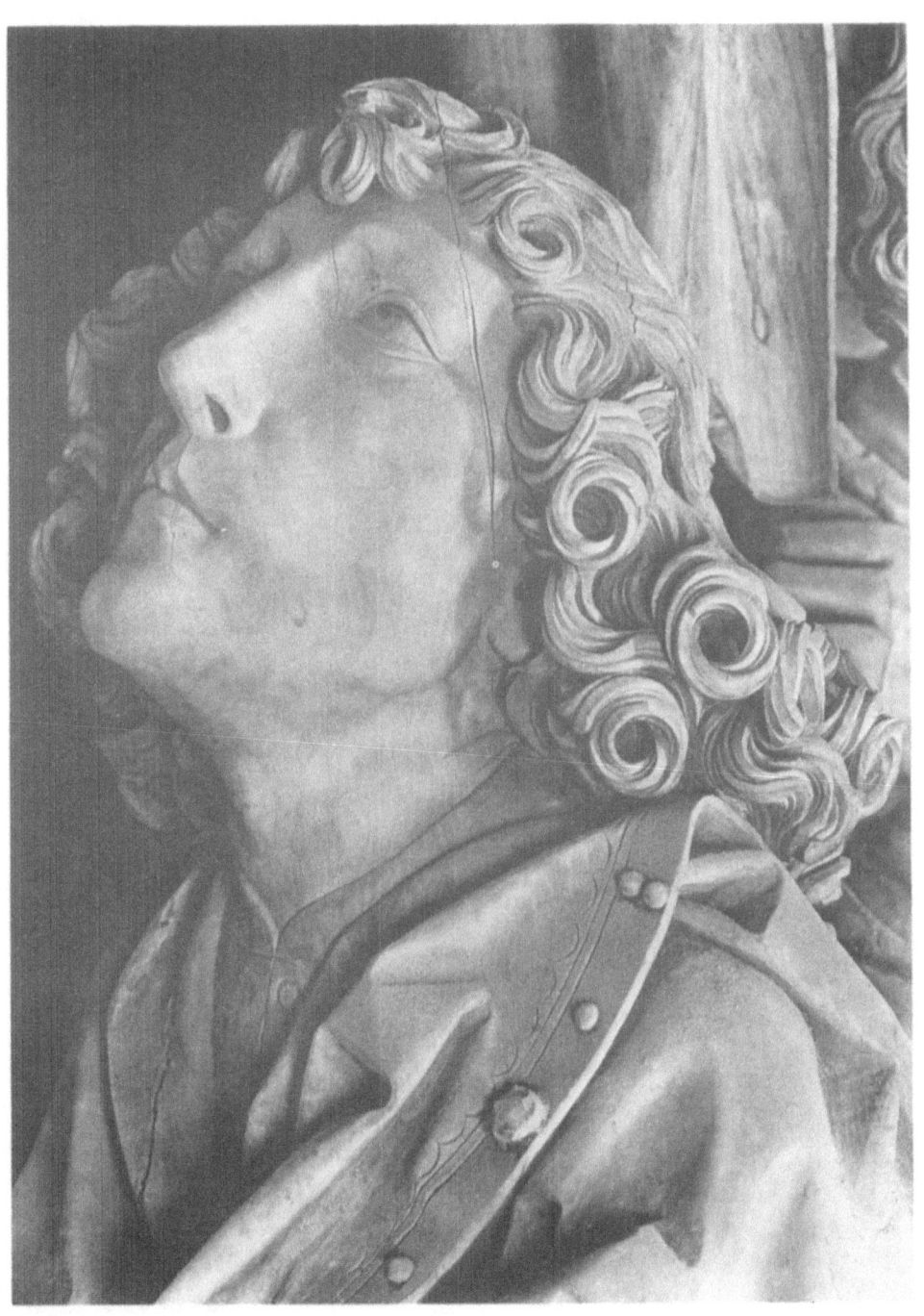

33H. John, detail of the shrine, Creglingen Altarpiece.

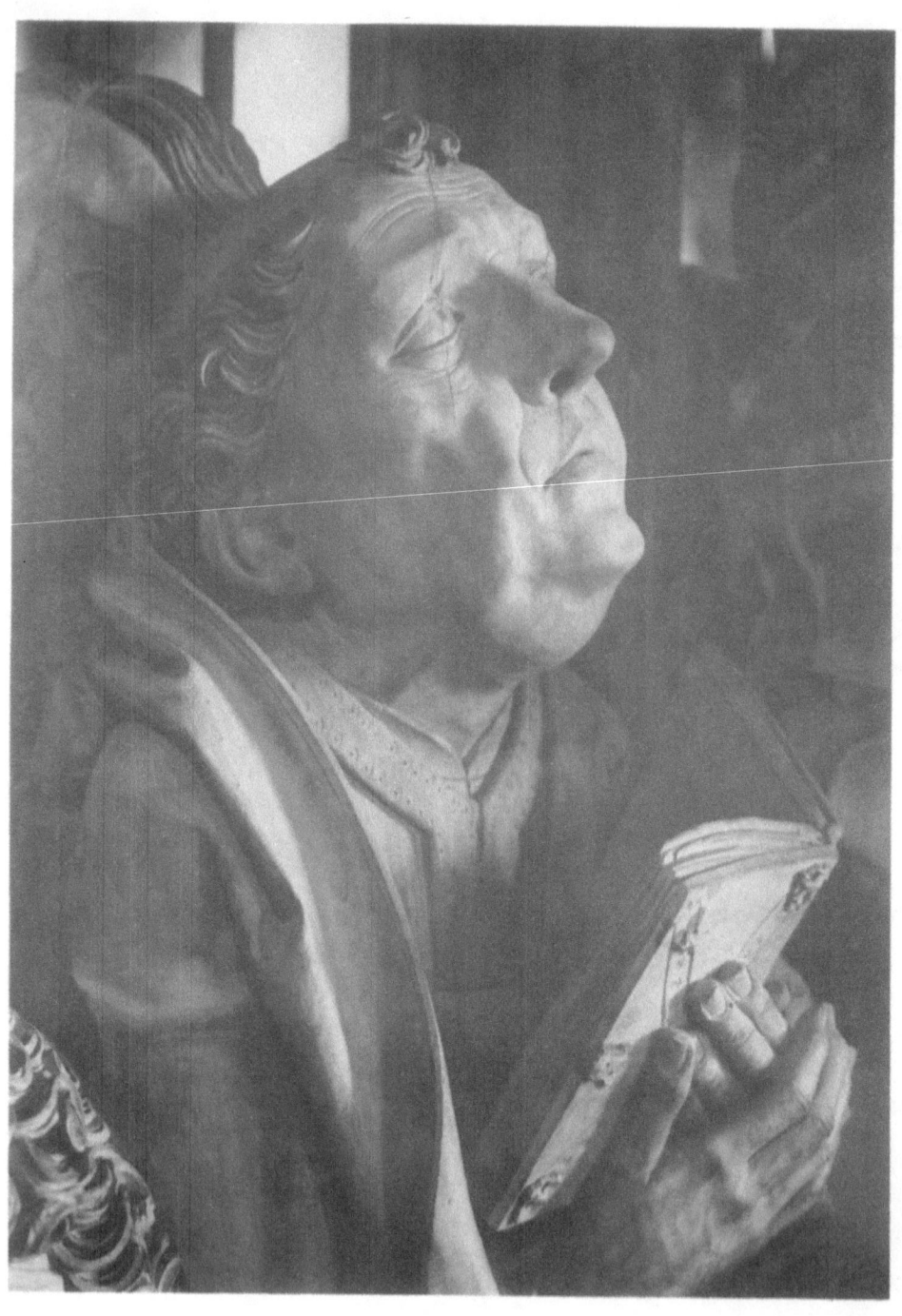

331. Philip, detail of the shrine, Creglingen Altarpiece.

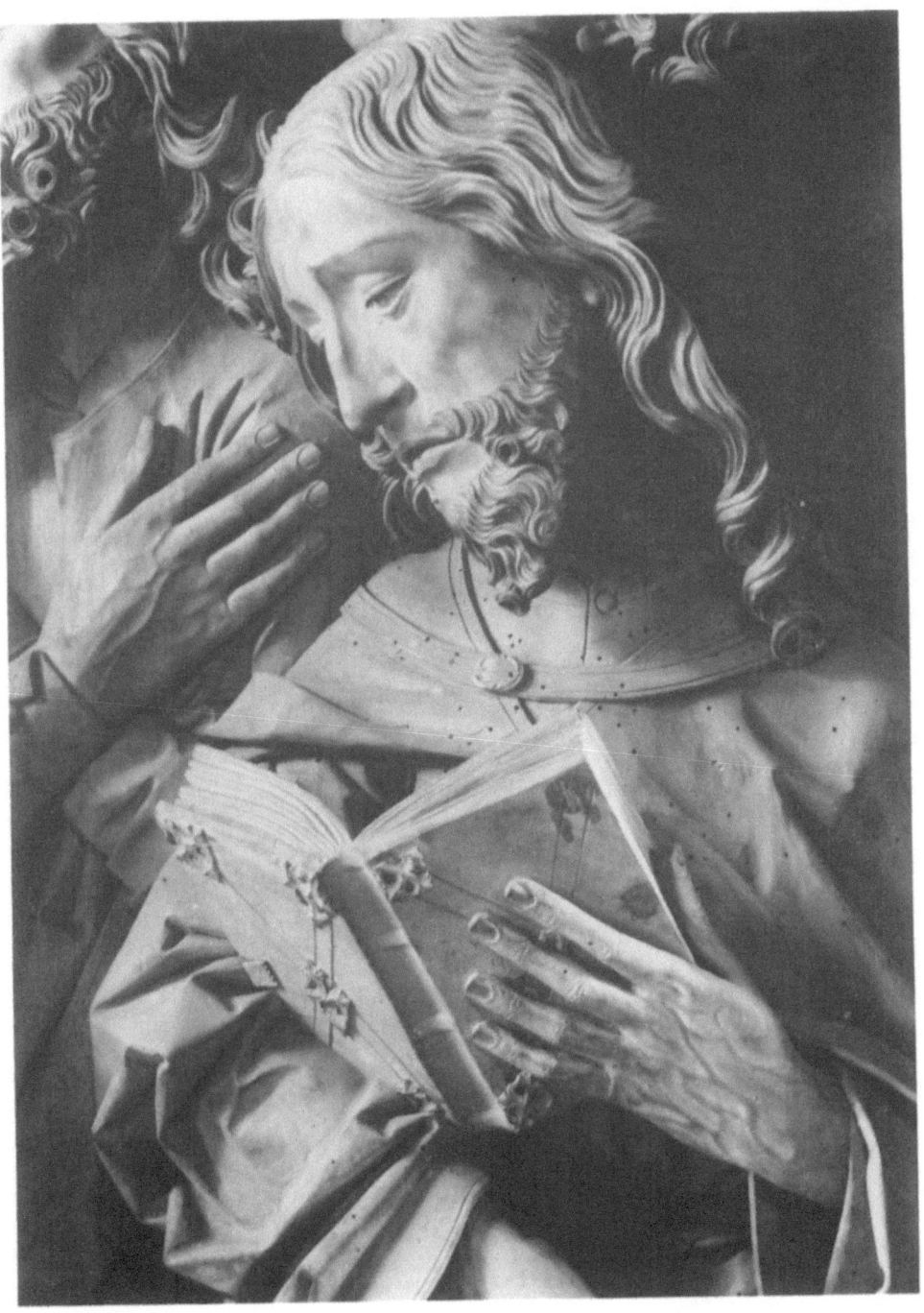

33J. James the Elder, detail of the shrine, Creglingen Altarpiece.

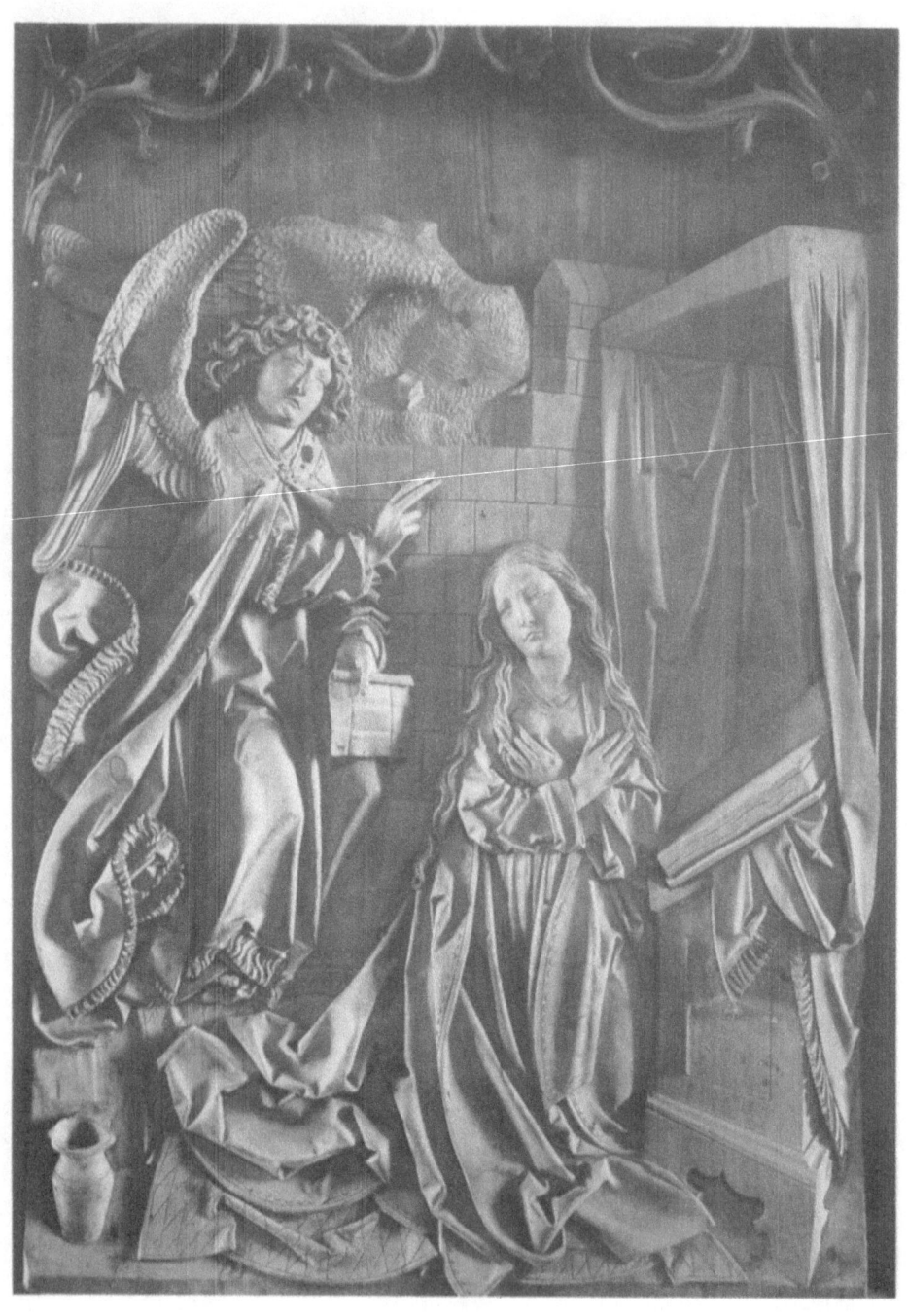

33K. The Annunciation. Lower left wing relief of the Creglingen Altarpiece.

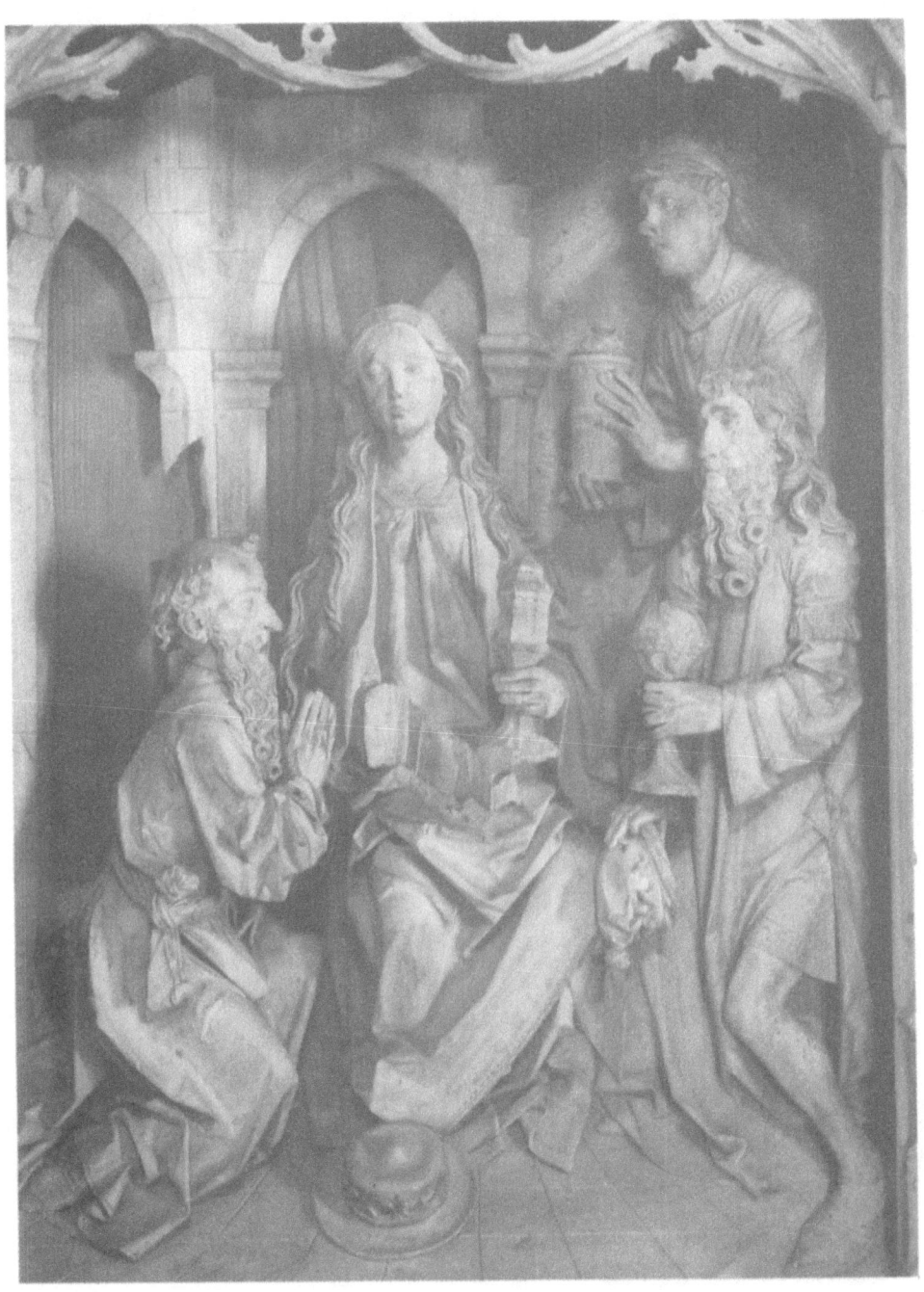

33L. The Adoration of the Magi. In the predella of the Creglingen Altarpiece.

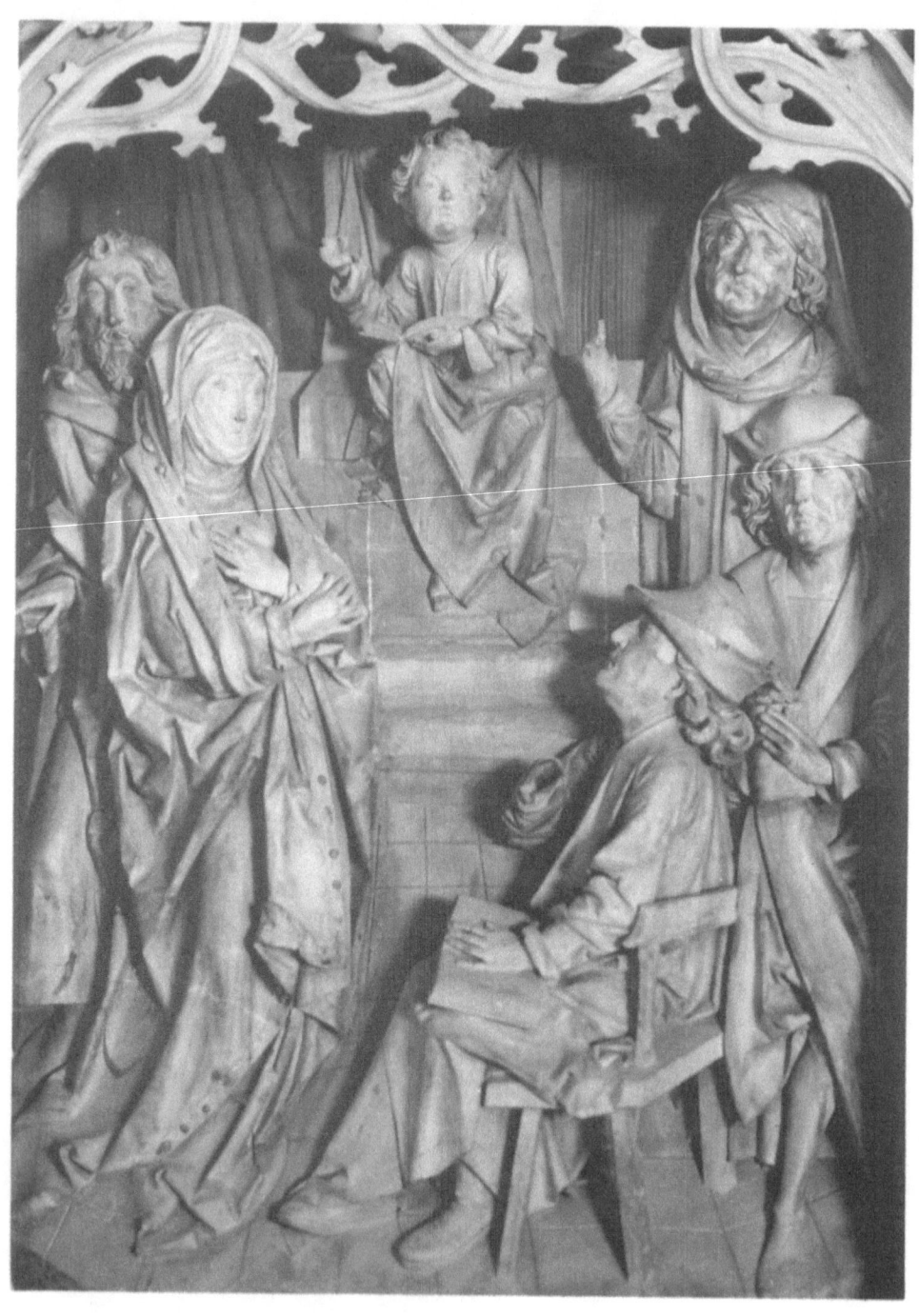

33M. Christ among the Doctors. In the predella of the Creglingen Altarpiece. *Opposite:* Two details of Christ among the Doctors. *Top:* 33N. The twelve-year-old Christ in the Temple. *Bottom:* 33P. One of the doctors (self-portrait of Tilmann Riemenschneider?).

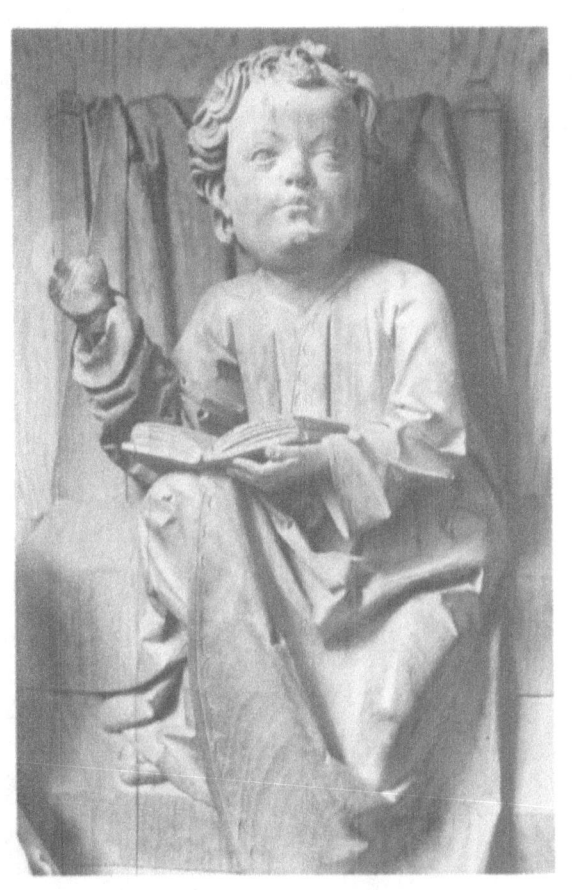

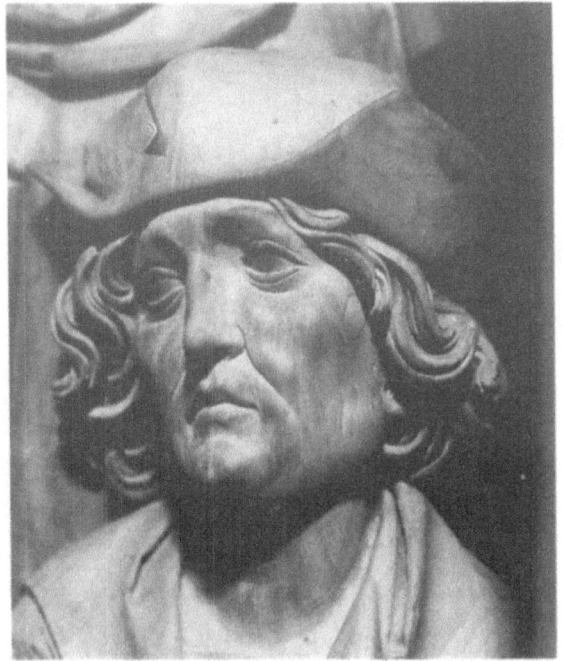

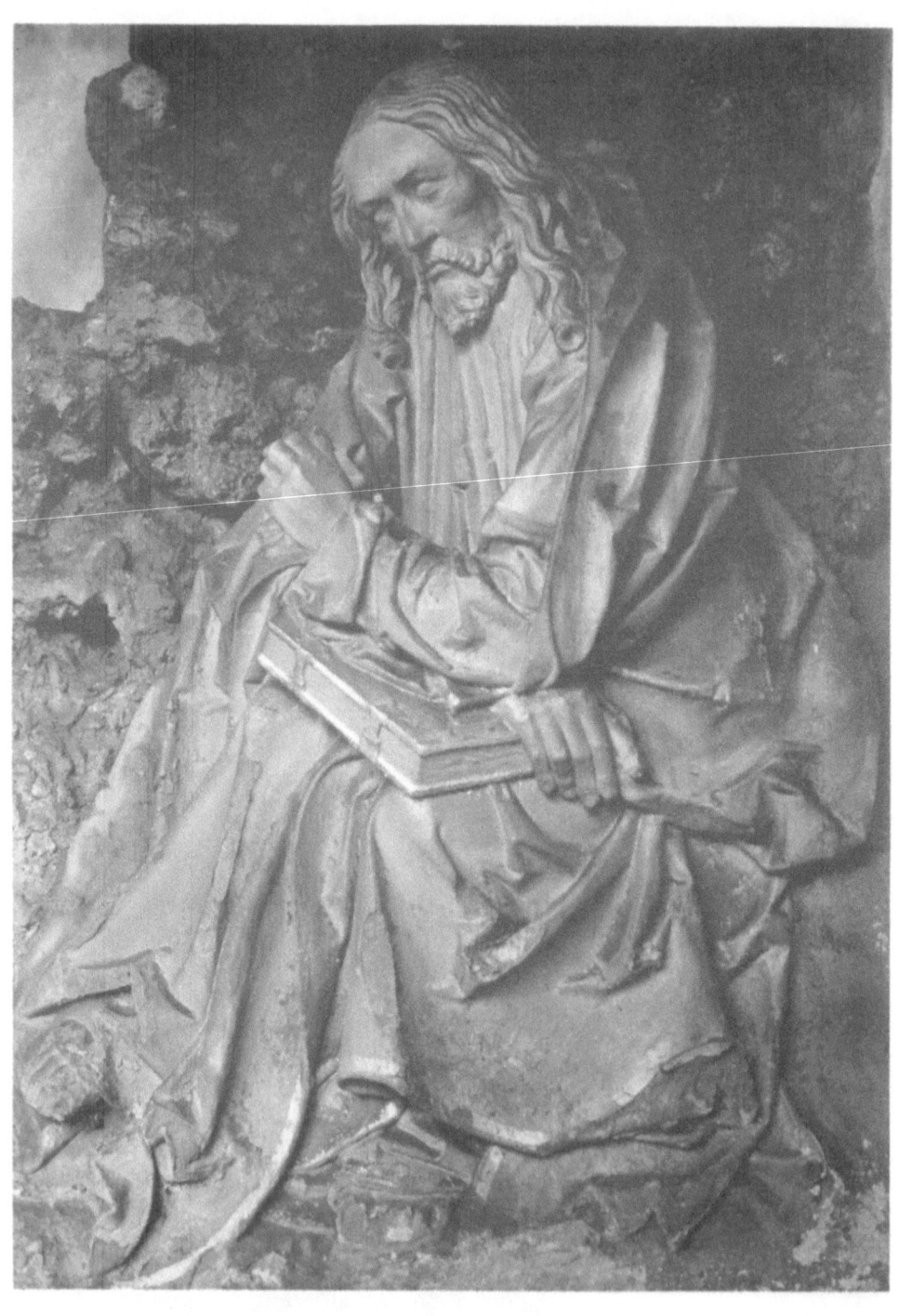

34A and (*opposite, top*) 34B. James asleep. 1510. Sandstone. From The Agony in the Garden (*opposite, bottom*, 34C), Parish Church, Heidingsfeld.

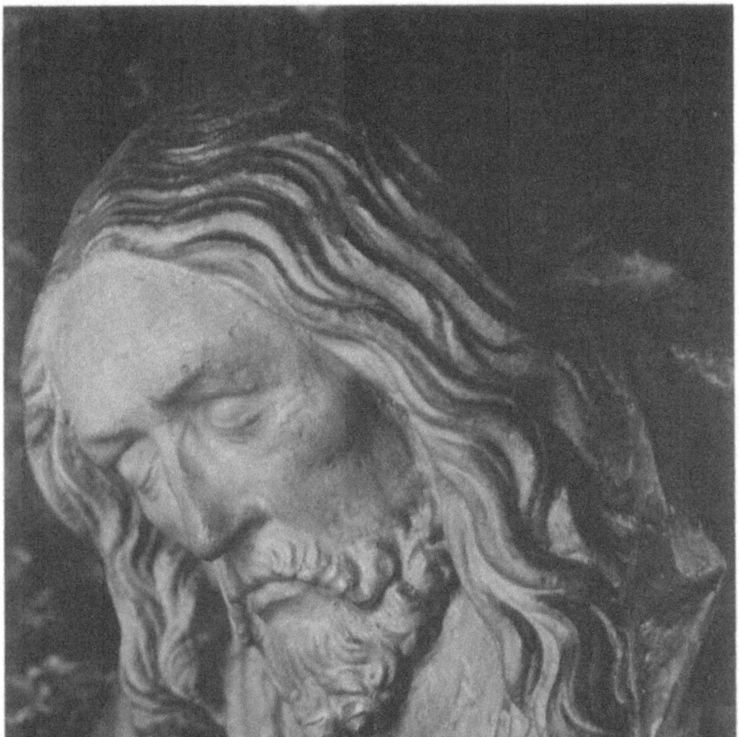

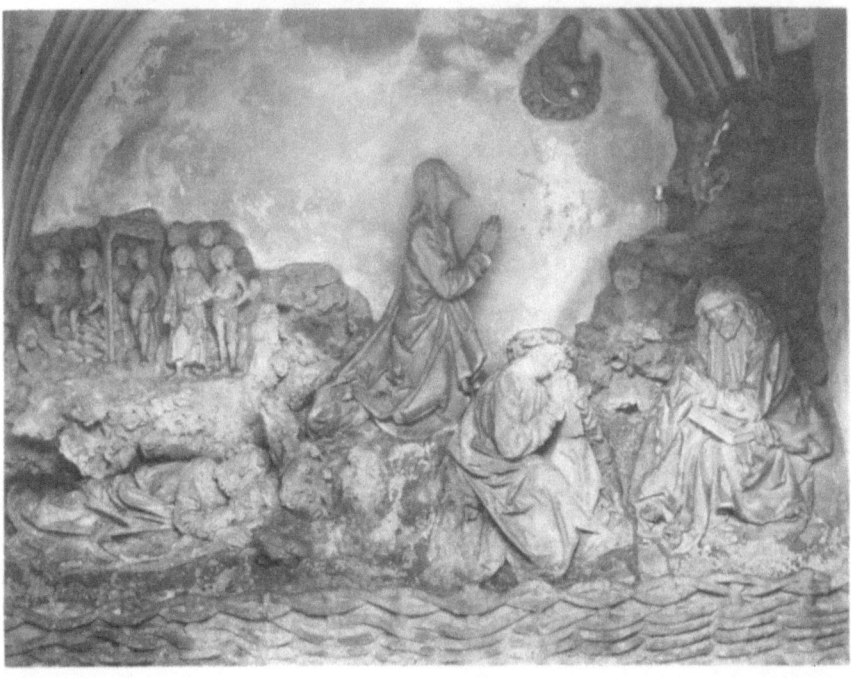

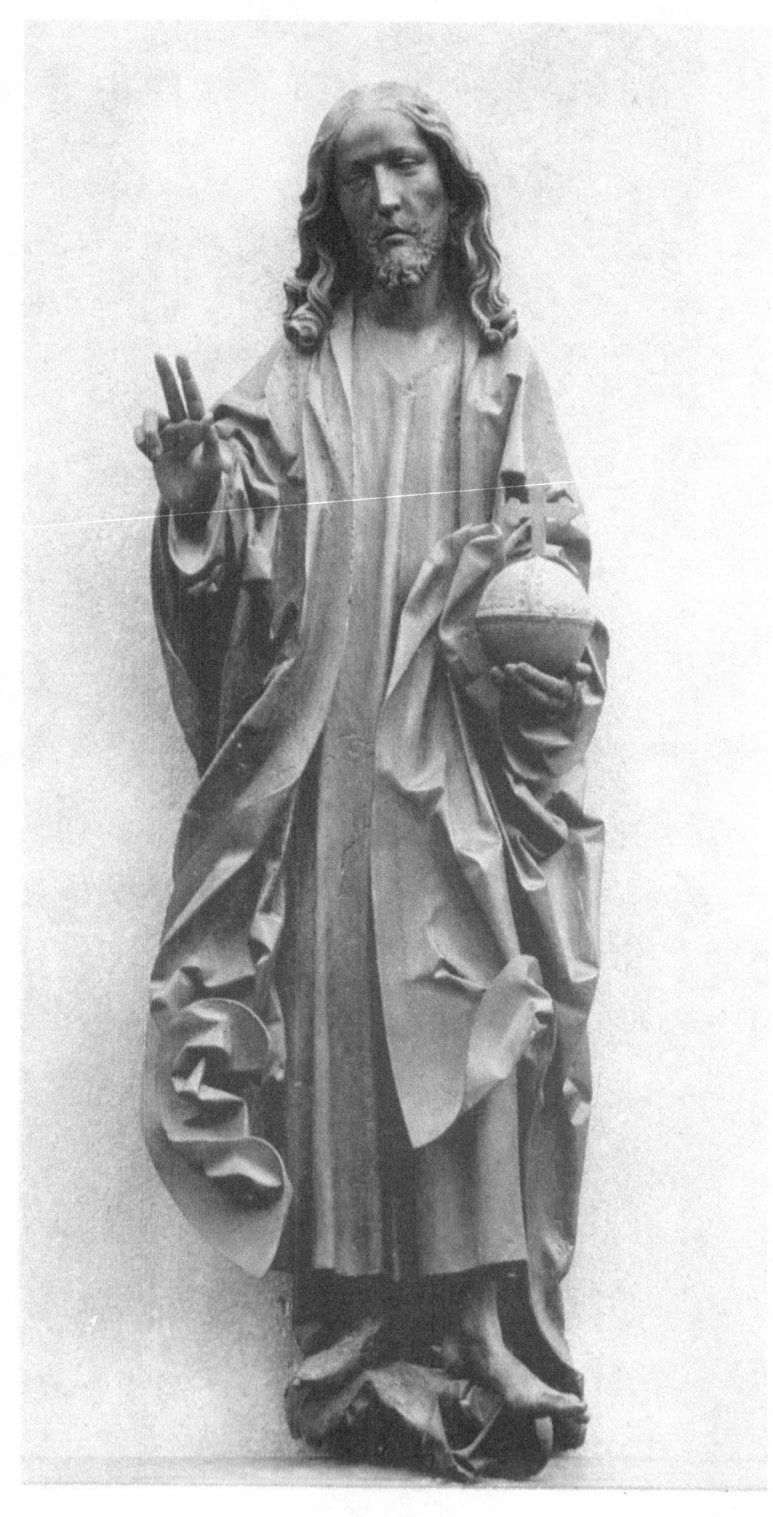

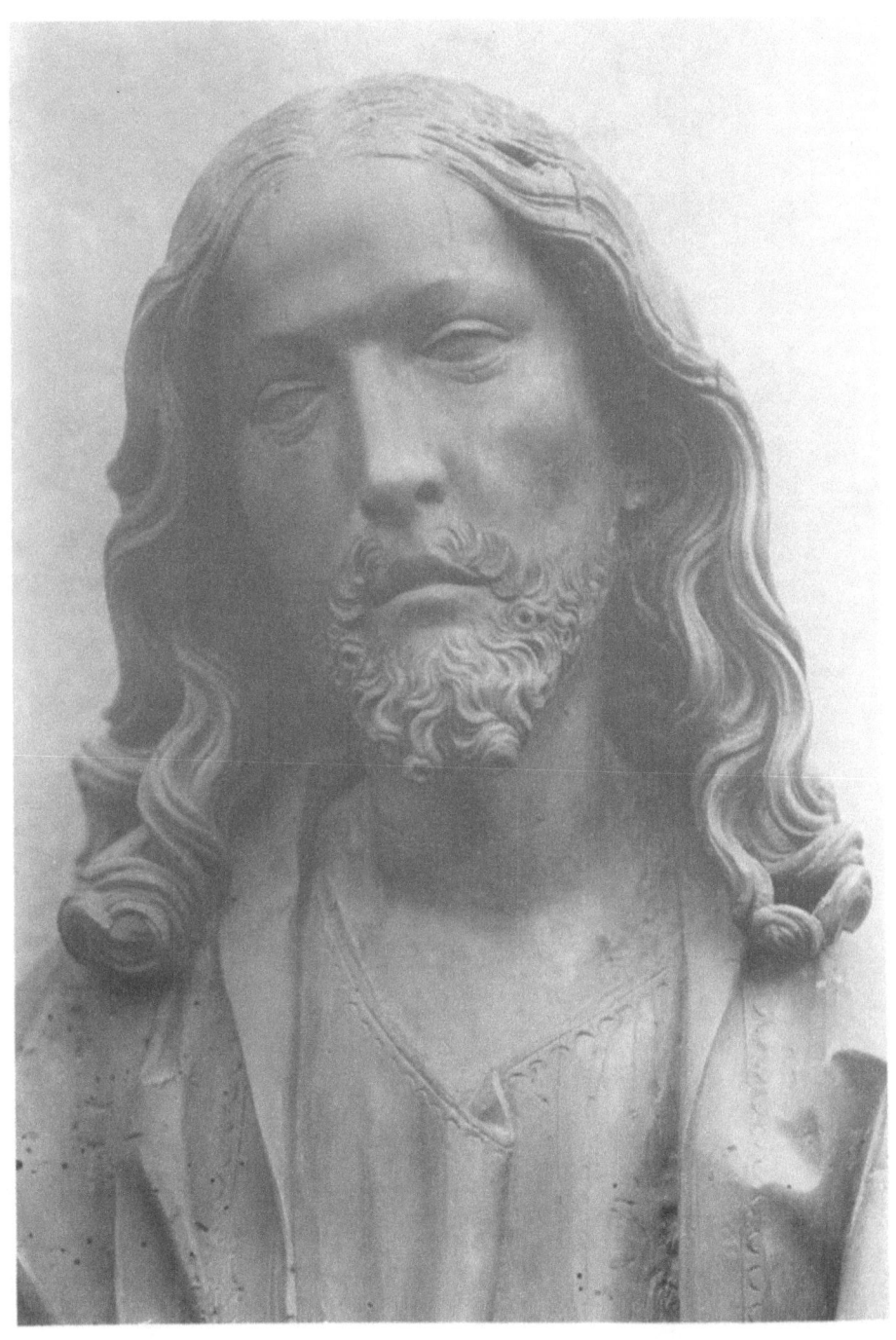

35A and B. The ascending Christ Salvator. From the High Altar of Würzburg Cathedral. 1508–1510. Lindenwood. Parish Church, Biebelried.

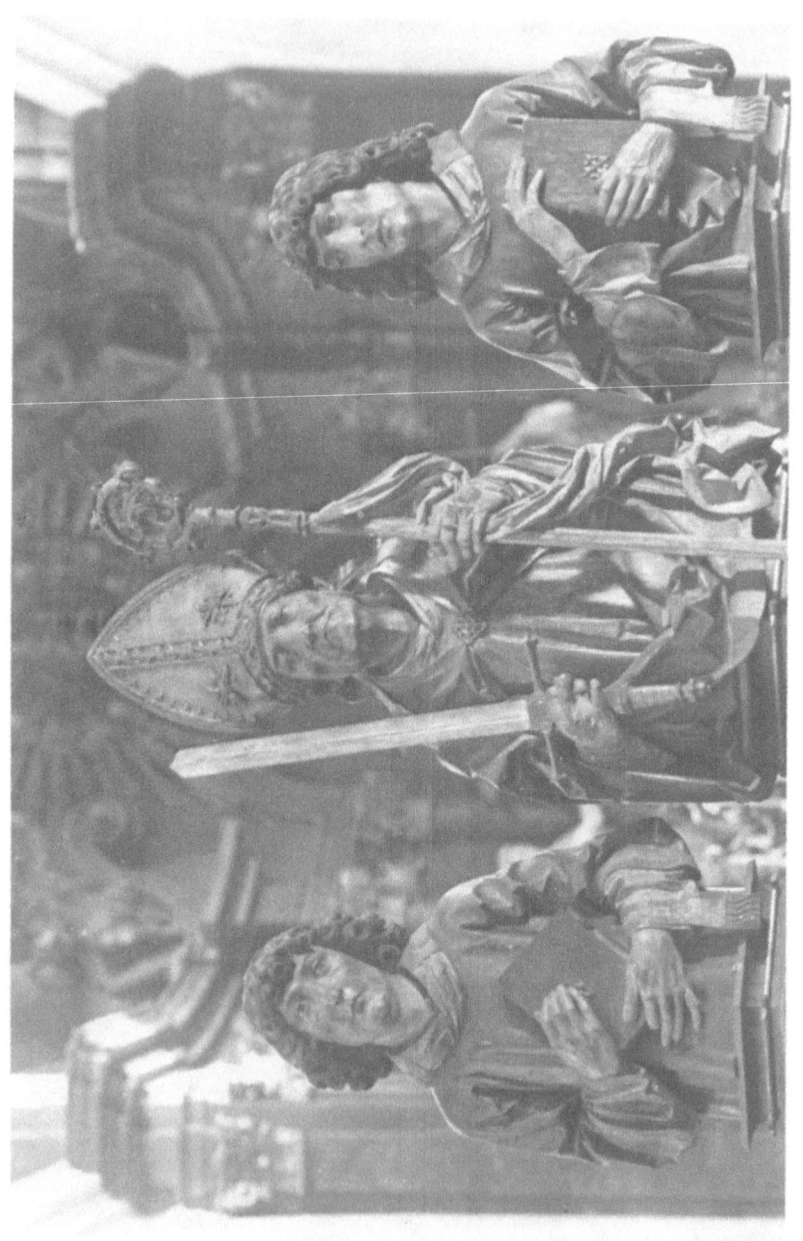

35C. The Three Franconian Apostles. Busts from the predella of the High Altar of Würzburg Cathedral. 1508–1510. Lindenwood. Destroyed in 1945. *Below, left:* 35D. St. Kilian. *Right:* 35E. Franconian Apostle.

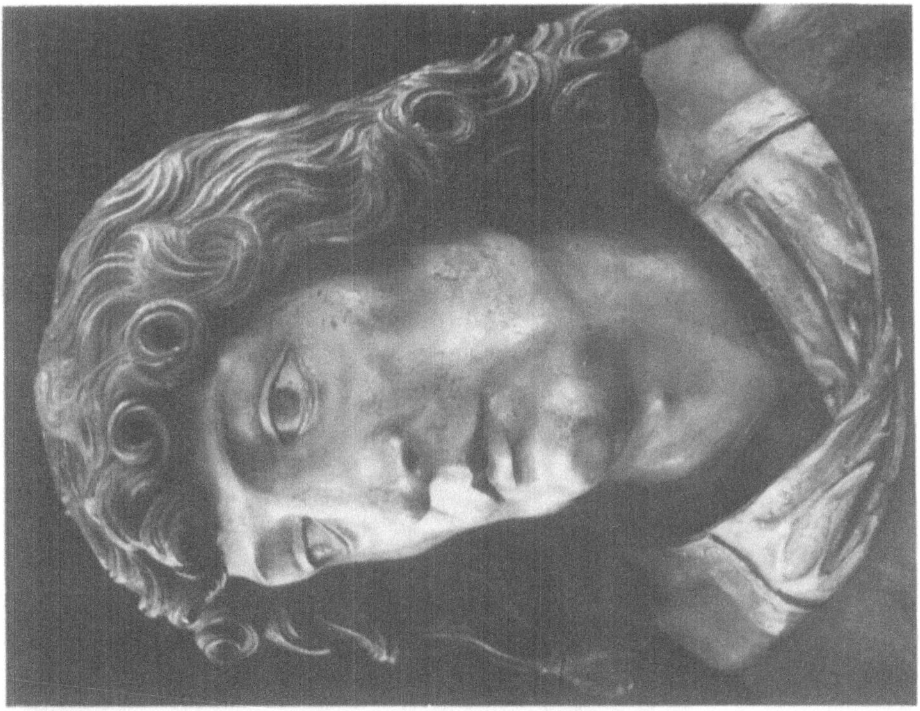
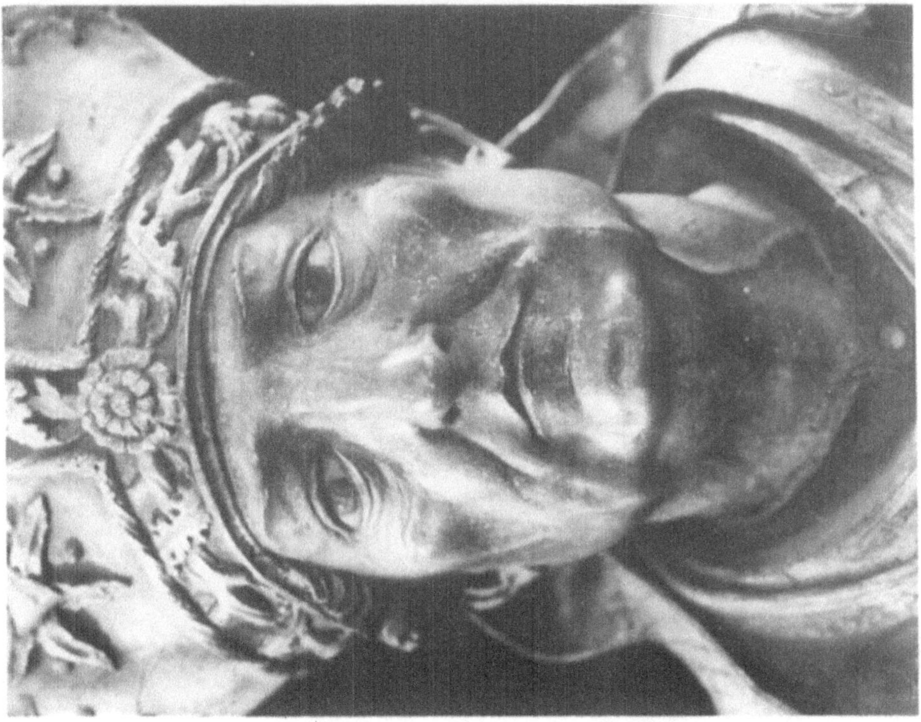

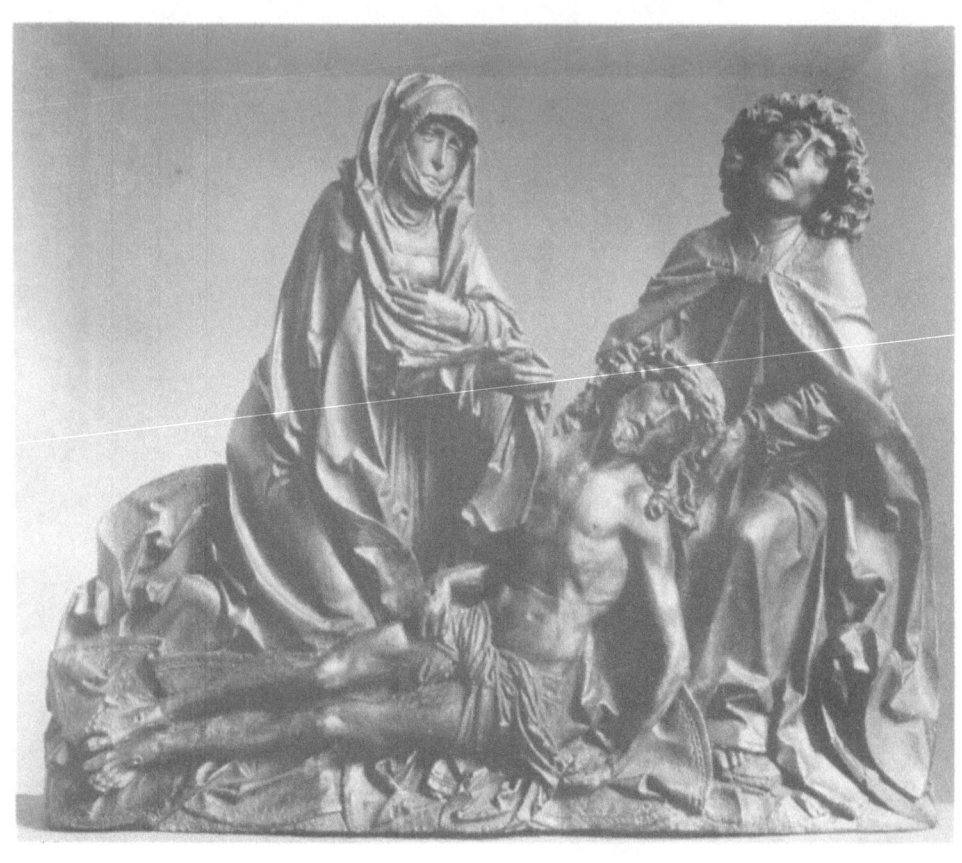

36. Lamentation for Christ. Before 1508. Lindenwood. Martin-von-Wagner Museum, University of Würzburg.

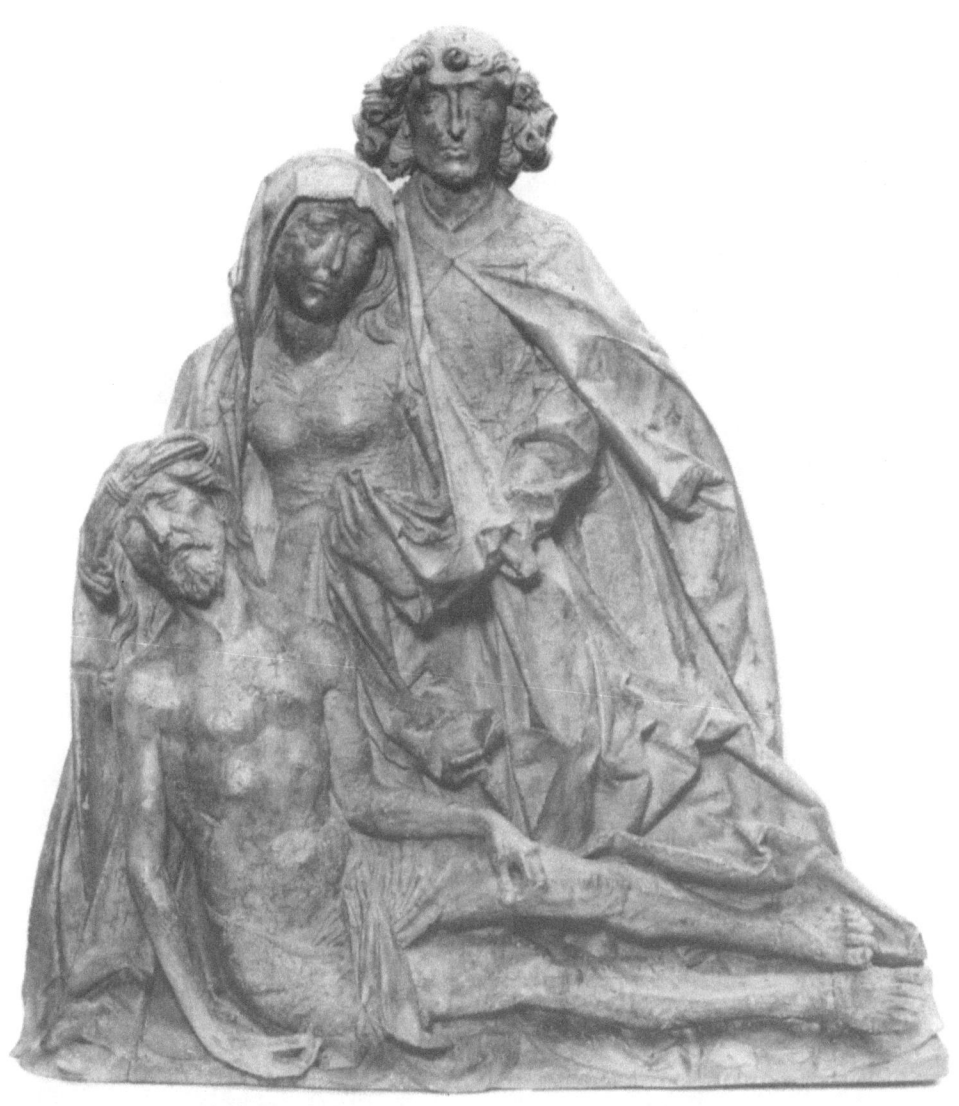

37. Lamentation for Christ. About 1515. Lindenwood. Ludwig-Roselius Collection in the Böttcherstrasse, Bremen.

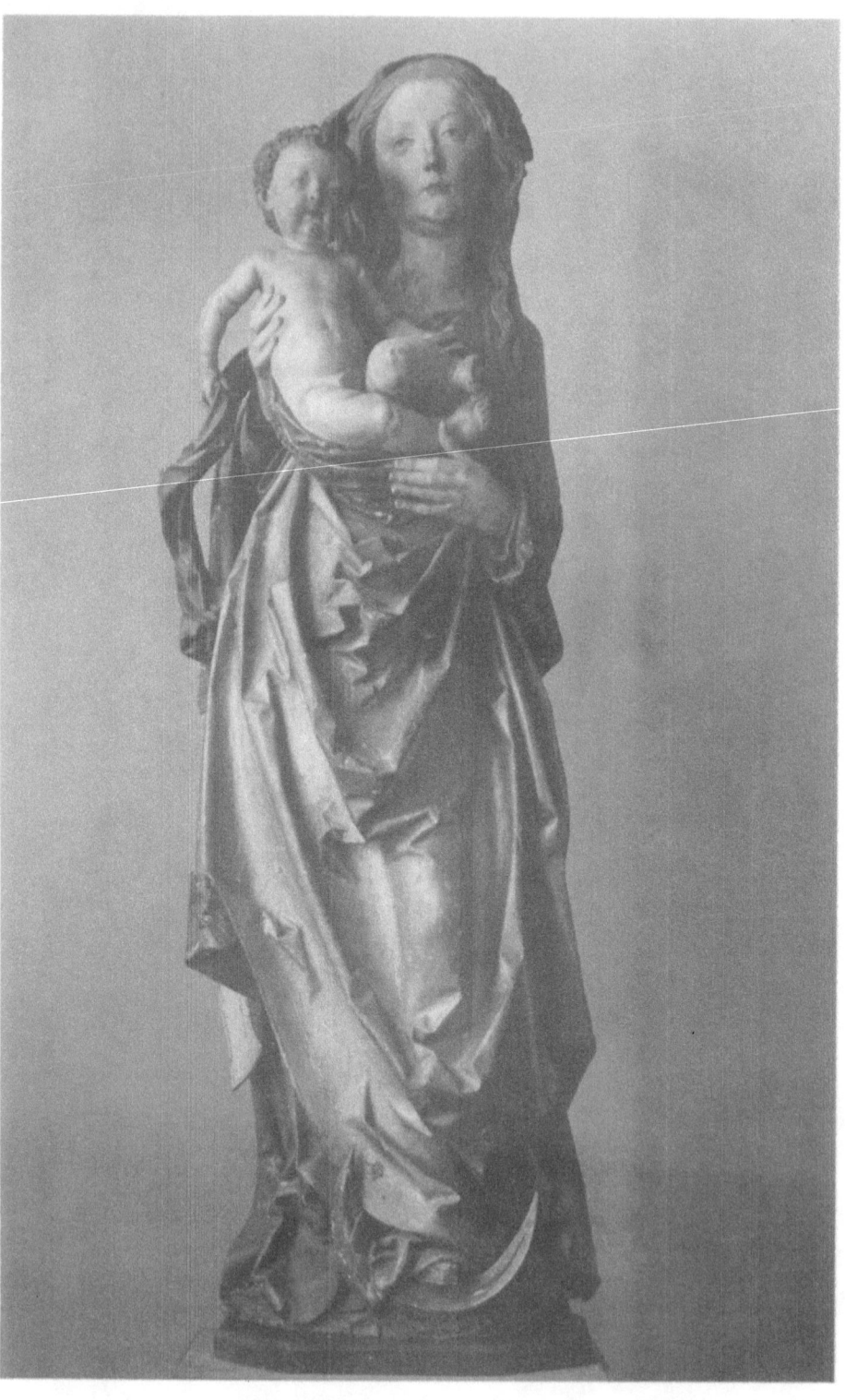

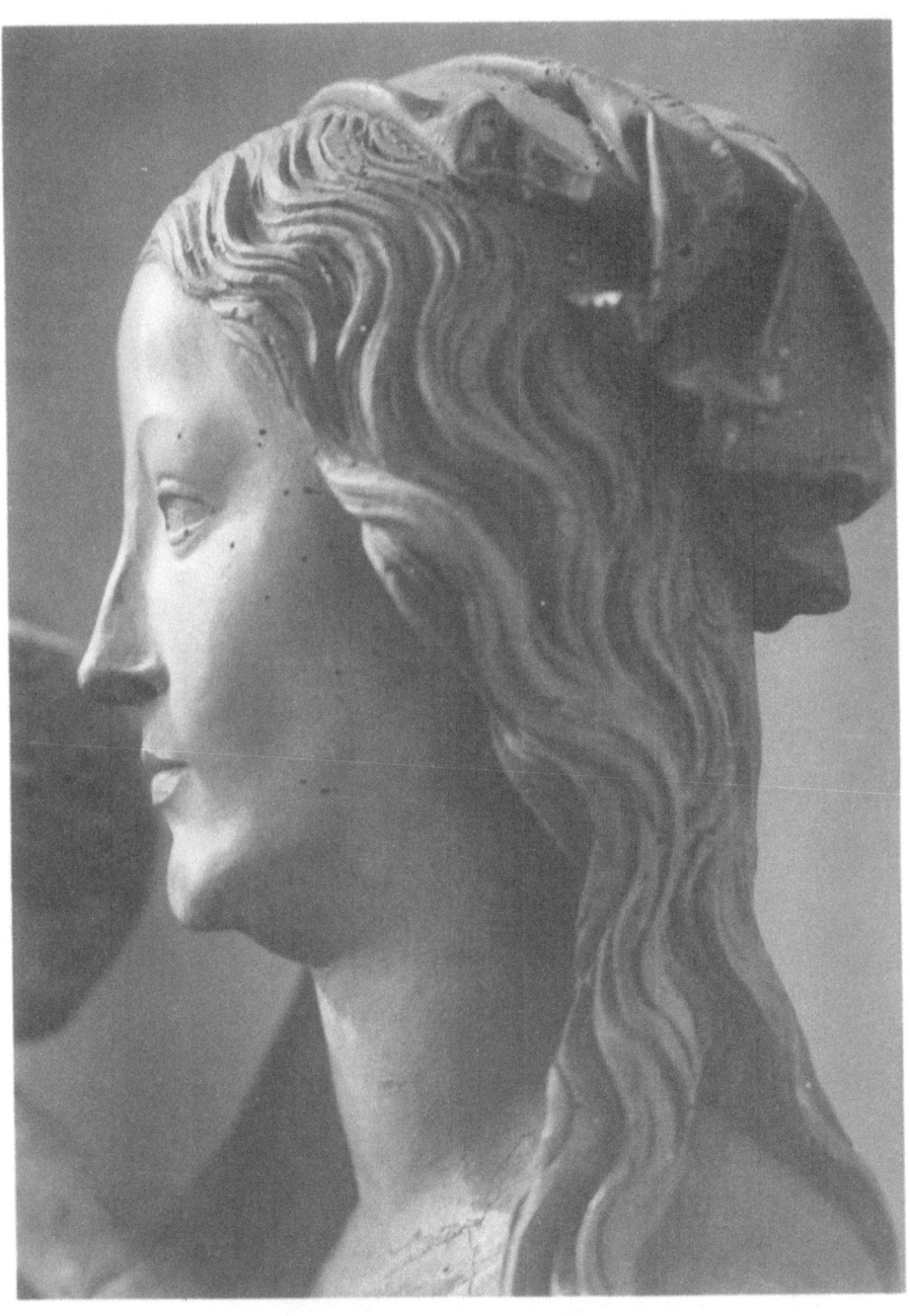

38A and B. The Virgin with the Christ Child. From an altarpiece in Gramschatz. About 1510–1515. Lindenwood. Landesgalerie, Hanover.

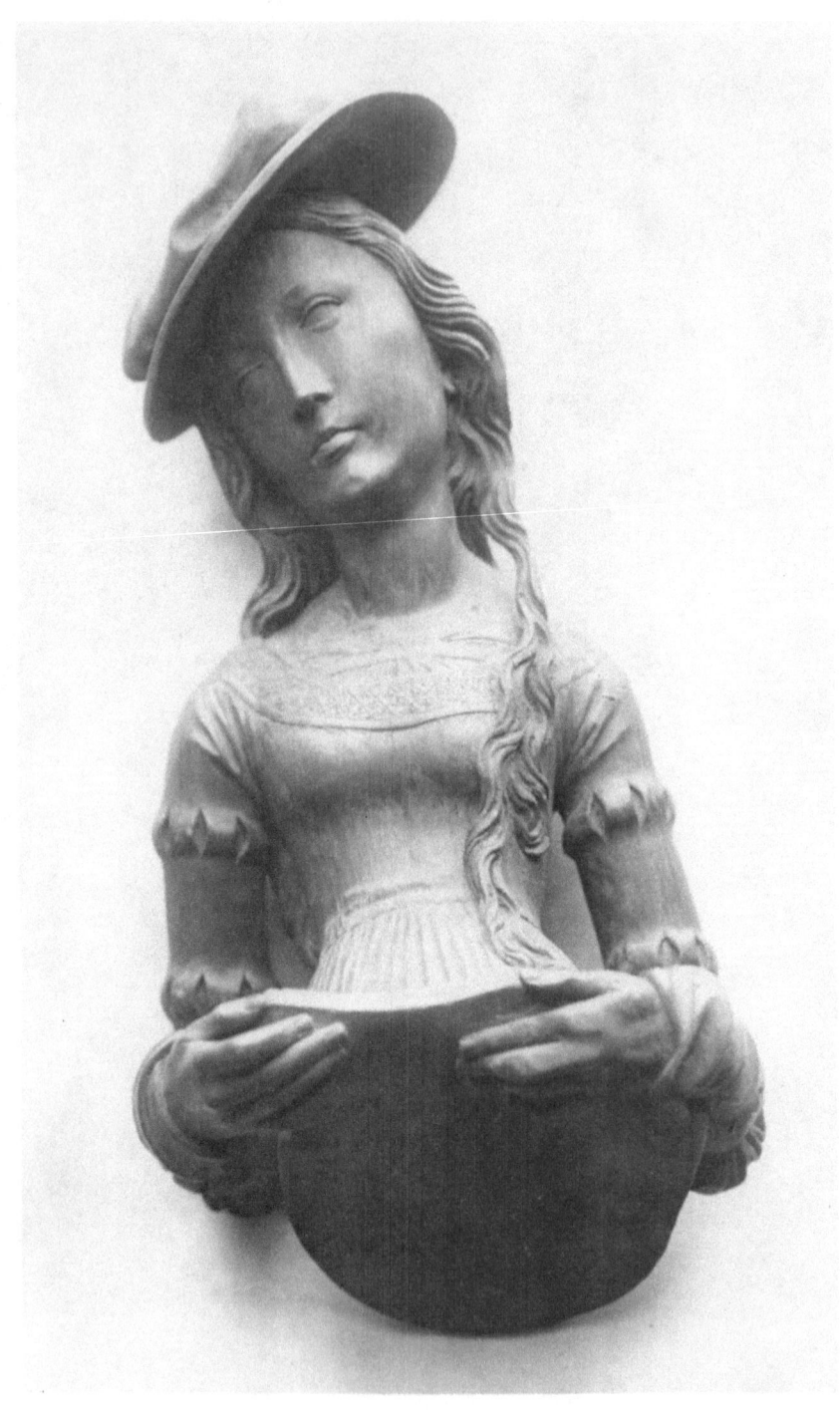

39. Female Bust for a Chandelier. About 1505–1510. Lindenwood. Landesgalerie, Hanover; Pelikan Collection.

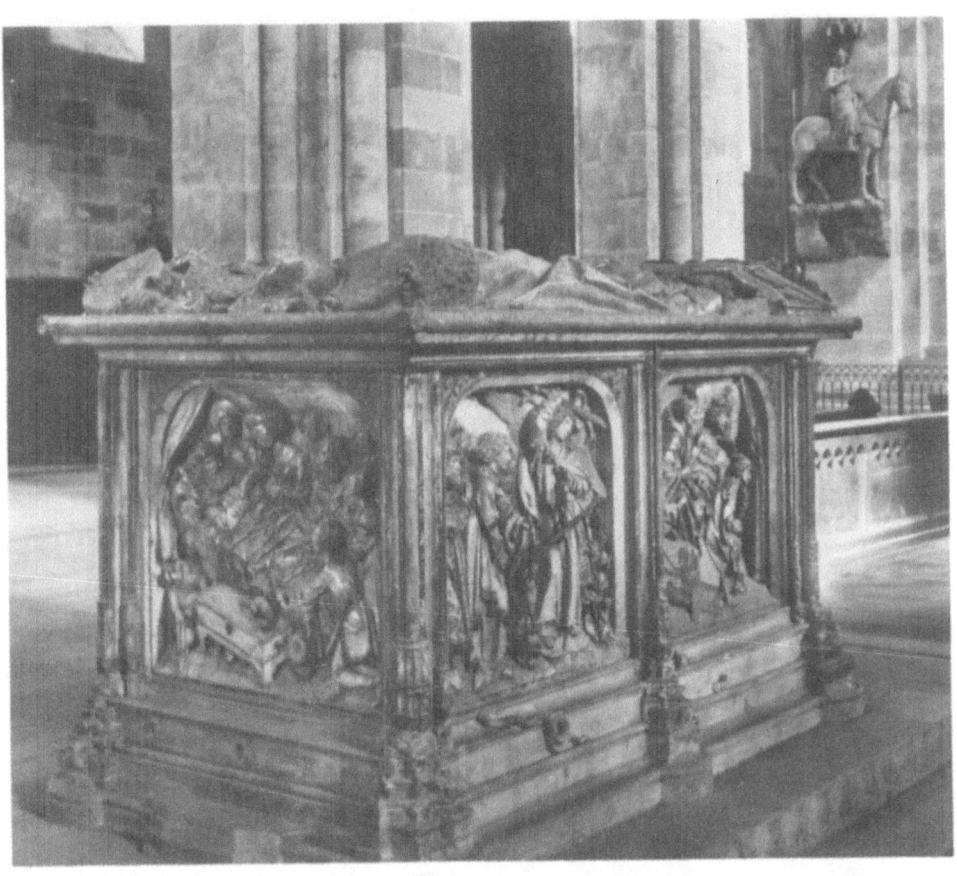

40A. Tomb of Emperor Henry II and Empress Cunegund. 1499–1513. Solnhofen limestone and sandstone. Bamberg Cathedral.

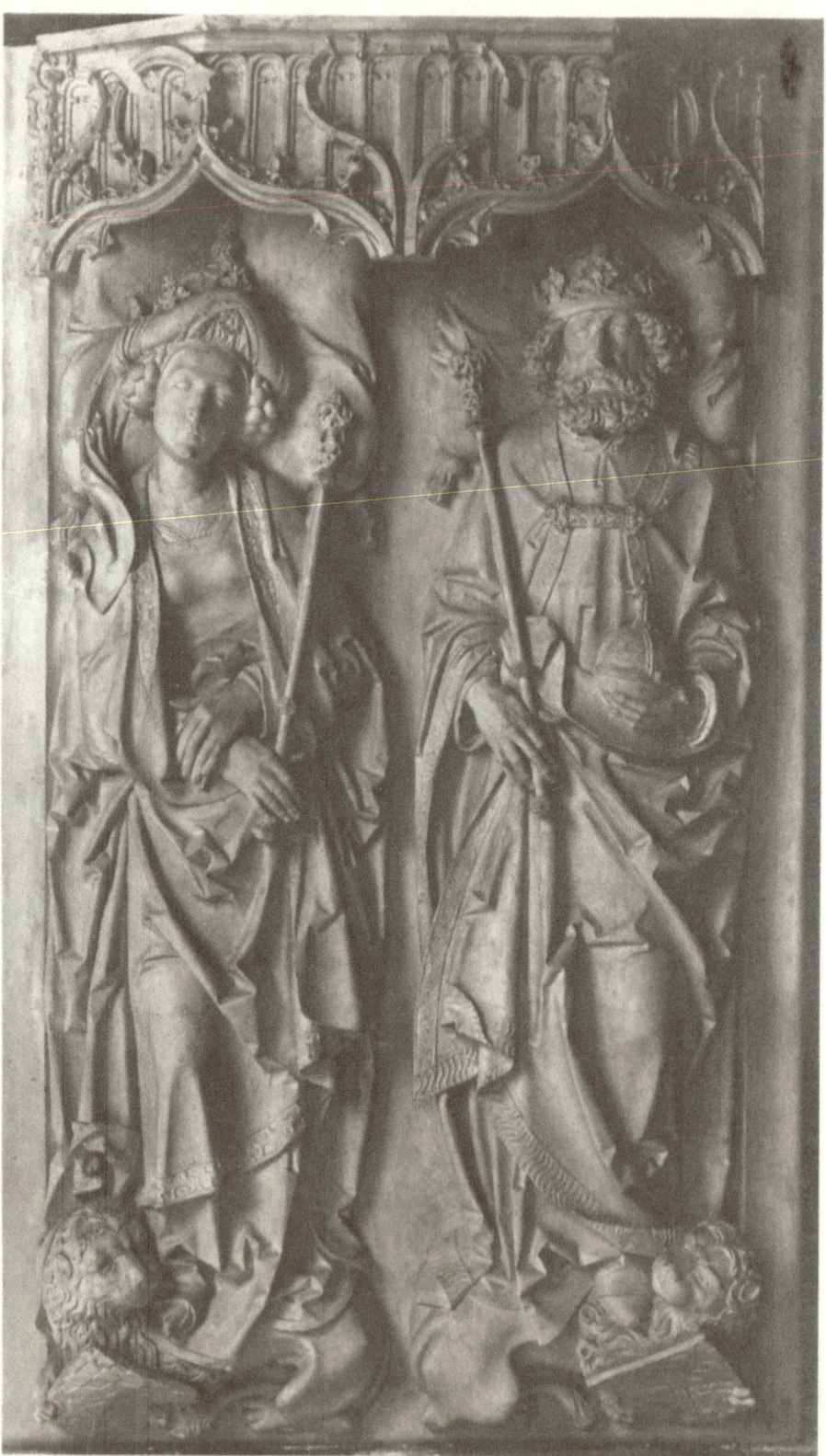

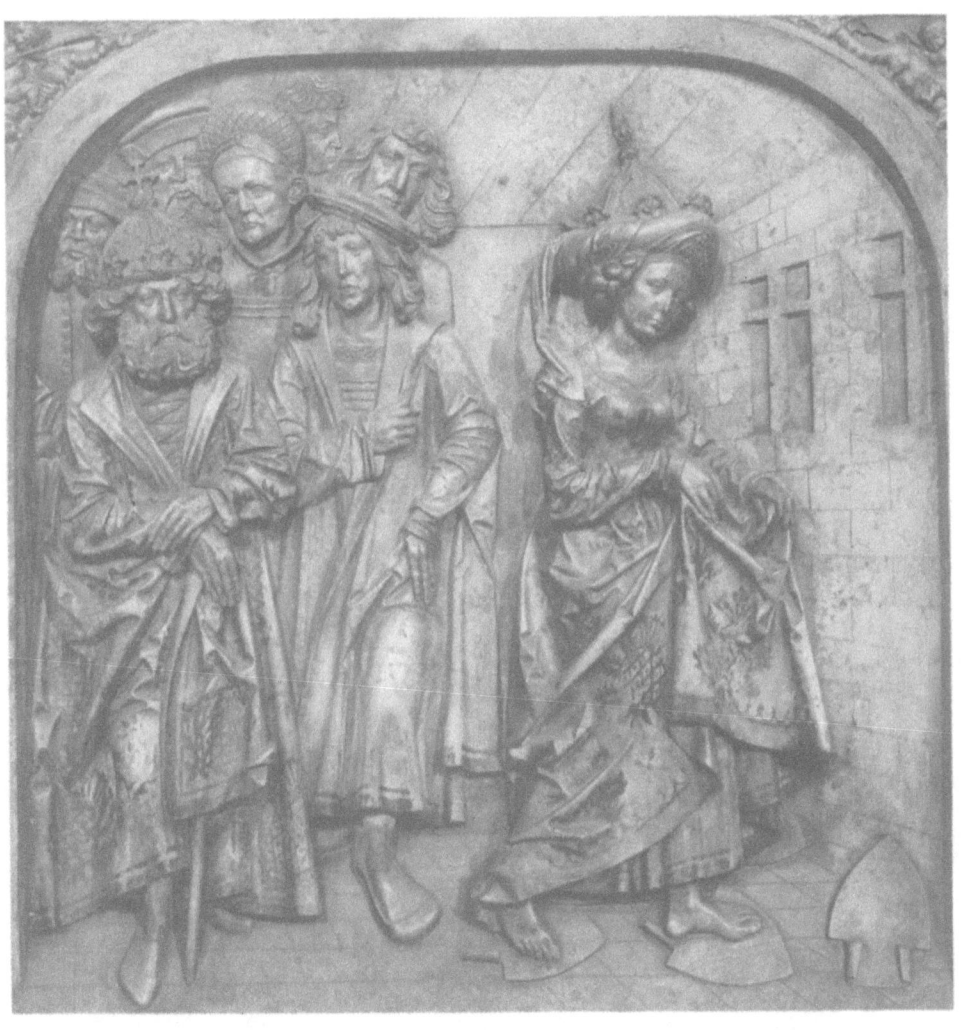

Opposite: **40B.** Emperor Henry II and Empress Cunegund. On the lid of their tomb in Bamberg Cathedral. *Above:* **40C.** Cunegund's Ordeal by Fire. Relief on the tomb of Emperor Henry II and Empress Cunegund. About 1501–1502.

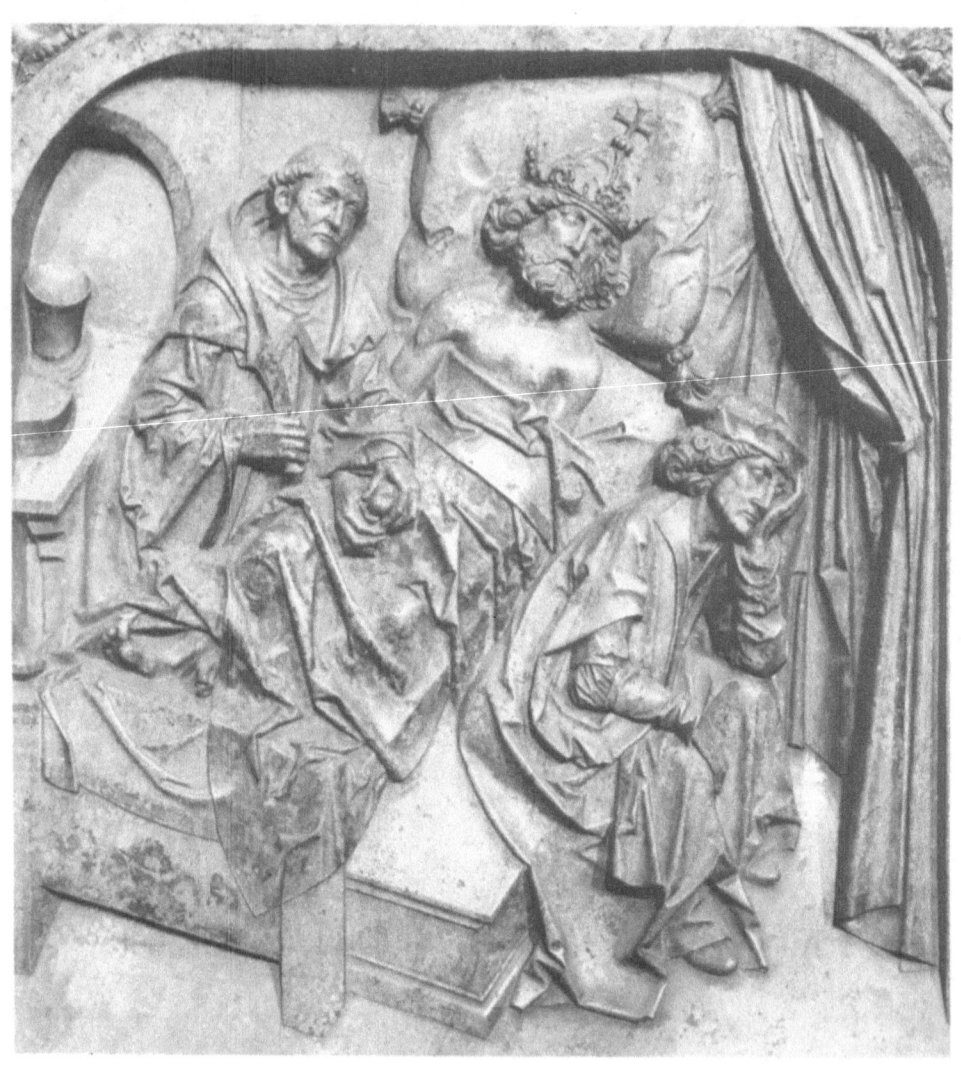

40D. The Removal of the Stone. Relief on the tomb of Emperor Henry II and Empress Cunegund. About 1505–1510.

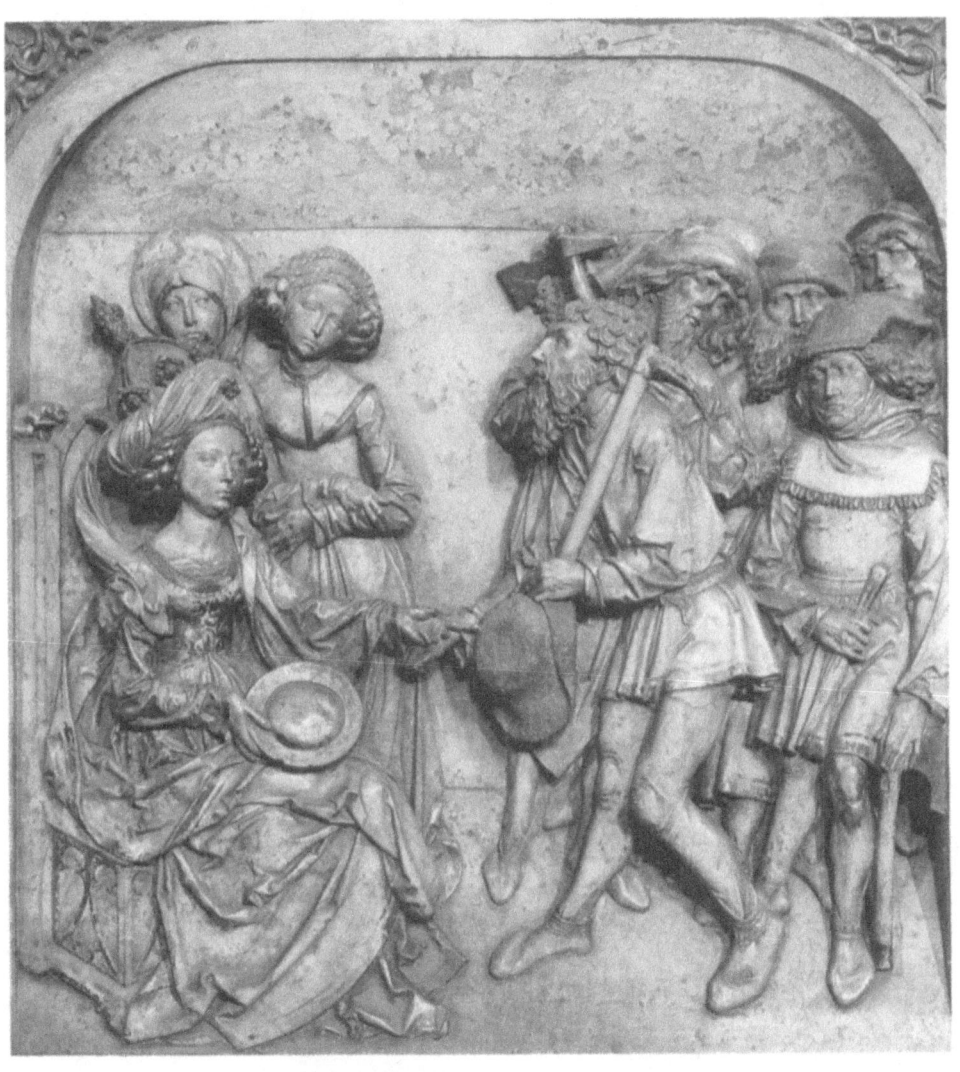

40E. The Miracle of the Crystal Bowl. Relief on the tomb of Emperor Henry II and Empress Cunegund. About 1505–1510.

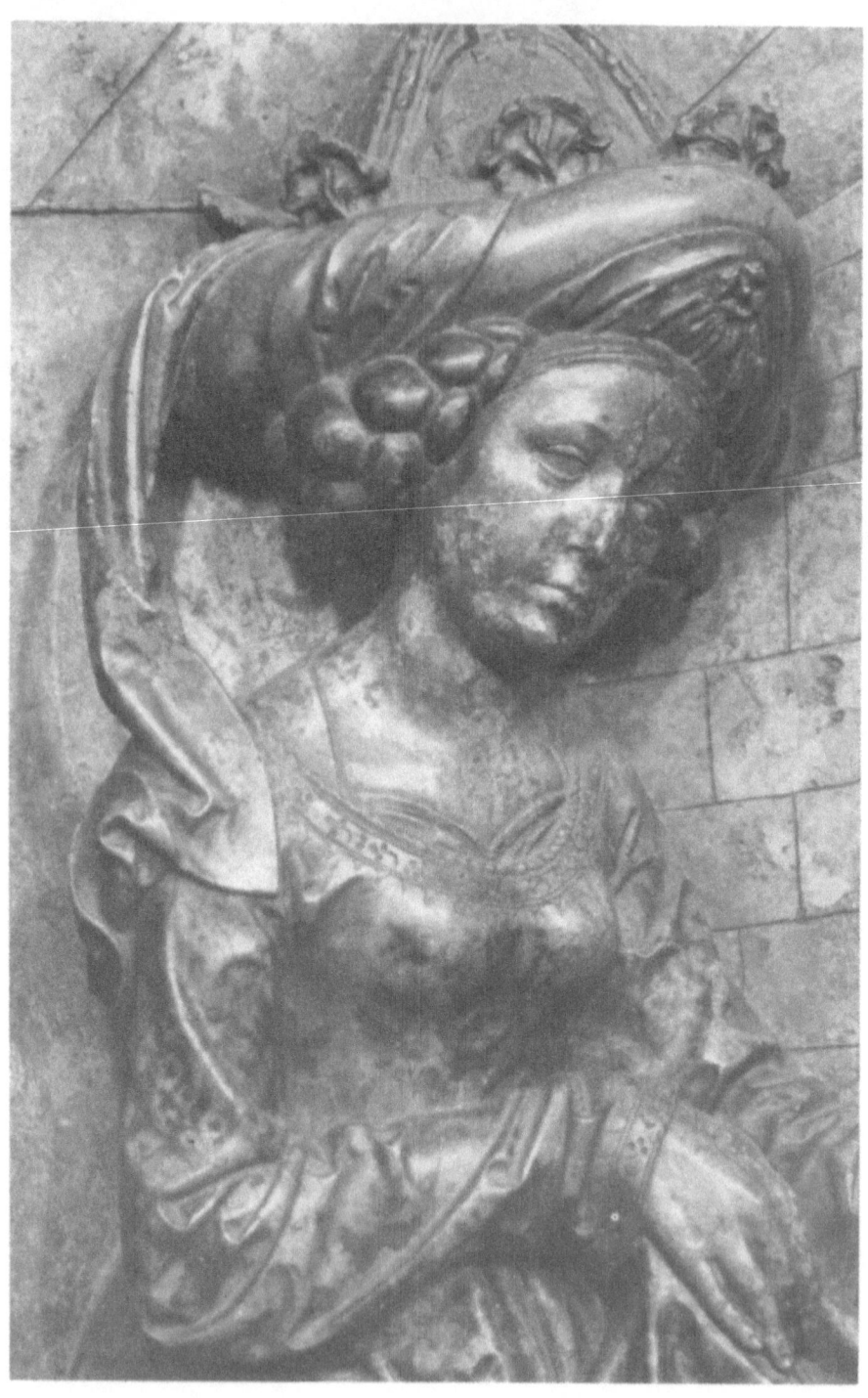

40F. Empress Cunegund, detail of Cunegund's Ordeal by Fire (Plate 40C).

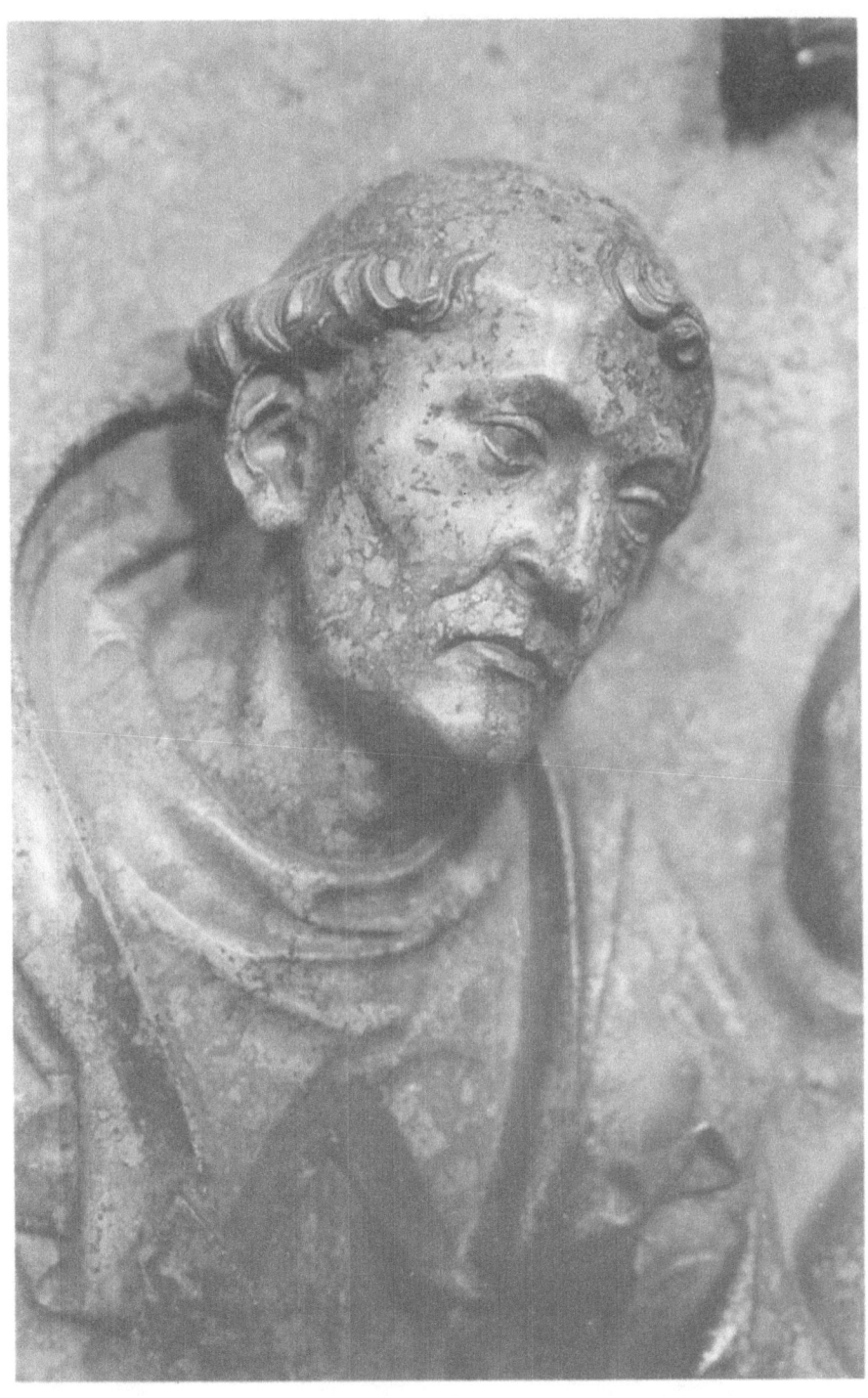

40G. St. Benedict as healer, detail of The Removal of the Stone (Plate 40D).

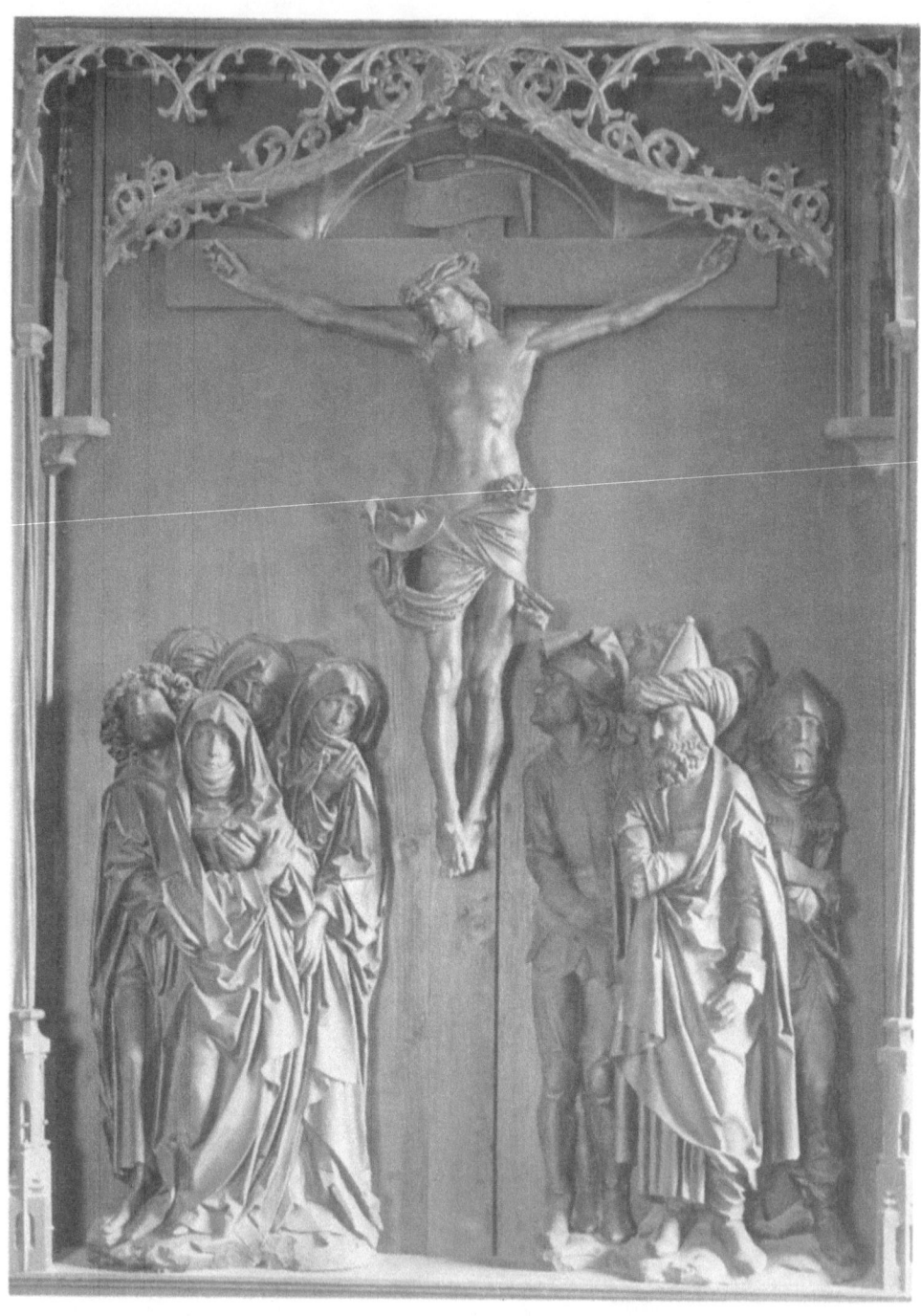

41A. The Crucifixion. Shrine of the altarpiece from the former Michaelskapelle in Rothenburg. About 1512–1513. Lindenwood. Village Church, Dettwang. *Opposite:* 41B. Group surrounding Mary, detail of the Dettwang Crucifixion.

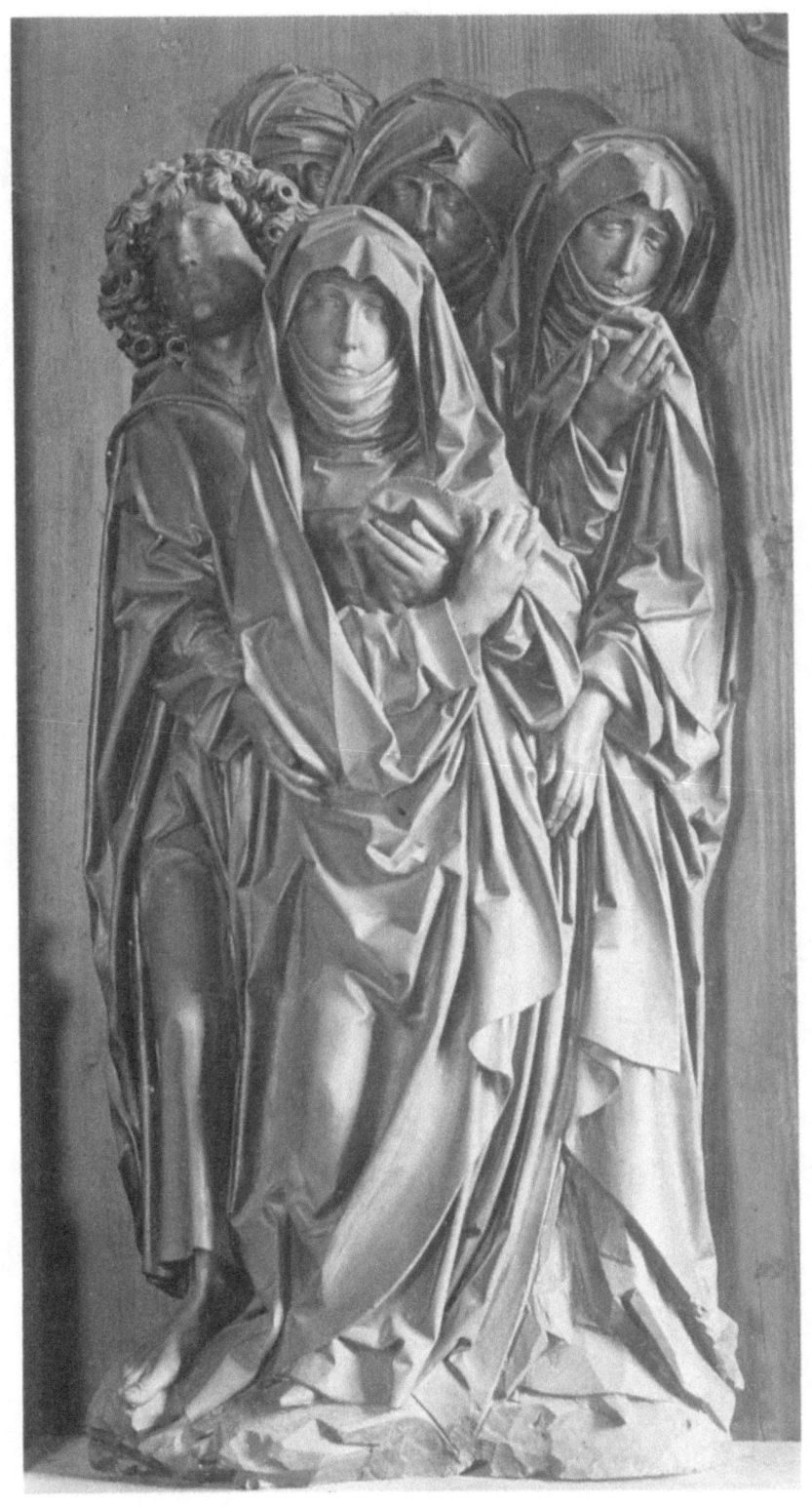

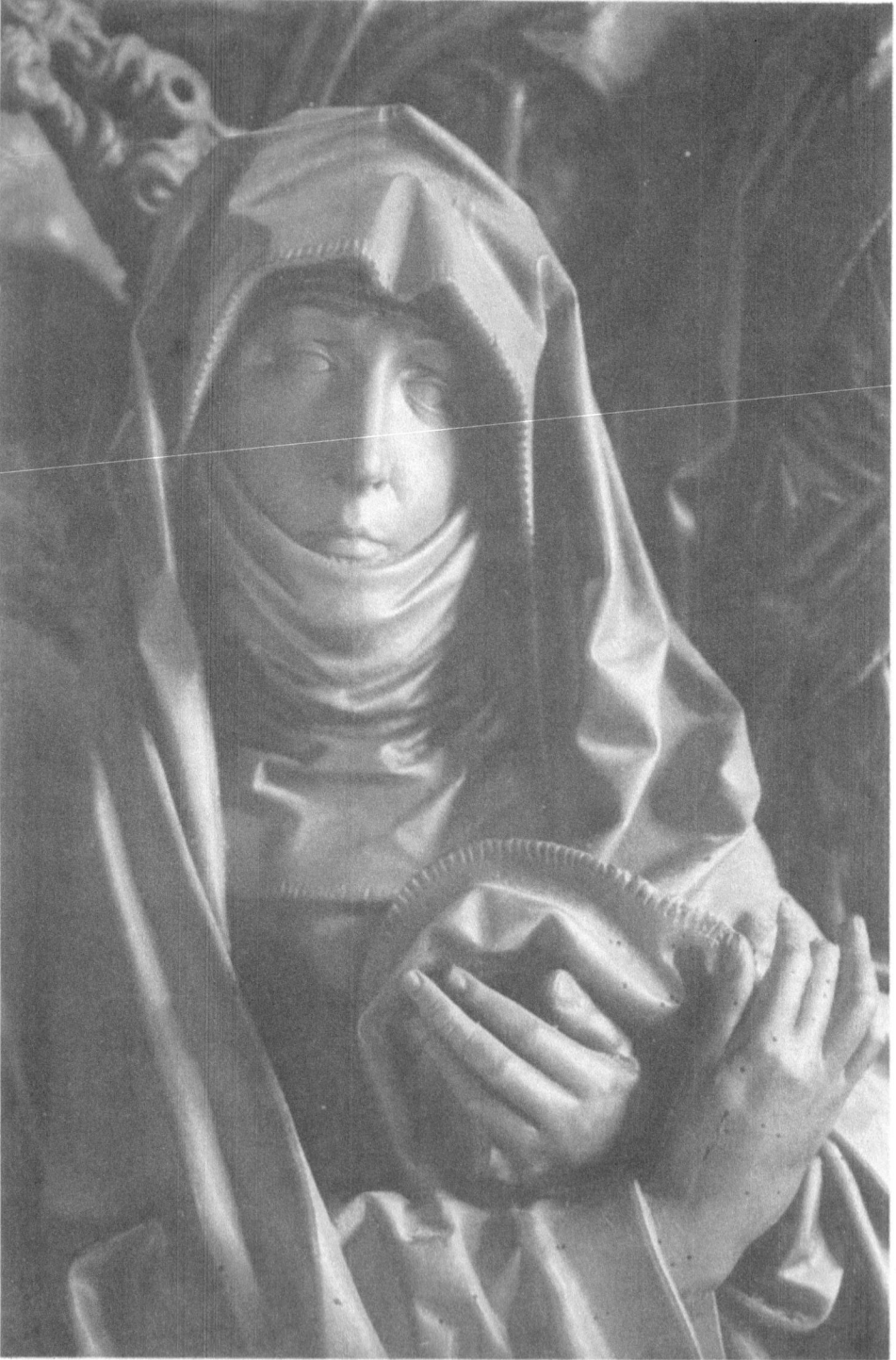

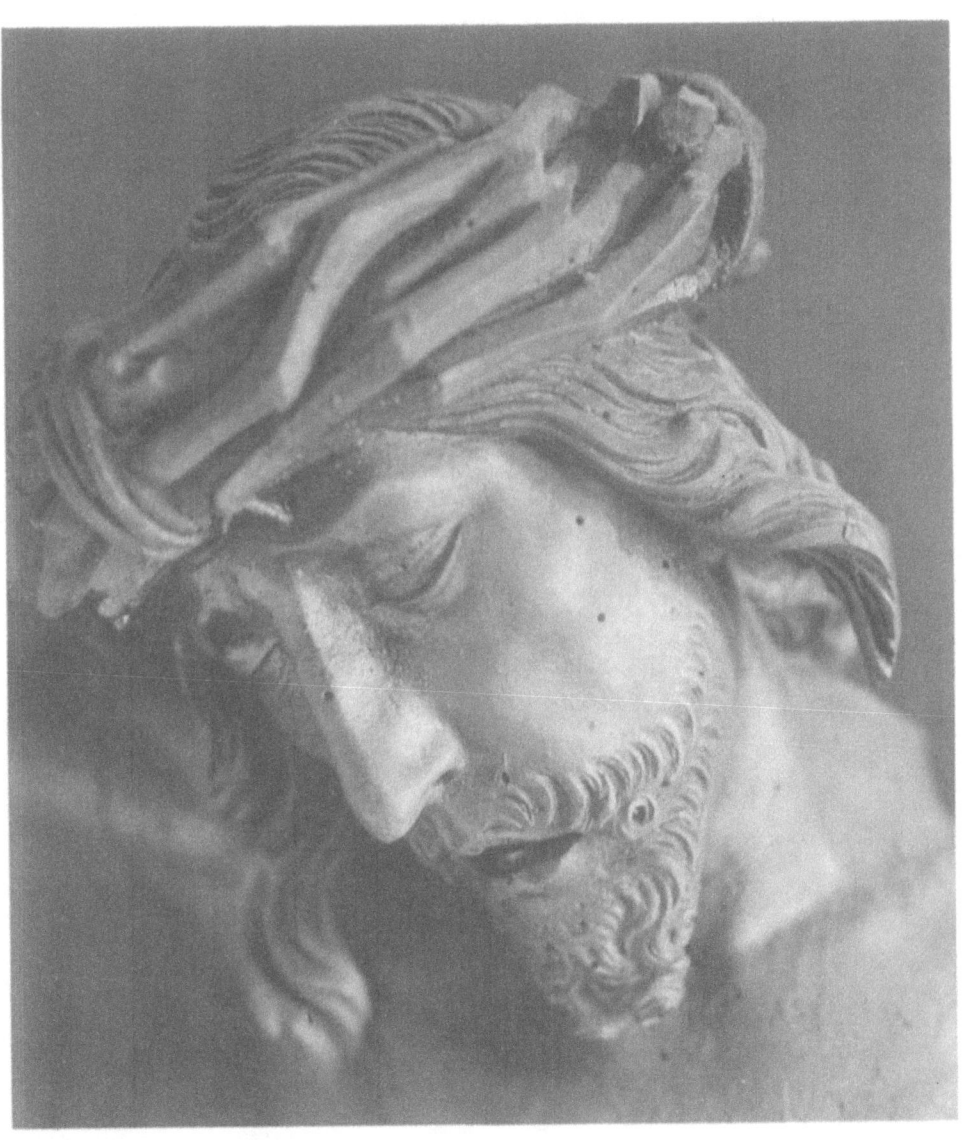

Two details of the Dettwang Crucifixion. *Above:* 41D. Head of Christ. *Opposite:* 41C. The grieving Mary.

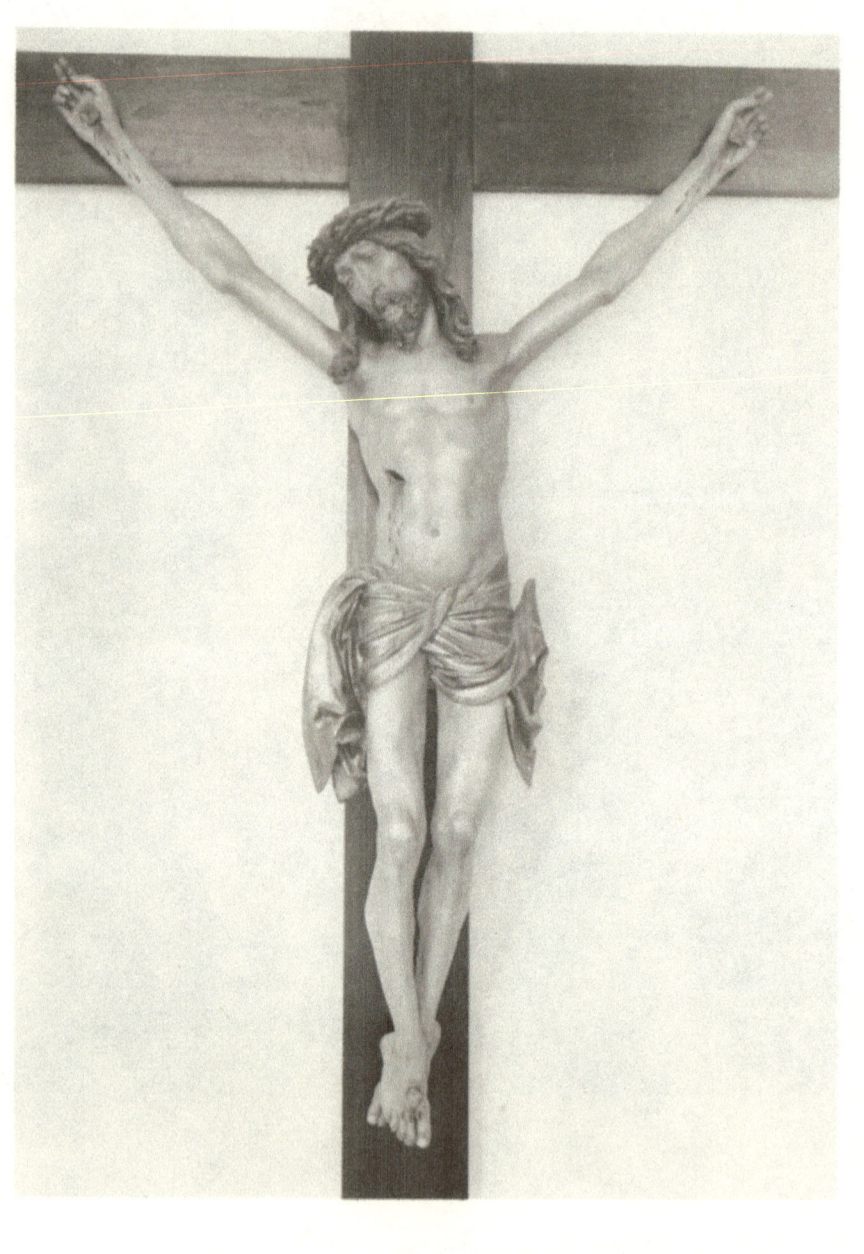

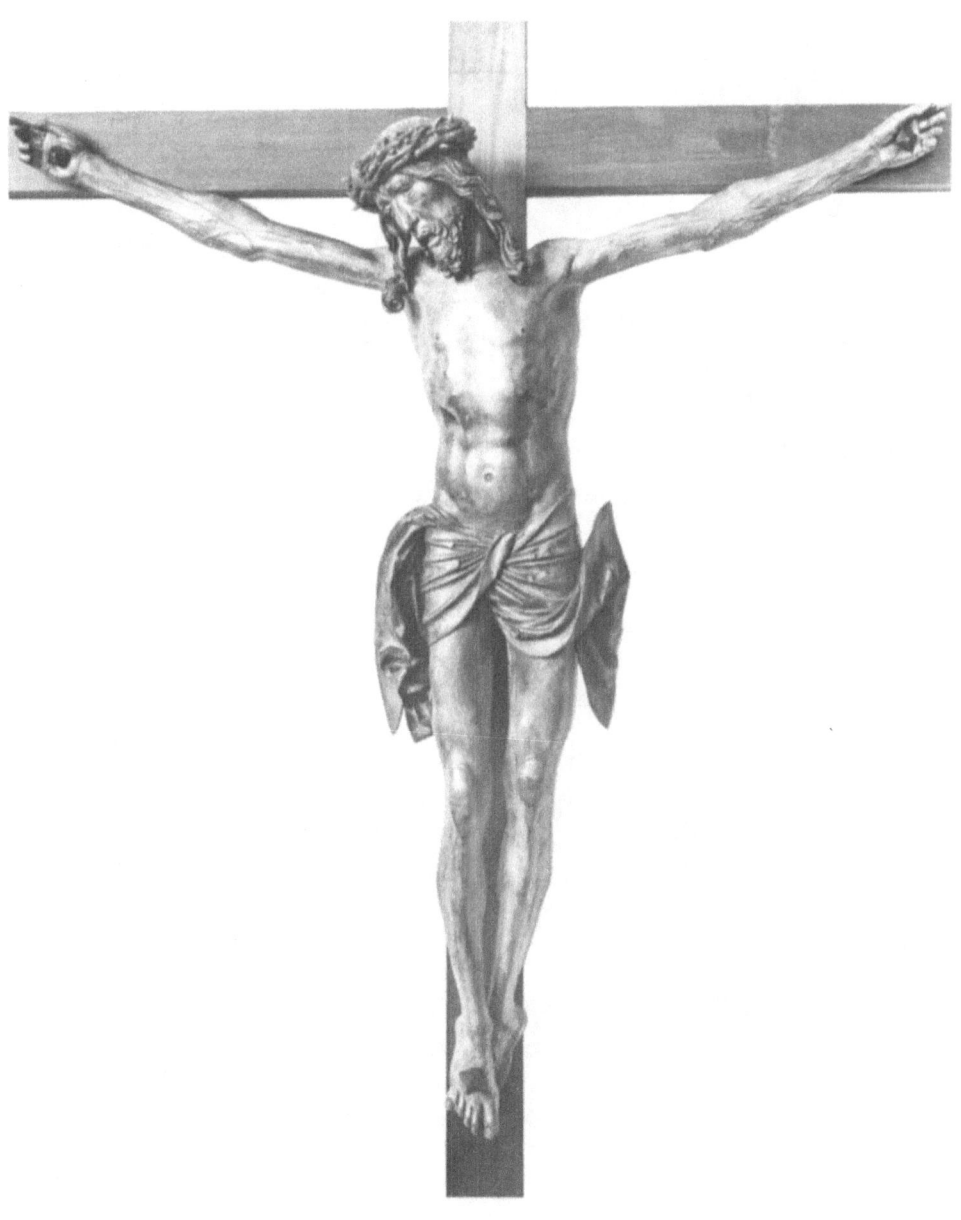

Opposite: 42A. Christ on the Cross. 1516. Lindenwood. Parish Church, Steinach an der Saale.
Before restoration. *Above:* 42B. Christ on the Cross, Steinach, after restoration.

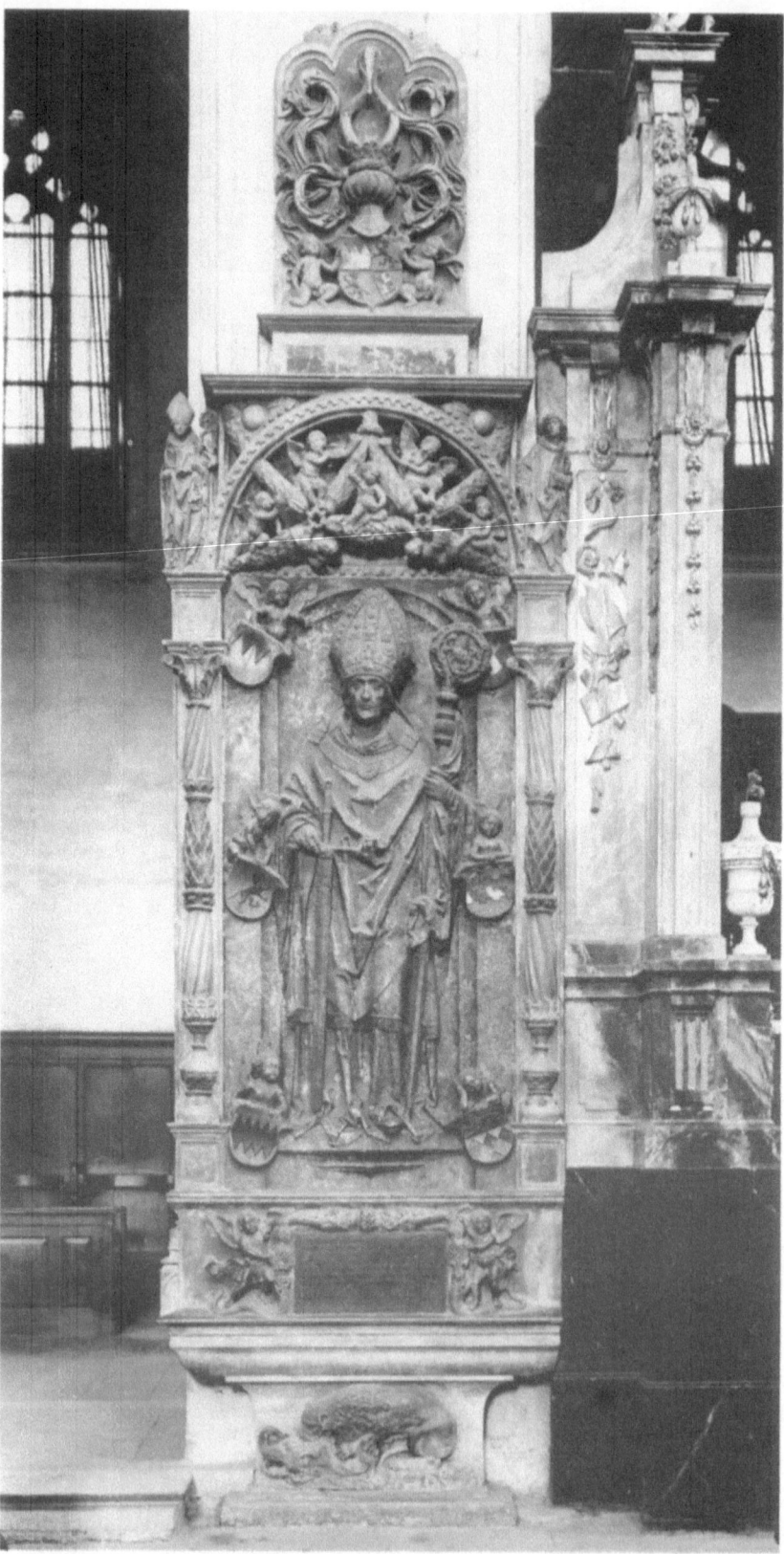

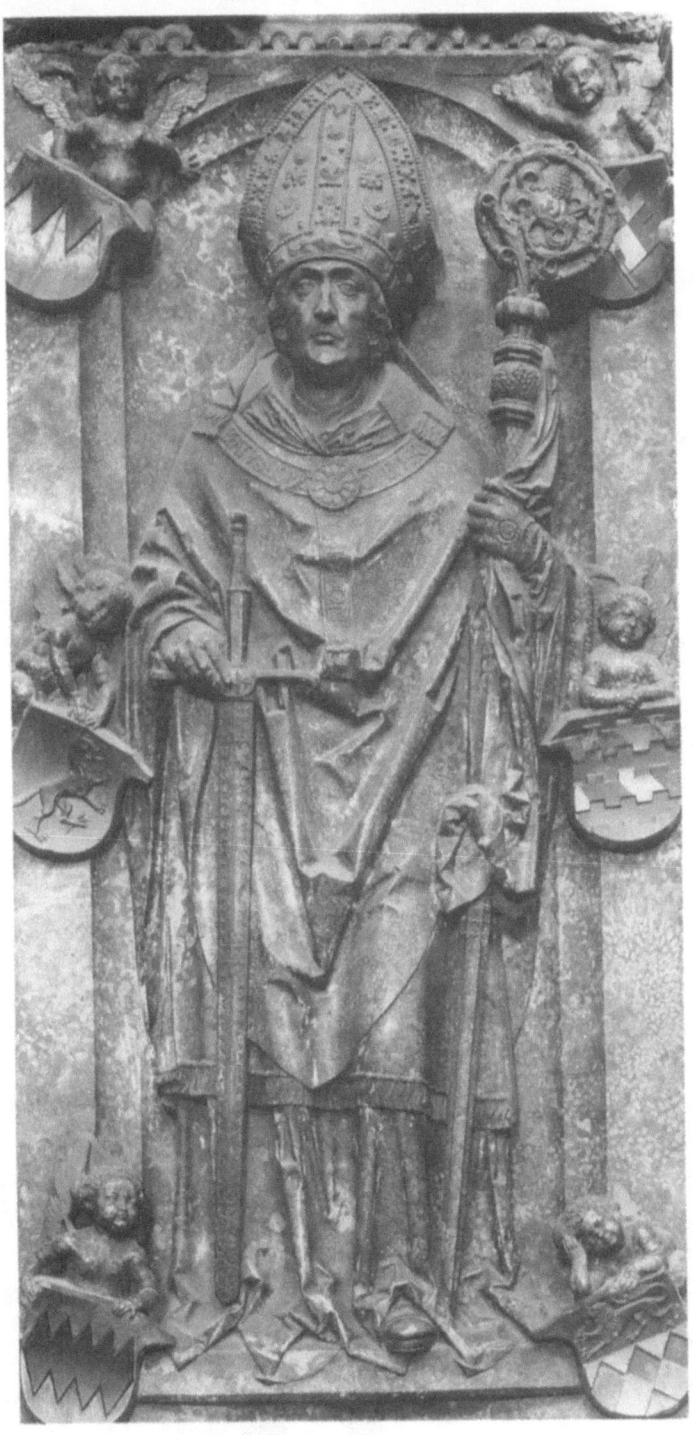

Opposite: 43A. Tomb-monument of Lorenz von Bibra (d. 1519).
About 1518–1522. Sandstone and marble. Würzburg Cathedral.
Above: 43B. Central section (marble slab).

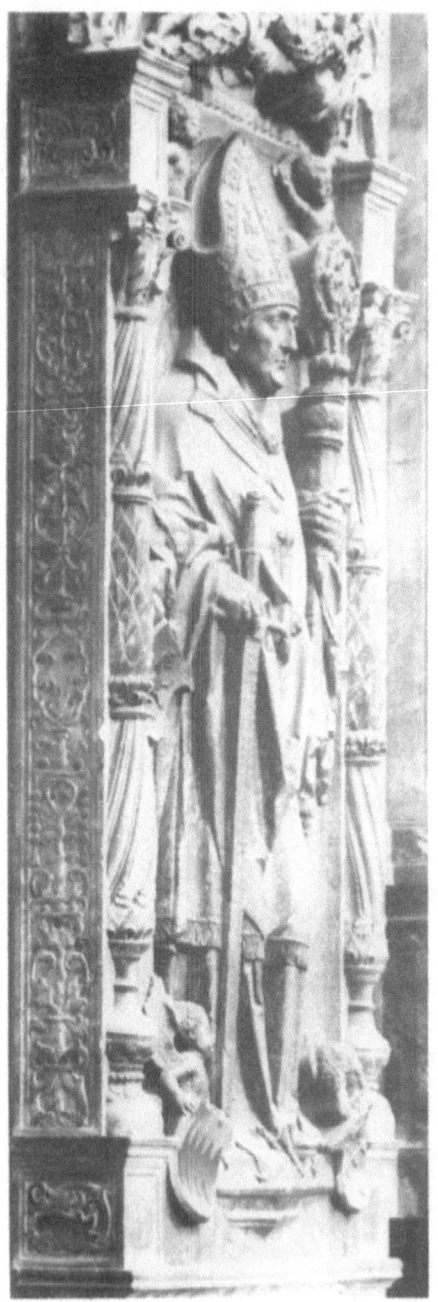

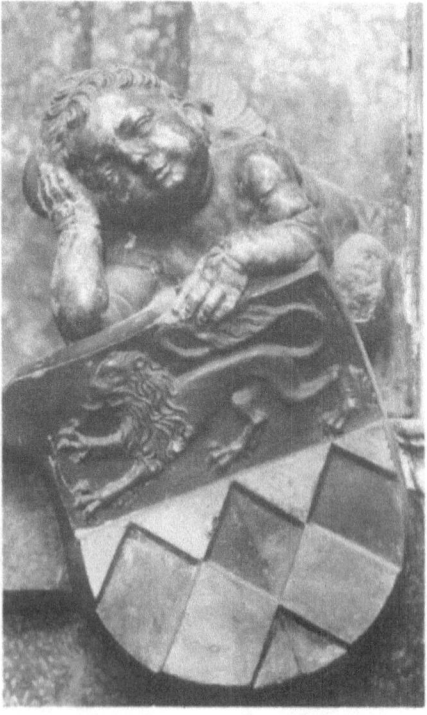

Left: 43C. Side view of the Tomb-monument of Lorenz von Bibra, showing frame with Gothic and Renaissance motifs. *Below:* 43D. Putto holding coat of arms, detail of the Tomb-monument of Lorenz von Bibra.

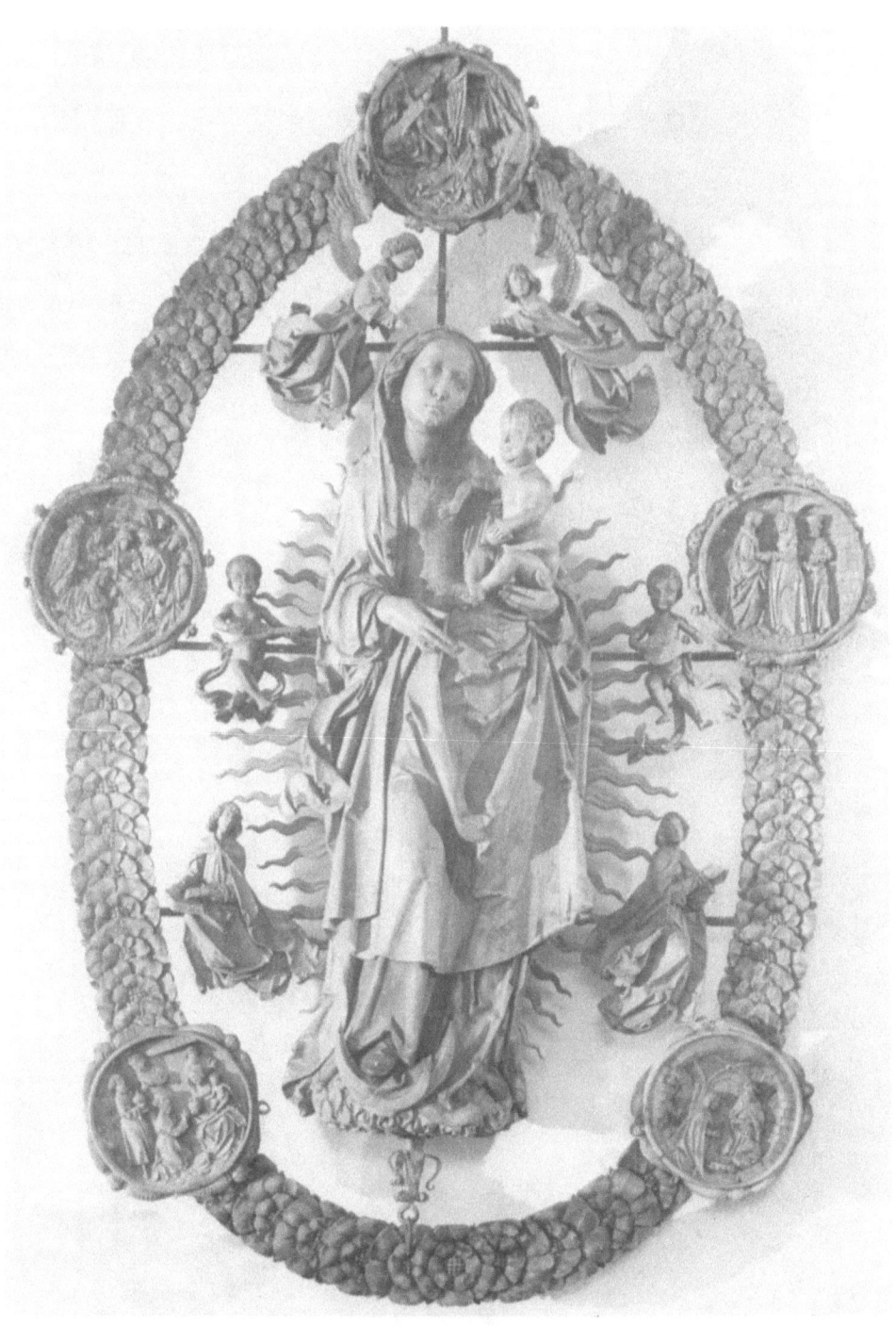

44. The Virgin and Christ Child in a Rosary. 1521–1522. Lindenwood. Pilgrimage Church, Kirchberg bei Volkach. After restoration.

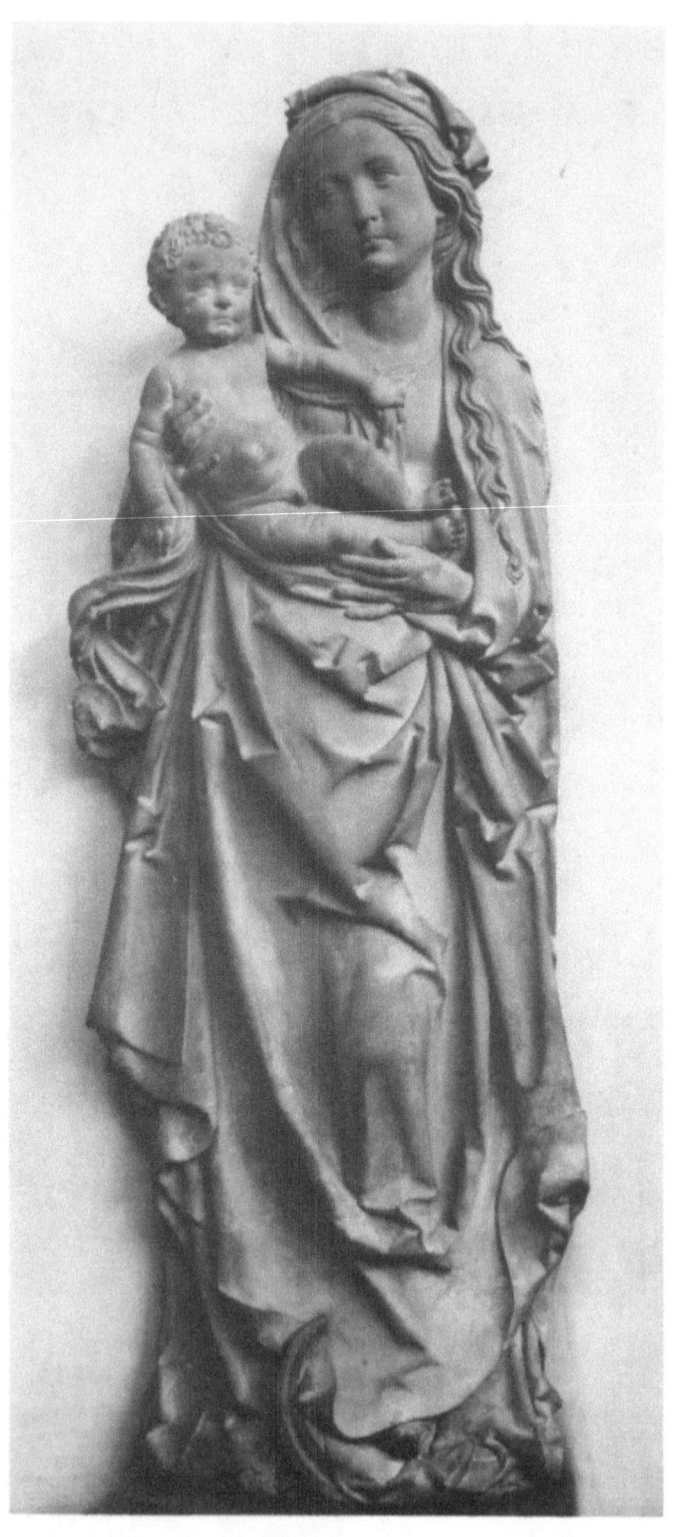

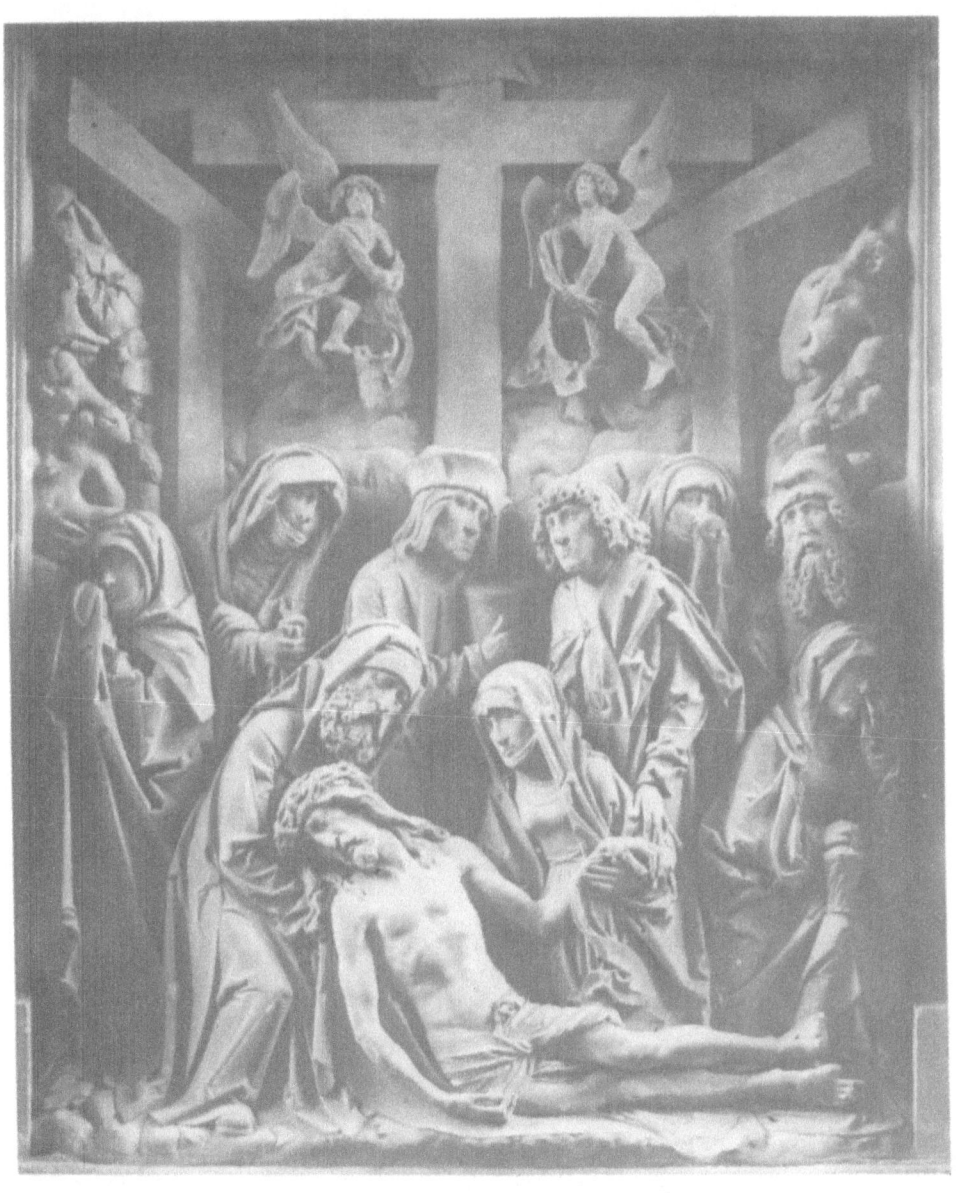

Above: 46A. Lamentation for Christ. 1519–1523. Sandstone. Parish Church, Maidbronn.

Opposite: 45. The Virgin with the Christ Child. From a canon's residence in Würzburg. 1516–1522. Sandstone. Liebieghaus, Städelsches Kunstinstitut, Frankfurt am Main.

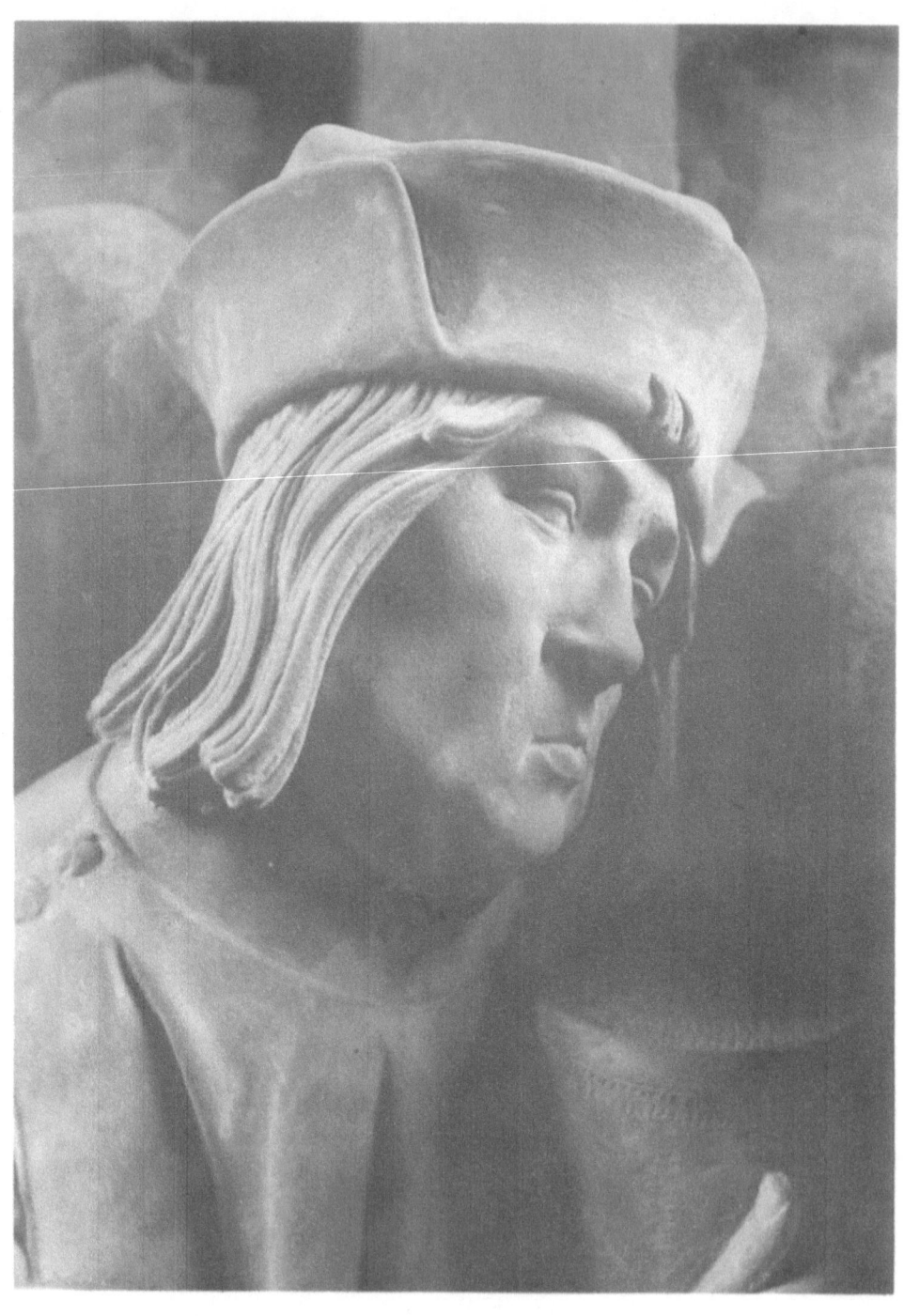

46B. Joseph of Arimathaea (self-portrait of Tilmann Riemenschneider?),
detail of the Maidbronn Lamentation.

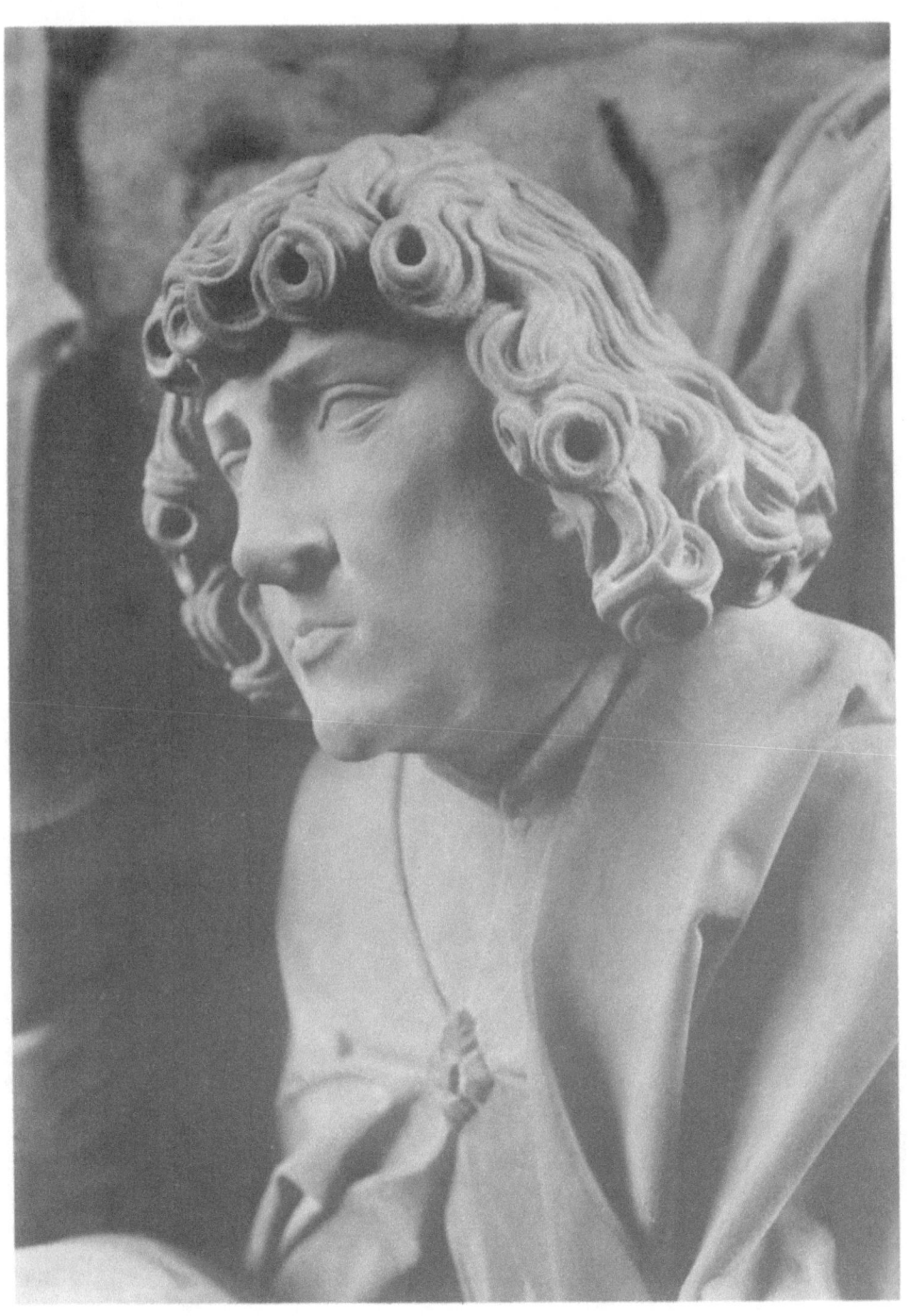

46C. St. John, detail of the Maidbronn Lamentation.

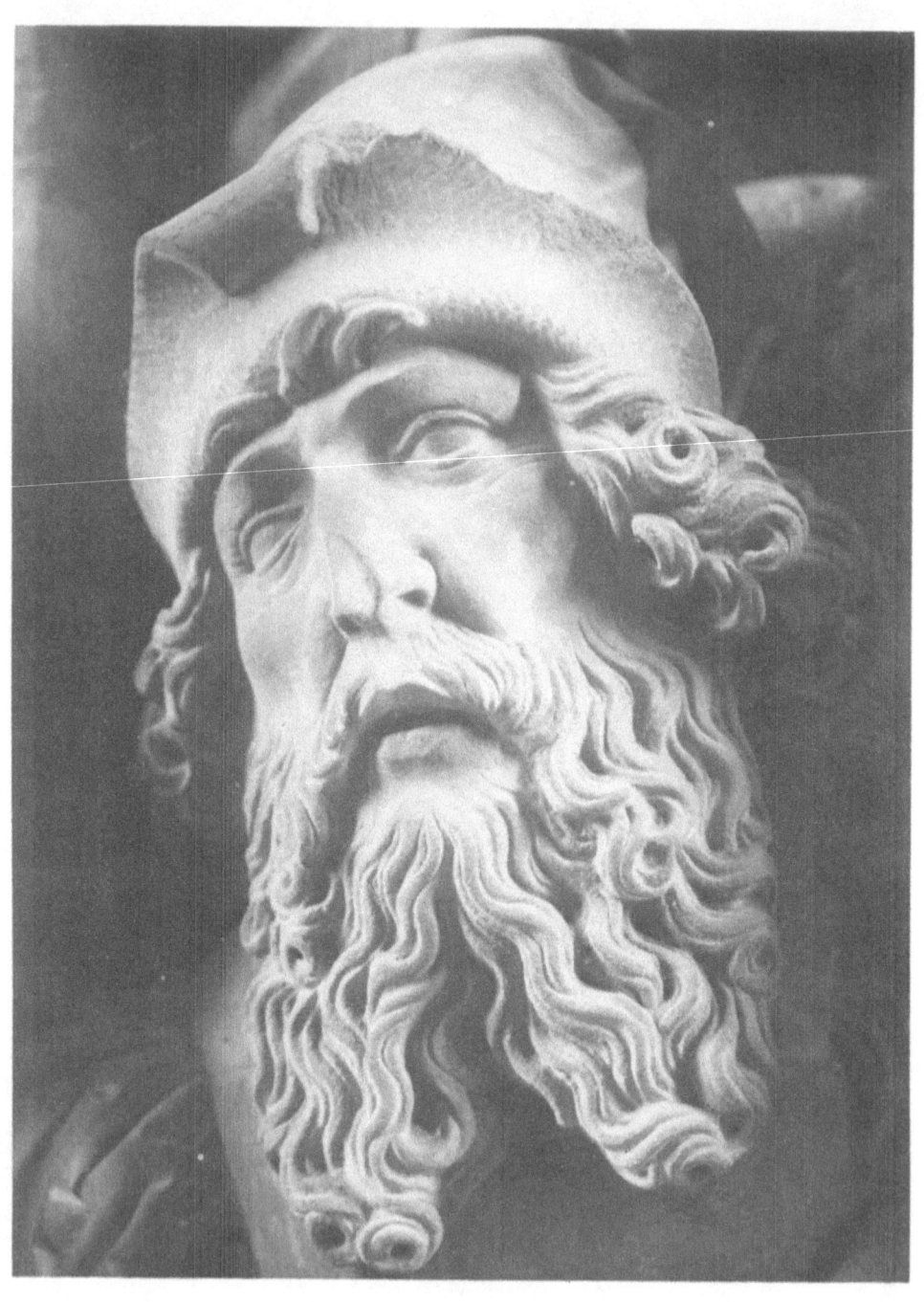

46D. Old man with a beard, detail of the Maidbronn Lamentation.

COMMENTARY ON THE SCULPTURES

Works in Public Collections in the United States and Canada

PLATE 1. **The Virgin with the Christ Child.** About 1490–1492. Museum of Fine Arts, Boston, Massachusetts. Lindenwood. Height 47¼ in. (120 cm).

The slender group of the Virgin and Child in the Boston Museum is an example of Riemenschneider's earliest representations of this theme. Though it is probable in this instance that an assistant helped in the actual carving of the figures, the composition is clearly Riemenschneider's own and the work was undoubtedly created under his supervision. The theme of the Virgin with the Christ Child occupied Riemenschneider through most of his working life, evolving gradually over the four decades from the early 1490s to the end of the 1520s. The Boston figures illustrate some of the special features of mood, composition, and style that distinguish the earlier renditions, particularly those of the early 1490s. Since the loss of the Werbach and Himmelstein Madonnas in World War II, the work has a special significance as one of the few surviving Madonnas from these years.

The Virgin in the Boston group stands tall and straight and with her head held erect, looking out towards the viewer. The pose here is similar to that of the Lawrence, Kansas, Madonna (Plates 3A, B), a figure dated a little later, at the end of the 1490s, though still from Riemenschneider's early period. In spite of the bulk of the drapery where it falls below the arms of the Virgin, the figure appears particularly slender and upright. The relatively high crown that Mary wears of course intensifies the impression of height and slenderness in the figure, as does the rather contrived narrowing of the drapery around the feet of the Virgin so that it is almost totally encompassed by the sickle-shaped moon on which Mary rests one foot. It is in fact possible that the particularly upright stance of the figure was necessitated by the use of the crown. Like the regal, statuesque bearing of Mary, the crown and the unusually large sickle moon make it clear that Mary appears here in her symbolic role as Queen of Heaven.

There are relatively few instances of Madonnas with crowns by Riemenschneider, and among these the Boston figure stands out in its prominent display of both the crown and the sickle moon. The only other figure that is close in this respect is the Virgin and Child in the Neumünster collegiate church in Würzburg. This again is an early work, important because it bears the date 1493 on its base and is the only definitely-dated statue of this subject from this period. Though the lifeless execution of the figure means that it must have been carved by an assistant, the composition is undoubtedly Riemenschneider's own, and in its general outline and the design of these particular features it is closely related to the Boston statue.

The arrangement of the drapery in the Boston Madonna is repeated more or less identically in the Neumünster group. In both these figures the mantle of the Virgin is drawn up on either side, and has the complication of a reversed lateral fold running from the Virgin's right shoulder diagonally down and over her left hip. With some variation, these motifs occur also in another early work, the Himmelstein Madonna of about 1493 (unfortunately destroyed by fire in 1945), and in several later works, including some from the mature period, notably the sandstone Virgin and Child of about 1505 in the Mainfränkisches Museum in Würzburg (Plates 28A, B).

Like the figure of Mary, the Christ Child in the Boston group (in a seemingly unique instance among the early renditions) is shown in a fully frontal position, looking directly out to the viewer. The small figure appears rather sedate despite the playful action of the Child's right hand clasping his left foot. This is a gesture Riemenschneider borrowed from the mid-fifteenth century Madonna on the central pier of the western portal of the Marienkapelle in Würzburg, and in a slightly different form the same motif appears in the Neumünster group. In a lesser degree, the conflicting nature of the Boston figure recalls the Christ Child of the Anna Selbdritt group of about 1502–1504 in the Walters Art Gallery in Baltimore (Plate 5B). The expression in the face and eyes of the Boston Child is greater and livelier, but in both cases the symbolic character predominates. Much the same contrast appears also in a work considered by the author to be Riemenschneider's earliest representation of the Virgin with the Christ Child, the Madonna from Werbach im Taubertal, of about 1490 (Plate 19). (This statue was also destroyed in 1945.) There, while the Child's right hand is raised in blessing and his head looks up, the rest of the small figure assumes a relatively natural, playful attitude.

The intimate gesture of Mary's right hand lightly holding the foot of the Child that is seen in the Boston figures also appears in the Werbach and Neumünster groups. In the Boston group, however, this informal gesture contrasts markedly with the Virgin's otherwise rather stiff stance and detached demeanor. In later renditions of the Virgin and Child, as for example the stone Madonna of about 1505 (Plates 28A, B), we find a much more tender and intimate attitude in the figures, with the emphasis on their relation-ship to each other rather than their symbolic relationship to the viewer.

The compositional similarities noted with other early figures of the Vir-gin and Child all point to a date in the first years of the 1490s. Stylistic fea-tures indicate the same period. The clear articulation of the often intricate forms, the distinct planes and rhythms and strong tactile and linear qualities of the work are all characteristics of Riemenschneider's style in the years up to 1503. Compared to the Werbach Madonna of about 1490, the greater ar-ticulation in the drapery of the Boston figure, together with the fact that the richly moving folds are arranged more on one plane, suggests that the Bos-ton group was created a little later. The group can in fact quite definitely be assigned a more precise date of about 1490–1492 on the grounds of the Vir-gin's strong resemblance in facial features and style of hair to the Mary Mag-dalene of that date from the Münnerstadt Altarpiece (Plates 20A, B) and, to a lesser degree, the figure of Eve from the Marienkapelle in Würzburg, com-pleted in 1493 (Plates 21B, D). The Boston Virgin has the same smooth oval face as these early figures, in distinct contrast to the more angular, more ar-ticulated faces of figures from around the end of that decade, such as the Kansas Madonna or the image of Empress Cunegund on the lid of the Bam-berg imperial tomb (Plate 40B).

The work was given to the Boston Museum of Fine Arts in 1941 by the widow of the late Felix M. Warburg of New York, in memory of her hus-band. The group had previously been in the Warburg collection in Ham-burg, Germany. Its earlier provenance is unknown.

Note: One other workshop figure representing Mary with the Christ Child, prob-ably also from the early 1490s, is now in the Detroit Institute of Arts. It is not in the scope of this survey, however, to include all workshop pieces in which Riemen-schneider had a hand in the finishing.

PLATES 2A-C. **The Three Helpers in Need.** 1494.
Cloisters Collection, Metropolitan Museum of Art, New York, New York.
Lindenwood. Height 21 in. (53.4 cm).

This finely-wrought group of three Helper Saints was only recently identi-fied as a work by Riemenschneider's own hand. The carving was discovered in a private English collection in 1952. A tentative attribution to Riemen-schneider on stylistic grounds was subsequently authenticated, and the work, which was at first unknown in regard to the master's oeuvre, was identified as a unique fragment of a 1494 commission thought to be totally lost. The group was acquired by the Metropolitan Museum of Art, for the Cloisters Collection, in 1961; it was first published by this author in 1963.

The figures of this fragment are easily recognized by their attributes, dress, and stance. They represent St. Christopher, St. Eustace, and St. Erasmus, three of the fourteen so-called "Helpers in Need." The twelve original Helpers (in addition to these three, George, Blaise, Pantaleon, Vitus, Acacius, Giles, Margaret, Barbara, and Catherine of Alexandria) were almost all martyr saints who were believed to have special powers of protection and intercession. Later, St. Dionysius (or Denis) and St. Cyriacus were included. The saint as intercessor and protector was of course a vital belief all through the Middle Ages. This particular association of the Fourteen Helper Saints had been a subject for art since the beginning of the fifteenth century, but reached its greatest popularity after 1446, when a shepherd named Hermann Leicht, from the Cistercian monastery of Langheim in Upper Franconia, reported seeing a vision of the saints asking to have a chapel built there in their honor. The famous Rococo church of Vierzehnheiligen (Fourteen Saints) by Balthasar Neumann now stands on this site.

The figure of St. Christopher is Riemenschneider's only known treatment of this patron saint of travelers and protector against accidents. He is ingeniously portrayed here in the act of wading ashore from a stream, helped by his gnarled but staunch staff. His left foot is already on firm ground while the right is still immersed in the swirling waters. His back is bent beneath the weight of the Christ Child he carries on his shoulders, and his face, which looks away from the companion figures in the group, shows both the strain of his labors and a sense of unease and mystification. Stance and expression alike imply a burden much greater than that he actually supports. This portrayal, which is a customary representation of the saint, relates to the incident in the legend of Christopher connected with his name, "Christophoros," meaning bearer of Christ. In his search for the most powerful master to serve, he became a convert to Christianity and was given the task of carrying travelers across a dangerous river. On one occasion, unknowingly, he bore the Christ Child on his shoulders, whose weight half-way over became such an immense burden that he barely succeeded in his task. Only after the crossing did the Christ Child reveal who he was. A confirmed believer thereafter, Christopher was martyred not long after this. The head and right arm of the Riemenschneider Christ Child are missing, following the recent removal of eighteenth-century restorations. It is probable that the Child's right hand was raised in a gesture of blessing. Also, the orb which he holds in his left hand would originally have had a small cross surmounting it.

Christopher's head is turned attentively to one side as if he were listening to the Christ Child's instructions.

Certain features of this figure are particularly characteristic of Riemenschneider's work. The bearded, expressive face of the saint is a type that appears frequently in his portraits of the Apostles, as for example in the figures of the Last Supper group in the Rothenburg Altarpiece of the Holy Blood (Plate 23B). Christopher also wears the same simple garments that many of the Apostles wear: a belted coat, buttoned in front, partly covered by a plain mantle which is thrown over the shoulders and gathered in rich folds. The same kind of slender, realistic hands, in which even the veins are carved, also occur in many works. Like the intense faces, these hands are a virtual hallmark of Riemenschneider's style.

Contrasting with the strained figure and face of St. Christopher is the stoic, resolute image of St. Erasmus at the other end of the group. Reputedly a bishop in Syria in the third century, he is shown in his bishop's robes, wearing gloves and rings on both hands. In his left hand he holds all that remains of his crozier—part of the staff and the sudarium—while the fragment in his right hand is almost certainly part of his attribute, the spindle (or windlass). This really was a misinterpretation of Erasmus's original emblem as the patron saint of sailors, which was a capstan with a cable coiled around. In inland areas this image was confused with the instrument of his supposed martyrdom by disembowelment and accordingly rendered as a spindle with entrails coiled round it. The loss of the spindle here may have been accidental, or, if the image was offensive to some previous owner, it may have been deliberately removed.

Another statue of St. Erasmus, which Riemenschneider made for a church in Kitzingen, is now in the Staatliche Museen in West Berlin. There are several other bishop-figures by Riemenschneider in existence, including the bust of St. Burchard, the first bishop of Würzburg, now in the National Gallery in Washington, D.C. (Plates 15A, B). The Erasmus of the Three Helpers group, however, is a more venerable figure than either of those two. In certain details of his costume and particularly in his expression of brooding concentration he bears a close resemblance to the effigy of the aged Prince-Bishop Rudolf von Scherenberg on the latter's tomb-monument of 1496–1499 in Würzburg Cathedral (Plate 22B). The two works were presumably carved within a few years of each other, and in this figure of Erasmus Riemenschneider seems almost to have given us a younger version of the old prelate. (The face of Scherenberg, it is worth noting, may be considered the prototype for most of Riemenschneider's depictions of old age.)

The middle figure of the group represents St. Eustace. He stands slightly behind the other two and is distinguished by his elegant attire and noble bearing. The legend of St. Eustace is as remarkable as those of his companions. He is reputed to have been a Roman general under Emperor Trajan who was converted to Christianity after seeing a vision of a stag with the figure of Christ on the Cross between its antlers, while out hunting one day. His conversion brought great suffering to his family, and ultimately all were imprisoned in a bronze bull and roasted to death. Eustace appears here as an aristocratic young knight. The gauntlet and breastplate he wears are of the kind used in Riemenschneider's time and are seen again in the tomb-monuments for the knights Eberhard von Grumbach (about 1488) and Konrad von Schaumberg (after 1502) (Plates 17, 25B). The cuffed leggings with pointed toe (which along with the tunic-like garment and hat are rather oddly combined with the armor) are also late Gothic in fashion. The hat, with its large, fluted, up-turned brim, was probably borrowed from Flemish art; it appears also in a figure in the early Lamentation altarpiece at Hessenthal. The knight's face, which is again the most fascinating element of the figure, appears withdrawn yet composed. It bears a certain resemblance to the face of Konrad von Schaumberg in his tomb-effigy in the Marienkapelle in Würzburg, and is even closer—especially in the eloquent, melancholy expression about the eyes—to the figure of St. Luke from the predella of the Münnerstadt altarpiece (Plate 20G).

As noted, all the works with which the Three Helpers may be compared are from a relatively early period of Riemenschneider's career. The earliest is the Münnerstadt Altarpiece of 1490–1492, and the latest is The Last Supper from the Rothenburg Altarpiece of the Holy Blood, of 1501–1502. The Three Helpers group shares with these the same sharply linear design, the complexity of interweaving forms, and all the restlessness and motion of late Gothic art in general. On these grounds alone it would be possible to place the New York group in the decade of the 1490s. However, we can also assign to the group the more precise date of 1494 on the grounds of the documentary evidence, now lost but referred to by Carl Becker in his 1849 monograph on Riemenschneider, of a commission for such a group (of all fourteen Helper Saints) given to Riemenschneider in 1494. The group was ordered by Johann von Allendorf, chancellor to Prince-Bishop Rudolf von Scherenberg, for the chapel of a Würzburg hospital he had endowed. Undoubtedly the fragment of the Three Helpers formed part of this commission. In the late eighteenth century the Gothic-style chapel of the hospital was replaced by a Neoclassic building on the orders of Prince-Bishop Ludwig von Erthal. During this period late Gothic art had little or no appeal, and it may well have been then that the Riemenschneider carving of the Fourteen Helper Saints was removed from the chapel, broken up, and the pieces scattered. Only this fragment of the three saints—portrayed with Riemenschneider's characteristic poignant blend of realism and intense emotional expression—has so far reappeared.

Another relief of the Fourteen Helpers, which is clearly of a later date than the New York group, is now in the Mainfränkisches Museum in Würzburg. In the author's opinion, this could well be the later carving of the Fourteen Helpers that is known to have been ordered from Riemenschneider's workshop by Lorenz von Bibra, in 1514, for the same hospital chapel. This relief remained on an outside wall of the chapel when Carl Becker was alive, and despite noticeable stylistic discrepancies, he assumed it to be the Riemenschneider work of 1494. The puzzle was only finally solved with the reappearance of the Three Helpers.

See also: Charles E. von Nostitz, Jr., "Two Unpolychromed Riemenschneiders at the Cloisters," *Metropolitan Museum Journal* 10 (1975): 51-62. Justus Bier, "Riemenschneider's Helpers in Need," *Metropolitan Museum of Art Bulletin* 21, no. 10 (June 1963): 317-26.

PLATES 3A-B. **The Virgin with the Christ Child.** Late 1490s.
Helen Foresman Spencer Museum of Art, University of Kansas, Lawrence, Kansas. Lindenwood. Height 47½ in. (120.7 cm).

In this commanding representation of the Virgin with the Christ Child, Mary appears as a slender, upright figure with her head held erect as she looks out towards the viewer. The proud bearing of the figure, together with the sickle moon under Mary's foot, makes it clear that she is portrayed here in her role as Queen of Heaven. While Mary seems almost to present the Christ Child to us, the Child himself turns towards the Virgin from the frontal position in which he is held, clutching her shoulder with his right hand and with his left hand tugging at her veil which he has drawn over one leg. His playful demeanor and intimate attitude contrast with the regal image of the Virgin. In spite of the latter's statuesque aspect, the sculptural theme of the group is based on actual movement, evident in the twist of the Christ Child's body and in the folds of Mary's mantle.

A look at some of the special features of the Kansas figures (such as the motifs of the Christ Child and the drapery, the face and stance of the Virgin) helps to determine the place of this group in Riemenschneider's gradual development of the Madonna theme. The playful, impetuous Christ Child, full of unruly movement, is characteristic of the sculptor's earlier representations and is found in varying poses in the slender group in the Boston Museum of

Fine Arts, of about 1490–1492 (Plate 1), the workshop statue in the Neumünster collegiate church in Würzburg, dated 1493, and in the now destroyed Himmelstein Madonna, also created about 1493. The concept of the
Virgin in these groups is similar also, and the arrangement of the drapery
shows the same motif of the mantle drawn up on both sides, except that in
these three cases the motif has the complication of a reversed lateral fold. The
restless, intricate arrangement of forms that is evident in the folds of the
mantle and the positioning of the Child in the Kansas statue and these other
groups is a distinguishing feature of Riemenschneider's early style which has
a final notable expression in the Last Supper group in the Rothenburg Altarpiece of the Holy Blood (Plates 23B-I). This group was carved between 1501
and 1502; the style of the slightly later figures by Riemenschneider in this
altarpiece, those of 1502 to 1504, demonstrates a change to a more static,
quiet arrangement of form and a reliance on light and shade as primary
agents in the carving, rather than on tactile and linear values. The swift
movements of the folds of the Virgin's mantle in the Kansas work recalls the
similarly restless arrangement in the mantle of St. Luke from the Münnerstadt Altarpiece of 1490–1492 (Plate 20I). The face of the Madonna, however, is much more articulated than the typical plain, oval countenance of
figures of this period, such as the Münnerstadt Mary Magdalene (Plate 20A),
the Madonna in the Boston Museum of Fine Arts (Plate 1), or Eve from the
Marienkapelle (Plate 21D). In its richness of planes and more angular form,
the face of Empress Cunegund on the lid of the Bamberg imperial tomb
(Plate 40B) offers the closest comparison. The lid of the tomb should be
dated 1499 to 1501. A date at the end of the 1490s for the Kansas group is
also indicated by the fact that the two figures are close in their total impression.

The figure should also be compared to the Madonna and Child from the
Clemens collection (Plates 24A, B), which again may be dated about
1501–1502. The face of the Clemens Virgin, the position of the Child, the
arrangement of the mantle and the folds within the mantle are all strikingly
similar, and vary only in that the Child in the Clemens group holds a pear in
his right hand and pulls more vigorously on the Virgin's veil with his left
hand. Finally, a revealing comparison may be made with the sandstone Madonna and Child of about 1505 now in the Mainfränkisches Museum in
Würzburg (Plates 28A, B)—a figure for which the Clemens Madonna may
well have served as model. There we find the same motifs as in the Kansas
and Clemens groups with regard to the Child's basic position and to the
general arrangement, but transformed according to the canons of Riemenschneider's mature style and his corresponding new concept of the figures:
the willful movement of the Child in the Kansas group, attempting to raise

himself up, is stilled; the Child also turns from a profile view at least half-way in the direction of the beholder (a concept that is fully developed in the later devotional images); the same more serene and calm arrangement of form is seen in the treatment of the drapery; and, in a feature that is already evident in the Clemens figure, the proud bearing of the Kansas Madonna is softened into a more gentle, tender attitude.

The Virgin with the Christ Child came to the Museum of Art of the University of Kansas in 1951, through the estate of Myrtle Elliott Thurnau, as a gift in memory of Professor Harry C. Thurnau. It was formerly in the collection of Hans Schwartz in Vienna (auctioned in 1910), and later of the Regierender Fürst von Liechtenstein.

See also: Justus Bier, "A Virgin with the Christ Child by Tilmann Riemenschneider," 2nd revised, enlarged ed., *Register of the Museum of Art, the University of Kansas* 2, no. 2 (June 1959): 2–15.

PLATE 4. **St. Urban.** About 1500.
Allen Memorial Art Museum, Oberlin College, Oberlin, Ohio. Linden-wood. Height 21¾ in. (55.2 cm).

Riemenschneider's bust of St. Urban which is now in the Allen Memorial Art Museum was first published in 1946 in an article by this author. The bust was formerly in the Eugen Schweitzer collection in Berlin. This collection was auctioned in 1918 and the catalogue of the collection, which attributes the bust to Riemenschneider, provides the only prior reference to the work that the author knows of.

St. Urban can be recognized in this figure of a pope by the bunch of grapes which is placed on the closed book. Originally representations of St. Urban, who was Pope Urban I from 222 until his death in 230, showed him with a chalice as his symbol, a reminder of Urban's papal decree that the chalice and paten used in the celebration of the Mass must be made of precious metal—silver or gold. In late Gothic times, however, because his feast day (May 25) came at the time of year when the grapes had reached a critical stage in their development and the blessings of Heaven had to be secured through a suitable mediator in order to ensure a good harvest later in the year, St. Urban was chosen as the patron saint of the vinegrowers and vineyards, and his symbol was changed to a cluster of grapes. The custom of having the vineyards blessed at the feast of St. Urban still persists in Franconia. Busts like the St. Urban were probably used in the ceremony of the blessing, carried in the processions that wound their way up the steep paths between the vineyards covering the bluffs on both sides of the Main River Valley in the region of Lower Franconia. Riemenschneider himself owned several vineyards in this region and must have participated in processions of this type. A declaration of his real estate which he made in 1525 lists, in addition to properties in the city of Würzburg, 17½ "morgen" of vineyards in various locations, some of which he had earlier turned over to his five children.

As was the practice with bust sculptures in Riemenschneider's time, since these were intended to be carried in religious processions and would be seen from all sides, the bust of St. Urban is carved full round in head and body. An interesting comparison in this respect can be made with the half-length figure of St. Burchard which is now in the National Gallery in Washington, D.C. (Plates 15A, B). The fact that the back of that figure is flat and hollowed out, in the manner of a full-length statue designed to be set against a pier or in the shrine of an altarpiece, where the unfinished state of the back would make no difference, proves that, unlike the St. Urban, the sculpture was not created as a bust but was cut down from a full-length figure.

Hollowing out a sculpture helps to prevent the wood cracking, and in some cases Riemenschneider used this procedure with his bust sculptures. But even then he preserved the appearance of sculpture in the round by closing the aperture at the rear of the bust with a panel, so that the carving could then be done as if the bust were solid. The busts of St. Kilian, St. Kolonat, and St. Totnan, which Riemenschneider carved between 1508 and 1510 for the high altar of Würzburg Cathedral (Plates 35C-E), were treated in this way. (Unfortunately all three of these works were destroyed in 1945.) The bust of St. Urban, in contrast, is carved from a solid block of lindenwood. This accounts for the remarkably good condition of the work. Apart from the missing cross-staff and some minor losses of parts of the tiara, the only damage the work has suffered is some vertical cracks, which are characteristic of such carvings from solid blocks. The worst of these cracks split the bust from St. Urban's left shoulder down the full length of the work; it is most noticeable on the back of the figure, where it has been filled in with spans of wood a quarter of an inch wide. These cracks probably developed shortly after the bust was finished. Since we can safely assume that the St. Urban bust is a relatively early work, we may surmise that Riemenschneider adopted the practice of hollowing out his bust sculptures after some years of working with solid blocks and observing the disadvantages of this method. The dark brown stain on the bust was no doubt applied to the lindenwood sometime in the nineteenth century in order to simulate the appearance of oak wood, which was then more fashionable.

The bust shows St. Urban in papal attire. The pontiff saint wears a cope which is fastened in front by a diamond-shaped clasp with a four-leaved flower design in its center; the tasselled hood is visible from the rear. Beneath the cope, part of the alb and the amice—the linen cloth folded around the neck and shoulders—can be seen, and under that, the shirt which is closed at the neck with a small button. Resplendent on St. Urban's head is the tiara, the pope's triple crown, a high conical cap encompassed by three crowns. The fringed infulae which hang from the back of this are brought forward and draped over his shoulders on top of the cope. Each of the crowns in the tiara is decorated with six cross-shaped leaves. Half of the leaves, most of them at the back, have broken off, as has the small orb and cross that doubtless surmounted the tiara. Originally St. Urban must have held a cross-staff in his right hand.

The saint's countenance shows him to be aging but still vigorous, and of a stern but benevolent disposition. The figure also expresses the same sadness and deep spiritual feeling that imbues almost all of Riemenschneider's figures, and which here contrasts with the robust realism with which every wrinkle of the face and every detail of the papal attire is rendered. This poignant blend of realism and emphasis on spiritual expression is one of the distinguishing characteristics of Riemenschneider's work.

Though there are no other representations of popes by Riemenschneider with which to compare the St. Urban, an instructive comparison can be made with some of the figures of bishops and of the Apostles. There is, for example, a striking similarity between St. Urban and Prince-Bishop Rudolf von Scherenberg, as the latter appears on his tomb-monument of 1496–1499 (Plate 22B). St. Urban has the same facial type as the prince-bishop, but in the case of St. Urban it is given a more youthful form; though more heavy-set and less lined, the face has the same distinctive almond-shaped eyes, down-turned mouth, prominent nose and cheekbones, and deep wrinkles around the eyes and on the neck. The prototype of both St. Urban and Rudolf von Scherenberg can be found in two works from the Münnerstadt Altarpiece, carved between 1490 and 1492, namely, the figure of St. Mark from the predella of the altarpiece (Plate 20J), now in the Staatliche Museen in West Berlin, and Bishop Maximin in one of the reliefs from the left wing, which is still in the Münnerstadt parish church. St. Urban is still more closely related to some of the figures of the Apostles in the Last Supper which Riemenschneider carved for the Rothenburg Altarpiece of the Holy Blood between 1501 and 1502. The figures share the same deeply religious expression which is intensified in each case by the outward gaze of the eyes and the tense, more emphatic modeling of form. The resemblance is greatest in figures such as the Apostle below St. James the Elder at the left end of the table and the seated Apostle facing Judas, in front of Christ (Plate 23c). Even the hands of St. Urban, which retain their expressive character despite the gloves he wears, find their counterpart in the hands of the Apostle Andrew which rest on the back of the bench. In light of these similarities of both spirit and style, we may conclude that the bust of St. Urban was carved about the same time as the Rothenburg Last Supper or even a little earlier.

See also: Justus Bier, "A Bust of St. Urban by Tilmann Riemenschneider," *Art Quarterly* 9, no. 2 (Spring 1946): 128-39.

PLATES 5A-B. **Anna Selbdritt.** About 1502–1504.
Walters Art Gallery, Baltimore, Maryland. Lindenwood. Height 39½ in. (100.3 cm).

This image of Anna Selbdritt shows St. Anne standing and holding in the crook of either arm the small, seated figures of the Christ Child and the Virgin Mary. The Christ Child is supported by her right hand, Mary by her left. "Anna Selbdritt" is the traditional name for this particular group of figures and means literally "St. Anne, herself the third." The composition of the Anna Selbdritt group may vary within certain well-defined types. In representations of this kind the Christ Child and Mary serve as symbols to identify St. Anne as the mother and teacher of the Virgin and grandmother of Christ.

St. Anne herself appears as a slender, dignified figure, her head inclined slightly to the left, her face pensive and seemingly untouched by age. Her right foot is set forward so that her knee and thigh appear beneath the drapery. The mantle she wears is drawn up in front in heavy, projecting folds that contrast with the verticality of the statue and enrich the light and shade design by means of the heavy shadow under the main bulge of the garment. This arrangement seems to have supplied the model for the drapery motif in several other similar groups attributed to Riemenschneider and his workshop. Under the mantle, St. Anne wears a dress with a fitted bodice and a full skirt that falls to the ground in a rich display of vertical folds. Her oval face is framed by the gentle curves of the widow's veil and wimple, the veil falling over her head and shoulders, the wimple drawn around the neck and chin and covering her shoulders like a cape. Typically, the iris and pupil of her eyes are tinted gray and black.

Though only slightly larger in size than the Christ Child, Mary is depicted as a young woman. She holds a prayer book on her lap and indicates a passage with her right hand. Her head is turned aside as if in contemplation. Her features and dress resemble those of St. Anne but lack their beauty.

The Christ Child is the only one in the group whose head is shown in an upright, frontal position, perhaps to emphasize that he is the object of adoration. Though there is some suggestion of natural childlike movement in the action of his feet and legs, the upper part of the body is stiffened into a cult-like pose. The right arm that holds the apple must be considered a late nineteenth-century restoration, since an earlier sketch of the group shows this hand raised in blessing.

Stylistically, the Christ Child seems close to the little Virgin and, like her, suffers in comparison with St. Anne. This difference in quality in the treatment of the figures leads the author to believe that an assistant was employed in the finishing of the two small lateral figures, whereas St. Anne was carved entirely by Riemenschneider's own hand.

We may easily establish the attribution of the group to Riemenschneider as responsible for the design and the greater part of the carving, through comparison of the sculpture with various documented works. This also shows how the group fits into Riemenschneider's development, and helps us to assign a date for it of about 1502 to 1504. In its general design the Anna Selbdritt shows a certain similarity to the figure of St. Elizabeth accompanied by the small figure of the cripple from the Münnerstadt altarpiece of 1492. A much more decisive comparison, however, involves the heads of the Mary Magdalene and Christ in the relief of The Meeting in the Garden from the same altarpiece (Plate 20c); the stylistic similarities in this case are alone sufficient to establish Riemenschneider's authorship of the Baltimore group. Other dominant stylistic features of the Anna Selbdritt appear in the tomb-effigy of Prince-Bishop Rudolf von Scherenberg, which Riemenschneider carved a few years later, between 1496 and 1499 (Plate 22A); the concentration on the weighty folds of the drapery as a main motif, the particular funnel shape they form, even the flexed leg beneath them—all these devices are found in both the Scherenberg figure and the St. Anne. Two other factors, however, point to a still later date for the Baltimore Anna Selbdritt, namely, the still more restrained style of the group and the development of the relief of the figure so that it depends more strongly on the action of light and shade. Both these features are characteristic of Riemenschneider's more advanced style which evolved during work on the Rothenburg Altarpiece of the Holy Blood (1501–1504) and is first evident in the figures of that altarpiece completed after 1502. The Mary of the Annunciation group above the shrine, and the wing relief of The Agony in the Garden (Plates 23J, P), both carved between 1502 and 1504, are close in style to the St. Anne. From this it may be concluded that the St. Anne group was carved about the same time, in the years following 1502. As additional evidence, we find that two other figures from the Rothenburg altarpiece, the angel of the Annunciation group and the angel to the right of the reliquary cross (Plate 23K), which were also delivered in 1504, show signs of having been worked on by the same assistant who finished the Mary and Christ Child of the Baltimore group.

It is unlikely that the Anna Selbdritt group was created much later than 1504. The distinct planes of the composition and the bulky volume of the forms here do not occur in Riemenschneider's later works from around 1510 on. In the Gramschatz Virgin and Child of about 1510–1515 (Plate 38A), for example, the Christ Child is so arranged in Mary's arms as to become part of a one-plane composition, with the same rhythm flowing through both figures. In contrast to this, the Child in the Anna Selbdritt group is set forward and apart from St. Anne, in a position that emphasizes rather than minimizes the volume of the figure. This would have been unacceptable to Riemenschneider in later years. The effigy of Prince-Bishop Lorenz von Bibra (Plate 43B), carved around 1518–1522, shows the same reduction in the bulk of the figure that occurs in the Gramschatz Virgin and Child.

Though the provenance of the Baltimore Anna Selbdritt remains unknown, an interesting conjecture may be made about its possible origin. There are, in the records of the Jakobskirche in Rothenburg, several entries relating to an altarpiece of St. Anne which Riemenschneider carved for a small lateral altar in the Marienkapelle in Rothenburg during the years 1505 and 1506. This is the only reference we have to a representation of St. Anne by Riemenschneider. There is no description of this St. Anne altarpiece, and a good case can be made to connect it with the Anna Selbdritt fragment now in the Bayerisches Nationalmuseum in Munich (Plate 29). On the other hand, it is also conceivable that the Baltimore St. Anne was made to be the central figure of this Rothenburg altarpiece. The sculpture fits the requirements of size and style for such an altarpiece; other Rothenburg altarpieces from the same period, still extant on lateral altars, have a single statue in the center; and there is, moreover, an 1888 description of one such complete altarpiece, now lost, with a standing St. Anne Selbdritt attributed to Riemenschneider which seems almost identical to the Baltimore piece.

Restorations to the group (in addition to the Christ Child's right arm) include the entire front of the base, with the drapery attached to it, and St. Anne's right foot, a small piece of the funnel-shaped fold in the cloak, the part of the book above Mary's left hand, and the noses of both small figures. Some recutting of parts of the hair and eyes of the small figures, which in the case of the Christ Child has obliterated Riemenschneider's customary delineation of the lower eyelid, probably took place sometime in the nineteenth century. The brown stain which now covers the entire surface of the group is probably also of that period.

The Anna Selbdritt groups derive from the cult of St. Anne which flourished in the late Middle Ages. The veneration of Anne as the mother of the Virgin had long existed in the Eastern Church. In the West it fluctuated with the theological disputes concerning Mary's conception, receiving particular impetus after the acceptance of the doctrine of the Immaculate Conception by the Ecumenical Council of Basel in 1439. The cult was already established in Würzburg prior to Riemenschneider's settling there in 1483, as we know from the far older images of Anna Selbdritt in the area; but in the next decades, when Riemenschneider was active in Würzburg, it did have a noted and ardent adherent in Johannes Heidenberg of Trittenheim, called "Trithemius," who wrote extensively in defense and praise of St. Anne in the 1490s, and who became, at the invitation of Riemenschneider's patron, Prince-Bishop Lorenz von Bibra, abbot of the monastery of St. James in Würzburg in 1506. When Trithemius died, Riemenschneider's workshop provided for his monument in the abbey church, the Jakobskirche. But whether Riemenschneider carved one of his St. Anne groups for this church we do not know.

The other St. Anne sculptures that have been attributed to Riemenschneider and his workshop are of various compositional and iconographical types. One, in a private collection in Tiefenbrunn, shows a seated St. Anne in semiprofile with her three legendary husbands standing beside her. This is a fragment from an altarpiece of the Holy Clan in which the three figures of the Anna Selbdritt group are supplemented by other family members traditionally connected with Anne and Mary. A second fragment from this altarpiece, representing one of the two supposed sisters of Mary with her husband, is now in a private collection in Harburg. One other fragment from a second Holy Clan altarpiece is preserved in the Victoria and Albert Museum in London. All three carvings show Riemenschneider's own hand.

In the Anna Selbdritt groups, St. Anne may appear seated or standing. The images which show the saint seated also take different forms. One is the relatively statuesque group in which St. Anne supports the small figures of the Christ Child and Mary, which has as its most famous examples the sandstone sculpture from Kitzingen, now in the Mainfränkisches Museum in Würzburg, and the wood group from Rimpar now in the Bayerisches Nationalmuseum in Munich. The wood figure was for a long while on the facade of a house in Rimpar, and it is possible that the Kitzingen figure served a similar decorative and protective purpose. Both of these are works by Riemenschneider. The other carvings of this type are workshop or school pieces of lesser quality.

One other figure, also in the Bayerisches Nationalmuseum, represents a quite different, much more naturalistic concept of the Anna Selbdritt group. This is the fragment (Plate 29) already mentioned in connection with the documented Rothenburg altarpiece of St. Anne; its association with that altarpiece is based mainly on the grounds that the fragment is reputed to come from the neighborhood of Rothenburg. The complete composition in this case probably resembled the famous Anna Selbdritt group by Nicolaus Gerhaert van Leyden in the sculpture collection of the Staatliche Museen in West Berlin. There, the Virgin and St. Anne are shown seated together on a bench, playing with the Christ Child, who stands on Mary's lap. The Riemenschneider fragment shows only the figure of St. Anne, carved in high relief, in profile, and with her right arm outstretched to support the missing Christ Child.

The extant groups that represent St. Anne standing also vary in composition, though they always retain a statuesque quality. In some St. Anne carries both the Virgin and the Christ Child in the manner of the Baltimore piece; in others the diminutive figure of the Virgin stands beside St. Anne. The Baltimore sculpture, however, is the only one among these groups that can claim to be a work largely by Riemenschneider's own hand. In its well-balanced composition and serene, melancholy mood it stands out as a fine example of Riemenschneider's craft.

See also: Justus Bier, "An 'Anna Selbdritt' by Riemenschneider," Journal of the Walters Art Gallery 7-8 (1944–1945): 10-37.

PLATES 6A-B. **St. Lawrence.** About 1502.
Cleveland Museum of Art, Cleveland, Ohio. Lindenwood, polychromed and gilded. Height 37¼ in. (94.6 cm).

The figure of St. Lawrence is one of two companion statues of young martyr saints which are now in the possession of the Cleveland Museum of Art. The other statue represents St. Stephen (Plates 14A, B), who is associated with St. Lawrence in legend and frequently portrayed with him in art. Both figures have been known and attributed to Riemenschneider from the late 1880s and since then they have remained together through several changes of ownership in private European collections prior to their acquisition by the Cleveland Museum in 1959.

Though it is clear the two figures were designed as counterparts, each figure has its own distinctive character. While St. Stephen stands erect and resolute, the figure of St. Lawrence sways to one side, forming a gentle curve that is echoed in the position of the head as it inclines to the right, and in the flow and predominant folds of his deacon's robes. In sharp contrast to this are the short broken folds in the center of his robe, caused by its being drawn up to one side, and the whorled forms of the deeply carved locks of hair. Framed by these curls, the face of the saint is modeled into a soft, smooth fullness. The expression is soulful and pious, and, like the yielding stance of the figure, suggests meekness and humility. In his right hand St. Lawrence holds before him an open book, his fingers elegantly spread to support it. With his left hand he displays a gridiron, the attribute of this saint.

From the fourth century, St. Lawrence was venerated as one of the most famous martyrs of the city of Rome. Born in Spain, he became one of the seven deacons of Rome under Pope St. Sixtus II. Both he and the pontiff were martyred in the city in 258 A.D. According to tradition St. Lawrence was roasted to death on a gridiron for his defiance of the city prefect in refusing to hand over the Church's treasure and presenting instead all the assembled poor and sick people of the city. The legend that associates St. Lawrence with St. Stephen alleges that when St. Stephen was eventually reburied beside St. Lawrence, the latter moved to one side, yielding the place of honor to Stephen.

The gridiron that St. Lawrence holds here, apart from the handle, is a replacement, probably made in the early nineteenth century. The hand that holds the gridiron is carved from a separate piece of wood. To prevent cracking, the back of the figure has been neatly hollowed out. Modern layers of paint, as well as the late eighteenth- or early nineteenth-century additions of gold foil dots on the alba of the saint, were removed in the Cleveland Museum's restoration workshop and the statue now stands with much of the original polychromy, gold leaf and silver foil, revealed.

The original location of the St. Lawrence and St. Stephen figures is largely a matter of conjecture. Based on a report that the sculptures, together with two statues of female saints (now in the Historisches Museum in Frankfurt) belonged to an altarpiece from the Rothenburg region, a reasonable connection may be made with the lost altarpiece that is known to have been carved by Riemenschneider in 1510 for an All Saints altar in the Church of the Dominican Nuns in Rothenburg. This church was demolished in 1813 and the altarpiece presumably dismantled at that time. In spite of the altar dedication, the Riemenschneider altarpiece could have depicted only a few saints who were particularly venerated, and it is possible that all four of these figures—St. Lawrence, St. Stephen, and the two unidentified female saints—were included in this group.

Various points can be made in support of this theory. First of all, there is no evidence of any altarpiece by Riemenschneider on the theme of "All Saints." Nor, as has already been indicated, is there a necessary correlation between the consecration of an altar and the iconographic content of the altarpiece. There is documentary evidence, on the other hand, that the altarpiece in question contained two angels, which would be unlikely in the case of a many-figured All Saints altarpiece. There is also documentary evidence indicating the possible size of the altarpiece and showing it suitable to accommodate in the shrine some six figures of the stature of St. Lawrence and St. Stephen. Finally, and most important, there is the fact that the dates connected with the altarpiece correspond to the dates that this author would assign to St. Lawrence and St. Stephen. On stylistic grounds these two figures should be dated about 1502 and about 1510, respectively. We know from documents, on the other hand, that the Riemenschneider altarpiece for the All Saints altar was completed by 1510; payments for this work were made between 1507 and 1510. Quite possibly, though—since many of Riemenschneider's works are known to have taken considerable time between commission and completion (fourteen years, from 1499 to 1513, in the case of the Bamberg tomb of Emperor Henry II and Empress Cunegund, for example)—the altarpiece was already commissioned at the beginning of the century. The dates of the two saints, therefore, fall within the probable period of work on the altarpiece, and thus offer convincing evidence that the figures were originally intended for this altarpiece.

In both cases, the dates assigned to the statues derive from comparisons with other works by Riemenschneider. In certain stylistic characteristics the St. Lawrence clearly relates to other figures carved in the first years of the sixteenth century. The relative fullness of the drapery and of the figure generally, together with the particular motif of the broken folds in the robe drawn up to one side, recalls the image of Empress Cunegund on the lid of the Bamberg imperial tomb (Plate 40B). The lid evidently was the first part of the sarcophagus to be carved and was probably completed by 1501. As William D. Wixom first observed, the face of St. Lawrence recalls another figure from the Bamberg tomb: that of the young prince behind the empress's father at the extreme right of the relief depicting the death of the emperor. This is one of the earlier reliefs of the tomb and should be dated shortly after the lid, about 1501 to 1502. Though it is a softer, fuller version in this instance, the face of St. Lawrence, framed with curls, also bears a resemblance to the face of the knight Konrad von Schaumberg on his tomb-monument in the Marienkapelle in Würzburg, carved probably shortly after 1502 (Plates 25A, B).

The provenance of both the St. Lawrence and the St. Stephen can be traced back to the collection of the Frankfurt merchant von Gontard in the 1880s. The statues later passed into the collection of Richard von Passavant-Gontard in Frankfurt. (A catalogue of this collection, published in 1929, gives the date of acquisition of the St. Lawrence figure by the Gontard family as 1855, and of the St. Stephen as 1881.) From there the figures entered the collection of Baronesse Catalina von Pannwitz, at De Hartekamp near Bennebroke in the Netherlands. The statues were on the New York art market prior to their acquisition by the Cleveland Museum of Art.

As we find in the case of the companion figure of St. Stephen, a comparison of Riemenschneider's statue with the engravings of St. Lawrence and St. Stephen by Martin Schongauer (before 1440–1491) makes it clear that these engravings influenced the design of Riemenschneider's figure. The characterization and expression of mood and feeling, on the other hand, are highly individual and distinctively Riemenschneider's own. Equally, the sensitivity with which both figures are finished, especially evident in the expressive faces and hands, leaves no doubt that in each case Riemenschneider himself was responsible for the decisive work on the figure.

See also: Justus Bier, "Two Statues: St. Stephen and St. Lawrence by Riemenschneider in the Cleveland Museum of Art," *Art Quarterly* 23, no. 3 (Autumn 1960): 214-27. William D. Wixom, "Two Lindenwood Sculptures by Tilmann Riemenschneider," *Bulletin of the Cleveland Museum of Art* 46, no. 9 (November 1959): 187-97.

Plates 7a-b. **St. Andrew.** About 1505.

Samuel H. Kress Collection, High Museum of Art, Atlanta, Georgia. Lindenwood. Height 40½ in. (102.9 cm).

The standing figure of St. Andrew, which is now in Atlanta, is one of four such representations of this saint made by Riemenschneider or his workshop over a period of years, yet all within the first decade of the sixteenth century. Each figure displays a quite different concept of the saint, and a comparison of the four versions shows us how widely Riemenschneider explored the iconographic theme. The earliest of these single figures is the sandstone statue of St. Andrew from the Marienkapelle in Würzburg, now in Würzburg Cathedral. This figure is one of the twelve stone figures of the Apostles that were carved in the workshop between the years 1500 and 1506, and it should itself be dated about 1500. A painted wood figure of St. Andrew, which is now lost but was formerly in the chapel of the Ehehaltenhaus in Würzburg, and which was most probably a work by Riemenschneider's own hand, was made about 1505, about the same time as the Atlanta St. Andrew, which is also considered a work from the master's hand. Finally, there is the lindenwood statue in the Altarpiece of the Twelve Apostles in the Kurpfälzisches Museum in Heidelberg, which was originally in the Church of St. Kilian in Windsheim and for a long time was thought to have been destroyed in the fire that razed the town and that church in 1730. This statue, which is again by Riemenschneider's own hand, is dated 1509.

Of these four representations, the Atlanta St. Andrew seems closest to the description of this saint in the *Heiligenleben* (The Lives of the Saints) published by Anton Koberger in Nuremberg in 1488. Riemenschneider would no doubt have been familiar with this edition of Jacobus de Voragine's work which describes St. Andrew as the "worthy apostle" who "loved God and served Him with diligence by day and night, with praying, with fasting, with staying awake, and with much other good exercise." St. Andrew does appear here as a venerable, "worthy" figure. An aging man with a long full beard, he stands erect, with only his head bent slightly forward, deeply engrossed in reading and thought. The serious face shows a determined and intense concentration. His right hand supports an open book, while the left loosely clasps one arm of the X-shaped cross that is his attribute and the symbol of his martyr's death by crucifixion. His attire is simple, in both its nature and its arrangement. Over a long robe he wears a capacious cloak. Beneath the robe one bare foot appears. The cloak is drawn tightly over the saint's narrow shoulders and fastened in front: on his right side it is gathered up in voluminous folds and held by the arm which supports the book, while on his left side the other end of the cloak is slung over the center part of the cross in a movement that echoes the fall of the gathered-up end. The abstract language of the drapery and folds, the expressive nature of the face, even the treatment of the hair and hands, are all in perfect accord, and nothing detracts from the grave mood inherent in Riemenschneider's concept of the figure.

Hands of the same serious character, expressing an equally deep emotion, are found among the figures in the shrine of the Creglingen Assumption Altarpiece of about 1505–1510. St. Andrew's right hand, for example, finds a counterpart in the right hand of St. Philip in that group, while his more relaxed left hand has its equivalent in the left hand of James the Elder (Plates 33I, J). The statue also has affinities with several of the stone figures of the Apostles from the Marienkapelle, mentioned earlier. It is not, however, the St. Andrew of that stone series that is most closely related to the Atlanta statue, though there is a similar severity about these two figures, but rather the apostle Jude Thaddaeus (Plate 26c). This figure not only shows the use of an identical central motif in the arrangement of the cloak, with the folded-over end hanging below the arm of the figure, but also the same reliance, in the carving, on the play of light and shade. It is in fact quite possible that the wood figure of St. Andrew served as the model for the stone figure of Jude Thaddaeus, which (to judge from the style) could well have been carved towards the end of the series, in about 1505. Whether or not this was the case, Riemenschneider's working drawings of the one figure must have been recalled in the design of the other. The particular motif of the drapery also appears in the figure of Mary in the relief showing Christ among the Doctors in the Creglingen Assumption Altarpiece (Plate 33M) and is developed more monumentally in the figure of St. James the Elder in the shrine of that altarpiece (Plate 33B). We may judge the St. Andrew to be close in time to the Creglingen Altarpiece not only because of this specific correspondence but also on the grounds of its more general stylistic conformities: the works are alike in the integration of all elements into a fluid and unified composition (as against the additive approach of earlier works), in the use of light and shade to suggest volume and space, and in the subtle individuation of character.

The Atlanta St. Andrew is in good condition, and the only restoration has been to the bridge of the nose, parts of the top section of the book, the back arm of the upper fork of the cross, and some small sections at the base. The wormholes are partially filled with wood putty. The statue is unpainted but the original color of the natural lindenwood has been lost through the application of a brown stain to the figure. This was probably done towards the latter part of the nineteenth century, when it became the practice to apply such a stain in order to simulate the appearance of the then more fashionable oak wood.

The original location of this figure is unknown, and its provenance goes back only to the 1930s, when the work was in the author's own collection in Widdersburg, having been acquired from a dealer in the Rhineland. Confiscated by the Nazi authorities and auctioned in Hamburg, the work was acquired by the Museum für Kunst und Gewerbe in Hamburg at the beginning of World War II, but was restored to its previous owner (by then in this country) after the end of the war. The figure was later acquired by the Samuel H. Kress Foundation in New York, and, in 1958, as part of the Kress Collection for Atlanta, it entered the Atlanta Art Association. It is now displayed in the High Museum of Art.

See also: Justus Bier, "St. Andrew in the Work of Tilmann Riemenschneider," *Art Bulletin* 38, no. 4 (December 1956): 215-23.

PLATES 8A-B. **St. Catherine.** About 1505–1510.
North Carolina Museum of Art, Raleigh, North Carolina. Lindenwood. Height 37¾ in. (96 cm).

This graceful figure of St. Catherine of Alexandria may well be considered one of Riemenschneider's finest representations of a female saint. Every detail of the carving, the face and the finely-articulated right hand in particular, indicates Riemenschneider's own hand, and there is nothing to suggest the help of assistants in the execution of the piece. The figure compares in quality to the famous statue of St. Dorothea from the Marienkapelle in Würzburg, and in light of the wartime destruction of that work the preservation of the St. Catherine statue is particularly fortunate.

St. Catherine wears a crown signifying her royal lineage as the daughter of King Costus (according to the *Legenda Aurea*). In her left hand she holds the sword that is the symbol and instrument of her martyrdom, and in the right, an open book indicating her great learning. All three symbols relate to the legend of St. Catherine of Alexandria and can be found in the numerous representations of this saint in Gothic and Renaissance art. Catherine's other special attribute, a spiked wheel, does not appear here. In keeping with the fashion of the times, the mantle St. Catherine wears is rectangular in shape and is draped around without any fastening. One end of this is pressed against the saint's waist, creating a group of folds that radiate towards the ground. On the left side of the figure, the edge of the mantle turns outwards, while on the right, the corner opens up in an ear-like fold. The dress she wears under this cloak has a low, V-shaped neck in which a small part of her shirt is visible. Wide sleeves fall to the wrists and the bodice is tightly gathered in at the waist, which produces a flare of rectangular folds that jut forward and create deep shadows between them. The tip of the saint's left foot can be seen between the dress and mantle, close to the point of the sword. St. Catherine's beautiful oval face turns a little to the left, as she gazes into the distance. Traces of Riemenschneider's customary gray and black tinting of the pupil and iris of the eye are still apparent. The nose and mouth are delicate and neatly formed, and beneath the heavy coils of thickly-braided hair both earlobes are just visible. The crown gives the appearance of being a flexible band, since it fits the shape and follows the line of her head and braids. Five pierced, cross-shaped leaves decorate the crown, and a fringed lappet hangs from the back.

Though the figure is undocumented, stylistic comparison with other works by Riemenschneider, some of which are documented, serves to establish a date of about 1505–1510 for the sculpture. In the shape of the face and style of the hair, as well as the general bearing and elegant air, the image of St. Catherine bears a distinct resemblance to the relief figure of St. Cunegund on the lid of the imperial sarcophagus in Bamburg Cathedral (Plate 40B). The commission for this sarcophagus took fourteen years (1499–1513) to execute. The lid appears to have been the first part of the tomb to be worked on and was probably completed by the middle of 1501. The image also corresponds to the Cunegund figures in the reliefs on one side and end of the tomb, particularly the early relief of about 1501–1502, depicting

Cunegund's Ordeal by Fire (Plate 40c). A striking similarity to St. Catherine's facial expression is found in a still earlier work, the statue of Eve from the Marienkapelle (Plate 21D), completed in 1493 and now in the Mainfränkisches Museum in Würzburg. But the closest, most convincing similarity to the features of St. Catherine occurs in a relatively late work, the figure of Mary in the shrine of the Creglingen Altarpiece of the Assumption of the Virgin, created in the years 1505–1510 (Plate 33c).

In addition to the facial expression, the treatment of the drapery is particularly important in assigning a date to this figure. The dominant motif of the great, sweeping curve of St. Catherine's mantle appears in Riemenschneider's work as early as the decade of 1480–1490: the alabaster statuette of St. Barbara, created in the 1480s and now in the Böttcherstrasse in Bremen, is one example; the statue of St. John the Baptist in the parish church of Hassfurt (Plate 18), carved before 1490, is another example. The figure of St. Catherine, however, shows this motif handled in a more relaxed and natural way. Similar assurance and ease of treatment are apparent in the draperies of the Virgin and Child of about 1510–1515 from an altarpiece in Gramschatz (Plate 38A), now in the Landesgalerie in Hanover. The deeply-cut folds common to the draperies of both the Gramschatz Madonna and the Raleigh St. Catherine definitely belong to Riemenschneider's mature period, in the years around 1503–1510; so too does the eloquent face of St. Catherine, which, in its emotional expression and individual nature, goes beyond the more restrained countenances of Riemenschneider's earlier figures.

The figure is carved in lindenwood, of which there was a plentiful supply in the southern part of Germany in Riemenschneider's time, and which has the advantage of carving easily but hardening with age. As it appears now, the statue has the deep golden-brown tone of natural lindenwood that has been darkened by preservation treatment with wax. The loss of the original left hand (sometime prior to 1898) is the only serious damage the work has sustained. Both the present left hand and the sword are restorations made in the early years of this century, between 1904 and 1918. Losses of this kind are not uncommon since in many cases the hands of a figure were carved from separate pieces of wood and set into the sleeves; they were therefore particularly susceptible to loss or breakage. (The figure of St. Anthony Abbot in the Busch-Reisinger Museum in Cambridge [Plate 12A] has suffered a similar loss.) Apart from this and minor damage to the crown and restored sword (one leaf of the crown and the quillons of the sword are missing, and the two lateral leaves of the crown are broken) the St. Catherine remains in remarkably good condition. The back of the figure is partially hollowed out, as was Riemenschneider's customary practice with his larger statues whenever the placing of a work permitted. This was done to remove the soft strains in the wood and to allow it to dry out evenly, which to a large extent prevented cracking of the surface. Some of the wormholes (often found in lindenwood sculptures) have been filled in with a slightly darker-tinted wood putty. A hole still visible on the top of the head reminds us that in Riemenschneider's time, to facilitate carving, the block of linden-wood would be held in place on the workbench by the insertion of two horizontal iron spikes; this allowed the work in progress to be rotated in horizontal position as though it were a large roast on a spit.

Nothing definite is known about the original location of the Raleigh St. Catherine, or about its provenance prior to the end of the last century. The fact that the figure is not carved in the round but is flat at the back and hollowed out suggests that the statue was intended for, and was originally placed against, one of the piers of a church, with a baldachin above and a bracket, probably displaying the donor's coat of arms, below. Alternatively, the figure may have been created as part of a shrine of an altarpiece, where it would also be viewed only from the front. (Images of St. Catherine, frequently paired with St. Barbara—the two figures flanking a statue of the Virgin and Child—are often found in small shrines.)

The St. Catherine was acquired by the North Carolina Museum of Art in 1968. It was formerly owned by the late Dr. Franz Haniel of Munich. At the end of the nineteenth century the figure formed part of the extensive collection belonging to Wilhelm Gumprecht in Berlin. The Gumprecht collection was sold at auction in Berlin in 1918, and, as far as the author can establish, it was at this time or shortly afterwards that the figure passed to Franz Haniel.

See also: Justus Bier, "Riemenschneider's St. Catherine in the North Carolina Museum of Art," *North Carolina Museum of Art Bulletin* 14, no. 1 (1977): 14-32.

PLATES 9A-D. **St. Jerome and the Lion.** About 1505–1510. Cleveland Museum of Art, Cleveland, Ohio. Alabaster. Height 15 in. (37.8 cm).

The small alabaster group of St. Jerome and the Lion deserves to be regarded as one of Riemenschneider's most important works. The artistry of carving and strength of feeling achieved on such a small scale are, in their way, as remarkable as the grandiose display of these same qualities in the great Creglingen Altarpiece. The group was acquired by the Cleveland Museum in 1946 (the first of three Riemenschneider works to enter this collection). It remains the only example in a collection in the United States of Riemenschneider's rare use of alabaster.

Dressed in cardinal's robes, St. Jerome is seated on a bench set on grass-covered ground, the grass indicated through shallow relief cutting and the use of green paint, of which only traces remain. (The same color appears in one of the reliefs on the Bamberg imperial tomb and on several other works in alabaster. Riemenschneider quite often used touches of color and gold to enrich the surface of his stone sculptures.) The bench is visible only from one side and from the rear. The saint's head inclines to the left as he looks down with compassion on the docile lion sitting close to his left side. The lion's left foreleg is held up for the saint's surgery. With his left hand Jerome holds the leg in a firm but gentle grip: with his right, he tries delicately, by means of a "scalpel," to extract the thorn from the injured paw. His cardinal's hat rests on his knee, helping to keep his arm and hand steady. The fine-featured face of the saint is careworn. Deep lines are etched around his eyes and on his brow, and the spare flesh reveals wide cheek-bones, a long lean jaw, and pointed chin. The countenance as a whole not only shows the concentration and compassion of the moment but seems also to bear witness to years of an ascetic, spiritually rigorous existence.

The incident that Riemenschneider represents here—that of St. Jerome extracting the thorn from the lion's paw—comes from one of the legends told about this great scholar-saint. This incident was particularly popular with artists of the fifteenth century, who set the scene either in the saint's study or in an open landscape representing the desert of Chalcis, where Jerome lived as a penitent and hermit for some years. A panel-painting of the second type by the Flemish artist Rogier van der Weyden, which is now in the Detroit Institute of Arts, seems to have furnished the basic model for Riemenschneider's sculpture. The main difference is that, while van der Weyden's figure is seated on a rock ledge, Riemenschneider continues the tradition of showing St. Jerome "in cathedra" and thereby characterizing him as the great Latin doctor even in the outdoor scene. Riemenschneider has also added a feature of his own invention by changing the position of the cardinal's hat and placing it on the saint's knee, to support his arm and steady his hand as he extracts the thorn. (The representation of St. Jerome in the desert as a cardinal was generally accepted in spite of the historical confusion it entailed. Jerome would only have been made a cardinal, if at all, after his years in the desert, when he returned to Rome in 382 and became adviser to Pope Damasus. But his image in art, of course, reflects more than historical fact.)

The iconographic idea which Riemenschneider uses here in fact goes considerably farther back than Rogier van der Weyden's panel. It was introduced in the first half of the fourteenth century by a professor of law, Joannes Andreas of Bologna, who made the promotion of the Jerome cult his chief object in life. In Riemenschneider's lifetime, another humanist, Johannes Trithemius, made the intensification of the cult of St. Anne his main concern (see p. 49, above). Both men had considerable influence on the spread of the cults of their chosen saints and on the artistic development of the requisite devotional images. It was Joannes Andreas who prescribed that Jerome be painted, as we see him here, basically, "seated 'in cathedra,' with the hat which the cardinals now use laid beside him and with the tamed lion." In the interests of popularizing the saint, he wisely included the miracle of the tamed lion in the new devotional image he suggested; clearly this had much greater popular appeal than the rather forbidding image of a man of great learning at his studies or in meditation. Though it was undoubtedly Jerome the humanist that appealed to Joannes Andreas, he chose the legendary character of the saint as the most effective means of making him known.

The tale of the tamed lion has, of course, an existence independent of the Jerome legend and, through such stories as Androcles and the Lion and Aesop's Fables, can be traced back to ancient times. The nature of the story changed in medieval times from a tale or fable about simple gratitude to a tale of an animal tamed by the miraculous power and exemplary goodness of the saint. The legend was attached to St. Jerome as a way of explaining the lion symbol that was given to him as one of the four great doctors of the Church. The four Latin doctors shared their symbols with the evangelists, so that Jerome is connected in this way with St. Mark. St. Jerome's lion, therefore, is ultimately derived from the winged lion among the apocalyptic beasts.

The Cleveland alabaster group was first attributed to Riemenschneider in 1909 by Otto Grossmann, but no date for the work was given at that time. Though later writers considered the group to be an early work, carved shortly before 1500, the author has assigned to the sculpture a date of about 1505–1510, placing it in the years of the Creglingen Assumption Altarpiece when Riemenschneider's mature style was at its peak. Several comparisons bear this out: there is a close relationship between the figure of St. Jerome and the old, kneeling king in the Adoration of the Magi, one of the predella groups in the Creglingen altarpiece (Plate 33L). This relief and its counterpart depicting Christ among the Doctors were probably created about 1510. There is also a notable correspondence between the alabaster group and the Solnhofen stone tomb of Emperor Henry and Empress Cunegund in Bamberg Cathedral. The figure of St. Jerome resembles the imperial effigies on the lid of this sarcophagus but by far the most striking feature is the relationship to the figure of St. Benedict in the relief of The Removal of the Stone on one side of the sarcophagus (Plate 40D). The two figures may differ in age and in physical type, but they share the same expression of feeling. Both are original versions of Riemenschneider's refined and spiritual concept of the great doctors of the Church; and both display—in the slight tilt of the head, in particular—the Christian humility that marks all his saintly figures. The Bamberg tomb was begun in 1499 and completed in 1513. The Removal of the Stone is one of the most mature parts of the work and was most probably executed about, or even after, 1510. The group of St. Jerome, however, should be dated a little before this. St. Jerome is more individual, livelier, and less idealized in treatment, and this feature places the group somewhat closer to the Apostle figures of the Creglingen Assumption, carved probably between 1505 and 1510.

Although there are reputed to have been alabaster works by Riemenschneider in Würzburg Cathedral, evidence points to the former Church of St. Peter in Erfurt as the likely place of origin for the Cleveland St. Jerome. Together with the alabaster Virgin by Riemenschneider which is now in the Louvre, the group has been traced back to the collection of a cleric, *Domprobst* Würschmidt, who resided in Erfurt prior to about 1860, when he retired to Dieburg near Darmstadt. Both works are said, by a contemporary source, to have been carved from alabaster quarried near Erfurt, and since the same source describes the Virgin as coming from the former Church of St. Peter in Erfurt, given the other connections betwen the two works, we may reasonably attribute this location to the group of St. Jerome also.

Because the Virgin is more turbulent in style than the group of St. Jerome, it is unlikely that the figures came from the same altarpiece, although it could be assumed that the Annunciation (of which the Virgin formed part) was ordered first and the altarpiece was later enlarged by lateral figures. On the other hand, Riemenschneider, after he had executed the Annunciation for St. Peter's, may well have received the order for a second altarpiece, either with a St. Jerome alone, or in arrangement whereby the four Latin Fathers flanked a central figure. The use of alabaster for both works was probably stipulated in the contract by the church authorities or the donor who commissioned the Annunciation and the St. Jerome group. And since alabaster was quarried near Erfurt, the material was probably provided and sent to Riemenschneider's workshop in Würzburg. Providing the material for the sculptor was a common practice. We have a documented instance of this in the tomb-monument of Prince-Bishop Rudolf von Scherenberg, for which the marble and sandstone were supplied by his successor, Lorenz von Bibra.

The alabaster statuettes of St. Jerome and the Virgin were offered for sale by the heirs of the cleric Würschmidt in 1892, the Virgin being placed in the

Louvre in 1904. St. Jerome became the property of Mme C. Lelong of Paris; her collection was sold in 1902 and the group passed to Edouard Aynard in Lyon. When this collection was sold in 1913, the carving returned to Germany. It entered the collection of Harry Fuld of Frankfurt am Main, to be ultimately acquired by Cleveland from Fuld's sister, Mrs. Clementine Cramer, who left Germany in the 1930s and went first to England and later to the United States. In recent years, restoration of the figure by the Cleveland Museum removed the unnecessary paint over the cracks in the sculpture. The plates show the statuette after restoration.

Besides the Cleveland group and the Virgin in the Louvre (which for stylistic reasons must be dated in the early 1490s) there are three other alabaster statuettes attributed to Riemenschneider: a figure of St. Barbara in the Böttcherstrasse in Bremen, and a kneeling Virgin and Angel forming an Annunciation, now in the Rijksmuseum in Amsterdam. On stylistic grounds all three alabasters must be considered among Riemenschneider's earliest works, from the decade of the 1480s. Though most of Riemenschneider's works are lindenwood or stone, this series of alabaster sculptures proves that the master's use of this medium, though infrequent, was not just incidental. Riemenschneider must have started working in this material in the early 1480s, when he was a journeyman, and continued using it at least into the first decade of the sixteenth century. Alabaster was a material frequently used in the Upper Rhine region as well as in the Erfurt area, and the contact Riemenschneider must have had with alabaster works in such places as Erfurt and Strasbourg, both before and during his journeyman years, undoubtedly stimulated his own interest in this material.

See also: Justus Bier, "Riemenschneider's St. Jerome and His Other Works in Alabaster," *Art Bulletin* 33, no. 4 (December 1951): 226-34. William M. Milliken, "'St. Jerome and the Lion' by Tilmann Riemenschneider," *Bulletin of the Cleveland Museum of Art* 33 (December 1946): 175-77. Grete Ring, "St. Jerome Extracting the Thorn from the Lion's Foot," *Art Bulletin* 27 (1945): 188-94.

PLATES 10A-B. **Pietà.** About 1505-1510.
Museum of Art, Rhode Island School of Design, Providence, Rhode Island. Lindenwood. Height 17¾ in. (45.2 cm).

In this moving representation of the Pietà, the body of the dead Christ rests on the ground in front of his grieving mother. Mary kneels behind her son, supporting his head and shoulders with her left arm. Her face, shrouded by the veil and wimple she wears, is turned away in deep and private sorrow; her right hand raises the veil to her tear-filled eyes. A long cloak with a scallop design along the border, is draped around her shoulders. One end of this cloak falls forward over the naked feet of Christ, while the other end reaches still further forward, around the raised body of Christ, to the same frontal plane as his limply dangling arms, giving an especially intimate character to the piece. At the same time the poignancy of the image is intensified, for while the figure of Mary, it seems, seeks to encompass her Son, as much with her "pity" as physically with the end of her cloak, the figure of Christ—turned wholly outwards to the viewer, and occupying a relatively shallow plane as it extends across the foreground and projects beyond the pyramidal mass formed by the base and figure of Mary—remains apart.

In so displaying the dead Christ, Riemenschneider has preserved in the figure something of Christ as the symbolic image; the limply hanging arms with the wounds from the nails showing in the hands recall the image of the "crucifixus." But combined with this is Riemenschneider's characteristic naturalism in the rendition of such features as Christ's face, his strained neck, his tortured hands and feet, with veins and tendons showing, and in the very lifelessness of the figure, with its lolling head and drooping arms. Mary, in contrast, is entirely human: her compassion and her grief, which, rather than in any action, are the real subject of the sculpture, as a true Pietà composition, are beautifully expressed not only in her face but in the whole stance of the figure, the flow and fall of the mantle and veil, and the gesture of the hand raising the veil to her eyes.

The Pietà theme of Mary mourning the dead Christ, a scene which occurs between the Deposition and the Entombment, appears in German sculpture from the beginning of the fourteenth century, and, in spite of its Italian name, is a peculiarly German theme. Through the fifteenth century two basic formulations evolved: one strongly realistic, particularly in its emphasis on the agony and suffering of Christ; the other more classically restrained. The first type remained essentially a German form of expression, with many fine examples occuring in the Late Gothic period, while the other spread throughout Europe from Denmark to Northern Italy and has as one of its most famous examples Michelangelo's Pietà of 1497 in St. Peter's in Rome.

Riemenschneider's workshop is known to have produced a considerable number of Pietà and Lamentation images (the latter containing one or more figures in addition to those of Mary and Christ). These carvings are among the finest examples of a third group of Pietà works which combine the characteristics of the two types discussed above. Among the representations originating in Riemenschneider's workshop, the small Providence Pietà has a special significance: from its first mention in the Riemenschneider literature by Eduard Tönnies in 1900, it has been accepted as a work by Riemenschneider's own hand, and in one instance at least (Hubert Schrade, *Tilman Rie-*

menschneider, 1927) is considered to be one of only two representations of
the Pietà by Riemenschneider himself. (The other is the relief in the collection of the University of Würzburg [Plate 36], which in the strict iconographic sense is a Lamentation rather than a Pietà.) Small enough that Riemenschneider required no assistance in carving it, the Providence Pietà is a
precious document of the master's most personal style. It is also very probable that the group is one of Riemenschneider's few extant model figures.
What is evidently a direct copy of the Providence piece can be found in the
Church of St. Anne in Obernburg, south of Aschaffenburg. This, together
with the small size of the original Pietà, indicates that the latter (like the figure of St. Sebastian in the Montreal Museum [Plates 11A, B] served as a
model for the use of assistants in Riemenschneider's workshop, who could
work independently and produce copies on their own without constant
supervision by the master. The need for models of this kind would be particularly great in the case of a famous workshop like Riemenschneider's, where
many journeymen must have sought employment for short periods of time,
without staying long enough to become a real part of the workshop team.
Letting them work from a model on their own was a safe way of using their
services, and ensured a supply of works that could be kept in stock for sale to
smaller churches requiring standard devotional images. The workshop copy
in this case is—characteristically for such copies—larger than the original and
also lacks the inspired motifs of Riemenschneider's original invention, such
as the unusual turning away of Mary's head, the symbolic positioning of
Christ's arms, and the lyrical arrangement of Mary's veil.

The composition of the Providence Pietà appears to have its first formu-
lation here. A survey of other Pietà and Lamentation groups from Riemenschneider's workshop shows the compositional development in his renditions of this theme and also helps in assigning a date to the Providence work.
The early Lamentation group in the pilgrimage church of Hessenthal, carved
probably shortly after Riemenschneider became an assistant in a Würzburg
workshop in 1483, continues the traditional motif of the body of Christ
placed across the lap of his seated mother. This arrangement is repeated in
two later works of about 1515: the Lamentation in the parish church in
Grossostheim, by Riemenschneider and an assistant, and the Pietà in the
Church of the Franciscans in Würzburg, a workshop piece. A new variation
working towards the Providence composition appears in Riemenschneider's
Pietà in the village church of Hassenbach, carved probably in the early 1490s:
here Mary remains seated but the body of Christ now lies on the ground in
front of her in essentially the position of the Providence sculpture. From this
evolves the classic solution of Mary kneeling behind the body of her Son,
which appears in the Providence group and all Riemenschneider's later rep-

resentations of this theme, in which the body of Christ lies on the ground. The Lamentation relief belonging to the University of Würzburg (Plate 36), the Lamentation in the Böttcherstrasse in Bremen (Plate 37), the Lamentation Altarpiece in the parish church of Maidbronn (Plate 46A), and various workshop pieces—all contain the kneeling figure of Mary.

Other stylistic considerations, besides compositional features, place the Providence Pietà in Riemenschneider's mature period. In contrast to the more linear definitions of form found in his early works, light and shadow are the decisive factors here in the organization of the sculpture. This is a primary characteristic of Riemenschneider's mature style as it developed in works carved after 1502. The richer orchestration in light and shade, together with the expressive quality of the work, strongly suggests that the Providence group was carved about the same time as the Creglingen Assumption Altarpiece, in the years between 1505 and 1510.

In the nineteenth century, the Pietà formed part of the collection of Carl Streit, the early biographer of Riemenschneider and owner of various carvings by him. In 1890 this collection was acquired in its totality by the Bayerisches Nationalmuseum in Munich. The Pietà was later sold by the museum and was ultimately acquired by the Museum of Art of the Rhode Island School of Design in 1959.

See also: Justus Bier, "A Pietà by Tilmann Riemenschneider," *Bulletin of Rhode Island School of Design* 46, no. 3 (March 1960): 1-12.

PLATES 11A-B. **St. Sebastian.** About 1505–1510.
Montreal Museum of Fine Arts, Montreal, Canada. Lindenwood. Height 28½ in. (72.1 cm).

Despite its fragile state, the figure of St. Sebastian now in the Montreal Museum of Fine Arts remains a fine illustration of the particular beauty and sensitivity of Riemenschneider's art. The sculpture was acquired by the Montreal Museum in 1971. Before that it was, for twenty-five years, in a private collection in Canada (that of L.V. Randall of Berne, Switzerland, and Montreal). Its provenance goes back to the Gedon collection in Munich in the 1880s. Later, the figure entered the Pfälzische Landesgewerbeanstalt museum collection in Kaiserslautern, where it was kept in storage awaiting restoration. This, however, never took place, and in its extremely delicate but untouched state the work was acquired by the English sculptor William F.C. Ohly, who lived for many years in Frankfurt. Practically unknown up to this time, the sculpture was found in Ohly's collection by Dr. Edmund

Schilling in the early 1930s and was published by the present author in 1936, the figure being then in Berne.

At that time the author was able to determine that the Montreal St. Sebastian was one of Riemenschneider's rare extant model figures. (A good number of these must have existed but only a very few have come down to us—notably, the still smaller Pietà in the museum of the Rhode Island School of Design [Plates 10A, B] and the somewhat larger Virgin with the Christ Child in the Dumbarton Oaks Collection in Washington, D.C. [Plates 16A-C].) The existence of this model figure had been presupposed by the discovery, throughout Germany, of a number of Riemenschneider workshop figures of St. Sebastian, none of which were able to claim the distinction of being the model for the others. To date, ten copies, all larger than the model, have been identified, an indication of the popular demand for this Sebastian composition. In 1962 this author recorded the location of these figures as follows: Munich, Bayerisches Nationalmuseum (Gerolzhofen Altarpiece); Grosslangheim, Pfarrkirche; Nordheim vor der Rhön, St. Sebastianskapelle; Rothenburg ob der Tauber, Wolfgangskapelle; Munich, Galerie Karl Büchs, in 1936; Bremen, Böttcherstrasse; Sulzfeld, Pfarrhof; Traustadt, St. Kilianskirche; Gabolshausen, St. Laurentiuskirche; Schloss Haidenburg, collection Freifrau Myrrha von Aretin. Since each of the extant copies is by a different hand, it would seem likely that Riemenschneider kept this model figure in his workshop for a considerable number of years, to be used as an example to copy or follow by the journeymen who sought temporary employment with him and whom he set to work on their own. The comparatively late date of the one copy that has a documented date—the Rothenburg St. Sebastian of 1514—also supports this assumption. The need for model figures from which assistants could produce copies on their own, without constant supervision, must have been particularly great in the case of a famous workshop like Riemenschneider's, where many journeymen would seek work but not stay long enough to make it worthwhile for the master to make them a real part of the workshop team. (Guild rules prescribed that any journeyman seeking employment must be taken in.) Letting them work from a particular model on their own would be a safe, profitable, and efficient way of using their services, since a certain number of pieces were undoubtedly kept in stock for sale to smaller churches, and the works produced in this way could be used for that purpose. (Larger works were still produced only on a commission basis at this time.) In this respect the Dumbarton Oaks Virgin and Child is a little different: rather than serving as a model figure for general use in the workshop, possibly over a number of years, this group in the author's opinion was specifically created as the model for the commissioned sculpture of the Volkach Madonna and Child in a Rosary.

In Riemenschneider's portrayal, St. Sebastian appears as a slender, wistful figure, with his head inclined to one side, his right arm bound tightly behind his back, and his left leg set slightly forward. The flowing ends of his loincloth form a distinctive motif, as does the mantle which falls from his left shoulder in a graceful configuration that both echoes and encloses the movement of the figure, like a mandorla. Because the workshop figures of St. Sebastian are almost identical to the original in respect to the movement of the figure and the richness of its articulation, it is possible to use these figures to reconstruct the missing forms of the Montreal St. Sebastian, and as a result we may safely assume that the left arm and hand reached down to catch up the mantle on that side.

Two of the copies (the Gerolzhofen and Grosslangheim figures) are mirror images of the original, possibly reversed in order to give some change of movement to the drapery, but still very close to the original design. In spite of the close imitation, however, none of the derivative figures displays the grace or pathos of the original, which remains far superior in both feeling and execution.

In the Montreal St. Sebastian the emphasis is on the expression of spiritual strength and feeling, which are so clearly apparent in the slender, gentle face, with its delicate features, its air of calm acceptance, and its fleeting tender smile that seems to show the saint transcending all earthly suffering and looking to the world beyond. The figure demonstrates Riemenschneider's characteristic avoidance of any element of harshness in both form and emotional content, with the result in this instance that the predominant impression is not of the cruel nature of the martyrdom or the suffering endured but of the poignant, ethereal beauty of the figure. In its depiction of youthful beauty and saintliness the image of St. Sebastian recalls such figures as St. Lawrence (Plates 6A-B) and John the Evangelist (Plate 33H), and like all Riemenschneider's portrayals of this kind it is totally convincing.

A fundamental element in the extraordinarily fine carving is the play of light and shade on the figure, and this in turn is important in assigning a date to the sculpture. The rich orchestration of light and shadow produces an effect of vivid three-dimensionality which can only be associated with Riemenschneider's mature period, in particular the years between 1505 and 1510, which saw the creation of the Creglingen Assumption Altarpiece. A date within these years for the St. Sebastian is again supported by the fact that the one copy of this figure (the St. Sebastian from the Wolfgangskapelle in Rothenburg) is known to have been carved in 1514.

See also: David Giles Carter, "Riemenschneider's St. Sebastian: Haunting Beauty and Nobility of Form," M^{11} (a Quarterly Review of the Montreal Museum of Fine Arts) 3, no. 3 (December 1971): 17-23. (This comprehensive article discusses the Montreal Sebastian in a much wider context and touches on many aspects not mentioned here: for instance, the different iconographical traditions followed by northern and Italian artists in their depictions of this saint; an antecedent for Riemenschneider's preferred form in a statuette of 1497 attributed to an Augsburg master; a possible further connection with Ulm in the "reticence"—akin to that found in both Michael Erhart and Riemenschneider—of a youthful St. Sebastian attributed to the Ulm sculptor Jörg Syrlin the Younger; and an instructive comparison between Riemenschneider's figure and the Sebastian of Mathias Grünewald in a wing of the Isenheim altarpiece, to illustrate the different nature of the Late Gothic and the Renaissance.)

PLATES 12A-B. **St. Anthony Abbot.** About 1510.

Busch-Reisinger Museum, Harvard University, Cambridge, Massachusetts. Lindenwood. Height 47 in. (119.4 cm).

St. Anthony is portrayed here as a tall, lean figure, standing with feet slightly apart on stony ground. He wears a long cloak that reaches to the ground. Apparently fastened at the neck, this cloak falls open in front to reveal the simple robe worn underneath. His slippered feet are visible below the robe. Part of the saint's mantle is drawn up across the front of his robe and pressed, apronlike, to the body by each arm. The predominant funnel-shaped folds of this piece of drapery, and the short, broken folds within, contrast sharply with the otherwise strongly vertical organization of the drapery which is especially evident in the straight, narrow folds of the robe above the saint's feet and in the long, unbroken line of the cloak sweeping down on the left side of the figure.

On his head the saint wears a high hat, Gothic in style, which is pulled right down to his brows and which curves outward at both sides. The face of St. Anthony is that of an elderly man, long and lean, with almond-shaped eyes surrounded by heavily lined areas, a long, straight nose, and sunken cheeks. The mouth is slightly open. The rest of the face is hidden by a long, luxuriant, curly beard and flowing locks of hair that fall abundantly about his shoulders, emphasizing the careworn, ascetic aspect of the face they frame. The saint's expression is pensive and a little sad.

The hands of the saint, which were probably carved from separate pieces of wood and set into the sleeves, are lost. This is the only serious loss the figure has suffered. There are some splits in the wood but generally the condition of the figure is good. The base and toe of the left shoe have been restored. As it appears now the lindenwood figure is without paint. Traces of gesso, however, would indicate that it was polychromed at one time.

The statue was acquired for the Busch-Reisinger Museum of Harvard University from the New York Art Market in 1969. Nothing is known about the original location of the work or about its provenance prior to the late nineteenth or early twentieth century. However, the fact that the figure is hollowed out at the back indicates that it was intended to be placed in a setting where it would be viewed only from the front, as in the shrine of an altarpiece or against the pier of a church.

The identification of the Cambridge figure as St. Anthony Abbot can be safely assumed from its close resemblance in dress and pose to the wood figure of St. Anthony Abbot in the Roman Catholic chapel dedicated to this saint in Grosslangheim. It is possible that the Cambridge figure originally held a staff and book in his hands, as did the Grosslangheim St. Anthony. A relief in the same chapel showing the burial of St. Paul by St. Anthony further supports the identification.

St. Anthony Abbot is generally considered the first of the Christian hermits, the so-called "desert fathers." Born in Egypt in the middle of the third century A.D., he lived a solitary, ascetic existence most of his life, first by the Nile river and in later years in a cave on a mountain near the Red Sea. Tradition has it that he was over one hundred years old when he died, having survived by several years his latter-day companion, St. Paul the hermit. As one story goes, during their sojourn in the desert together, both old men were sustained by bread brought to them each day by a raven—a scene Grünewald depicted in his Isenheim Altarpiece. St. Anthony's influence and following, which included the hermit monastic communities he established, were considerable during his lifetime, and veneration of him continued for many centuries after his death.

Stylistically, the Cambridge St. Anthony is closely related to the figures in the Riemenschneider Altarpiece of Christ and the Twelve Apostles, which was completed and delivered in 1509 for the Church of St. Kilian in Windsheim (Plate 31B). The Windsheim figures show the same narrow proportions, vertical emphasis and relatively simple outline. The figure at the outer end of the group in the right wing of the altarpiece (as viewed), though it is one of a group of three relief figures carved as a single sculpture, is particularly similar in the position of the head, the tilt of the upper part of the body, the motif of the drapery, and the simple, straight left edge of the figure contrasting with the angle and broken line made by the arm and drapery folds on the right side. These similarities could indicate that the Cambridge St. Anthony was designed as part of a group composition similar to that of the Windsheim Altarpiece, where the organization of the figures is controlled by the restrictions of the shrine and wing spaces; in this case, the straight left edge of the figure would suggest that the carving was intended to be placed close to the parallel edge of the shrine. On the other hand, these characteristics could equally well apply to a single-figure composition, intended, for example, to be set against a pier. And indeed Charles Kuhn has argued in a recent article that the "self-sufficient design of the drapery contained within the closed silhouette" makes the single image thesis more plausible.

While this remains an open question, the stylistic correspondence of the St. Anthony to the Windsheim Apostles clearly suggests a date close in time, of about 1510. The characteristics shared by these figures, which relate not only to the organization of the figures but also to the carving of the drapery and the facial type of the St. Anthony, which recurs in the Windsheim figures of St. Andrew and St. James the Elder, are all typical of Riemenschneider's mature work in the years between 1503 and 1510.

Though appearing more simple in design and perhaps less rich in effect than the Windsheim figures, the Cambridge St. Anthony is a work of high quality and in the opinion of the author it was undoubtedly carved by Riemenschneider's own hand. The expressive character of the head is typical of Riemenschneider's figures and the particular funnel-shaped motif of the folds in the drawn-up part of the saint's cloak is reminiscent of the motifs used in the marble monuments of the Prince-Bishops Rudolf von Scherenberg and Lorenz von Bibra (Plates 22A, 43B) and in the stone figure of Empress Cunegund on the lid of the imperial tomb at Bamberg (Plate 40B). On individual figures in wood, comparable motifs appear on the Baltimore statue of St. Anne (Plate 5B) and the model figure of "Sant Mathias" (Plate 26A), which is now in the sculpture collection of the Staatliche Museen in West Berlin.

See also: Charles L. Kuhn, "Riemenschneider in the Harvard Collections," *Art Bulletin* 56, no. 2 (June 1974): 244-47.

PLATES 13A-B. **The Mourning Virgin.** About 1510.
William Rockhill Nelson Gallery of Art, Atkins Museum of Fine Arts, Kansas City, Missouri. Lindenwood. Height 23 in. (58.1 cm).

Since it was first published in 1854, this figure of the Mourning Virgin has been singled out in several instances as a most expressive work by Riemenschneider's own hand. In the author's opinion it is one of Riemenschneider's finest small statuettes, a document of his highly refined and sensitive craftsmanship.

This representation of the Virgin (which is also known as "Mary under the Cross") is based on Mary's presence at the Crucifixion and shows Mary mourning the death of her Son. Figures of this kind are found in Crucifixion groups, where, together with St. John the Evangelist and others, they flank the Crucifixus. An example of this can be seen in the shrine-work of the Dettwang Altarpiece (Plate 41A). The statuette now in Kansas City is known to have been part of a Crucifixion group on an altar of the Stiftskirche in Aschaffenburg. The Virgin in this instance stands with her hands clasped slightly to one side, in a prayerlike gesture, and with her veil caught up between them. Her head is turned aside in sorrow and her eyes cast down. The face—which must be among Riemenschneider's most eloquent—is wonderfully expressive of sadness mixed with compassion; the contours of the cheek and mouth, and the eyes and drawn brows in particular reveal the intensity of grief and suffering. The Virgin wears the customary mourning apparel of veil and wimple covering her head and neck. The end of this veil forms a characteristic Gothic S-curve where it falls below the clasped hands of the Virgin. A loose mantle is draped around her shoulders and covers much of the long robe she wears, which reaches to the ground and below which only the tip of her left foot protrudes. The mantle is gathered up on both sides under the arms of the figure in a way that produces a rich display of folds both above and below. Between the folds are smooth, calm areas. The motif of the reversed lateral fold of the mantle which appears here is also found in many of Riemenschneider's figures of the Madonna, as, for example, the sandstone Madonna of about 1505 in the Mainfränkisches Museum in Würzburg, and the later stone Virgin and Child of 1516–1522 belonging to the Städelsches Kunstinstitut in Frankfurt. The same motif occurs in the Mary of the Annunciation, of 1502–1504, in the Rothenburg Altarpiece of the Holy Blood. Despite its small size, the figure of the Mourning Virgin projects a certain grandeur. At the same time, the richness of the drapery and the relative bulk this gives to the figure only emphasize the poignancy of the slender grieving face, shrouded by the veil and wimple.

Both the style of the figure—the abstract language of the drapery and folds—and the particularly expressive character of the head indicate that this is a work from Riemenschneider's mature period. Most probably the Mourning Virgin was created about the time of the Creglingen Altarpiece of the Assumption of the Virgin, when Riemenschneider was at the very height of his powers. On stylistic grounds, the Creglingen Altarpiece should be dated about 1505 to 1510. In the author's opinion the Mourning Virgin was carved by Riemenschneider probably in 1510 or shortly thereafter. In its stylistic qualities and the general arrangement of the drapery, the Mourning Virgin is closely related to the figure of Mary in the shrine of the Creglingen Altarpiece (Plate 33B). We find a similar arrangement of the veil and mantle, many of the same motifs, and a similar treatment of the drapery in the use of wide, unbroken areas between the folds. Both figures illustrate the more advanced concepts of Riemenschneider's mature style, not only in the clearer, calmer arrangement of forms, but in the new importance of light and shade in the carving to create a feeling of space and depth and at the same time heighten the emotional expression. The Mourning Virgin can also be compared to the figure of Mary in the relief of Christ among the Doctors in the predella of the same altarpiece, while the expressive quality of the face is found in several of the Apostles in the Creglingen shrine group, most notably in the figure of James the Elder (Plate 33J), who seems to express the same sorrowful feeling.

The small Pietà in the collection of the Rhode Island School of Design (Plates 10A, B), which dates from roughly the same period, about 1505 to 1510, and which is again an example of Riemenschneider's personal style, shows the same richer instrumentation in light and shade as the Creglingen figures and the Mourning Virgin. There, too, the focus of the work is on Mary's grief and compassion.

The figure of the Mourning Virgin is in unusually fine condition. Apart from two tiny triangular pieces set into the base, where very slight damage had occurred, the only restoration the statuette has received is the application of a brown stain over the entire surface of the figure. This was almost certainly applied sometime in the latter part of the nineteenth century. Restorers of that period were accustomed to use this brown stain on lindenwood carvings (naturally grayish white in color) in order to simulate the appearance of oak, which was then more fashionable.

The provenance of the Mourning Virgin has been thoroughly investigated by the author, who has known this sculpture since the 1920s. The Crucifixion group of which the figure was originally part was removed from the altar of the Stiftskirche in Aschaffenburg in the early nineteenth century. (A Neo-Gothic altarpiece was erected in its place in the mid-nineteenth century.) In 1851 the Mourning Virgin was acquired by Dr. Jakob von Hefner-Alteneck prior to his appointment as the first director of the Bayerisches Nationalmuseum. The statuette quickly gained fame after being published by von Hefner-Alteneck in his work on medieval costume, in 1854, and discussed by Wilhelm von Bode in his history of German sculpture, of 1886, and by Wilhelm Lübke in an essay on Tilmann Riemenschneider in 1891.

After the death of Jakob von Hefner-Alteneck, the figure was successively in the collections of Hans Schwarz, Dr. Walter von Pannwitz, and, after the latter's death in 1920, Frau Catalina von Pannwitz at De Hartekamp near Bennebroek in the Netherlands. It was then acquired by a New York dealer and in 1964 became the property of the William Rockhill Nelson Gallery of Art.

The Crucifixus from the group containing the Mourning Virgin was acquired for the Berlin Staatliche Museen and is today in the Bode-Museum in East Berlin. The figure of St. John is lost and is known only through nineteenth-century copies made by the Würzburg restorer and sculptor, Andreas Halbig.

PLATES 14A-B. **St. Stephen.** About 1510.
Cleveland Museum of Art, Cleveland, Ohio. Lindenwood, polychromed and gilded. Height 36½ in. (92.7 cm).

The figure of St. Stephen, together with the figure of St. Lawrence (Plates 6A, B), was acquired by the Cleveland Museum of Art in 1959. In spite of the later date assigned to this figure, it is clear that St. Stephen was designed as the counterpart to St. Lawrence and was intended to serve in the same altarpiece. The high quality of both figures and the sensitivity with which they are finished, especially evident in the expressive faces and hands, leaves no doubt that both figures were carved by Riemenschneider's own hand.

Like St. Lawrence, Stephen is portrayed as a devout, saintly young man, dressed in the deacon's robes customary in representations of both saints. He is identified by his attribute and the instrument of his martyrdom, namely, the stones he carries in the fold of his robe. The story of this first martyr for Christ is recorded in the Acts of the Apostles, chapters six and seven. As recounted there, Stephen was the first of the seven helpers taken by the Apostles in Jerusalem: "full of faith and power," he "did great wonders and miracles among the people," until, falsely accused of blasphemy by his detractors, he was taken before the Jewish Council, whom he in turn denounced and so provoked that they "cast him out of the city, and stoned him" to death. Legend relates that some centuries later his body was miraculously found and reburied in Rome beside St. Lawrence. Allegedly St. Lawrence moved to one side, yielding the place of honor to St. Stephen. This legend of the burial explains the frequent association of these saints, who in fact lived two centuries apart and in very different circumstances.

In composition and character, the image of St. Stephen presents an interesting contrast to his counterpart. Whereas the St. Lawrence has a gentle sway to the figure and a predominance of curves in the design, the figure of Stephen stands erect and has a strongly vertical emphasis. Face, figure, and drapery are all of leaner, less full proportions, sharp and angular in character where the same features of St. Lawrence are soft and gently rounded. The contrast is greatest in the folds of the mantle and in the modeling of the face and neck. The pose and demeanor of St. Stephen combine with the treatment of these features to suggest a character that is both more ascetic and more resolute, without quite the resignation and humility we find in St. Lawrence. A comparison of the engravings of St. Lawrence and St. Stephen by Martin Schongauer makes it clear that, as in several other instances that we know of, the design of Riemenschneider's figures was influenced by the Schongauer engravings. The sensitive characterization and expression of mood and feeling in the figures, however, are Riemenschneider's alone. (Illustrations of 1921 and 1929 show St. Stephen holding a palm leaf in his left hand, corresponding to those held by both saints in the Schongauer engravings, but this has since disappeared.)

The St. Stephen and St. Lawrence figures may have formed part of the lost altarpiece that is known to have been completed by Riemenschneider about 1510 for an All Saints altar in the Church of the Dominican Nuns in Rothenburg (see pp. 51–52, above). A date of about 1510 for the figure of St. Stephen, placing it in the last years of work on the altarpiece, is indicated on various counts. The figure is similar in style to the two female saints in the Frankfurt Historisches Museum, which are thought to have come from the same altarpiece. They, in turn, on the basis of the resemblance of one saint to the figure of Elisabeth Stieber on her tomb-monument in the parish church in Buttenheim, and from their own stylistic relationship, can both be dated about 1508. St. Stephen is also similar in style to several of the Apostles in the shrine of the Creglingen Assumption Altarpiece which this author considers to have been carved between 1505 and 1510: in facial features St. Stephen is very close to John the Evangelist (Plate 33H); the free treatment of the loosely curling hair recalls the two Apostles at the back of the group on the right (Plate 33F); and the surprising twist of his robe is not unlike the swirling drapery of the angels surrounding Mary. Other pertinent comparisons have been made by William Wixom, both with the bust sculptures of St. Totnan and St. Kolonat, known to have been carved between 1508 and 1510 for the high altar of Würzburg Cathedral (Plate 35C), and with the slender figure of St. Andrew from the Windsheim Altarpiece of the Twelve Apostles (Plate 31A), which was delivered in 1509.

Like the St. Lawrence, the lindenwood figure of St. Stephen is neatly hollowed out at the back to prevent cracking. Later layers of paint, as well as the gold foil dots added to the alba in the late eighteenth or early nineteenth century, were removed in the Cleveland Museum's restoration workshop, with the result that much of the original sixteenth-century polychromy, gold leaf and silver foil, is again evident.

For the provenance of St. Stephen, see pages 52–53, above.

See also: Justus Bier, "Two Statues: St. Stephen and St. Lawrence by Riemenschneider in the Cleveland Museum of Art," *Art Quarterly* 23, no. 3 (Autumn 1960): 214-27. William D. Wixom, "Two Lindenwood Sculptures by Tilmann Riemenschneider," *Bulletin of the Cleveland Museum of Art* 46, no. 9 (November 1959): 187-97.

PLATES 15A-B. **St. Burchard.** About 1519–1523.

Samuel H. Kress Collection, National Gallery of Art, Washington, D.C. Lindenwood. Height 32½ in. (82.6 cm).

This bust of a bishop, which has long been considered to represent St. Burchard, the first bishop of Würzburg, demonstrates the final evolution in Riemenschneider's style as this first appeared in works carved towards the end of the second decade of the sixteenth century. It is one of the few late works by Riemenschneider that we have in the United States. Though the original location of the figure is unknown, its provenance can be traced back to the first half of the nineteenth century, when the figure formed part of the well-known Sattler collection in Castle Mainberg, near Kitzingen. This collection was started by Wilhelm Sattler, who bought Castle Mainberg from the Bavarian government in 1822, and was enlarged by his son Jens Sattler. Together with other works by Riemenschneider, such as the figure of Mary Magdalene borne aloft by angels (Plates 20A, B) and two wing reliefs, all from the Münnerstadt Altarpiece, the bust remained in the Sattler Collection through the nineteenth century. After the death of Jens Sattler, the collection was auctioned in 1901. The St. Burchard bust then entered the collection of Benoit Oppenheim in Berlin and was later acquired through a Munich dealer by the late Henry Goldman of New York. Since 1945, as part of the Kress donation, the bust has been in the National Gallery of Art in Washington, D.C.

The identification of the figure as St. Burchard, as has already been indicated, is a matter of tradition and has on occasion been disputed. No reason exists to discredit the designation, however, and it is especially plausible when we consider that Carl Streit, who first used the name in 1888, may have taken it from Sattler, who probably bought the bust from the church for which it was made. St. Burchard was consecrated bishop of the new See of Würzburg by St. Boniface in 741. He was responsible for the building of the Cathedral of Christ in Würzburg, and after his death in 754 he was greatly venerated in that region. In the early eleventh century the Church of St. Burchard in Würzburg was built in his honor, and his remains were transferred there from their original resting-place in the Cathedral.

The bust is cut from lindenwood, which is the only wood Riemenschneider used in his figural carvings. Traces of paint and linen in the depths of the mantle folds prove that the figure was originally polychromed, although this would not have taken place in Riemenschneider's workshop. (Riemenschneider was listed as a sculptor among the masters of the Würzburg Guild of St. Luke, and as such, he was allowed to do only incidental polychroming and gilding of his sculptures. Works that were to be fully painted had to be turned over to a painter's workshop.) A later coat of paint was removed in the early twentieth century, and apart from the delicate marking of the pupil and iris of the eyes in black and gray—as was Riemenschneider's customary practice with his figures—the bust is now without paint.

Though called a "bust," the St. Burchard is more aptly described as a half-length figure. Whereas all the busts that Riemenschneider designed as such (for instance, the bust of St. Urban and the three busts of the Franconian Apostles [Plates 4, 35c]) are carved full round in both head and body, only the head of the St. Burchard is treated this way; the back of the body remains flat and unworked. This kind of treatment, on the other hand, is typical of Riemenschneider's statues that were intended to be placed in boxlike shrines or in front of piers, where they would be seen only from the front. Probably the bust of St. Burchard was cut from a full-length figure at the time the figure was converted to a reliquary. This may have taken place in the early years of the nineteenth century as a result of the secularization of ecclesiastical treasures by the state in 1803; with the seizure of reliquaries in precious metal, new accommodation for relics had to be found. The style of certain additions made to the figure at the time of its conversion, namely, the relic box, the restored staff, and the decorations to the miter, which appear in a late nineteenth-century illustration, certainly supports this argument. These additions were all removed early in this century. The crude cutout now seen on the breast of St. Burchard is where the relic box was attached, placed so that it seemed to hold the cope together like a clasp. Only the Gothic-style crosier that St. Burchard now holds is a more modern addition, made to replace the nineteenth-century restoration.

St. Burchard is shown here in the full regalia of a bishop, wearing a miter with fringed infulae, a cope, alb, and amice. His right hand is raised in the gesture of benediction; his left holds the crosier and sudarium. The head inclines slightly to one side, which seems to emphasize the expression of humility on the rather youthful, ascetic-looking face. The basic structure of this face, with its prominent nose and cheekbones, finely-cut almond-shaped eyes, down-turned mouth, and strong, broad chin, is a type Riemenschneider used repeatedly in his representations of bishops, adapting it only to the different ages of his subjects. Examples are found in the figure of St. Kilian from the Münnerstadt Altarpiece of 1490–1492, now in the Münnerstadt parish church; the effigy of Prince-Bishop Rudolf von Scherenberg on his tomb-monument in Würzburg Cathedral, of 1496–1499 (Plate 22B); and the bust of St. Kilian from the high altar of Würzburg Cathedral, carved between 1508 and 1510 (Plate 35D). The St. Burchard head lacks the expression of dominating power found in the heads of these older subjects, but in its subtle beauty and air of calm resignation and spiritual dedication it exemplifies instead the peculiar charm of Riemenschneider's youthful faces.

Among other statues of bishops attributed to Riemenschneider, the figure of St. Erasmus from Kitzingen, now in the sculpture collection of the Staatliche Museen in West Berlin, seems particularly close to the St. Burchard. Though the face is again that of an older man, the general movement of the figure—with the slight inclination of the head and the left half of the mantle drawn over to the right side, breaking the vertical flow of the folds of the vestment below—is very similar. Unique to the St. Burchard bust, however, is a new purity of form and simplicity of treatment which is apparent in the smoother planes of the face and the emphasis on the tectonic structure, and in the clear, uncomplicated arrangement of the drapery: the bishop's choir-mantle, which falls in a sweeping curve, sharply changes direction under the elbow, and is thrown simply over the left arm. The hand holding the crosier is thus completely visible and, in spite of the glove, is shown with very articulate expression. The clarity of form and restraint of expression which characterize the St. Burchard bust clearly indicate that the figure belongs in Riemenschneider's late period and should be dated about the same time as his great masterpiece of these years, the Maidbronn Lamentation Altarpiece of about 1519–1523. A comparison with the figure of St. John from this altarpiece (Plate 46C) shows the two figures particularly close in their simplicity of form, delicacy of detail, and strength of religious feeling.

See also: Justus Bier, "The Bust of a Bishop by Tilmann Riemenschneider," *Art Quarterly* 6, no. 3 (1943): 158–66.

PLATES 16A-C. **The Virgin with the Christ Child.** 1521.
Dumbarton Oaks Collection, Washington, D.C. Lindenwood. Height
37½ in. (95.2 cm).

This model figure was introduced into the Riemenschneider literature in
1937, when it was still in a private collection in Germany. Since 1940 it has
formed part of the Dumbarton Oaks House Collection belonging to Harvard University, installed in the Dumbarton Oaks mansion in Georgetown,
Washington, D.C.

The small figure of the Virgin and Child is an outstanding work, significant for many reasons. Because of its close relationship to the much larger
Madonna in a Rosary in the Pilgrimage Church in Kirchberg near Volkach
(Plate 44), the Dumbarton Oaks Madonna is considered by the author to
have been created as the model for that figure. Since the Volkach Madonna is
known to have been commissioned from Riemenschneider in 1521, the
model figure may safely be assigned that same date. The figure thus adds a
(circumstantially) documented work to the master's oeuvre, which is so
often elusive in regard to exact dating.

Considering the evident size of Riemenschneider's workshop and the
steady flow of commissions he received over a period of more than three decades, a considerable number of model figures, like the Dumbarton Oaks Madonna, must have existed, which enabled his numerous assistants to proceed
with work on hand without constant supervision or direct help from the
master. However, though we may reasonably infer the existence of such
models, very few of these are known to us. Of those that are, the most notable (besides the present figure) are the Pietà in the Rhode Island School of
Design (Plates 10A, B) and the figure of St. Sebastian in the Montreal Museum of Fine Arts (Plates 11A, B), both now in North America. These, however, belong to the years 1505–1510, in Riemenschneider's mature period
more than a decade earlier; the Dumbarton Oaks Madonna is the only extant
model from Riemenschneider's late period.

(A tiny figure of the Virgin and Child acquired by the Mainfränkisches
Museum in Würzburg in 1969 has been assumed to have been either a model
for a large figure or the centerpiece of a chandelier, similar to that still hanging in the nave of the Church of St. Lawrence in Nuremberg. The author,
however, would again place this in Riemenschneider's mature period, considerably earlier than the Dumbarton Oaks figure.)

Unlike the Volkach Madonna in a Rosary, which is largely a workshop
piece, the Dumbarton Oaks Madonna and Child is clearly by Riemenschneider's own hand. Small enough for Riemenschneider to execute on his own,
without the help of assistants, the figure serves as a fine example of the mas-

ter's most personal style during his late period. The superb composition and sensitive treatment of the surface show that the sculptor preserved an outstanding vitality and mastery of his craft well into his advanced age (he was then about sixty) and should dispel any notion that his work became stereotyped or repetitious in his later years. The wood figure also proves that Riemenschneider continued working in this medium as well as in stone, and that he achieved the same classic simplicity and grandeur—the hallmarks of his late style—in his wood carvings as he did in such stone masterpieces as the sandstone Madonna of 1516–1522 in the Liebieghaus in Frankfurt (Plate 45), the tomb-monument of Prince-Bishop Lorenz von Bibra (Plates 43A-D), completed in 1522, and the majestic Maidbronn Altarpiece created between 1519 and 1523 (Plates 46A-D). Though these stone sculptures are perhaps better known examples of Riemenschneider's late works, wood carvings such as the Dumbarton Oaks Madonna and the Steinach Crucifixus of 1516 (Plate 42B) are certainly their equal.

While most of Riemenschneider's sculptures in wood are hollowed out at the back, the Dumbarton Oaks Virgin is carved in the round and carefully finished front and back. Since we know that the Volkach Madonna in a Rosary was originally hanging freely from the arch of the choir (as it is again now) and was intended to be seen from front and back, further proof is provided that we are indeed dealing with a figure created as a model. The back view of the model figure (Plate 16c) shows the long full tresses of the Virgin's hair flowing rhythmically down over the simple vertical folds of her mantle cloak, and falling well below her waist. The head and body of the Christ Child are likewise fully carved behind.

The Dumbarton Oaks Virgin and Child is far superior to the large figure of the Madonna (well over twice the size) for which it served as model. The small figures are full of natural grace and feeling: instead of lifeless doll-like features, there is grief and fervor in the model's face; in place of a Child awkwardly enthroned, the infant in the Dumbarton Oaks group is supported gracefully and convincingly on his mother's hip. Her left hand is protectively positioned around the Child's thigh and knee, the thumb raised as though anticipating sudden movement by him. This safer placement leaves the Virgin's right arm free and her hand resting lightly on her mantle, neither holding nor supporting the Christ Child. This novel feature is not found in any other representation of the theme, though it is reminiscent of the very early Werbach (Plate 19), Boston (Plate 1) and Neumünster Madonnas all from the first years of the 1490s, with the difference that, in the early examples, the Child's foot is held or caressed by the Virgin's right hand. The motif of the Virgin's mantle gathered up in front of her lap and held by the hand which supports the Child also recalls the early Werbach figure.

The Dumbarton Oaks Christ Child extends his arms in what may be interpreted as a welcoming gesture toward the beholder; the same feeling is found in the faint but definite smile on his face and the way he leans forward in his mother's arms. This graceful little figure (much less stilted than those in the early groups, despite their more playful pose) here wears a short-sleeved garment with a low neckline, lightly secured in the front and falling open. This garbed Child, which is highly unusual in Riemenschneider's work, must not have found approval with his patrons, since in the Volkach group the Christ Child is again naked. (Madonnas with the clothed Christ Child are a rarity in South German sculpture of the period. The author knows of only one other Riemenschneider Virgin with a clothed Child, which perished with the building of the Fränkisches Luitpold Museum in Würzburg during the last days of World War II.)

While we have noted that the general stance of the Dumbarton Oaks group harks back to Riemenschneider's earliest figures of the Virgin and Christ Child, particularly to the Werbach Madonna, incorporating the typical Gothic S-curve that is found in that work, in other respects there is a close resemblance to the much later stone Virgin and Child of 1516–1522, in the Liebieghaus in Frankfurt (Plate 45). In both the stone figure and the Dumbarton Oaks group the lines of the drapery are greatly simplified and there is a notable absence of Late Gothic swirls in the folds. The composition and motifs are transformed, in each case, according to the canons of Riemenschneider's late style, and both figures display the characteristic simplicity and grandeur of the works of this period.

Except for some breakages in the Christ Child's hands and some gouging and obliteration of the Virgin's hair around the top of her head, presumably to accommodate the later addition of a crown (since lost), the group is for the most part intact. (A recent report on the condition of the figure notes the loosening of a large carved, vertical board inserted sometime after 1787.) The sculpture is not polychromed and preserves the natural off-white color of aged lindenwood. Riemenschneider's customary tinting of the pupil and iris of the eyes can be clearly seen in Plate 16B.

The provenance of this model figure cannot be traced beyond the early years of this century. In 1937 the figure was acquired by Mr. and Mrs. Robert Woods Bliss, the founders of the Dumbarton Oaks Collection, which they donated to Harvard University in 1940. The author first saw this work in Munich during the winter of 1935–1936, at which time he learned that the dealer Wilhelm Böhler had acquired it in Vienna around 1910.

See also: Charles L. Kuhn, "Riemenschneider in the Harvard Collections," *Art Bulletin* 56, no. 2 (June 1974): 244-47.

Selected Works in Germany

PLATE 17. **Tomb-Monument of Eberhard von Grumbach.**
About 1488.
Parish Church, Rimpar. Gray sandstone. Height 215 cm; width 86 cm
(84¾ in.; 34 in.)

The tomb-monument of the knight Eberhard von Grumbach, who died on
October 7, 1487, is the earliest work by Riemenschneider that can be connected with a definite date. The monument is still in the Grumbach chapel in
the choir of the parish church in Rimpar. When the church was rebuilt in
the middle of the nineteenth century, the choir and lower section of the
tower were the only part of the early Gothic edifice left intact. The inscription surrounding the figure reads: "Anno d[omi]ni 1487 an sant Affra tag
starbe der gestreng und vest her Ebierhart von Grumbach, Ritter zu Rimpar, dem [got] gnad am[en]." (In the year of our Lord 1487 on St. Affra's
day died the severe and honorable lord Ebierhart von Grumbach, Knight of
Rimpar, may God grant him grace amen.) The nose, scabbard, and mace are
restored. Riemenschneider was also responsible for the tomb-monument of
Eberhard von Grumbach's daughter, Elisabeth; see Plate 30.

PLATE 18. **John the Baptist.** Before 1490.
Parish Church, Hassfurt. Lindenwood, polychromy removed. Height 180
cm (71 in.)

The large figure of John the Baptist must have been carved by Riemenschneider around the same time as, or earlier than, the Münnerstadt Altarpiece of Mary Magdalene (1490–1492), since one of the workshop figures
from the superstructure of that altarpiece clearly derives from it. (The figure
is still in the parish church in Münnerstadt.) The index finger and middle
finger of the saint's right hand and the front legs of the lamb have been restored. Polychromy probably dating from the baroque period has been removed.

Plate 19. **The Virgin with the Christ Child**. About 1490. Destroyed 1945.

Formerly Deutsches Museum, Berlin. Lindenwood. Height 143 cm (56¼ in.)

This figure of the Virgin with the Christ Child is said to have come from Werbach in the Tauber Valley. Its origin in Werbach is of particular interest, since we know that Johann von Allendorf, chancellor to Prince-Bishop Rudolf von Scherenberg and one of the executors for Tilmann Riemenschneider's uncle, Nikolaus Riemenschneider, had property in Werbach. It is a documented fact that Johann von Allendorf gave several commissions to Riemenschneider (one of these being a commission of 1494 for a representation of the Fourteen Helpers in Need, a fragment of which is now in the Cloisters Collection in New York [Plates 2A-C]), and it is conceivable that he commissioned this figure of the Madonna and Child from the young sculptor. The work was acquired for the Berlin Museums in 1884 from Tauberbischofsheim, near Werbach, and exhibited in the Deutsches Museum in Berlin until World War II. Ironically, it appears that the figure was destroyed by fire in 1945 in the depot to which it had been taken for safekeeping to escape the bombing.

In the author's opinion, the figure is Riemenschneider's earliest representation of the Virgin with the Christ Child, the first of many Madonna figures which range in date from the first years of the 1490s to the late 1520s and which span his career as a sculptor. Unlike the later figures of the Madonna, the Werbach Madonna conveys a strong impression of three-dimensional depth, which is due to the spiralling, upward movement of the figure of the Virgin, as well as to the lateral position of the Christ Child, who is balanced on his mother's hip and supported by her left hand. The richly moving folds of the drapery, the sudden movement of the mantle drawn up to one side, and the slightly melancholy expression of the young Madonna, contrasting with the lively Christ Child, also indicate an early date. The figure may be compared, especially in regard to its expression of youthful innocence, to the figures of Mary Magdalene from the Münnerstadt Altarpiece of 1490–1492 (Plates 20A-E).

Plates 20A-K. **Sculptures from the Münnerstadt Altarpiece of Mary Magdalene**. 1490–1492.

The Altarpiece of Mary Magdalene for the high altar of the parish church in Münnerstadt is Riemenschneider's earliest documented work. It was commissioned from Riemenschneider by the City Council of Münnerstadt on June 24, 1490, for the sum of 145 guilders. The altarpiece, which was also Riemenschneider's first large-scale work, was completed by September 30, 1492. Contrary to the prevailing practice, Riemenschneider left the light-colored lindenwood in its natural state, without the customary polychromy and gilding. (There are indications, however, that as a final step a pigmented glaze was applied by the workshop, as apparently was done with the later Rothenburg altarpiece; traces of an original glaze have been found on the figures of the Evangelists from the predella of the altarpiece.) This innovative treatment was not tolerated by the citizens of Münnerstadt for long, and about ten years after the altarpiece was erected, a commission to polychrome and gild it, as was then still the custom, was given to the Nuremberg sculptor Veit Stoss. The Münnerstadt altarpiece was dismantled in 1831 and its finest pieces sold. Only the works by Riemenschneider's own hand are illustrated here. Originally the shrine of the altarpiece contained the figure of St. Kilian to the right of Mary Magdalene, and St. Elisabeth to the left. The superstructure showed God the Father flanked by the Virgin Mary and St. John the Evangelist, and surmounting these, the figure of John the Baptist. The two reliefs of the left wing, upper and lower, depicted The Last Communion of Mary Magdalene and The Burial of Mary Magdalene.

PLATES 20A-B. *Mary Magdalene Borne Aloft by Angels.* From the shrine. Bayerisches Nationalmuseum, Munich. Lindenwood, polychromy removed. Height of Mary Magdalene 186 cm. (73¼ in.)

The group of the ascending Mary Magdalene and the six angels bearing her aloft filled the center of the shrine of the altarpiece, with the figures of St. Elizabeth and St. Kilian placed on either side. The contract of 1490 describes the group as follows: "And in the middle shall stand Mary Magdalene, as the 7 angels bear her aloft in the wilderness, wearing a coarse-spun garment as one paints John the Baptist; and on either side three angels, with their bodies extended, and the seventh angel above the head with a crown. And under her feet shall stand an altar, decorated with lights, candlesticks and other ornaments as befit an altar; and beside the altar a desert with rocks, stones, trees, herbage and other things." The seventh angel is lost or was never executed. The summary carving on the back of the saint's head, seen in Plate 20B, indicates that Riemenschneider intended the figure to be viewed only from the front.

PLATE 20c. *The Meeting in the Garden* (Noli Me Tangere). Lower relief of the right wing.

Skulpturenabteilung, Staatliche Museen, West Berlin. Lindenwood, polychromy removed. Height 143.5 cm (56½ in.)

The contract for this relief called for "the appearance of Christ to Mary Magdalene after his resurrection."

PLATES 20d-e. *Supper in the House of Simon.* Upper relief of the right wing.

On loan to the Bayerisches Nationalmuseum, Munich. Lindenwood, polychromy removed. Height 143.5 cm (56½ in.)

The contract here specified that the relief should show "how Mary Magdalene anointed Christ's feet as he sat at the table in the house of Simon."

PLATES 20f-k. *Figures of the Evangelists.* From the predella.

Skulpturenabteilung, Staatliche Museen, West Berlin. Lindenwood, polychromy removed. Height 72–78 cm (28¼–30¾ in.)

Luke is shown with his symbol the ox, and Mark with the lion. The angel and eagle, attributes of Matthew and John, are lost. In the 1960s traces of an original pigmented glaze, similar to the glaze discovered on both the Rothenburg and Dettwang altarpieces, were found beneath the very small amount of polychromy remaining on these figures.

PLATES 21a-d. **Adam and Eve.** 1491–1493.

Mainfränkisches Museum, Würzburg. White sandstone. Height of Adam 189 cm (74½ in.); Eve 185 cm (73 in.)

The figures of Adam and Eve were carved by Riemenschneider for the Marienkapelle in Würzburg. The statues were removed from the south portal of this church in 1894 and are now in the Mainfränkisches Museum in Würzburg, on permanent loan from the Marienkapelle Foundation. Replicas were made to take their place at the Marienkapelle. During World War II, for safekeeping, the figures were stored underground in a cellar belonging to a brewery in Ochsenfurt, thanks to Dr. Max H. von Freeden, who thus saved these figures from the damage suffered by so many art works in the bombing of Würzburg. The statues were commissioned from Riemenschneider by the "burgermeister und rathe" (mayor and council) of the City of Würzburg on May 5, 1491. On December 19, 1492, the council decreed "that Adam, whom master Tyll was carving in stone, should be made with-

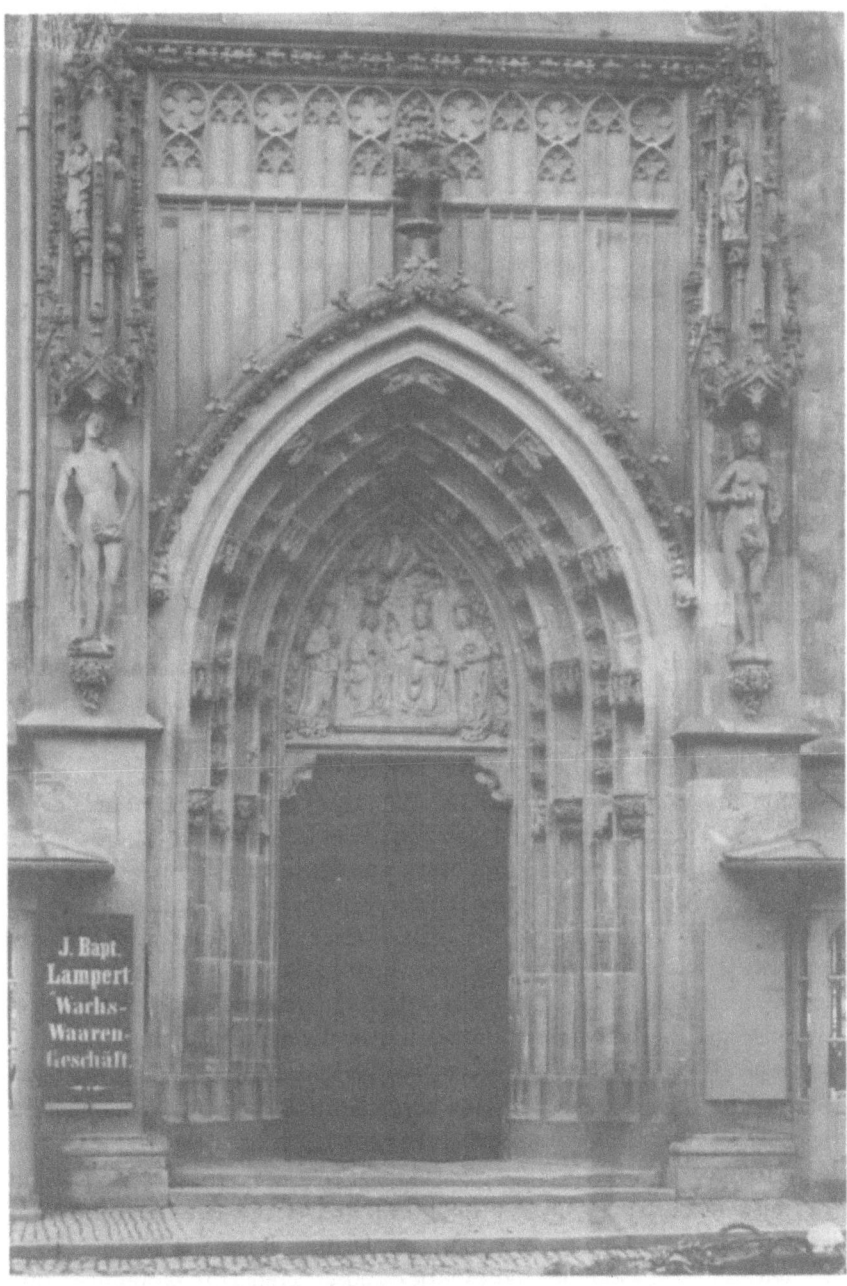

The south portal of the Marienkapelle in Würzburg before removal of the figures of Adam and Eve in 1894.

out a beard." Evidently Riemenschneider asked for this decision in order to give Adam a youthful appearance. On September 10, 1493, 120 guilders were paid for the statues complete with baldachins, the small figures in the baldachins, and the brackets on which the statues stand. The amount, which exceed the contract by 10 guilders, was given to him "because they were made by the master's own hand, artful, graceful and in an honest manner." Parts of the arms of Adam and Eve, Eve's left foot, and part of the serpent have been restored. The photograph here shows the statues in their original location.

PLATES 22A-E. **Tomb-Monument of Rudolf von Scherenberg.** 1496–1499.

Würzburg Cathedral. Salzburg marble and sandstone, some polychromy. Height of monument including base and baldachin 490 cm (6 ft. 1 in.), total height originally more than 6 m (20 ft.); height of red marble slab with figure 252 cm (99¼ in.)

The tomb monument of Prince-Bishop Rudolf von Scherenberg, who died on April 29, 1495, at the age of ninety-three, was ordered from Tilmann Riemenschneider by Scherenberg's successor, Prince-Bishop Lorenz von Bibra. Riemenschneider received the commission, amounting to 250 guilders, on October 21, 1496. By July 15, 1499, the work on the monument was completed. The central slab of Salzburg marble shows the figure of the prince-bishop framed by two lions below and two angels above holding four of the six coats of arms, with the other pair of coats of arms placed at medium height. The angels display the coats of arms of the Bishopric of Würzburg (left, as viewed) and the Duchy of Eastern Franconia (right). The four remaining escutcheons contain the ancestral armorial bearings of Rudolf von Scherenberg. The base, outer frame, and baldachin of the monument are sandstone. There is some polychromy on the Prince-Bishop's face, the coats of arms, the angels' wings, and the borders of the garments. The relief on the base that is partially embedded in the ground has been obliterated. As on the tomb-monument of Lorenz von Bibra (Plate 43A), this depicted a lion battling with a dragon; only the tip of the lion's tail is extant. The baldachin is slightly damaged, and the crowning coat of arms is missing entirely (compare with Plate 43A). Protected by brick and concrete, the monument survived the bombing of 1945 and the subsequent collapse of the cathedral in 1946 without serious injury. The photograph here shows the ruined interior of the cathedral as it was in 1946, with the walled-up tomb-monuments of

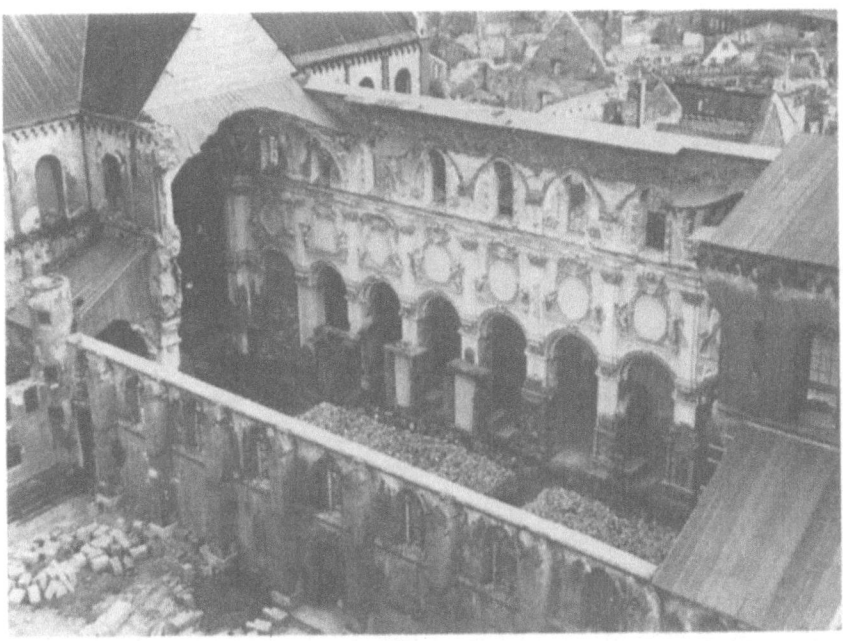

Würzburg Cathedral in 1946, showing the walled-up tomb-monuments of Rudolf von Scherenberg and Lorenz von Bibra.

both Rudolph von Scherenberg and Lorenz von Bibra. Since 1967, when the rebuilding of the cathedral was completed, both monuments have occupied new positions on the north side of the nave.

PLATES 23A-S. **Altarpiece of the Holy Blood.** 1501–1504.

St. Jakobskirche, Rothenburg ob der Tauber. Lindenwood figures in pine-wood framework. Height including mensa 10.83 m; width 416 cm (35 ft. 6½ in.; 13 ft. 8 in.)

The altarpiece takes its name from the relic of a drop of Christ's blood pre-served in the gilded cross upheld by angels in the central niche above the shrine. Only the figures of the altarpiece are by Riemenschneider, or, in some cases, his assistants. The architectural framework, with the exception of the decorative leaf-work carving above the wing reliefs, is from the work-shop of the Rothenburg carpenter Erhard Harschner. This pinewood frame-work was ordered as early as 1499, whereas the lindenwood sculptures were only commissioned from Riemenschneider on April 10, 1501. Harschner and Riemenschneider were to receive 50 guilders each. Harschner, however, ultimately got twice that amount, not "auf sein arbeyt" (for his work) but "geschenkt" (as a gift). Riemenschneider received an additional 10 guilders as a mark of esteem, and his assistants a one guilder gratuity when the final settlement was made on January 12, 1505. The sculptures were delivered in the following order: on July 3, 1502, the Last Supper group and the two pairs of angels; on July 14, 1504, the reliefs for the wings and the figures of Mary and the Angel for the Annunciation group above the shrine; on January 19, 1505, the last piece, the Ecce Homo figure surmounting the reliquary cross. In the nineteenth century the altarpiece was stained dark brown; also a group of Christ and John the Baptist, carved in 1584 by an unidentified sculptor, was placed in the central section of the predella of the altarpiece, which had previously been reserved for the exhibition of the chalice and paten. This has since been replaced by a crucifix. The altarpiece stood in the west choir of the church from 1502 until 1575; from 1575 till the 1860s it was in the east choir, and from the 1860s until 1964, at the eastern wall of the southern aisle. In 1965, after complete restoration, it was finally returned to its original location, the west choir. The restoration work of the early 1960s made it clear that, as surmised, the altarpiece was originally unpolychromed, apart from the touches of color on the eyes, lips, and nostrils of the figures. At the same time the restoration revealed the existence of a pigmented glaze ("lasur") directly over the surface of the lindenwood, which must have been applied in Riemenschneider's workshop as a final step, after Riemenschneider himself had applied the touches of color to the facial features. The glaze consists of oil, egg white, and traces of ocher, gypsum, white lead, and carbon. Possibly it was intended to unify the appearance of the whitish lindenwood, if this was marred by irregularities. As a result of the restoration, the original glaze is again exposed.

The restoration of the Rothenburg altarpiece is a striking illustration of the different aims of contemporary conservation as opposed to the nineteenth-century practice. Present-day restorers favor uncovering as much of the original surface as possible, and, together with the work now going on at the Berlin State Museums, the Rothenburg altarpiece is evidence of the great strides German restorers have made in this field.

PLATES 23B-I. *The Last Supper.* In the shrine. 1501–1502.
Height of shrine 244 cm; width 230 cm (96¼ in.; 90½ in.)

PLATES 23J-K. *The Annunciation* and *Pair of Angels Holding the Reliquary Cross.* In the superstructure, above the shrine. 1502–1504.
Height of Mary 117 cm (46 in.); Angel 119.5 cm (47 in.); angels with cross 51 cm (20 in.)

The two angels holding the reliquary cross, which dates from the thirteenth century, were delivered in 1502; they are the work of assistants. The two figures of the Annunciation, Mary and the Angel, were delivered in 1504. Only Mary is by Riemenschneider's own hand.

PLATES 23L-M. *Pair of Angels Holding the Pillar of Christ's Martyrdom and His Cross.* In the predella. 1501–1502.
Height of angels to top of head 53 cm and 55 cm (21 in.; 21¾ in.)

The wings of the angel holding the cross have been restored.

PLATES 23N-S. *The Entry into Jerusalem* and *The Agony in the Garden.* Wing reliefs. 1502–1504.
Height of *Entry* 147.5 cm; width 79.5 cm (58 in.; 31¼ in.). Height of *Agony* 145:5 cm; width 78 cm (57¼ in.; 30¾ in.)

The relief on the left wing of the altarpiece (as viewed) depicting Christ's Entry into Jerusalem is probably the work of assistants. The relief on the right wing representing the Agony in the Garden is by Riemenschneider's own hand, except for the group of Judas and the soldiers in the background. This relief shows characteristics of Riemenschneider's mature style and must have been done slightly later than the Entry into Jerusalem.

PLATES 24A-B. **The Virgin with the Christ Child.** About 1501–1502.
Kunstgewerbemuseum, Cologne. Lindenwood, polychromy removed. Height 76 cm (30 in.)

This small statue of the Virgin and Child has been in the Kunstgewerbemuseum in Cologne since 1921. It was given to the museum by the painter Wilhelm Clemens, who had acquired the work in Munich in 1909. Because of the nature of the nineteenth-century polychromy on the figure (in particular the damask flower pattern on the bodice, which indicated French rather than German workmanship), it has been possible to connect this figure with the Virgin and Child that is known to have been bought in Paris by the collector Brauer sometime before 1884. The provenance of this figure, which the author assumes to be the same as the Cologne Clemens Madonna, can be traced back through two private collections in Würzburg, namely, that of the merchant Ferdinand Broili and that of a canon of the cathedral, Wickenmayer, to the collection of Councillor Martinengo of Würzburg. Martinengo was a member of the Secularization Commission entrusted with the disposal of church property in the early years of the nineteenth century.

The nineteenth-century polychromy on the figure was removed during restoration in the early 1960s. The traces of seventeenth- or eighteenth-century polychromy and gilding found underneath the later polychromy, and the subtlety of the carving, established the authenticity of the piece both as a Late Gothic work and as one by Riemenschneider's own hand, which the general appearance of the figure had suggested but which had previously been in dispute. The removal also of the baroque polychromy restored the figure to what can be judged to have been its original condition, though it is possible that the carving had a monochromatic pigmented glaze as its original finish, similar to that found, and now exposed, on a work of the same period, the Rothenburg Altarpiece of the Holy Blood of 1501–1504 (Plate 23A). The date of 1501–1502 that I have assigned to the Clemens Virgin and Child is based on stylistic considerations and comparisons. Conceptually, the figure bears a striking resemblance to the sandstone Virgin and Child of about 1505 in the Mainfränkisches Museum in Würzburg (Plates 28A, B). The works correspond in the general organization of the figures and in the particular motifs of the playful Child raising his right arm towards the Virgin and pulling at her veil with his left hand. The Clemens figure, however, lacks the monumental aspect of the stone image, and in its more intricate, restless arrangement of the drapery and the twist of the Child's body, is allied to the earlier figures of the Rothenburg Altarpiece, those of 1501–1502, and to the Virgin and Child of the late 1490s, in the University of Kansas Museum of Art. Given the similarity of the Würzburg stone Madonna and the small size of the Clemens figure, it seems likely that the Clemens Madonna served as, and might even have been carved as, the model for the later stone figure. The toes of both feet of the Christ Child and the little fingers of both hands are missing. Small parts of the Virgin's veil are also missing, and the crown shows minor damage. The Child's left arm and Mary's left hand have been restored.

PLATES 25A-B. **Tomb-Monument of Konrad von Schaumberg.** After 1502.

Marienkapelle, Würzburg. Sandstone, some gilding. Height of figure including lion 201 cm (79¼ in.)

On February 12, 1500, the City Council of Würzburg, as owner of the Marienkapelle, decided to grant the last wish of the Knight and Marshal

Konrad von Schaumberg to place "ein stein und wappen in die capellen" (a stone and coat of arms in the chapel). Konrad von Schaumberg died on November 30, 1499, while returning from the Holy Land. On stylistic grounds it would seem that the monument was made no earlier than 1502 and was probably carved around the same time as the relief of The Agony in the Garden and the figure of Mary in the Rothenburg Altarpiece of the Holy Blood, both of which were delivered in 1504. The tomb-monument is a work entirely by Riemenschneider's own hand. The inscription above the head reads: "Anno domini 1499 am sampstag noch Katherine starb der gestreng und ernvest her Conrad von Schawmberg Knoch, ritter, marschalk, an der widerfart von dem heiligen grab uff dem mere, dem got gnad, amen." (In the year of our Lord 1499 on Saturday after [St.] Katherine's day died at sea the severe and honorable lord Conrad von Schawmberg Knoch, knight, marshal, on his return from the holy grave, may God grant him mercy, amen.) "Knoch" (meaning "Bone") was the knight's nickname. Originally the monument had a raised base. Some gilding is found on the coat of arms, the groove around the monument, and the knight's armor. The scabbards of both the sword and the dagger are missing. Parts of the hair, armor, and hands which broke off in the fire that engulfed the Marienkapelle during the air raids on Würzburg in March 1945 have been successfully restored.

PLATES 26A-F. **Figures of the Apostles for the Marienkapelle in Würzburg.** 1500–1506.

On February 4, 1492, the City Council of Würzburg decided "to have the twelve holy messengers hewn from stone for the empty spaces around the outside of the chapel." The chapel in question was the council's own church, the Marienkapelle. This rare commission to Riemenschneider followed the council's earlier commission for the figures of Adam and Eve for the Marienkapelle. Though the decision was made in 1492, the figures of the Apostles were executed only in the years 1500 to 1506. Besides the twelve Apostles, the series includes statues of Christ and John the Baptist. The figures are carved from sandstone, and, as decreed, were designed to fill the fourteen empty spaces on the buttresses of the Marienkapelle. The figures vary considerably in quality. Some are strictly workshop pieces, done by assistants after Riemenschneider models; others show Riemenschneider's hand in part. For each figure Riemenschneider received 10 guilders, considerably less than the amount he received for the figures of Adam and Eve for the same church, which were ordered to be "meysterlichen" (by the master's

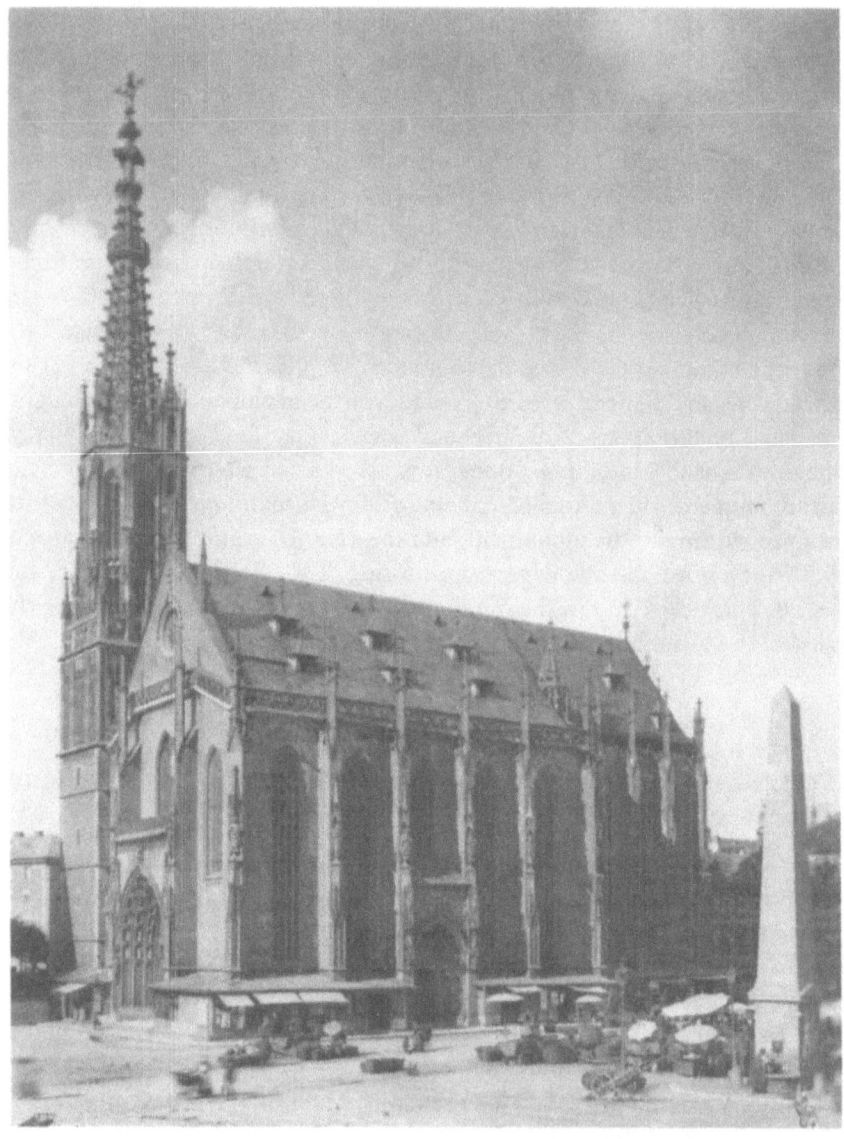

The Marienkapelle in Würzburg before removal of Riemenschneider's Apostle figures sometime before World War I.

own hand). Only the figure of James the Elder remains in its original location. The figures of Christ, John the Evangelist, Peter, and Andrew are now placed in an altarpiece in the Cathedral of Würzburg. The other nine figures were removed to the Fränkisches Luitpold-Museum in Würzburg, which subsequently burned to the ground on March 16, 1945. The Riemenschneider statues appeared to have been destroyed with the museum, but, in an operation directed by Dr. Max H. von Freeden, they were later unearthed from the ruins and pieced together. They are now installed in the Mainfränkisches Museum in Castle Marienburg, overlooking Würzburg. The photograph here is from the early years of this century showing the stone figures of the Apostles still in their original location.

PLATE 26A. *The Apostle Matthias.* After 1502.
Skulpturenabteilung, Staatliche Museen, West Berlin. Lindenwood. Height 104.5 cm (41¼ in.)

Carved by Riemenschneider's own hand, this lindenwood figure of the Apostle Matthias clearly served as the model for the stone statue of Matthias in the series of Apostle figures created for the Würzburg Marienkapelle. The sandstone St. Matthias was probably one of the last figures in the series to be executed, about 1504–1505. The lindenwood figure was carved not earlier than 1502. The left hand of the figure has been restored, and in the nineteenth century the work was stained dark brown.

PLATES 26B-F. *The Apostles Bartholomew, Jude Thaddaeus,* and *Philip.*
Mainfränkisches Museum, Würzburg. Sandstone. Height 180–185 cm (71-73 in.)

These three figures are part of the series of twelve stone statues of the Apostles created in the years 1500 to 1506.

PLATE 27. **St. Dorothea.** About 1500–1505. Destroyed 1945.
Formerly in the Marienkapelle, Würzburg. Lindenwood. Height 116 cm (45¾ in.)

This figure of St. Dorothea was one of Riemenschneider's most beautiful female figures. The statue stood in the arch leading into the choir of the Marienkapelle, opposite a somewhat inferior figure of St. Margaret. Both statues might originally have been created for the shrine of one of the altarpieces of the church, since lost. Both were destroyed in the great fire of March 16, 1945, while temporarily stored in the crypt of the Marienkapelle. A replica of the Dorothea, made in 1973, today stands in the Ratskeller in Würzburg.

PLATES 28A-B. **The Virgin with the Christ Child.** About 1505.
Mainfränkisches Museum, Würzburg. Gray sandstone, traces of polychromy. Height 155 cm (61 in.)

This fine sandstone statue of the Virgin with the Christ Child was acquired by the City Council of Würzburg for the Mainfränkisches Museum and installed there in 1956. Federal, state, and private funds contributed to the purchase of this figure, enabling its return to Würzburg after a century of absence while it was in private ownership, lost to public view. The statue had been the property of the Neo-Gothic sculptor Andreas Halbig (born in 1807), who moved from Würzburg to Vienna in 1857. The figure remained in Halbig's collection until his death in 1869, when it passed to his niece in Florence, Italy, and ultimately from there into the Swiss Art Market. Its rediscovery in 1956 had a special significance in view of the wartime destruction of Riemenschneider works such as the Himmelstein Madonna, lost in the Würzburg fire of 1945 that consumed almost the whole city. There are two acceptable theories concerning the possible origin of the figure in Würzburg. One is that it came from the exterior of the Marienkapelle, since the grooves found on the back of the head, where welded metal hooks attached it to a stone wall, are identical to those found on the stone figures of the Apostles from the Marienkapelle. The other is that it came from the exterior of a Neumünster canon's residence (now Bahnhofstrasse no. 9), where Andreas Halbig lived while he was a resident of Würzburg.

As with the Clemens Madonna and most of Riemenschneider's representations of this theme, the date assigned to this figure derives from stylistic analysis and comparison. Though a later date has been suggested, this author thinks that the figure must have been created in Riemenschneider's mature period (1503–1511), about the year 1505. The figure corresponds in particular to two works in the Rothenburg Altarpiece of the Holy Blood: the wing relief of The Agony in the Garden, and the figure of Mary of the Annunciation, both of which were delivered in 1504. The works are alike in showing a new spatial effect and a rich modulation of light and shadow through the use of wide, unbroken areas between the drapery folds that does not occur in earlier figures. The main motif of the drapery of the Madonna is also closely related to the motif of the mantle worn by Mary in the shrine group of the Creglingen Altarpiece of the Assumption of the Virgin, of about 1505–1510, and to that seen in the kneeling figure of St. John the Evangelist in the same group. Finally, the Christ Child displays a naturalness and a playful character not found in Riemenschneider's later renditions of the Virgin and Child, in which the Christ Child is presented more as a devotional image. Motifs similar to those of the Christ Child in the Würzburg sculpture are employed in the Madonna and Child of the late 1490s belonging to the University of Kansas at Lawrence. The closest resemblance among Riemenschneider's works of this kind, however, is found in the Virgin with the Christ Child from the Clemens collection, now in the Kunstgewerbemuseum in Cologne (Plates 24A, B). This figure may be dated a few years earlier, about 1501–1502. In this case the figures correspond not only in the composition and character of the playful Christ Child but also in the stance and demeanor of the Virgin and the tender relationship this expresses. Such differences as the simplified, compact outline of the Würzburg stone Madonna and the more monumental aspect of the figure may be explained in part by the use of stone for the carving, as well as by developments in Riemenschneider's style. In view of the similarities between the works, it may be supposed that the much smaller lindenwood figure served as, and might even have been carved as, the model for the sandstone Madonna.

PLATE 29. **St. Anne.** About 1505–1506 (?)
Bayerisches Nationalmuseum, Munich. Fragment. Lindenwood, polychromy removed. Height of fragment 75 cm; width 51 cm (29½ in.; 20 in.)

This figure of St. Anne is known to have come "from the region of Rothenburg" and is generally thought to have formed part of the documented but lost Altarpiece of St. Anne carved by Riemenschneider for the Marienkapelle in Rothenburg in 1505–1506. For the architectural framework and the figures of the St. Anne Altarpiece, Riemenschneider received a total sum of 50 guilders. The small altarpiece was presumably dismantled or destroyed when the Marienkapelle was demolished in 1810. This fragment showing the seated figure of St. Anne was acquired by the Bayerisches Nationalmuseum in 1892. The figure of the saint is in high relief. Originally the composition must have shown the Virgin Mary and St. Anne seated together on the bench, with the Christ Child standing between them or on Mary's lap, supported by St. Anne's outstretched arm. The saint's thumb, the tip of her shoe, and parts of the front edge of the base have been restored.

PLATE 30. **Tomb-Monument of Elisabeth Stieber.** After 1507.
Parish Church, Buttenheim. Sandstone. Height 219 cm; width 100 cm (86¼ in.; 39½ in.)

Elisabeth Stieber von Buttenheim died on August 30, 1507. Her husband, Heinrich Stieber, lord of the village of Buttenheim, died three weeks later.

Elisabeth's tomb-monument in the parish church in Buttenheim is a work by Riemenschneider's own hand, while the slightly larger tomb-monument of her husband, in the same church, was executed by assistants. Both were intended to be standing wall-monuments. Originally the tomb-monuments were placed inside the church, where noblemen were customarily buried, but when the church was rebuilt in 1757 they were moved outside and placed against the wall of the churchyard. In 1835 they were brought back into the church, to their present location in the tower chapel.

Elisabeth was the daughter of Eberhard von Grumbach, whose own tomb-monument in the parish church of Rimpar (Plate 17) is the earliest of Riemenschneider's works that can, like this one, be connected with a definite date and dated by inference from it. The inscription on Elisabeth's tomb reads: "Anno domini MCCCCC und im sybende am montag nach Augustini [starb] die erber tugenthaffd fraw Eliczabet Stiberin, geporn von Grunbach." (In the year of our Lord 1500 and in the seventh year on Monday after [St.] Augustine's day died the honorable and virtuous lady Eliczabet Stiber, née von Grunbach.) The nose of the figure, the fingers of her left hand, and one escutcheon show damage, probably caused by the monument's long exposure at the churchyard wall.

PLATES 31A-B. **Windsheim Altarpiece of the Twelve Apostles.** Before 1509.

Kurpfälzisches Museum, Heidelberg. Lindenwood, polychromy removed. Height of shrine 160 cm; width 110 cm (63 in.; 43¼ in.); width of each wing 48 cm (19 in.)

This altarpiece has been in the collection of the city of Heidelberg since 1879, but it was only after extensive restoration in 1948–1949 that it was established as a work largely by Riemenschneider's own hand and identified as the Windsheim Altarpiece of the Twelve Apostles—supposedly lost or destroyed. Records in Windsheim show that Riemenschneider carved this altarpiece and two other works (both lost) for the Church of St. Kilian in Windsheim. His payment for the altarpiece was 75 guilders. The altarpiece was taken from Würzburg to Windsheim and erected in St. Kilian's, at the eastern end of the southern aisle, between February 12 and April 8, 1509. It was then without polychromy. In 1512 it was polychromed for the first time by the painter Jakob Mülholtzer. The altarpiece was subsequently assumed to have been lost in the fire of December 1730 that completely destroyed St. Kilian's together with much of the city of Windsheim. As charred marks on the wing panels show, however, it must have been carried out of the burning church. In 1840 the altarpiece is known to have been back in Würzburg, where it was restored by the journeyman cabinetmaker Johann Weidner of Retzbach. For a while it was in the collection of Councillor Martinengo of Würzburg. In 1861 (the year the Martinengo collection was auctioned) it was acquired by Count Karl von Graimberg, and was subsequently included in his bequest of 1879 to the City of Heidelberg. This bequest founded the Heidelberg Collection.

Prior to the restoration (Plate 31A) a thick layer of nineteenth-century polychromy and heavy gilding obscured the quality of the altarpiece and led to its being generally considered a workshop piece. When this polychromy and gilding was removed, the delicate carving of the hands, faces, and drapery that was revealed clearly indicated Riemenschneider's own hand. The figures are now as they were originally, without polychromy except for Riemenschneider's customary touches of gray and black on the pupil and iris of the eyes and red on the lips. The restoration also revealed a chalk inscription on the right wing panel (as viewed) which stated that the altarpiece was painted in 1617 by the painter and citizen of Windsheim Daniel Schultz. It was this inscription together with the evidence of the fire damage that enabled the ultimate identification of the altarpiece.

The present arrangement of the figures in the shrine of the altarpiece dates from the restoration: Christ stands in the center, with the single figures of Peter and Andrew on the left and right respectively, the group of John and Thomas to the left of Peter, and the group of James the Younger and James the Elder to the right of Andrew. The reconstruction was based on discoveries made during the restoration of particular relationships among the carved figures. It was found, for example, that the upper part of Andrew's cross was indented to fit exactly to the right edge of the figure of Christ (as viewed), and that the carving of the group of James the Younger and James the Elder was incomplete and thereby dictated a position to the right of Christ and partially behind Andrew. As a comparison of the two plates shows, this arrangement reveals a rhythm and harmony in the work not found in the previous presentation (which was probably of mid-nineteenth-century origin). The wings of the altarpiece remain unchanged: each contains one group of three low-relief figures—Bartholomew, Matthias, and Simon on the right, and Paul, Jude Thaddaeus, and Philip on the left. The figures of the shrine and right wing are by Riemenschneider's own hand; those of the left wing, by an assistant.

Unlike the earlier Rothenburg Altarpiece of the Holy Blood, of 1501-1504, which represents the Apostles in the story of the Last Supper (Plate 23B), the Windsheim Altarpiece presents the Apostles as symbolic figures. Eight of the Apostles are identifiable by the attributes they display (for example, Paul with the sword, Peter with the key, Simon with the saw) while the others can be tentatively named through comparison with the slightly earlier stone figures of the Apostles carved for the Marienkapelle in the years 1500 to 1506. In many instances there is a definite correspondence between the two sets of Apostle figures.

The altarpiece also contains one of only three extant drawings attributed to Riemenschneider: The Dance of Salome, a sketch in black chalk and red ocher on the back of the relief group in the right wing. This was discovered during the restoration and has been proved to date from the time the altarpiece was carved. Riemenschneider presumably found this flat surface simply a convenient place on which to make a quick sketch illustrating some idea or concern of the moment.

For a detailed discussion of this altarpiece, see: *Der Windsheimer Zwölfbotenaltar von Tilman Riemenschneider im Kurpfälzischen Museum zu Heidelberg*, ed. Georg Poensgen (Munich and Berlin, 1955). See also Georg Poensgen, *The Windsheim Altar of the Twelve Apostles by Tilman Riemenschneider in the Kurpfälzisches Museum in Heidelberg*, rev. ed. (Heidelberg, 1967).

PLATES 32A-B. **The Virgin with the Christ Child.**
About 1505–1510.
Bayerisches Nationalmuseum, Munich. Lindenwood, polychromed and gilded. Height 98.5 cm (38¾ in.)

This figure of the Virgin with the Christ Child was acquired by the Bayerisches Nationalmuseum in Munich from the Munich Art Market as recently as 1974. It was previously unknown and its provenance has not been determined. If we consider the small size of the figure, however, it is clear that the work was destined to hang in a small church or in a chapel within a church.

There are several points of interest about the work. The figure of the Madonna is surrounded by a carved border of clouds, painted blue, reaching the level of her chin, and indicating her role as Queen of Heaven. Thirty-two transverse notches on the back edge of the figure show that originally there must have been a halo made up of individual rays attached to the figure and radiating from it, behind the border of clouds, hence the name "Strahlenkranzmadonna" used to refer to this figure and others of the type. The term means literally "Madonna in a wreath of rays."

The back of the figure is carefully planed flat, with a shallow vertical opening in the middle, 60 centimeters long. The treatment of the back and the fact that the figure is carved in bas relief prove that the figure is one half of a "Double Madonna," the two figures being placed back to back and not necessarily completely identical, designed to hang freely and be seen from all sides. The opening in the back may have served to attach the second figure if it had a complementary vertical projection. It also may have accommodated an iron hook used to suspend the figures. One example of such a Double Madonna, of about 1510–1520 (with both figures extant), also originally surrounded by a halo of rays, and considered to be from Riemenschneider's workshop, is now in the Mainfränkisches Museum in Würzburg. It seems that in South German Gothic sculpture Riemenschneider's workshop was the only one to produce this type of double figure. Usually such a double figure served as embellishment of a chandelier. There are three grooves at the back of the base of this figure, which may have held the branches of a chandelier.

The Virgin and Christ Child in a Rosary for the pilgrimage church near Volkach (Plate 44) is also an example of a Madonna surrounded by a halo of individual rays and designed to hang freely in space, though the Madonna in this case is a single figure only. This documented figure was carved in 1521, but, as the Munich figure proves, Riemenschneider had already prepared this type considerably earlier.

Recent restoration has revealed in full the polychromy and gilding on the Munich figure that was partly visible before. This undoubtedly dates from the Late Gothic period, though it must have been done in a painter's workshop and not by Riemenschneider himself, in accordance with a Würzburg city ordinance; in an attempt to spread out work between various workshops, this ordinance allowed sculptors no more than incidental coloring and gilding of their works, not the full polychromy displayed here. The cloak of the Virgin is gilded (well preserved) on a dark bole; the blue lining shows some damage; the base is green, badly scratched; the Virgin's gown and shirt, of which only small parts are visible, are silver on a yellow bole; the white veil has a brownish, faded pattern of horizontal stripes and clusters of dots; and the flesh of both figures is a warm orange with reddish-brown highlights. Two gold rings are painted, not carved, on the index and ring fingers of the Virgin's left hand. The figure as it appears now is in good condition in other respects also. Only the tip of the Virgin's right foot, the right half of the crescent moon, some small parts of the crown, and the big toe of the Christ Child's left foot are missing.

The fine facial features of the Virgin, her beautifully carved hands, the articulation and spontaneous movement of the Christ Child, and the motifs of the mantle and gown all show this to be a work by Riemenschneider's own hand from his mature period. The Christ Child held in the position in which it is here, cradled by the Virgin's veil or mantle, appears frequently in Riemenschneider's figures of the Madonna, especially those created after 1503, in his mature and late periods. Compare, for example, the stone Madonna in the Mainfränkisches Museum in Würzburg (Plates 28A, B), the Gramschatz Madonna in the Landesgalerie in Hannover (Plates 38A, B), and the Madonna of the Städelsches Kunstinstitut in Frankfurt am Main (Plate 45). Similar too are the Madonna carved after 1503, now in the Hamburg Museum für Kunst und Gewerbe, and the Gerolzhofen Madonna, of about 1515, also in the Bayerisches Nationalmuseum. The Munich rendition is particularly individual in respect of the Christ Child being more enfolded in and supported by the veil and having one hand pulling at one of the Virgin's long tresses rather than at the veil. The treatment of the figure of the Virgin and of the drapery also corresponds to the other Madonna figures considered to have been carved in Riemenschneider's mature period. Comparisons should be made too with the figures of the imperial tomb in Bamberg Cathedral, particularly with the image of Cunegund holding the crystal bowl in the side relief of 1505–1510 (Plate 40E), and with the figure of Mary of the Annunciation above the shrine of the Rothenburg Altarpiece of the Holy Blood (Plate 23J), carved between 1502 and 1504.

Much of the information in this note derives from the article by Dr. Alfred Schädler, "Eine Strahlenkranzmadonna von Tilman Riemenschneider im Bayerischen Nationalmuseum," *Pantheon* 33, no. 2 (April–June 1975): 99–106; and from a discussion the author had with Dr. Schädler when he inspected the figure in the summer of 1976.

Plates 33A-P. **Altarpiece of the Assumption of the Virgin.** About 1505–1510.

Herrgottskirche, Creglingen. Lindenwood figures in pinewood framework. Height including mensa about 10 m, width 372 cm (32 ft. 10 in.; 12 ft. 2½ in.)

The Altarpiece of the Assumption of the Virgin in the Creglingen Herrgottskirche marks the place where a miracle is said to have occurred, when a peasant found a sacred wafer at that site. Long in question, the designation of this altarpiece for the Hergottskirche is now substantiated by documentary evidence. A date for the work can only be assigned on the basis of stylistic comparison, however. On these grounds the altarpiece must be consid-

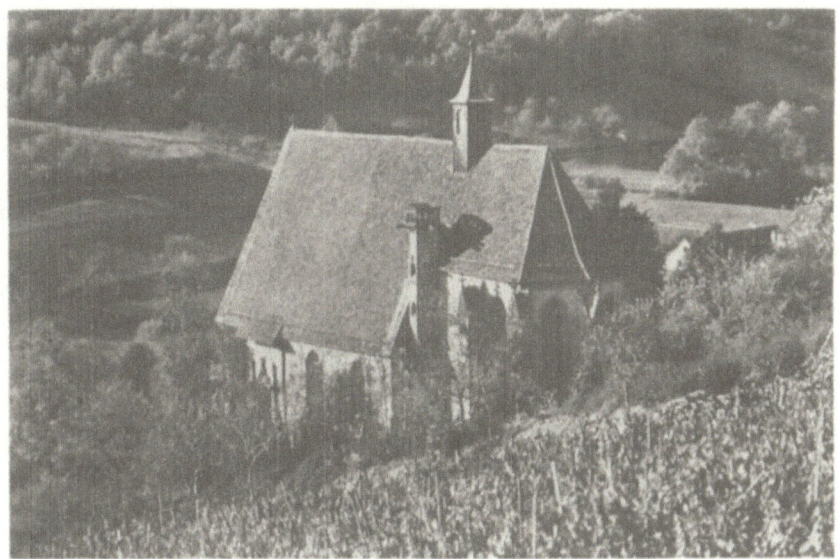

Herrgottskirche, Creglingen, which contains Riemenschneider's Altarpiece of the Assumption of the Virgin.

ered a work from Riemenschneider's mature period, when his powers were at their peak. It would appear that the entire altarpiece, both the figures and the architectural framework, came from Riemenschneider's workshop. This is the only altarpiece by Riemenschneider that escaped staining in the nineteenth century: it preserves unchanged the original effect of the pale-colored lindenwood used for the figures and the slightly reddish pinewood used for the architectural framework. The altarpiece was restored in 1959. The restoration revealed instructions in Riemenschneider's own hand on the back of the wing reliefs, indicating their placement in the altarpiece. It also showed that the hair of the figures had been treated with vinegar to create gradations of tone in the wood.

PLATES 33B-J. *Assumption of the Virgin.* In the shrine.
Width 186 cm (73¼ in.)

This central group of the Creglingen Altarpiece conveys almost better than any other work the essence of Riemenschneider's art in his mature period. Close examination of these figures shows clearly the delicate gray and black tinting of the eyeballs, rims of eyelids, and eyebrows, and the red markings of the nostrils and lips. These are the only touches of color and paint on the pale lindenwood. While Riemenschneider preferred to leave his figures un-polychromed, he usually liked to highlight the facial features in this way.

PLATE 33K. *The Annunciation.* Lower relief of the left wing.
Width 69 cm (27¼ in.)

Of the four wing reliefs, this is the only one by Riemenschneider's own hand.

PLATES 33L-P. *Adoration of the Magi* and *Christ among the Doctors.* Reliefs in the lateral niches of the predella. About 1510.

These reliefs, which are at least partly workshop pieces, were probably the last part of the altarpiece to be completed. They are stylistically related to the reliefs of The Removal of the Stone and The Miracle of the Crystal Bowl on the tomb of Emperor Henry II and Empress Cunegund in Bamberg Cathedral (Plates 40D-E), and must have been made about 1510. The superior figure of the Doctor seen in Plate 33P, which is probably by Riemenschneider's own hand, may well be a self-portrait, judging by its resemblance to the effigy on his tombstone (p. 21). The figure of the Christ Child belonging in the Adoration of the Magi (Plate 33L) has been missing for a very long time.

PLATES 34A-C. **The Disciple James in the Heidingsfeld Agony in the Garden.** 1510.
Parish Church, Heidingsfeld. Sandstone, polychromy removed. Height 120 cm (47¼ in.)

This figure of the disciple James is by Riemenschneider's own hand and is not, as was once assumed, a workshop piece. The figure forms part of The Agony in the Garden housed in the small chapel adjoining the Heidingsfeld parish church. Both the church and the chapel were rebuilt in 1951, after the church was almost completely levelled during World War II. The Riemenschneider sculpture miraculously escaped destruction at that time, and after restoration, including the removal of the nineteenth-century stone-colored paint, it was replaced in the newly-built chapel. The original chapel, which adjoined the south side of the church, was built specifically to house the Riemenschneider group and was completed in 1510. The date "1510" was carved on the wall of the chapel above the arch which framed the work. The Agony in the Garden was presumably delivered the same year, though the commission must have been given to Riemenschneider a few years earlier. The Heidingsfeld figures of James and John show a close stylistic relationship to the figures in the shrine of the Creglingen Assumption Altarpiece of about 1505–1510. Also, James's countenance is very similar to that of the sleeping emperor in the Bamberg relief of The Removal of the Stone (Plate 40D), which should be assigned a similar date. Like the figure of James, the other central figures of the work, Christ and John, are by Riemenschneider's own hand. The figure of Christ, however, is based on an engraving of The Agony in the Garden by Schongauer, whereas the superior design of the figures of James and John is Riemenschneider's own invention. The group represents an important new presentation of the theme which Riemenschneider depicted earlier in the wood relief of 1502–1504 on the wing of the Rothenburg Altarpiece of the Holy Blood (Plate 23P).

PLATES 35A-E. **Sculptures for the High Altar of Würzburg Cathedral.** 1508–1510.

The sculptures of the altarpiece for the high altar of Würzburg Cathedral, which was ordered from Riemenschneider by the Cathedral Chapter, were carved between 1508 and 1510. Since a bequest had been made for an altarpiece in 1505, it is possible they were ordered as early as 1506. The entire altarpiece, however, with its architectural framework, was only completed as late as 1519, and in 1522 Riemenschneider was still contending with the Cathedral Chapter for a final payment. Ultimately, Riemenschneider received at least 260 guilders for this work. The altarpiece was shaped like a tabernacle; the three busts of the so-called Franconian Apostles, Kilian, Kolonat, and Totnan, were contained in the predella, while the figure of Christ Salvator was originally in the shrine. With the exception of one Apostle (on the left, as viewed in Plate 35c), the sculptures are by Riemenschneider's own hand.

PLATES 35A-B. *The Ascending Christ Salvator.*
Parish Church, Biebelried. Lindenwood, polychromy removed. Height 103 cm (40½ in.)

The figure of Christ Salvator from the shrine of the altarpiece on the high altar of Würzburg Cathedral was given to the parish church in Biebelried (near Würzburg) probably about 1701, when the busts from the predella were removed. The hand raised in blessing and the orb have been restored. The polychromy has been removed and the figure has been stained brown.

PLATES 35C-E. *The Franconian Apostles.* Destroyed by fire in 1945.
Formerly in the Neumünster church in Würzburg. Lindenwood, polychromed. Height of figures with base (from left to right) 96 cm, 124 cm, 94 cm (37¾ in., 48¾ in., 37 in.)

The three busts from the predella of the altarpiece on the high altar of Würzburg Cathedral were given to the Neumünster church in Würzburg probably when the altarpiece was dismantled in 1701. The busts were carved in the round and polychromed. All three works were subsequently lost in the fire that destroyed the Neumünster church in 1945. (The busts were then in the crypt of the church.)

PLATE 36. **Lamentation for Christ.** Before 1508.
Martin-von-Wagner Museum, University of Würzburg (Residenz). Lindenwood, polychromy removed. Height 48 cm; width 56 cm (19 in.; 22 in.)

The small wood relief from the collection of the University of Würzburg is among the finest of Riemenschneider's representations of the Lamentation for Christ. This carving probably served as the model for the stone relief of the Lamentation in the parish church in Heidingsfeld, which includes the figure of Mary Magdalene and is a workshop piece of 1508. The wood relief must have been done about the same time or a little earlier. The figure of St. John in this group is closely related to the figure of John in the later Dettwang Crucifixion Altarpiece (Plate 41B). The kneeling figure of the Virgin evolved from Riemenschneider's earlier arrangement of the seated Virgin, and seems first to appear in the Providence Pietà of about 1505–1510 (Plates 10A, B). A further development in composition is seen in the equally fine Lamentation group in Bremen (Plate 37). Like the Würzburg relief, both of these are works by Riemenschneider's own hand.

PLATE 37. **Lamentation for Christ.** About 1515.
Ludwig-Roselius Collection, Böttcherstrasse, Bremen. Lindenwood. Height 103 cm; width 95 cm (40½ in.; 37½ in.)

See under Plate 36, above.

PLATES 38A-B. **The Virgin with the Christ Child.**
About 1510–1515.
Niedersächsische Landesgalerie, Hanover. Lindenwood, polychromed.
Height 145 cm (57¼ in.)

This was originally the central figure of an altarpiece in the parish church in
Gramschatz, near Würzburg. It was acquired in 1863 by the Welfenmuse-
um in Hannover, which was incorporated into the Landesgalerie in 1955.
The figures of Cyriacus and John the Baptist, which stood on either side of
this statue in the shrine of the altarpiece, were acquired at the same time.
The Gramschatz Virgin with the Christ Child is one of the finest and best-
preserved examples in a number of closely related figures of the Madonna
and Child by Riemenschneider, particularly the Virgin with the Christ
Child created about 1515, from Gerolzhofen, now in the Bayerisches Nationalmuseum in Munich, and the Virgin and Child from Wiesloch, after
1503, now in the Museum für Kunst und Gewerbe in Hamburg.

PLATE 39. **Female Bust for a Chandelier.** About 1505–1510.
Pelikan Collection, Landesgalerie, Hanover. Lindenwood. Height 55 cm
(21¾ in.)

Only two secular sculptures by Riemenschneider have been preserved, both
busts for chandeliers of the type known as "Lüsterweibchen." As the name
implies, the busts underneath these chandeliers were usually of women,
shown in the fashionable dress of the day. The bust reproduced here was formerly in the collection of the Broili family in Würzburg. Its origin is not
known. The other "Lüsterweibchen" figure by Riemenschneider, now in
the Böhler collection in Munich, is known to have come originally from the
City Hall in Ochsenfurt. The precise notching of the ornamental borders of
the gown on the Hannover figure indicates that Riemenschneider intended
this maiden—with the necessary exception of the coat of arms she holds—to
remain unpolychromed. The right hand of the figure has been restored.

PLATES 40A-G. **Tomb of Emperor Henry II and Empress Cunegund.** 1499–1513.

Bamberg Cathedral. Solnhofen limestone and white sandstone, some poly-chromy and gilding. Height excluding modern steps 152 cm; length 240 cm; width 142 cm (60 in.; 94½ in.; 56 in.)

The commission for the tomb of Emperor Henry II (d. 1024) and his wife, Empress Cunegund (d. 1033), in Bamberg Cathedral was given to Riemen-schneider in 1499. The tomb was probably supposed to be erected the fol-lowing year, to mark the tercentenary of Cunegund's cannonization in 1200, but the work was not in fact completed until 1513. Records show that Riemenschneider received at least 307 guilders as payment. The tomb is of Solnhofen limestone on a base of white sandstone. Some polychroming and gilding can be observed, as, for example, in the patterns of the brocade gowns, in the ornamental borders, and on the crowns. The tomb was never completely painted but color and primarily gilt were used to render or em-phasize details of texture and design.

The lid of the tomb was evidently begun first. It corresponds stylistically to the Last Supper group of 1501–1502 in the shrine of the Rothenburg Holy Blood Altarpiece, and was probably completed by June 5, 1501, when payment of 200 guilders was made to Riemenschneider. Of the five reliefs on the sides and foot-end of the tomb, Cunegund's Ordeal by Fire and The Death of the Emperor can both be dated shortly after the lid, in 1501–1502, while The Weighing of the Soul, The Removal of the Stone, and The Mir-acle of the Crystal Bowl are, judging by the style, all later works belonging to the years 1505–1510.

Since 1971 the tomb has been situated at the eastern end of the nave be-tween the new stairways to the east choir. Before that it was placed in the very center of the cathedral. Plate 40A shows the sarcophagus in its former location, as viewed from the southwest. The relief on the foot-end of the tomb depicts the death of Emperor Henry II. The two reliefs on the side show scenes relating to the legend of the emperor: The Weighing of Emper-or Henry's Soul and The Removal of the Stone.

PLATE 40B. *Lid of the Tomb with the Figures of Empress Cunegund and Emperor Henry II.* About 1499–1501.

Length 240 cm; width 142 cm (94½ in.; 56 in.)

Framed by the baldachin above their heads and the two small lions lying at their feet, the imperial figures repose side by side, the slightly smaller figure of Cunegund on the emperor's right. Their heads rest on cushions. Neither gesture nor look unites the figures, yet harmony is achieved through such factors as the incline of the scepters, and the general curvature of the figures and of the folds and borders of their gowns. In spite of their rich attire and the regalia displayed, the most striking feature is the expression of inner strength on the faces of the figures.

PLATES 40C, F. *Cunegund's Ordeal by Fire.* Side relief. About 1501–1502. Height 82 cm; width 84 cm (32¼ in.; 33 in.)

The relief shows Cunegund walking over red-hot plowshares to clear herself of the charge of adultery. The devil as the accuser stands next to the emperor and is dressed as a courtier. Behind them is the smith who heated the irons.

PLATES 40D, G. *The Removal of the Stone.* Side relief. About 1505–1510. Height 82 cm; width 84 cm (32¼ in.; 33 in.)

This scene shows St. Benedict appearing to the ailing emperor. According to the legend (as related in the German translation of the *Legenda Aurea, Summertayl der heiligen leben* [Nuremberg: Anton Koberger, 1488]), while the emperor slept, St. Benedict "gently cut out the stone and laid it in the emperor's hand." Beside the bed sits the chamberlain who has fallen asleep and rests unaware of the miraculous happening.

PLATE 40E. *The Miracle of the Crystal Bowl.* Side relief. About 1505–1510. Height 82 cm; width 84 cm (32¼ in.; 33 in.)

Here the empress is seen inviting the workers who were building the Church of St. Stephen to take their pay from a bowl full of pennies. "And put each one his hand into the bowl and received not more than he had honestly earned after he had begun to work. Whoever comes early can take no more than he has earned, likewise whoever came late or slow, took no more than was his due." Originally the individual coins were distinguished by gilt and paint, but due to frequent touching the gilt and paint have worn off and the pennies appear now only as an unbroken mass.

PLATES 41A-D. **Altarpiece of the Crucifixion.** About 1512–1513. Village Church, Dettwang. Lindenwood figures in pinewood framework. Height of shrine 234 cm (92¼ in.); width 156 cm (61½ in.) (originally 204 cm [80½ in.]); width of each wing 102 cm (40¼ in.)

This altarpiece has been in Dettwang since 1653. Originally it belonged to the Michaelskepelle in Rothenburg ob der Tauber, until it was demolished in 1811, stood in the cemetery adjoining the Jakobskirche. In moving from Rothenburg to Dettwang the figure of Mary Magdalene kneeling at the foot of the Cross was lost. Also the shrine of the altarpiece was made narrower in order to fit it into the small choir of the Dettwang church. There is no mention of the altarpiece in the records of the Jakobskirche for the years up to 1508, or in those for 1511, 1514, and 1516. (The account books for the intervening years are lost.) On stylistic grounds, it seems probable that the altarpiece was made in the years 1512–1513. The altarpiece in Dettwang is a more mature repetition of an earlier Crucifixion Altarpiece formerly in Wiblingen. Only the figures in the shrine of the Dettwang Altarpiece, of which the figure of the Centurion is modeled after a copper engraving by Dürer, are by Riemenschneider's own hand. The wing reliefs were carved by assistants. The altarpiece was originally without polychromy and gilding. Traces of an original pigmented glaze have been found on the right wing; chemical analysis has shown this to be closely related to the glaze found on the Rothenburg Altarpiece of the Holy Blood. Staining applied in the nineteenth century accounts for the dark color of the wood today.

PLATES 42A-B. **Christ on the Cross.** 1516.
Parish Church, Steinach an der Saale. Lindenwood, polychromy removed. Height 123 cm; width 98 cm (48½ in.; 38¾ in.)

A small lead receptacle discovered in 1903 in the back of the crucified Christ contains a strip of parchment with an inscription which translates: "In the year of our Lord 1500 and 16 this image was cut by master Dyl, [member] of the [city] council of Würzburg, and painted by Johann Wagenknecht, building supervisor for the cathedral foundation, painter, also burgher and member of the city council. At this time ruled Bishop Lorenz, of the Bibra family, and Provost Albertus, Margrave of Brandenburg, Dean Thomas de Stein. In the reign of Emperor Maximilian." The image was painted by Wagenknecht because Riemenschneider, unlike the sculptor Veit Stoss, was not trained as a painter and was therefore prohibited (by a city ordinance) from doing more than incidental coloring and gilding of sculptures in his own workshop. In 1903 both the original paint and the later baroque polychromy were removed, and the image was then repainted. Restoration of the work, which had also suffered changes in the seventeenth or eighteenth century, was carried out in 1938. As comparison of the two plates shows, the modern coat of paint was removed, the placement of the arms was changed from the diagonal back to the Late Gothic horizontal, the feet were returned to their original position, and the thumbs were made extended instead of bent. The image is today placed above the high altar of the Steinach parish church.

PLATES 43A-D. **Tomb-Monument of Lorenz von Bibra.**
About 1518–1522.
Würzburg Cathedral. Salzburg marble and sandstone, some polychromy.
Height 652 cm (21 ft. 4¾ in.)

The tomb-monument was commissioned from Riemenschneider by Prince-Bishop Lorenz von Bibra during von Bibra's lifetime for the sum of 277 guilders. The prince-bishop died on February 6, 1519. The tomb-monument was not completed however until February 8, 1522. The central slab showing the figure of Lorenz von Bibra is of Salzburg marble and was carved by Riemenschneider's own hand. The architectural framework, including the base, baldachin, and surmounting coat of arms, is of sandstone and shows some polychroming. The frame uses mainly Renaissance forms and is the work of an assistant whose mark appears on it. As the motifs on the one side of the epitaph section show (Plate 43c), the frame was originally started in Gothic style. The change of style may well have been inspired by the tomb of George III, Schenk von Limpurg, in Bamberg Cathedral, which was carved by Loy Hering in pure Renaissance forms during the same period. The work remains in good condition, with all parts intact. Protected by brick and concrete, the monument survived the wartime bombing of 1945 and the subsequent collapse of Würzburg Cathedral in 1946 without major damage. The photograph on p. 87 shows the ruined interior of the cathedral as it was in 1946, with the walled-up tomb-monuments of both Lorenz von Bibra and Rudolf von Scherenberg. Since 1967, when the rebuilding of the cathedral was completed, both monuments have occupied new positions on the north side of the nave.

PLATE 44. **The Virgin and Christ Child in a Rosary.**
1521–1522.
Pilgrimage Church, Kirchberg bei Volkach. Lindenwood, polychromy removed. Total height 280 cm; width 190 cm (9 ft. 2¼ in.; 74¾ in.); height of Mary 171 cm (67¼ in.)

The Virgin and Christ Child in a Rosary for the pilgrimage church on the hill near Volkach known as the Kirchberg was "accorded with Master Dill

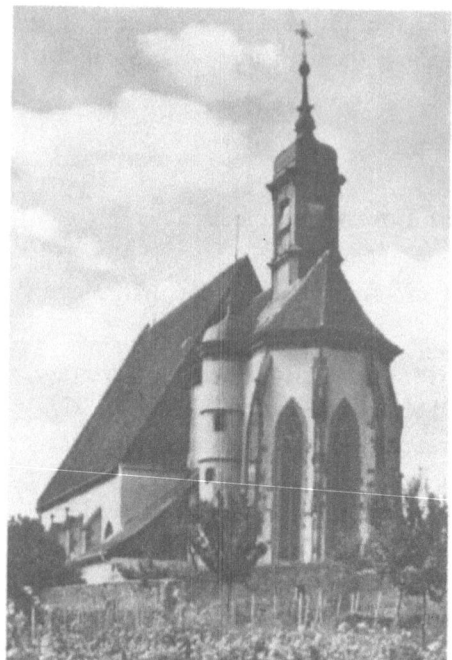 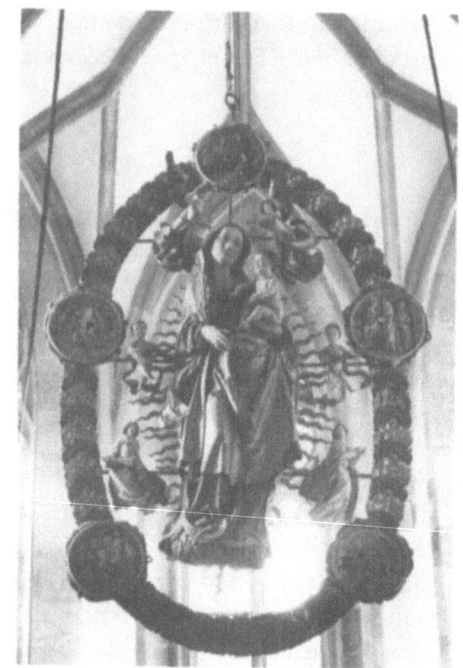

Left: The Pilgrimage Church at Kirchberg bei Volkach, which contains Riemenschneider's Virgin and Christ Child in a Rosary. *Right:* A photograph from the 1930s showing the work hanging from the arch leading into the choir, its present location.

in the year 1521 and hung the following year." The work was executed by assistants after a model carved by Riemenschneider. This model figure is now in the Dumbarton Oaks Collection in Washington, D.C. (Plates 16A-c). The Volkach Virgin and Christ Child is approximately twice the size of the model figure. During World War II, the figure was removed from the church for safekeeping. Major restoration, including the removal of the nineteenth-century paint and remains of baroque polychromy, was carried out before the reinstallation of the figure in 1954. The work made headlines when it was stolen from the pilgrimage church in August 1962. It was returned three months later, badly damaged. Successful restoration was accomplished by the Bayerisches Landesamt für Denkmalpflege (Bavarian State Office for the Upkeep of Monuments) in Munich. Exactly one year after the theft, the work was reinstalled in the Kirchberg church.

As it did originally, the figure once again hangs from the arch of the choir, as in the right-hand photograph here, which was taken in the 1930s when the work was still polychromed. In this position, light passes through the open-work, enhancing the filigree effect and covering up to some extent the coarse finish of the carving that becomes apparent in a close-up view.

PLATE 45. **The Virgin with the Christ Child.** 1516–1522.

Liebieghaus, Städelsches Kunstinstitut, Frankfurt am Main. Sandstone, traces of polychromy. Height 156.5 cm (61¾ in.)

Originally this sandstone Virgin and Christ Child was placed on the exterior of the residence of a canon of the Neumünster collegiate church in Würzburg. There the figure was set to the right of and slightly above the front entrance of the house. In the middle of the nineteenth century the statue was sold to Carl Becker, the early biographer of Riemenschneider, by a later owner of the building. (The building, which had been acquired for the Neumünster endowment in 1310, had been sold earlier in the century in the wake of the secularization of church property.) In this way the figure escaped destruction when the building itself, together with much of the central part of the city, was razed by fire on March 16, 1945. The statue has been the property of the Städelsches Kunstinstitut in Frankfurt am Main since 1871 and is now displayed in the Liebieghaus, the museum housing Frankfurt's municipal sculpture collection.

The statue is considered to be one of the finest single figures from Riemenschneider's late period. In place of the spontaneity and vigor of earlier representations of this theme, the figure demonstrates great restraint and a quiet dignity. Stylistically, it resembles Riemenschneider's last major work, the Maidbronn Lamentation Altarpiece of 1519–1523; it is also closely related, in its almost calligraphic beauty, to the figure of Lorenz von Bibra on his tomb-monument in Würzburg Cathedral, completed in 1522. Several layers of paint were removed by Becker during his ownership, which revealed that underneath this the hair was gilded, the veil was white, the mantle cloth blue, and the gown red. There are still traces of polychromy on the figure.

PLATES 46A-D. **Altarpiece of the Lamentation for Christ.** 1519–1523.

Parish Church, Maidbronn (originally the church of the former Cistercian convent in Maidbronn). Gray sandstone. Height 205 cm; width 166 cm (80¾ in.; 65½ in.)

Though the Maidbronn Lamentation Altarpiece is not documented, there is good reason to believe that work on this altarpiece was not begun before 1519 and was completed not later than 1523. The evidence is as follows: on May 16, 1519, the Bishop of Würzburg was obliged to donate a sum of money as aid to the convent of Maidbronn, it "being in a state of decay and disorder"; and, in the accounts from 1523 on, there is only one payment of 11 guilders recorded, for the year 1526. On account of the small amount, this cannot relate to the main relief of the altarpiece but only to the relief in the predella, added in 1526 with an inscription commemorating the suppression of the Peasants' Revolt. This dating is corroborated by the existence of an assistant's mark on the upper part of the framework identical to that on the frame of the Lorenz von Bibra monument of 1518–1522. The upper section of the main relief with the rather awkward angels is the work of this assistant. The figure of Joseph of Arimathaea (Plate 46B) must be considered a self-portrait of Riemenschneider in view of its resemblance to the effigy on his tombstone (p. 21), carved by his eldest son Georg Riemenschneider.

This last major work by Riemenschneider achieves an almost classic simplicity and unity of effect in its placement and subtle connecting of the ten figures that distinguish it from all the earlier altarpieces, which concentrate more on detail than on rhythmic harmony. Here, in a monument that is carved from one solid slab of sandstone, an illusion of depth and space is created both by the light and shadow falling on the figures and their drapery and by the design that does crowd the figures onto one plane, yet interconnects and draws them into an organic whole.

Monographs on Tilmann Riemenschneider

Becker, Carl. *Leben und Werke des Bildhauers Tilmann Riemenschneider.* Leipzig, 1849.

Bier, Justus. *Die Jugendwerke Tilmann Riemenschneiders.* Inaugural Dissertation. Zürich, 1924.

———. *Tilmann Riemenschneider.* Vol. 1, *Die Frühen Werke.* Würzburg, 1925. Vol. 2, *Die Reifen Werke.* Augsburg, 1930. Vol. 3, *Die Späten Werke in Stein.* Vienna, 1973. Vol. 4, *Die Späten Werke in Holz.* Vienna, 1978.

———. *Tilmann Riemenschneider: Ein Gedenkbuch zur vierhundertjährigen Wiederkehr seines Todestages.* Augsburg, 1931; 2nd enlarged edition, Vienna, 1936; 3rd edition, Vienna, 1937; 4th enlarged edition, Vienna, 1937; 5th edition, Vienna, 1938; 6th enlarged edition, Vienna, 1948.

Demmler, Theodor. *Die Meisterwerke Tilman Riemenschneiders.* Berlin, 1936.

Freeden, Max H. von. *Tilman Riemenschneider.* Munich and Berlin, 1954. 4th edition, *Tilman Riemenschneider: Leben und Werk.* Munich and Berlin, 1972.

———. *Tilman Riemenschneider.* Hamburg, 1976.

Gerstenberg, Kurt. *Tilman Riemenschneider.* Vienna, 1941; 5th edition, Munich, 1962.

Muth, Hanswernfried, and Schneiders, Toni, *Tilman Riemenschneider und seine Werke.* Würzburg, 1978.

Poensgen, Georg, ed. *Der Windsheimer Zwölfbotenaltar von Tilmann Riemenschneider im Kurpfälzischen Museum zu Heidelberg.* Munich and Berlin, 1955.

Schrade, Hubert. *Tilman Riemenschneider.* Heidelberg, 1927.

Streit, Carl. *Tylmann Riemenschneider: Leben und Kunstwerke des fränkischen Bildschnitzers.* 2nd edition, Berlin, 1888.

Tönnies, Eduard. *Leben und Werke des Würzburger Bildschnitzers Tilmann Riemenschneider.* Studien zur deutschen Kunstgeschichte, 22nd issue. Strasbourg, 1900.

Weber, Anton. *Til Riemenschneider: Sein Leben und Wirken.* 3rd edition. Regensburg, 1911.

List of Riemenschneider's Works
with Selected References

Only those works that the author considers to be entirely or partially by Riemenschneider's own hand are listed here. The works, both sacred and secular, are grouped first according to whether they are documented or attributed on the basis of style; and second, whether or not they are extant; they are then further subdivided according to type and material. Within each of the categories the works are arranged chronologically. Works discussed and illustrated in this book are marked with an asterisk (*).

Since this list is intended mainly as a convenient guide to the location of Riemenschneider's works, little beyond the title, date, and present location of each work has been given. In the case of altarpieces, the itemized sculptures include only those by Riemenschneider's own hand, either entirely or in part. The distinction between the autograph works and those showing workshop participation is not generally noted here. For this and other information about a specific work, the Riemenschneider literature should be consulted. For this purpose one or more references to the literature are included. Where publications in English exist, depending on their nature, these are given as the sole or subsidiary reference.

Certain abbreviated forms are used in the case of literature quoted frequently:

Bier, *Riem.* = Justus Bier, *Tilmann Riemenschneider*, vol. 1, *Die Frühen Werke* (Würzburg, 1925); vol. 2, *Die Reifen Werke* (Augsburg, 1930); vol. 3, *Die Späten Werke in Stein* (Vienna, 1973); Vol. 4, *Die Späten Werke in Holz* (Vienna, 1978).

Müller, *Bildwerke* = Theodor Müller, *Die Bildwerke in Holz, Ton und Stein, Kataloge des Bayerischen Nationalmuseums München* 13, pt. 2 (Munich, 1959).

Riem. Cat. = *Sculptures of Tilmann Riemenschneider* (Raleigh: North Carolina Museum of Art, 1962).

W.-R.-J. = Justus Bier, "Riemenschneiders Marienstatuen und die Clemens-Madonna im Kölner Kunstgewerbemuseum," *Wallraf-Richartz-Jahrbuch* 37 (1975): 41-64.

All other references are given in full.

Since the number of documented works is very small, this remains a tentative rather than a definitive listing of Riemenschneider's work. The author hopes it will give an idea of Riemenschneider's oeuvre and will prove a useful reference.

I. DOCUMENTED WORKS

A. Works Extant or Partially Extant

Münnerstadt Altarpiece of Mary Magdalene, 1490–1492
    *Mary Magdalene borne aloft by angels: Munich, Bayerisches Nationalmuseum
    *Figures of the Evangelists: West Berlin, Staatliche Museen, Skulpturen-
    abteilung
    *The Meeting in the Garden: West Berlin, Staatiche Museen, Skulpturen-
    abteilung
    *Supper in the House of Simon: Munich, Bayerisches Nationalmuseum
    (on loan)
        Bier, *Riem.,* 1: 9-59, 92-99, Pls. 4-32.

Adam and Eve for the Marienkapelle, 1491–1493: Würzburg, Mainfränkisches
Museum
        Bier, *Riem.,* 1: 65-72, 99-101, Pls. 39-42

Three Helpers in Need, 1494: New York, Metropolitan Museum of Art,
Cloisters Collection
        Justus Bier, "Riemenschneider's Helpers in Need," *Metropolitan Museum
        of Art Bulletin* 21, no. 10 (June 1963): 317-26. Charles E. von Nostitz, Jr.,
        "Two Unpolychromed Riemenschneiders at the Cloisters," *Metropolitan
        Museum Journal* 10 (1975): 51-62.

Tomb-Monument of Rudolf von Scherenberg, 1496-1499: Würzburg Cathedral
        Bier, *Riem.,* 1: 78-86, 101-03, Pls. 52-61

Tomb of Emperor Henry II and Empress Cunegund, 1499–1513: Bamberg Cathedral
        Bier, *Riem.,* 3: 1-48, 166-77, Pls. 145-72. Justus Bier, "Riemenschneider's
        Tomb of Emperor Henry and Empress Cunegund," *Art Bulletin* 29,
        no. 2 (1947): 95-117, 287

Figures of the Apostles for the Marienkapelle, 1500–1506
        James the Elder: Würzburg, Marienkapelle
        Christ Salvator: Würzburg Cathedral
        John the Evangelist: Würzburg Cathedral
        Peter: Würzburg Cathedral
        Andrew: Würzburg Cathedral
        *Nine remaining figures: Würzburg, Mainfränkisches Museum
            Bier, *Riem.,* 2: 126-45, 185-89, Pls. 129-36

Rothenburg Altarpiece of the Holy Blood, 1501–1504: Rothenburg ob der Tauber,
St. Jakobskirche
    *The Last Supper (shrine)
    *Mary of the Annunciation (superstructure)
    *Angels holding pillar of Christ's martyrdom and his Cross (predella)
    *The Agony in the Garden (wing relief)
        Bier, *Riem.,* 2: 11-43, 169-75, Pls. 70-85

Eichstätt Table, 1506: Würzburg, Mainfränkisches Museum
>Bier, *Riem.,* 2: 148-51, 190-91, illus. p. 149

*Windsheim Altarpiece of the Twelve Apostles, before 1509: Heidelberg,
Kurpfälzisches Museum
>*Christ and Apostles (shrine)
>*Apostles (right wing)
>>Georg Poensgen, ed., *Der Windsheimer Zwölfbotenaltar von Tilman Riemen-
schneider* (Berlin, 1955). Justus Bier, "St. Andrew in the Work of Tilmann
Riemenschneider," *Art Bulletin* 38, no. 4 (December 1956): 215-23

*Sculptures for the High Altar of Würzburg Cathedral, 1508–1510
>*Christ Salvator: Biebelried, Parish Church
>>Bier, *Riem.,* 2: 110-15, 179-82, Pls. 116-17

*Christ on the Cross, 1516: Steinach an der Saale, Parish Church
>Bier, *Riem.,* 4: 59-82, Pls. 248-49

*Tomb-Monument of Lorenz von Bibra, about 1518–1522: Würzburg Cathedral
>Bier, *Riem.,* 3: 97-117, 177-78, Pls. 190-200

*Maidbronn Altarpiece of the Lamentation for Christ, 1519–1523: Maidbronn,
Parish Church
>Bier, *Riem.,* 3: 126-63, 178, Pls. 201-10

*The Virgin and Christ Child in a Rosary, 1521–1522: Kirchberg bei Volkach,
Pilgrimage Church
>Bier, *Riem.,* 4: 83-97, Pl. 251

B. Works Destroyed or Lost

1. Altarpieces and Single Works in Wood or Stone

Altarpiece for the choir of the parish church in Windsheim, 1494–1497. Church
destroyed by fire in 1730
>Bier, *Riem.,* 2: 1-5, 160-65

Altarpiece of the Virgin Mary for the Jakobskirche in Rothenburg, before 1496
>Bier, *Riem.,* 2: 6-9, 168

Crucifixion for the parish church in Windsheim, 1499–1500. Church destroyed
by fire in 1730
>Bier, *Riem.,* 2: 1-5, 165-66

Decorative work on the wood model for a small cannon (Schlangenbüchse) for
the City of Würzburg, 1504
>Bier, *Riem.,* 2: 190

Crucifixus for the Stiftskirche in Wittenberg, 1505–1506. Church destroyed by
fire in 1760
>Bier, *Riem.,* 2: 6, 167

Altarpiece of St. Anne for the Marienkapelle in Rothenburg, 1505–1506. Marienkapelle demolished in 1810
> Bier, *Riem.*, 2: 44-48, 175-76

Altarpiece of All Saints for the Church of the Dominican Nuns in Rothenburg, before 1510. Church demolished in 1813
> Bier, *Riem.*, 2: 9-10, 169

Armorial shield for the Konrad Gate in Würzburg, 1508. Gate demolished in nineteenth century
> Bier, *Riem.*, 2: 148, 191

Busts of the Franconian Apostles: St. Kilian, St. Kolonat, and St. Totnan for the high altar of Würzburg Cathedral, 1508–1510. Destroyed by fire in 1945
> Bier, *Riem.*, 2: 104-15, 179-85, Pls. 118-22

Altarpiece for the parish church in Frickenhausen, 1514. Replaced by baroque altarpiece
> Bier, *Riem.*, 4: 98-99

Lid for baptismal font for the parish church in Ochsenfurt, 1514. Replaced by Neo-Gothic bronze lid
> Bier, *Riem.*, 4: 99-101

Model for a silver bust of St. Kilian for Würzburg Cathedral, 1518
> Bier, *Riem.*, 4: 104-06

Model for a silver statue of the Virgin Mary for the Stiftskirche in Aschaffenburg, about 1519–1523
> Bier, *Riem.*, 4: 106

Bust of St. Kilian for Würzburg Cathedral, about 1520–1521
> Bier, *Riem.*, 4: 106-07

Decorative work on furnishings for the vestry of Würzburg Cathedral, 1523
> Bier, *Riem.*, 4: 107

2. Repair Work

Repairs to a case for carrying the bolts for a crossbow, 1500
> Bier, *Riem.*, 2: 148, 190

Restoration of carved altarpieces in the convent church in Kitzingen, 1527
> Bier, *Riem.*, 4: 107-14

Two replacement figures for the superstructure of an altarpiece in the convent church in Kitzingen, 1527
> Bier, *Riem.*, 4: 108

II. WORKS ATTRIBUTED ON THE BASIS OF STYLE

A. Extant or Partially Extant

1. Altarpieces and Fragments Associated with Identifiable Altarpieces

From an altarpiece of the Crucifixion for the abbey church in Wiblingen, about 1480–1483
 Crucifixus, 1480–1482: Graz, Vinzentinerinnen-Kloster
  Bier, *Riem.,* 4: 76-78, illus. p. 77
 Group with Mary under the Cross: Harburg, Schloss Harburg, Öttingen-Wallerstein Collection
  Bier, *Riem.,* 2: 100-103, illus. p. 102
 Group of Soldiers and Pharisees: Harburg, Schloss Harburg, Öttingen-Wallerstein Collection
  Bier, *Riem.,* 2: 100-103, illus. p. 103
 Mourning Women (fragment from an *Entombment*): West Berlin, Staatliche Museen, Skulpturenabteilung
  Bier, *Riem.,* 2: 100-103, Pl. 114
 Fragment from an Entombment: West Berlin, Staatliche Museen, Skulpturenabteilung
  Bier, *Riem.,* 2: 100-103, Pl. 115
 The Agony in the Garden and *Resurrection* (wing reliefs): Berchtesgaden, Schloss Berchtesgaden
  Bier, *Riem.,* 3: illus. p. 129; 4: 77.

From an altarpiece of the Lamentation for Christ in Hessenthal, about 1485–1490
 Lamentation for Christ: Hessenthal, Pilgrimage Church
  Bier, *Riem.,* 3: 147-51, illus. pp. 133-34

From an altarpiece in Aub
 Crucifixion, about 1500: Aub, Parish Church
  Bier, *Riem.,* 1: 29-30, Pls. 34, 36-37

From an altarpiece of the Holy Clan (origin unknown)
 St. Anne with Her Three Husbands, about 1500–1505: Tiefenbrunn, private collection
  Bier, *Riem.,* 2: 47-48; 3: 150-51, illus. p. 140; 4: 115-16, Pl. 255
 Couple from the Holy Clan, about 1505–1510: Harburg, Schloss Harburg, Öttingen-Wallerstein Collection
  Bier, *Riem.,* 2: Pl. 88; 4: 115-16

From the (documented) Altarpiece of All Saints for the Church of the Dominican Nuns in Rothenburg, before 1510
 *St. Lawrence, about 1502: Cleveland, Ohio, Cleveland Museum of Art
 *St. Stephen, about 1510: Cleveland, Ohio, Cleveland Museum of Art

William D. Wixom, "Two Lindenwood Sculptures by Tilmann Riemen-schneider," *Bulletin of the Cleveland Museum of Art* 46, no. 9 (Nov. 1959): 189-97. Justus Bier, "Two Statues: St. Stephen and St. Lawrence by Rie-menschneider in the Cleveland Museum of Art," *Art Quarterly* 23, no. 3 (Autumn 1960): 214-27.

From the (documented) Altarpiece of St. Anne for the Marienkapelle in Rothenburg, 1505–1506

> *Adoration of the Kings,* 1505–1506(?): London, British Museum
> Bier, *Riem.,* 2: 44-55, Pl. 89

> *St. Anne,* about 1505–1506 (?): Munich, Bayerisches Nationalmuseum
> Bier, *Riem.,* 2: 44-55, Pl. 87

*Creglingen Altarpiece of the Assumption of the Virgin, about 1505–1510: Creglingen, Herrgottskirche
> *Assumption of the Virgin (shrine)
> *Annunciation (wing relief)
> *Angels (predella, central section)
> *Adoration of the Magi (predella) (Riemenschneider and assistant)
> *Christ among the Doctors (predella) (Riemenschneider and assistant)
> Bier, *Riem.,* 2: 56-86, 176-78, Pls. 90-102

From an altarpiece of the Holy Clan (origin unknown)
> *Couple from the Holy Clan,* about 1510: London, Victoria and Albert Museum
> Bier, *Riem.,* 2: 88; 4: 115-16

From an altarpiece of the Crucifixion for the Stiftskirche in Aschaffenburg
> **The Mourning Virgin,* about 1510: Kansas City, Missouri, William Rockhill Nelson Gallery of Art, Atkins Museum of Fine Arts
> M. Stokstad, "Romanesque and Gothic Art," *Apollo* n.s. 96, no. 130 (December 1972): 490 (illus.)

From an altarpiece for the parish church in Gramschatz, about 1510–1515
> **The Virgin with the Christ Child:* Hanover, Landesgalerie
> *Cyriacus* and *John the Baptist* (largely by Riemenschneider's own hand): Hanover, Landesgalerie
> Bier, *Riem.,* 4: 23-31, Pls. 216-19. Gert von der Osten, *Katalog der Bild-werke in der Niedersächsischen Landesgalerie Hannover* (Munich, 1957), cat. nos. 227-29, p. 186, illus. pp. 185, 187-89

*Dettwang Altarpiece of the Crucifixion, about 1512–1513: Dettwang, Village Church
> *Crucifixion (shrine)
> Bier, *Riem.,* 2: 87-103, 178, Pls. 103-09, 112

From an altarpiece of the Lamentation for Christ in Grossostheim, about 1515
> *Lamentation* (Riemenschneider and assistant): Grossostheim, Parish Church. (The figures of Mary, Christ and Nicodemus are largely by Riemenschnei-der's own hand)
> Bier, *Riem.,* 3: 149-51, illus. p. 135

From an altarpiece of St. John from the Johanneskapelle in Gerolzhofen, about 1515
   The Virgin with the Christ Child: Munich, Bayerisches Nationalmuseum
   John the Baptist (partially by Riemenschneider's own hand): Munich, Bayer-
   isches Nationalmuseum
      Bier, *Riem.,* 4: 15-31, Pls. 217-19. Müller, *Bildwerke,* cat. no. 149, pp.
      154-57, illus. pp. 154-55

   2. Single Works or Fragments in Wood

John the Baptist, before 1490: Hassfurt, Parish Church
   Bier, *Riem.,* 1: 53-55, Pls. 20-21

Adoration of the Kings, about 1490: Nuremberg, Germanisches National-Museum
   Bier, *Riem.,* 2: 50-53, illus. p. 50. *Riem. Cat.,* no. IX, pp. 42-43, illus.

St. Sebastian, about 1490: Munich, Bayerisches Nationalmuseum
   Müller, *Bildwerke,* cat. no. 130, p. 140, illus. p. 141

Pietà, early 1490s: Hassenbach, Village Church
   Justus Bier, "A Pietà by Tilmann Riemenschneider," *Bulletin of Rhode
   Island School of Design* 46, no. 3 (March 1960): 3, illus. p. 11

The Virgin with the Christ Child (from the Warburg Collection), about 1490–1492:
Boston, Massachusetts, Museum of Fine Arts
   W.-R.-J., p. 47, illus. p. 45. *Riem. Cat.,* no. VI, p. 36, illus. p. 37

Ecce Homo, about 1490–1493: Würzburg, Mainfränkisches Museum
   J. Baum, *Unbekannte Bildwerke alter deutscher Meister* (Stuttgart, 1954), pp. 11,
   26, Pls. 46-47

The Virgin with the Christ Child, about 1490–1493: Detroit, Michigan, Detroit
Institute of Arts
   Riem. Cat., no. VII, p. 38, illus. p. 39

Seated Bishop, about 1495: New York, Metropolitan Museum of Art, Cloisters
Collection
   Charles E. von Nostitz, Jr., "Two Unpolychromed Riemenschneiders at the
   Cloisters," *Metropolitan Museum Journal* 10 (1975): 51-62

The Virgin with the Christ Child (statuette), 1496–1499: Würzburg, Mainfränkisches Museum
   W.-R.-J., p. 50, illus. p. 49

The Virgin with the Christ Child, 1496–1499: Buenos Aires, Argentina, Zichy-
Thyssen Collection
   W.-R.-J., p. 50, illus. p. 51

The Virgin with the Christ Child, 1496–1499: Vienna, Kunsthistorisches Museum
   W.-R.-J., pp. 49-50, illus. p. 49

Bishop Nikolaus, 1498: Ochsenfurt, Parish Church
   Bier, *Riem.,* 3: 92 (illus.); 4: 49

The Virgin with the Christ Child, late 1490s: Lawrence Kansas, University of Kansas, Helen Foresman Spencer Museum of Art
> Justus Bier, "A Virgin with the Christ Child by Tilmann Riemenschneider," rev. ed., *Register of the Museum of Art, University of Kansas* 2, no. 2 (June 1959): 2-15

St. George, about 1500: West Berlin, Staatliche Museen, Skulpturenabteilung
> Theodor Demmler, *Tilmann Riemenschneider* (Berlin, 1923), p. 8, illus. on cover. *Führer durch die Königlichen Museen zu Berlin,* Das Kaiser Friedrich Museum, 3rd ed. (Berlin, 1917)

Bust of St. Urban, about 1500: Oberlin, Ohio, Oberlin College, Allen Memorial Art Museum
> Justus Bier, "A Bust of St. Urban by Tilmann Riemenschneider," *Art Quarterly* 9, no. 2 (Spring 1946): 128-39

St. Matthias, after 1502: West Berlin, Staatliche Museen, Skulpturenabteilung
> Bier, *Riem.,* 2: 127, n. 1, Pl. 131

The Virgin with the Christ Child (from the Clemens Collection), about 1501-1502: Cologne, Kunstgewerbemuseum
> *W.-R.-J.,* pp. 41-64, illus. pp. 42-44

Bishop Erasmus (from Kitzingen), 1501-1504: West Berlin, Staatliche Museen, Skulpturenabteilung
> Bier, *Riem.,* 2: 111, n. 3; 4: 49

Anna Selbdritt, about 1502-1504: Baltimore, Maryland, Walters Art Gallery
> Justus Bier, "An Anna Selbdritt by Riemenschneider," *Journal of the Walters Art Gallery* 7-8 (1944-1945): 10-37

Fragments from a *Nativity*
> *Mary with the Infant Christ,* about 1502-1504: East Berlin, Bode Museum
> *Joseph with the Animals,* about 1502-1504: Aschaffenburg, Städtisches Museum
>> Justus Bier, "Riemenschneiders Weihnachtdarstellungen," *Aschaffenburger Jahrbuch für Geschichte, Landeskunde und Kunst des Untermaingebiets* 2 (1955): 168-72

The Virgin with the Christ Child (Strahlenkranzmadonna), after 1503: Munich, Bayerisches Nationalmuseum
> Alfred Schädler, "Eine Strahlenkranzmadonna von Tilman Riemenschneider im Bayerischen Nationalmuseum," *Pantheon* 33, no. 2 (April-June 1975): 99-106.

The Virgin with the Christ Child (from the Henkell Collection), after 1503: Germany, private collection
> *W.-R.-J.,* pp. 50-51, illus. p. 51

The Virgin with the Christ Child, after 1503: Würzburg, Martin von Wagner Museum, University of Würzburg (Residenz)
> *W.-R.-J.,* pp. 51-52, illus. p. 52

The Virgin with the Christ Child (from Wiesloch), after 1503: Hamburg, Museum für Kunst und Gewerbe
   W.-R.-J., pp. 52-53, illus. p. 52

*St. Andrew, about 1505: Atlanta, Georgia, High Museum of Art
   Justus Bier, "St. Andrew in the Work of Tilmann Riemenschneider," *Art Bulletin* 38, no. 4 (December 1956): 215-23

St. Elisabeth, about 1505: Nuremberg, Germanisches National-Museum
   Deutsche Kunst und Kultur im Germanischen National-Museum, ed. L. von Wilckens, 2nd enlarged ed. (Nuremberg, 1960), p. 101, illus.

The Virgin with the Christ Child (statuette), 1505–1510: Zurich, Bührle Collection
   W.-R.-J., p. 56, illus.

*Pietà, about 1505–1510: Providence, Rhode Island, Rhode Island School of Design, Museum of Art
   Justus Bier, "A Pietà by Tilmann Riemenschneider," *Bulletin of Rhode Island School of Design* 46, no. 3 (March 1960): 1-12

**Female Bust for a Chandelier*, about 1505–1510: Hanover, Landesgalerie, Pelikan Collection
   Justus Bier, *Tilmann Riemenschneider: Ein Gedenkbuch*, 6th ed. (Vienna, 1948), p. 34, Pl. 83

St. James the Elder, about 1505–1510: Munich, Bayerisches Nationalmuseum
   Müller, *Bildwerke*, cat. no. 134, p. 146, illus.

St. James the Elder, about 1505–1510: Stuttgart, Württembergisches Landes-museum
   Riem. Cat., no. XI, p. 48, illus. pp. 48-49

Twelve Seated Apostles, about 1505–1510: Munich, Bayerisches Nationalmuseum
   Müller, *Bildwerke*, cat. nos. 135-46, pp. 148-51, illus. pp. 147-51

*St. Catherine, about 1505–1510: Raleigh, North Carolina, North Carolina Museum of Art
   Justus Bier, "Riemenschneider's St. Catherine in the North Carolina Museum of Art," *North Carolina Museum of Art Bulletin* 14, no. 1 (1977): 14-32

*St. Sebastian, about 1505–1510: Montreal, Montreal Museum of Fine Arts
   David Giles Carter, "Riemenschneider's St. Sebastian: Haunting Beauty and Nobility of Form," *M[11]* (a quarterly review of the Montreal Museum of Fine Arts), 3, no. 3 (December 1971): 17-23. Bier, *Riem.*, 4: 26-29, Pls. 243-44

**Lamentation for Christ*, before 1508: Würzburg, Martin-von-Wagner Museum, University of Würzburg (Residenz)
   Justus Bier, "Riemenschneider's Use of Graphic Sources," *Gazette des Beaux-Arts*, 6th ser., 50 (October 1957): 204-05, illus. p. 207

*St. Anthony Abbot, about 1510: Cambridge, Massachusetts, Harvard University, Busch-Reisinger Museum

Charles L. Kuhn, "Riemenschneider in the Harvard Collections," *Art Bulletin* 56, no. 2 (June 1974): 244-47

St. Sebastian, about 1510: Munich, Beindorff Collection
Justus Bier, "Ein Sebastiansfragment von Tilmann Riemenschneider, Ein Beitrag zur Typologie der Riemenschneiderschen Sebastiansdarstellung," *Münchner Jahrbuch der bildenden Kunst*, 3rd ser., 5 (1954): 102-10

Bust of a Female Saint, about 1510: Hanover, Landesgalerie
Gert von der Osten, *Katalog der Bildwerke in der Niedersächsischen Landesgalerie Hannover* (Munich, 1957), cat. no. 230, p. 190, illus. pp. 190-91. *Riem. Cat.*, no. XVIII, p. 64, illus. p. 65

St. James the Elder (wing relief), about 1510: Basel, Öffentliche Collection
Benoit-Oppenheim, *Originalbildwerke aus der Sammlung Benoit-Oppenheim* (Berlin and Leipzig, 1907; with an additional note, 1911), no. 8, Pl. 5

Mourning Women (fragment from an *Entombment*), about 1510: Stuttgart, Landesmuseum
Bier, *Riem.*, 2: 101-02, Pl. 113

Bust of a Mourning Virgin, about 1510: Wolfsburg, Nordhof Collection
Unpublished

Two Angels with Candlesticks (from the chapel of the Wolferstetterhof near Külsheim), about 1510: London, Victoria and Albert Museum
Eduard Tönnies, *Leben und Werke des Würzberger Bildschnitzers Tilmann Riemenschneider* (Studien zur Deutschen Kunstgeschichte, 22) (Strassbourg, 1900), pp. 272-73. Bier, *Riem.*, 2: 38, n. 3.

St. Barbara, about 1510: Munich, Bayerisches Nationalmuseum
Müller, *Bildwerke*, cat. no. 147, p. 152, illus.

Bust of St. Afra, about 1510–1515: Munich, Bayerisches Nationalmuseum
Müller, *Bildwerke*, cat. no. 148, p. 153, illus.

Female Bust for a Chandelier, about 1510–1515: Munich, Böhler Collection
Kurt Gerstenberg, *Tilman Riemenschneider*, 5th ed. (Munich, 1962), p. 216, Pl. 143. Bier, *Riem.*, 4: 103, Pl. 254

Crucifixus, 1510–1520: Heroldsberg, Church
Bier, *Riem.*, 4: 72-80, illus. p. 80

Bust of St. Anne, 1510–1520: Mönchengladbach-Hardt, Schwartz Collection
Riem. Cat., no. XIX, p. 66, illus. p. 67

God the Father and Christ (fragment from a *Trinity*), about 1510–1520: West Berlin, Staatliche Museen, Skulpturenabteilung
P. Metz, *Berlin Staatliche Museen, Bildwerke der Christlichen Epochen* (Munich, 1966), cat. no. 363, p. 75, Pl. 60

*Lamentation for Christ, about 1515: Bremen, Böttcherstrasse, Ludwig-Roselius-Collection
Bier, *Riem.*, 3: 154, illus. p. 138

*Bust of St. Burchard, about 1519–1523: Washington, D.C., National Gallery of Art
 Justus Bier, "The Bust of a Bishop by Tilmann Riemenschneider," *Art
 Quarterly* 6, no. 3 (1943): 158-66

Crucifixus, about 1520: East Berlin, Bode Museum
 Katalog aus 1000 Jahren Stift und Stadt Aschaffenburg, Jubiläums-Ausstellung
 (June–September 1957), p. 76, illus. p. 36

*The Virgin with the Christ Child (model for the Volkach Madonna), 1521:
 Washington, D.C., Dumbarton Oaks Collection
 Bier, *Riem.,* 4: 95-97, Pls. 252-53. Charles L. Kuhn, "Riemenschneider
 in the Harvard Collections," *Art Bulletin* 56, no. 2 (June 1974): 244-47

The Virgin with the Christ Child (from Tauberbischofsheim), 1525–1531: West
 Berlin, Staatliche Museen, Skulpturenabteilung
 W.-R.-J., p. 60, illus. p. 59. P. Metz, *Berlin Staatliche Museen, Bildwerke
 der Christlichen Epochen* (Munich, 1966), cat. no. 364, p. 75, Pl. 61

3. Single Works or Fragments in Sandstone

Christ (fragment from a *Meeting in the Garden*), about 1480–1482: Freiburg im
 Breisgau, Augustinermuseum
 Justus Bier, "Ein Werk Riemenschneiders aus seiner Strassburger Zeit,"
 Jahrbuch der Berliner Museen 1, no. 2 (1959): 190-97

*Tomb-Monument of Eberhard von Grumbach (d. 1487): Rimpar, Parish Church
 Bier, *Riem.,* 1: 60-64, Pls. 64-65

Christ (fragment from a *Meeting in the Garden*), 1492–1493: Würzburg, Main-
 fränkisches Museum
 Justus Bier, "Ein Werk Riemenschneiders aus seiner Strassburger Zeit,"
 Jahrbuch der Berliner Museen 1, no. 2 (1959): 190-97

Tomb-Monument of Baltasar Hemech (d. 1496): Teilheim bei Würzburg, Church
 Bier, *Riem.,* 3: 75-77, illus. p. 76

*Tomb-Monument of Konrad von Schaumberg (d. 1499): Würzburg, Marienkapelle
 Bier, *Riem.,* 1: 87-90, Pls. 62-63, 66

*The Virgin with the Christ Child, about 1505: Würzburg, Mainfränkisches Museum
 Bier, *Riem.,* 4: 141-42, Pl. 229. *W.-R.-J.,* pp. 53-55, illus. p. 54

*Tomb-Monument of Elisabeth Stieber (d. 1507): Buttenheim, Parish Church
 Bier, *Riem.,* 3: 49-55, Pls. 173-74. Justus Bier, "Tilman Riemenschneider's Monuments of Heinrich and Elisabeth Stieber," *Art in America* 31
 (1943): 172-83

Tomb-Monument of Georg von Liechtenstein (d. 1508): Würzburg Cathedral
 Bier, *Riem.,* 3: 78-79, Pl. 185

*The Agony in the Garden, 1510: Heidingsfeld, Kapelle auf dem Kirchplatz
 Bier, *Riem.,* 3: 63-69, Pls. 177-83

Tomb-Monument of Heinrich and Johannes Schodt von Schottenstein (d. 1472, 1512): Würzburg Cathedral
Bier, *Riem.*, 3: 78-81, Pl. 186

**The Virgin with the Christ Child*, 1516–1522: Frankfurt am Main, Liebieghaus, Städelsches Kunstinstitut
W.-R.-J., pp. 59-60, illus. p. 57. Bier, *Riem.*, 4: 21-23, Pl. 234

St. James (fragment from *The Agony in the Garden* from the Burkarduskirche in Würzburg), about 1520: Würzburg, Mainfränkisches Museum
Bier, *Riem.*, 3: 70-74, Pl. 184

Anna Selbdritt (from Kitzingen), about 1520: Würzburg, Mainfrañkisches Museum
Bier, *Riem.*, 2: 86; 4: 141

4. Single Works or Fragments in Alabaster

St. Barbara, 1480s: Bremen, Böttcherstrasse, Ludwig-Roselius-Collection
Riem. Cat., no. I, p. 20, illus. p. 21

Annunciation, 1480s: Amsterdam, Rijksmuseum
Riem. Cat., no. II, pp. 22-24, illus. pp. 23-25

Virgin (fragment from an *Annunciation*), 1490s: Paris, Musée du Louvre
Riem. Cat., no. IV, p. 30, illus. p. 31

**St. Jerome and the Lion*, about 1505–1510: Cleveland, Ohio, Cleveland Museum of Art
Justus Bier, "Riemenschneider's St. Jerome and His Other Works in Alabaster," *Art Bulletin* 33, no. 4 (December 1951): 226-34

5. Graphic Work (Sketches)

Portrait Sketch of a Young Man, 1502–1510: Frankfurt am Main, Städelsches Kunstinstitut
Justus Bier, "Eine dritte Zeichnung Tilmann Riemenschneiders: Wilhelm Worringer zum 80. Geburtstag," *Niederdeutsche Beiträge zur Kunstgeschichte* 1(1961): 219-24, illus. no. 157 following p. 224

Dance of Salome, about 1506–1508: Heidelberg, Kurpfälzisches Museum
Justus Bier, "Riemenschneider als Zeichner," in *Der Windsheimer Zwölfbotenaltar von Tilman Riemenschneider*, ed. Georg Poensgen (Munich and Berlin, 1955), pp. 100-113, illus. pp. 103, 107. Bier, *Riem.*, 4: 39, illus.

Portrait Sketch of Abbot Johannes Trithemius, about 1515: Leningrad, Hermitage Museum
Justus Bier, "Riemenschneider als Zeichner," in *Der Windsheimer Zwölfbotenaltar von Tilman Riemenschneider*, ed. Georg Poensgen (Munich and Berlin, 1955), pp. 100-113, illus. p. 107

B. Works Destroyed during World War II

The Virgin with the Christ Child (from Werbach), about 1490: formerly Berlin, Deutsches Museum
> *W.-R.-J.*, pp. 44-47, illus. p. 45. Bier, *Riem.*, 4: 16-18, Pls. 220-22

The Virgin with the Christ Child (from the Himmelstein Collection), about 1493: formerly Würzburg Cathedral
> *W.-R.-J.*, pp. 47-49, illus. p. 46. Bier, *Riem.*, 4: 19, Pls. 223-24

St. Dorothea (from an altarpiece in the Marienkapelle in Würzburg), about 1500–1505: formerly Würzburg, Marienkapelle
> Justus Bier, *Tilmann Riemenschneider: Ein Gedenkbuch,* 6th ed. (Vienna, 1948), p. 32, Pl. 54

Sources of the Photographs

PHOTOGRAPHS IN THE TEXT

Karl Göbel: p. 87
Photo-Verlag Gundermann, Würzburg: pp. 21, 85, 92, 110 left
Foto-Schaffert, Creglingen: p. 101
Schnell, Munich: p. 110 right

PLATES

Allen Memorial Art Museum, Oberlin College: 4
Bayerisches Landesamt für Denkmalpflege, Munich: 18; 20D; 22D, E; 42B
Bayerisches Nationalmuseum, Munich: 20A, E; 29; 32A, B
Böttcherstrasse G.M.B.H., Bremen: 37
Busch-Reisinger Museum, Harvard University: 12A, B
Cleveland Museum of Art: 6A, B; 9A-D; 14A, B
Dumbarton Oaks Collection, Washington, D.C.: 16B
E. Gottmann, Heidelberg: 31A
Photo-Verlag Gundermann, Würzburg: 16A, C; 17; 20B; 21A-D; 22A-C; 23B,
    E-S; 25A, B; 26B-F; 27; 30; 33A, B, E, F, I-M, P; 34A-C; 35A-E; 38A, B; 39;
    40A, C-G; 41A-D; 43A-D; 44; 46A-D
Kunstgeschichtliches Seminar Marburg: 33N; 42A
Kurpfälzisches Museum, Heidelberg: 31B
Mainfränkisches Museum, Würzburg: 28A, B
Metropolitan Museum of Art, New York: 2A-C
Montreal Museum of Fine Arts: 11A, B
Museum of Art, Rhode Island School of Design, Providence: 10A, B
Museum of Fine Arts, Boston: 1
National Gallery of Art, Washington, D.C.: 15A, B
William Rockhill Nelson Gallery of Art, Kansas City, Missouri: 13A, B
North Carolina Museum of Art, Raleigh: 8A, B

Eike Oellermann, Heroldsberg: 23A, C, D
Preussische Messbild-Anstalt, Berlin: 19; 20H, I, K; 26A
Rheinisches Bildarchiv, Kölnisches Stadtmuseum: 24A, B
John D. Schiff, New York: 7A, B
Helen Foresman Spencer Museum of Art, University of Kansas, Lawrence:
    3A, B
Staatliche Bildstelle, Berlin: 20J; 40B
Staatliche Museen, Berlin: 20C, F, G
Städelsches Kunstinstitut, Frankfurt am Main: 45
Franz Stoedtner, Berlin: 33C, D, G, H
Martin-von-Wagner Museum, University of Würzburg: 36
Walters Art Gallery, Baltimore: 5A, B

www.ingramcontent.com/pod-product-compliance
Lightning Source LLC
Chambersburg PA
CBHW020735180526
45163CB00001B/248